Roadside History of
OREGON

Bill Gulick

Best Regards,

— Bill Gulick

MOUNTAIN PRESS PUBLISHING COMPANY
Missoula, 1991

Third Printing, March 1994

Cartography by Carla Majernik
Cover painting by Kendahl Jan Jubb

\

Library of Congress Cataloging-in-Publication Data

Gulick, Bill, 1916
    Roadside history of Oregon / Bill Gulick.
        p.   cm. — (Roadside history series)
    Includes bibliographical references and index.
    ISBN 0-87842-253-6 : $24.95. — ISBN 0-87842-252-8 (pbk.) : $16.00
    1. Oregon—History. 2. Oregon—Description and travel—1981—
-Guide-books. 3. Automobile travel—Oregon—Guide-books.
I. Title. II. Series.
F876.G85   19910   91-13733
917.9504 ' 43—dc20   CIP

Mountain Press Publishing Company
P.O. Box 2399
Missoula, Montana 59806
(406) 728-1900

For Larry Dodd, Penrose Library Archivist
at Whitman College—our long-time friend
and a good man to go up the river with.

Table of Contents

Walla Walla Union-Bulletin. —photo by John Froschauer

About the Author

Bill Gulick has been writing about the Pacific Northwest for thirty-five years. He and his wife Jeanne live six miles north of the Oregon border, near Walla Walla.

Twenty of his novels have been published, three of which have been made into movies—*Bend of the River, The Road to Denver,* and *Halle-lujah Trail.* In 1971 his *Snake River Country* won the Pacific Northwest Booksellers Award as Best Non-fiction Book. Ten years later, he wrote *Chief Joseph Country: Land of the Nez Perce,* another gem.

In *Roadside History of Oregon,* Bill Gulick blends his talent as story-teller with his knowledge and skill as historian.

Acknowledgements

Writing, for me, always has been a joint occupation with my wife Jeanne. Already a skilled secretary when we got married, after I learned that she liked to do research and was good at it, I asked her to look up some material for me at Whitman College's Penrose Library in Walla Walla; the next thing I knew, Librarian Ruth Reynolds had put her on the staff, where she remained for nine years as Pacific Northwest Librarian. She then resigned to assist me on the book *Snake River Country*, which required quite a bit of travel. A few years later Jeanne returned to Penrose when Librarian Arley Jonish requested a few months of her time as a temporary replacement for a staff member who was ill. By this time, the library was part of a Pacific Northwest computer network, and for three years she worked as Inter-library Loan Specialist, finally retiring once again to work with me on two more books.

Through all this, my bargain with Penrose was that we would share Jeanne's research skills. I am grateful to the late Ruth Reynolds, to retired Librarian Arley Jonish, and to current Librarian Henry Yapel for keeping their side of the bargain, while at the same time giving me free access to the library's excellent facilities. Further thanks go to Marilyn Sparks and Larry Dodd at Penrose, who not only helped immeasurably with research inside the library walls but also have shared some outside adventures in the depths of Hells Canyon.

Former Washington State Librarian Nancy Pryor, whose roots are in Walla Walla, returned to her native soil after retirement and now spends a great deal of time as a volunteer worker at Penrose. Her father, Russell Blankenship, from whose book *And There Were Men* I have quoted liberally, knew many of the area's colorful characters and wrote about them back in the 1940s while he was a Professor of English at the University of Washington. Nancy Pryor kindly has granted me permission to quote from his book, which has long been out of print.

O.C. Dugger and James S. Hackett, from the Public Affairs office of the U.S. Army Corps of Engineers in Walla Walla, supplied me with photos of the Columbia River dams and the fish-preserving truck and barge, as well as details on the building of jetties at the mouth of the Columbia River.

Steve Lee, at the Bonneville Power Administration in Walla Walla, put me in touch with Wes Taft of the Portland office, who promptly supplied me with photos and information regarding the Pacific Intertie, the Celilo Terminal, and BPA in general.

Fort Vancouver National Historic Site Curator David Hansen responded promptly to my request for photographs. As noted in the text of the book, the Oregon country originally delineated in the Joint Occupancy Treaty covered a much larger area than the present state. In fact, the deed to our own few acres south of Walla Walla, Washington, and six miles north of the Oregon state line, goes back to 1848 and and the old Oregon country. It was one of the first Donation Claims Land Act grants made by the Oregon Provisional Government to a settler named Ransom Clark, who had passed through the area while acting as a guide for Fremont.

Susan Seyl, Photographs Librarian at the Oregon Historical Society, and Ken House, responded quickly to my request for photos of the Vanport flood, the Rajneesh interlude, and the Chinese in John Day. Having dealt with OHS off and on for thirty-five years, I can testify to the fact that it is one of the best in the country.

Though of much more recent vintage, the Columbia River Maritime Museum in Astoria is unique in design and concept, and is located on a dramatic site just a few miles inside the Columbia River Bar. When we asked on our first visit if they had any historic photos, the lady said "a few—say, 50,000." Later, we went back and spent a long day going through the collection, ably guided by Assistant Director Larry Gilmore, who quickly perceived what we needed and found the photos for us.

Moving down the coast to the Tillamook County Pioneer Museum, we found Director Wayne Jensen quite helpful in finding and sending us photos. South of Lincoln City, Walla Walla friends Bal and Audrey Moore kindly gave of the use of their lovely condo overlooking a spectacular stretch of the Oregon Coast for a long weekend while we went through the collection of photos taken and acquired by Rose Troxell and her husband Bob at their home in Otter Rock.

Farther south at Coos Bay and Bandon, the excellent historical museums supplied us with needed reference material and information, not the least of which was that gorse still grows near Bandon; if any botanical genius can come up with a way to kill it, his fortune will be made.

Over in the Willamette Valley just south of Portland, Director Patrick Harris gave us an interesting tour of the Old Aurora Colony Museum, and showed us how some of the old tools and musical instruments worked.

In Salem, the state capital, the first thing we needed was a map showing where the offices were located, for they are spread over a wide area. Fortunately we began with the Department of Transportation's highway division, where Carol Mitchell marked a local map for us showing the locations of the offices we wanted to check. Later, she gave us up-to-date maps of Oregon. During our travels around the state, which we covered three times during the research and writing of the book, we drove so many winding miles of road we became convinced that, if straightened out, the Oregon highway system has enough paved roads to supply the state of Texas.

At the State Forestry Department, which as we noted in the text is located in a building designed by the architect who created Timberline Lodge and used wood products no longer available, Public Affairs Assistant Doug Decker went out of his way to be helpful by supplying photos and information about the Tillamook Burn.

In the State Parks Department, Public Information Specialist Monte Turner not only gave us a useful booklet containing sectional maps of the state parks, but also supplied us with a photocopy of the out-of-print book *Oregon's Historical Markers*.

In Eugene, long-time friend Mike Morris, of the U.S. Forest Service, quickly responded to an urgent phone request for information by steering us to the person who could answer our question. At the Lane County Historical Museum, Marty West, Curator of Special Collections, made a special trip to the museum to guide us through their photo collection, then promptly supplied us with the prints we wanted. Another long-time friend, Andy Maxon, and his wife Harri, with whom we share an interest in Western art, volunteered to send us their file of Lane County Historical Society publications, which proved quite useful.

East of the Cascades, Irene Helms, Director of the Crook County Historical Society, found some rare photos of the City of Prineville Railroad and the Crooked River Gorge bridge for us. In Bend, Betty Renk, Director of the Deschutes County Historical Society opened their outstanding collection to us, while Photo Archivist Chuck Sipman promptly made and sent us sharp prints.

At the High Desert Museum, Communications Director Jack Cooper told us how the museum began and about its ambitious plans for the future, as well as supplying us with a number of fine photos.

For the ZX Land and Cattle Company, Waynette deBraga responded promptly to my last-minute phone call requesting historic photos and information on the ZX Ranch, which I hope to learn more about some day.

South of the Malheur National Wildlife Refuge we stopped by the Frenchglen Hotel, where Judy and Jerry Santille, who supervise its eight rooms and family style meals for the state parks system, shared their knowledge of local history, wildlife, and road conditions with us.

Despite its classification as high desert, this lightly traveled region is one of the most beautiful in the state.

After a ride on the reconstructed Sumpter Valley Railroad narrow-gauge train manned by a volunteer engineer, J.D. Leathlean, conductor Bill Wilt, with Lorraine Myers acting as station agent, we stopped at Baker City, where Gary Dielman, President of the Baker County Library District, found some photos for us of the old trains and smoke-belching locomotives from the days when they operated.

In Pendleton, Librarians Carol Reeve and Leah Conner found some early day Round-Up photos for us, while Editor Mike Forrester of the *East Oregonian* made helpful suggestions on Chinese photo sources, which are scarce.

Grace Bartlett of Joseph, Oregon, who long has shared her first-hand knowledge of the Wallowa country with us, opened up the Wallowa County Historical Society Museum for us one cool Sunday morning and spent a couple of hours helping us find photos we wanted.

Several fellow writers deserve our thanks. Long-time friend Archie Satterfield not only got us involved with Mountain Press but then loaned us his personal copy of the best reference book ever written, WPA guide to Oregon, a book now so rare that we were willing to steal a copy, if and when we found one. Now Archie's problem is getting it back.

For a number of years, professional writer friends such as Francis Fugate, Elmer Kelton, and Winfred Blevins have urged us to convert to a computer. Having only recently changed from a battered manual portable to an electric typewriter, we have stubbornly resisted. But when Publisher Dave Flaccus and editors Dave Alt, Wendy Fox, and Dan Greer urged us during a visit to Missoula to try a computer, then showed us what theirs could do, we reluctantly agreed to give the gadget a try.

Their warning that we would be confused and baffled for a few weeks proved accurate; but after learning that the machine does exactly what you tell it, rather than what you meant to tell it, we began to get the hang of it. Now we wonder how we ever got along without it.

During the eighteen months spent researching and writing the book, we covered the state of Oregon three times. Though we thought we knew it pretty well, we found new places of interest and beauty on each trip. Even so, we're sure we missed quite a few more. When the book is published, readers will probably tell us what we missed and ask us why. To them, we can only say: "If the Lord is willing and the cricks don't rise, we'll be back. . ."

INTRODUCTION

The Great River of the West

Even before the Thirteen Colonies began to think about declaring independence from Great Britain and expanding west, dreamers and visionaries began speculating on a fabled land beside the distant Pacific shore. Jonathan Carver wrote prophetically of a land he never would see:

> To the west of these mountains may be found countries full fraught with all the necessities or luxuries of life and where future generations may find an asylum....

Although accounts vary on the exact origin of the word "Oregon," Carver had applied the name to the river now called the Columbia in his *Travels Through the Interior Parts of North America* in 1778. He said he had heard the word used two years before by Indians in what is now Minnesota. The Indian word means "River of the West." Eventually, the name was applied to the entire region drained by the river.

Geographers of that day, lacking factual information, theorized about the physical features of the North American continent. Convinced that great rivers ran to cardinal points of the compass, they called the Saint Lawrence the River of the East and the Mississippi the River of the South. The Indians along the lower Missouri told early explorers of a meadow near the river's headwaters, easily crossed in half a day by horse or on foot, beyond which flowed the waters of the River of the West. Down this stream, they said, the traveler could embark in a canoe and float tranquilly to the sea. While not the legendary Northwest Passage, for which explorers had been searching since the time of Columbus, a portage of only half a day would not be a bad interlude in a water trip from sea to sea.

But first the River of the West must be found.

Because Great Britain, the world's foremost sea power, was being challenged by the newly born United States, the two nations would

1

naturally compete fiercely in the search for and control of the distant river. Most believed it entered the sea somewhere between the fortieth and fiftieth latitudes along the Pacific Coast of North America—a sizable piece of real estate. Considering the time it took to travel vast distances in this age of sail, a surprisingly close contest to "get there first" ensued.

British sea captain George Vancouver—a bold, scientific geographer if ever there was one—listened skeptically when the Spanish explorer, Bruno Hecata, in 1775 claimed to have seen evidence of the mouth of a great river at forty-six degrees, seventeen minutes north. Noting currents too strong for his vessel to sail against between the headlands of a wide, mist-shrouded inlet, he wrote: "These currents and eddies of water caused me to believe that the place is the mouth of some great river, or of some passage into another sea." He named the entrance Assumption Inlet.

Unwilling to accept the Spaniard's claim of an important discovery, Vancouver sent a sea captain named Meares to check it out. After carefully examining the area, Captain Meares emphatically denied the existence of a great river there, naming the supposed inlet Deception Bay and its headland to the north Cape Disappointment.

A few years later American sea captain Robert Gray, meeting Vancouver in the Strait of Juan de Fuca, told him that on April 29, 1792, he had been "off the mouth of a river in latitude forty-six degrees, ten minutes north, where the current was so strong as to prevent our entering it." But Vancouver told Gray, an American with no scientific training, that the mouth of his great river was merely Hecata's Deception Bay, which Captain Meares had checked on and dismissed years ago.

Still curious, Captain Gray sailed south again, found the mouth of the river that wasn't there, and on May 11, 1792, "ran northeast between the breakers, having from five to seven fathoms of water. When we came over the bar, we found this to be a very large river with fresh water, up which we steered."

Dropping anchor at what he called Tongue Point, twenty-five miles upstream, Gray named the River of the West after his ship, the *Columbia*.

Hearing of his alleged discovery, Vancouver condescended to examine the area in October 1792, permitting Lt. William R. Broughton to cross the bar and go upriver in the small ship *Chatham*. Reaching a spot one hundred miles inland, Broughton named it Point Vancouver, then "took possession of the river and the country in its vicinity in his Britannic Majesty's name, having every reason to believe that the subjects of no other civilized nation or state had ever entered the river before."

This cast the first challenge in the war of words between Great Britain and the United States as to which country owned the land called Oregon. The bloodless contest lasted fifty years.

Meanwhile, in Europe, two men from different cultures with different motives prepared to step onto the stage of westering American expansion. One was a German merchant, John Jacob Astor; the other an American diplomat to France, Thomas Jefferson. Though of opposite personalities, the men had two things in common: each knew a bargain when he saw one, and each recognized the right moment for decisive action.

Astor's dream was to make a fortune buying and selling furs worldwide. Jefferson's dream was to build a nation stretching from sea to sea. Two years after he became president of the U.S. in 1801, Jefferson bought the Louisiana Territory and began preparations to send his two emissaries, Lewis and Clark, to the Pacific Coast to inspect his purchase. Five years later, Astor mounted an equally bold venture.

By accident or design, the Americans managed to keep a step or two ahead of their British rivals, who had the same goal in mind but were a little slower in acting. By then, the two English-speaking countries had discouraged other foreign claims to the region, pushing the Russians north and the Spanish south. Two costly wars had taught Great Britain and the United States the folly of fighting over territory in North America, so they made a unique agreement.

For ten-year terms, on a renewable basis, they allowed citizens of both countries to occupy the region called Oregon jointly. This was the Joint Occupancy Treaty. The idea was to let ownership of the country be settled by the people who wanted to live in it.

To the English, the only thing of value in the Oregon country was beaver, which the Hudson's Bay Company, a monopoly licensed by the British crown, had trapped for two hundred years. Daniel Webster, the American secretary of state, thought the Oregon country so worthless that a good bargain for the United States might be to trade its rights to Oregon for a codfish bank off the coast of Newfoundland.

Between the time the Joint Occupancy Treaty was signed in 1818 and its termination in 1846, Oregon began to develop as a unique part of the Pacific Northwest. Because the desires that drive men and women are not simply financial, but spiritually and physically inspired as well, the force that came to be called "Manifest Destiny" took many years to make its results evident.

Historically and geographically, Oregon consists of six parts:

The Columbia River: Since its discovery, this easily followed water route brought westering Americans to Oregon, at first from the sea, and later, along the Oregon Trail, from the points east.

The Oregon Coast: Although settlement started here, this area solidly retains its wild, rugged beauty.

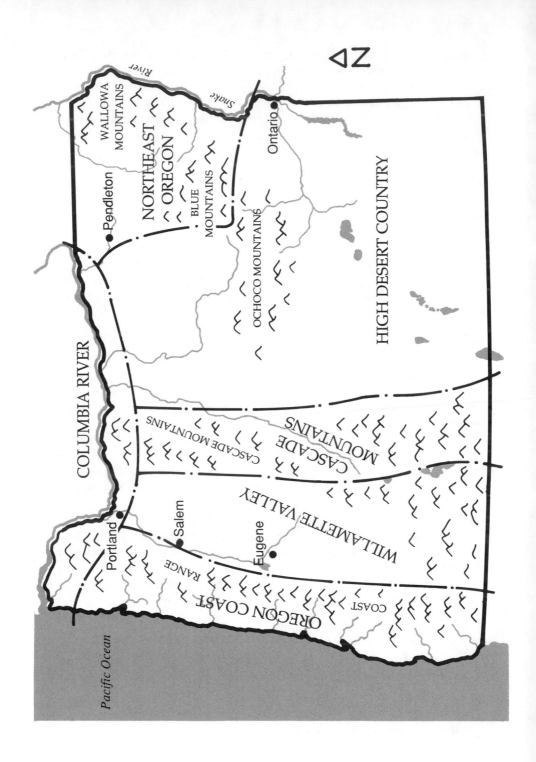

N

WALLOWA MOUNTAINS

River

Snake

NORTHEAST OREGON

Pendleton

BLUE MOUNTAINS

Ontario

OCHOCO MOUNTAINS

HIGH DESERT COUNTRY

COLUMBIA RIVER

CASCADE MOUNTAINS

CASCADE MOUNTAINS

WILLAMETTE VALLEY

Salem

Portland

Eugene

COAST RANGE

OREGON COAST

Pacific Ocean

The Willamette Valley: This broad, fertile valley stretching south from Portland between the Coast Range and the mighty Cascades proved a lodestar to land-hungry emigrants and community boosters.

The Cascade Mountains: A snow-covered, volcanic range, these giants split the state into two distinct regions, "east and west of the mountains."

The High Desert Country: Aridity, in stark contrast to the abundant rainfall west of the mountains, is the dominant characteristic of this central and southeastern portion of Oregon.

Northeast Oregon: Few people live in this area dominated by the Blue and the Wallowa mountains, the awesome depths of Hells Canyon and the Snake River that flows through it.

We start our journey where the Columbia River first touches Oregon in the eastern part of the state, for that is where where the kaleidoscopic history of Oregon began.

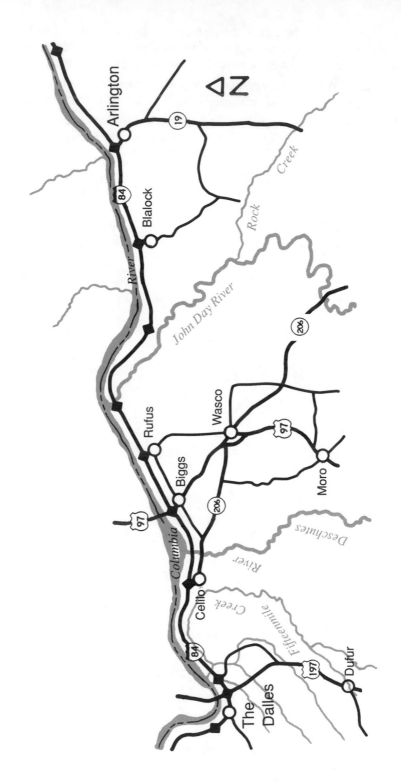

PART I

The Columbia River

OR 730, I-84
Washington Line—The Dalles
121 miles

Shortly after the Lewis and Clark party passed the westward bend of the Columbia on October 19, 1805, and entered the land to be called Oregon, it encountered a band of frightened local Indians.

"They said we came from the clouds ... and were not men." In his unique style of spelling and grammar, Clark continued, "as Soon as they Saw the Squar wife of the interperter they pointed to her ... the sight of This Indian woman, wife to one of our interprs. confirmed those people of our friendly intentions, as no woman ever accompanies a war party of Indians in this quarter."

The woman was Sacajawea, young Shoshone bride of the French-Canadian, Touissant Charbonneau, who had been hired as an interpreter and guide many months before in Mandan country on the Missouri River. Already she had proven her value to the explorers when they encountered the potentially hostile Shoshones just west of the Continental Divide. The head chief, Cameahwait, turned out to be her brother and rejoiced in her return home.

With the party of whites were two respected Nez Perce chiefs, Twisted Hair and Tetoharsky, who not only had agreed to look after the explorers' horses in Nez Perce country until the expedition returned east the next spring but had promised to travel down the Columbia with them as far as the great fishery, Celilo Falls, where many tribes met to trade.

Because the Nez Perces were the most powerful tribe in the upriver country, the presence of the two old chiefs guaranteed the Americans would be greeted in peace. To further demonstrate their friendship, a group of Nez Perces met the Lewis and Clark party at Celilo Falls on the return trip the following spring. When the white men found it difficult to move their clumsy dugout canoes against the strong spring current, the Indians gave them horses to pack their belongings and provided a guide who showed them an overland shortcut that saved the party eighty miles and a week's time.

During the fierce competition between Great Britain and the United States over ownership of the Oregon country, an important fur-trading post in the interior was built where the Columbia makes its big bend west. Called Fort Nez Perces when first built at the mouth of a small river in 1818, it soon adopted the name of that stream and became known as Fort Walla Walla.

Nothing remains of old Fort Walla Walla today. Ownership of Oregon was settled in favor of the United States in 1846, and the fort was burned by American volunteers during an Indian war in 1855 to prevent it falling into hostile hands. Later, in 1952, floodwaters of McNary Dam, twenty-four miles downriver, submerged its ruins. But its name survived in the form of a military post and a city called Walla Walla, twenty-nine miles to the east.

During the peak years of emigration along the Oregon Trail between 1843 and 1859, thousands of wagons wore deep ruts down the western slope of the Blue Mountains and across the sagebrush-covered desert flanking the Umatilla River. Faint traces of the trail can still be found in the area today, if a person knows where to look. What cannot be found is evidence of the feelings of those travelers of long ago who, having

Fort Walla Walla looking west down the Columbia River past towering bluffs known as Wallula Gap. —John Mix Stanley painting, 1847, Penrose Library, Whitman College

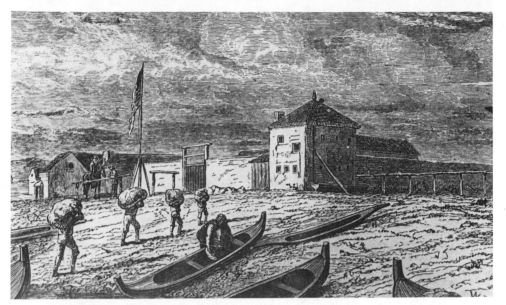

Old Fort Walla Walla, launching spot for brigades of trappers employed by the Hudson's Bay Company. —Oregon Historical Society

crossed most of the continent, finally reached the Columbia and knew that their long-sought goal lay only two hundred miles away.

By then, people and draft animals were exhausted, food supplies were short, shoes and clothes were worn out, and spirits were low. If the season were late, the thought of cold autumn rains catching them before they could get through the Columbia River Gorge between The Dalles and the Willamette Valley haunted the emigrants. After The Dalles, they knew the most difficult part of the journey lay ahead.

Numerous dams on the Columbia have made placid pools of what once were dangerous rapids. One of these dams is McNary, just three miles east of the town of Umatilla. Because all the dams on the Columbia are equipped with huge locks capable of lifting or lowering immense tug-and-barge carriers one hundred feet in a matter of minutes, the glamor of steamboat traffic is gone. However, between 1855 and 1900, passenger and freight transport on the Columbia River was just as colorful and busy as it ever was on Mark Twain's Mississippi.

During its boom years when gold rushes flourished in eastern Oregon, Idaho, and Montana, the windy, sand-drifted settlement called Umatilla Landing was a very lively place. Here, east-bound travelers could disembark and take a stagecoach or saddle train across the Blue Mountains to Boise, Salt Lake City, and the newly completed transcontinental railroad to Omaha, Chicago, and New York. Passengers could stay aboard for a few more hours and get off where the Columbia River

The Almota, *built by the Oregon Steam Navigation Co. in 1876, meeting the Nez Perce Indians at Lewiston, 1885.* —Idaho Historical Society

turned north at Wallula Landing, where a Spartan hotel made all other accommodations seem luxurious. After a night there, they could go by stern-wheeler on up the Columbia River to the Snake, which, after 140 miles of rapids, snags, ice floes, and other hazards, would land them in Lewiston, Idaho Territory, 470 river miles above the mouth of the Columbia.

For a few bonanza years, fortunes in gold were brought downriver to Portland on every boat. After the gold petered out, farmers in eastern Oregon and Washington discovered that fertile soil and good growing conditions on the rolling hills could produce tremendous quantities of grain year after year. Because population in the region was sparse, large amounts of wheat and other grains in 100-pound sacks were shipped downriver to a ready market.

Still later, cheap electricity from the dams, coupled with new pumps capable of irrigating the formerly arid lands high above the river promised even greater treasure through large-scale cultivation and marketing of crops such as potatoes. Today, along the stretch of river between the eastern border of Oregon and Arlington, long ricks of wheat piled outside overflowing grain elevators may be seen in late summer awaiting shipment downriver.

Where wind-blown sand drifts once covered railroads and highways, the region around Umatilla is now green and verdant, supporting vineyards and fruit and shade trees, and growing such tremendous crops of watermelons that the sides of the highway are lined each summer with stands where juicy melons sell by the truckload or by the chilled slice.

At McNary Dam, as at all the other dams on the Columbia River, salmon and steelhead migrating upriver to spawn are counted from special viewing stations in the base of the dam. The counters sit in darkened booths where they can see each fish as it passes across a white slab. Because there are several varieties of anadromous fish, as salmon and steelhead are called, counting them is important work. The livelihood of commercial fishermen, the treaty rights of native Americans, and the recreation of sports fishermen all depend on survival of the runs. Visitors are welcome at the counting stations.

The dam just east of Umatilla was named after Senator Charles McNary, a long-time advocate of cheap electricity, navigation, and irrigating the arid lands of eastern Oregon—all interests he represented in the United States Senate for many years.

Ninety miles west of McNary lies John Day Dam, completed in 1962 and named for an obscure, illiterate member of the overland section of the Astor party. Day's only enduring memorable event was that he went insane while traveling west in 1812. That he was immortalized by the most popular writer of the day, Washington Irving, probably had something to do with Day's notoriety, even though Irving killed him off a few years too soon in his book *Astoria.* Though accepted as fact for one hundred and fifty years, John Day survived his ordeal (explained later, in the section on Overland Astorians) and did not die until the 1820s. An

Three miles east of Umatilla, Oregon, McNary Dam was completed in 1952. It is one of four dams on the Columbia between eastern Oregon and Portland.
—Corps of Engineers

John Day Dam, ninety miles downriver from McNary Dam.
—Corps of Engineers

Idaho archivist found that the hunter-trapper lived and died for the second and final time in the wilds of Idaho. Obscure though John Day may have been, having a dam, river, and city in Oregon named after him, as well as a stream in Idaho, is an honor few men can claim.

When the Lewis and Clark party reached Celilo Falls in late October, 1805, the peak of the fishing season was past. But the immense stores of dried and powdered salmon made it clear to the explorers how important this fishery was to tribes both upriver and downriver. Furthermore, there was evidence that white traders cruising along the Pacific coast two hundred miles to the west had sent emissaries here. Clark wrote: "we Saw two scarlet and blue cloth blankets, also a Salors Jacket."

In the bleak sagebrush desert through which the Columbia flowed as it curved west toward the sea, it was clearly a big river, a quarter mile from bank to bank. But as it approached Celilo Falls, which at this low-water time of year had a vertical drop of twenty feet, sheer basalt bluffs on either shore literally forced the river to turn on edge, its might compressed for a fourteen-mile stretch into seething, boiling rapids that required portage by even the most skilled boatmen. At one point, Clark noted: "The whole of the Current of this great river must at all Stages pass thro' this narrow chanel of 45 yards wide." He estimated the speed of the current to be at least thirty miles an hour.

Whatever respect the Indians had for one another's property rights did not extend to the belongings of the whites. If left unguarded, a skillet of hot grease would be stolen in the blink of an eye. On April 20, 1806, Captain Lewis wrote in exasperation:

This morning I was informed that the natives had pilfered six tomahawks and a knife from the party in the course of the last night. I spoke to the chief on this subject. he appeared angry with his people and addressed them but the property was not restored. one horse which I had purchased and paid for yesterday and which could not be found when I ordered the horses into close confinement yesterday I was now informed had been gambled away by the rascal who sold it to me and had been taken away by a man of another nation. I therefore took the goods back from this fellow.

Some idea of the amount of fish caught in this part of the river may be gained from Clark's statement: "I counted 107 stacks of dried pounded fish in different places on those rocks which must have contained 10,000 lb of neet fish."

Twelve miles west of Celilo State Park, The Dalles Dam has an unusual appearance because its longest dimension runs parallel to, rather than across, the river. The reason for this, say the engineers who designed it, is that the bluffs on either side of the Columbia are so close together and the channel of the river so narrow that there would not be room enough for the necessary fish ladders, navigation locks, generators, and spillways if the dam was of a conventional design.

Why not find a site farther downriver that was wider? Because the placement of dams on the Columbia depends upon the amount of fall available to create a head for hydroelectric power; to make the most effective use of the river's might, the height of each dam must be approximately the same. On the lower Columbia, the ideal height for dams is one hundred feet.

All four barriers—Bonneville, The Dalles, John Day, and McNary—generate their power as "run-of-the-river" dams. That is, they take the amount of water running into the pool behind each dam, use its fall to

Celilo Falls just before this important Indian fishery was wiped out by the building of The Dalles Dam in 1956. —Yakima Nation Collection

Celilo Falls. —Yakima Nation Collection

Celilo Falls, a great salmon fishery on the Columbia River, where many Northwest Indian tribes met to fish and trade. —Yakima Nation Collection

create electricity, then let that water flow on to the next dam pool downstream, where it will be used again in the same way.

By law, the up-and-down fluctuations of the pools behind the lower Columbia River dams are limited to one foot per hour, with a total variation of only twelve feet per day. The reason for this is that navigation interests, migrating fish, and wild game birds nesting along the shorelines cannot live with sudden and severe variations in the level of the river. Storage is only a minor factor in the dam pools of the lower Columbia, unlike the "storage dam" pools in remote mountain areas designed to hold spring runoff water for irrigation use many miles downstream.

After portaging supplies around the rapids and lining their boats through in early November 1805, the explorers said goodbye to the two Nez Perce chiefs who had served them so faithfully. They embarked on a quieter stretch of river downstream from an area strewn with what appeared to be huge brown stepping stones. Some unknown French wanderer had already named this region The Dalles—French for "stepping stones." The name has endured.

The Dalles Lock and Dam. Looking west down the river, the fish ladder is in the foreground, the power bays in the middle, and the navigation lock on the upper right. —Corps of Engineers

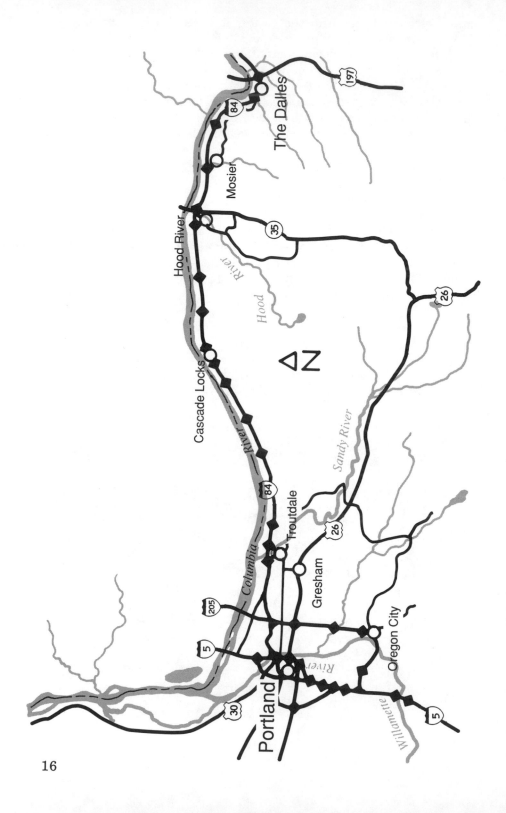

The Dalles of the Columbia River with Mount St. Helens in the background. —John Mix Stanley painting, Penrose Library, Whitman College

I-84
The Dalles—Portland
84 miles

West of The Dalles, the look of the country changes dramatically as the Cascade Mountains close in, trying but failing to block the great river's journey to the sea. In contrast to the dry, flat country to the east, trees begin showing up in scattered clumps of low-growing pines at first, then, as moisture increases, stately ponderosas and towering firs appear. As the river moves into the depths of the gorge, the color of the foothills and mountain slopes turns rich green. Before the dams created a series of tranquil pools, a six-mile stretch of rapids called the upper, middle, and lower cascades forced Lewis and Clark and those who followed to portage again and again. In this wild water no boatman could survive.

In places, the river was so filled with tumbled dark lava rocks that the local Indian legend "Bridge of the Gods" could readily be accepted. Many years ago a natural bridge crossed the Columbia River at this spot, so the legend goes, with a sacred flame, tended by a beautiful young maiden named Loo-Wit, burning at its center. But the two sons of Tyhee Sahale, the Supreme Being, had fallen in love with the young lady and began quarreling so violently over her that their father decided to teach the trio a lesson.

Destroying the natural bridge in a cataclysm that turned the six-mile stretch of river into a series of tumbling rapids, he changed the two young men and the girl into mountains, which are now known as Mount Hood, Mount Adams, and Mount St. Helens. Looming eleven thousand feet above the Columbia River on the Oregon side is Mount Hood; well to the north on the Washington side is Mount Adams at twelve thousand feet; nearest the river on the Washington side stands Mount St. Helens, formerly a perfect cone of ninety-six hundred feet.

After many years of silence, Mount St. Helens erupted in May 1980, losing more than a thousand feet from its cap.

Physical evidence that a geological disaster of some kind occurred in the area was frequently noted by steamboat travelers on the river back in the 1860s, before dam pools quieted the rapids. Under certain water conditions, they saw large blocks of submerged rock with trees growing out of them fifty feet or so beneath the surface, as if deposited there by the collapse of a natural bridge.

Around the turn of the century, a popular writer, Frederic Homer Balch, wrote the romantic novel *The Bridge of the Gods* based on the Indian legend. At Hood River, one of the first bridges to span the Columbia was built a few years later and is still in use. Taking its name from the legend, it, too, is called the "Bridge of The Gods."

Captain Meriwether Lewis almost declared war against a band of local Indians who kidnapped his big Newfoundland dog, Scannon, near this area. Having already done what no other dog in history had by crossing the continent to the Pacific Ocean, Scannon was making the return trip in April 1806 when he disappeared near the lower cascades. Clark wrote that the Indians were "great thieves, so arrogant and intrusive that nothing but our number saves us from attack. We were told by an Indian who spoke Clatsop that they had carried off Captain Lewis's dog to their village below. Three men, well armed, were instantly dispatched in pursuit of them, with orders to fire if there [was] the slightest resistance or hesitation. At the distance of two miles they came in sight of the thieves, who, finding themselves pursued, left the dog and made off."

With the Cascade Mountains and the last of the rapids behind them, the explorers put their dugout canoes into the broad, quiet waters of the lower Columbia, feeling effects from the tide 150 miles from the sea. On November 4, Clark wrote: "Tide rose last night 18 inches perpendicular at Camp." He also noted an abundance of beautifully fashioned seaworthy canoes. "I counted 52 canoes on the bank in front of this village maney of them verry large and raised in bow."

Manned by fifty or more paddlers, these canoes could transport large quantities of freight and people in the roughest currents and seas. With these, the Indians could cross the treacherous bar at the mouth of the river and range widely up and down the coast in their hunts for seals, sea otters, and whales.

In contrast to its low-water stage on the downriver trip in the fall, by spring the Columbia River was running in full flood through the lower, middle, and upper cascades. Passing through the gorge at Hood River, the explorers noted a feature still prevalent today: "The wind continued violently hard all day, and threw our canoes with such force against the shore that one of them split before we could get it out." That same violent wind now makes Hood River famous to adventurous souls as the windsurfing capital of the Western world.

During the 1830s, when Americans were trying to compete with the monopolistic Hudson's Bay Company for the fur and fish business in Oregon country, two enterprising businessmen saw their ambitious schemes fall apart in the lower cascades area. One was a New England ice seller and merchant named Nathaniel Wyeth, who had chartered a ship out of Boston, loaded it with empty barrels, salt, and ice, and sent it around the Horn to the lower Columbia.

Wyeth hoped to earn a fortune selling Northwest salmon and furs back east. Though he labored hard and long for several years, neither the Hudson's Bay Company nor the local Indians cooperated with him, so eventually he gave up and left the country. But he managed to build a trading post in the Snake River country—Fort Hall—which the Hudson's Bay Company owned for a while and later became an important way-station on the Oregon Trail. Some of Wyeth's former employees settled in the Willamette Valley and became the vanguard of American civilization in the region. For a time, a whistle stop on the railroad just west of Multnomah Falls marked the point where he finally gave up the battle, but otherwise no evidence of Wyeth's efforts remains.

A far more flamboyant character named Captain Benjamin Louis Eulalie de Bonneville explored the country and tried to compete with the Hudson's Bay Company with no better success. Exactly what Captain Bonneville was up to in the Oregon country is as unclear today as it was then. A career army officer of French descent he somehow raised enough money too equip a large body of men whose vague purpose was to trade in and explore the Pacific Northwest. He was granted a leave of absence from August 1831 to October 1833, which his letter of authorization from the War Department stated was for:

> The purpose of carrying into execution your design of exploring the country to the Rocky Mountains and beyond, with a view to ascertaining the nature and character of the several tribes inhabiting those regions, the trade which might be probably carried on with them; the quality of the soil, the productions, the minerals, the natural history, the climate, the geography and topography, as well as the geology of the various parts of the country.

19

Though his operation was unsuccessful during its first two years, he never seemed to run out of funds or enthusiasm, blithely requesting that his leave of absence be extended for two more years. When his request was lost and he was suspended from the service, he asked President Andrew Jackson to reinstate him with no loss in rank or pay, which the president did. Before long, he was promoted and became the hero of the day when his friend and benefactor, John Jacob Astor, introduced him to best-selling author Washington Irving, who wrote a book about him and made him famous.

To further ensure his enduring fame, a few years after resolution of the Joint Occupancy Treaty required the Hudson's Bay Company to turn Fort Vancouver over to the United States, Colonel Bonneville returned as its commandant. And the first dam to block the flow of the mighty Columbia in 1938 received the name Bonneville, as did the small town below it on the north bank.

Oregon Trail Days

Peak years of emigration over the Oregon Trail spanned from 1843 to 1859. Many latter-day pioneer societies rule that if a person's ancestors came to Oregon after 1859, they cannot be called "pioneers." Reaching The Dalles after long, weary months on the trail, the emigrants were dismayed to learn that the most difficult part of their trip across the continent lay just ahead of them. If they arrived late in the autumn, the specter of cold rains catching them in the Columbia River Gorge haunted them.

At river level, the sheer walls of the gorge closed in to make land travel impossible. In the fifty-mile stretch of river ahead tumbled three sets of rapids—the upper, middle, and lower cascades—so wild that no boat could shoot them and remain intact, let alone a wagon box with its wheels removed and seams calked, the method normally used to cross rivers. "Wagons had to be sold or dismantled here," writes Oregon historian Robert Ormond Case, "and rafts built of logs or sawed lumber."

The typical raft was made of twelve logs, eighteen inches thick and forty feet long. Wheelless wagons lay on the raft bed, ropes secured all the loose gear, and, with or without skilled boatmen, the terrified emigrants committed their safety to the river. They withstood icy water and wet clothes for weeks at a time, making only a few miles each day. When it got too dark to see, they waited for daylight, only to face another day of rough water and increasingly cold weather.

A typical trip, like the one endured by Elizabeth Smith and her family in the fall of 1847, took twenty-six days. A few excerpts from her diary, beginning at The Dalles, tell how their party suffered:

[Nov. 1] We are lying by waiting for the wind to blow downstream in order that we may embark with our raft.

[Nov. 2] We took off our wagon wheels, laid them on the raft, placed the wagon beds on them and started. There are three families of us, Adam Polk, Russell Welch, and ourselves, on twelve logs eighteen inches through and forty feet long. The water runs three inches over our raft.

[Nov. 3] Still lying by and waiting for calm. Cold and disagreeable weather.

[Nov. 4] Rain all day. Laid by for the water to become calm. We climbed up a steep hillside among the rocks and built a fire and tried to cook and warm ourselves and children, while the wind blew and the waves rolled beneath.

[Nov. 7] Put out in rough water. Moved a few miles. The water became so rough that we were forced to land. No one to man the raft but my husband and my oldest boy, sixteen years old.

[Nov. 8] Waiting for wind to fall. We have but one day's provision ahead of us here. My hands are so cold I can hardly write.

[Nov. 9] Waves dashing over our raft and we are already stinting ourselves in provisions. It is very cold. The icicles are hanging from our wagon beds to the water. Tonight about dusk Adam Polk expired.

[Nov. 18] My husband is sick. It rains and snows. We started around the falls this morning with our wagons. We have five miles to go. I carry my babe and lead, or rather carry, another through snow, mud, and water almost to my knees.

[Nov. 19] My husband is sick but can have but little care. Rain all day.

[Nov. 20] I froze or chilled my feet so that I can not wear a shoe, so I have to go around in the cold water in my bare feet.

[Nov. 27] Passed Fort Vancouver in the night. Landed a mile below. My husband has never left his bed since he was taken sick.

Even after the family reached Portland and moved into a small, leaky, frame building with two other families, Elizabeth's husband did not improve. Her diary continues in early 1848:

[Feb. 1] Rain all day. This day my dear husband, my last remaining friend, died.

[Feb. 2] Today we buried my earthly companion. Now I know what none but widows know: that is, how comfortless is a widow's life; especially when left in a strange land without money or friends, and the care of seven children.

Meanwhile, the young men and boys of the family drove the milk cows and beef cattle over a trail two thousand feet up the mountainside; nimble-footed goats might have negotiated it without difficulty, but cattle found it nearly impossible. The search for new routes through or over the Cascades did not yield an easy solution. One of the emigrant's first options to shooting the three sets of formidable rapids was the Barlow Road, but few embraced the choice.

In those days of totally free enterprise, a man could easily obtain a franchise for a road or bridge and charge travelers a toll. After as little improvement as felling a tree across a stream or moving a rock or some dirt with crowbar or shovel, he could go to whatever political body regulated commerce in that area, pay a fee, request a monopoly, and conduct business. Such a man was Samuel K. Barlow, who, after crossing the Cascades in 1845, did a bit of token work and was given a franchise by the provisional government to "operate" a toll road across the last mountain crest.

Actually, Barlow did not pioneer the road himself. A pair named Joel Palmer and William Rector were trying to take sixty wagons over the Cascades by a new, unexplored route. Reaching a spot near the top of a 5,000-foot plateau, Palmer explored the country north and south for fifty miles, declared it impassable, and recommended that the wagons turn back. Rector objected; he wanted instead to take Samuel Barlow and go on to the Willamette Valley settlements for help while his partner brought the wagons on up to the summit, where they could be left until the next June. Palmer told him to go ahead and try.

Traveling light, with only two-days' rations, the forty-year-old Rector soon found that his sixty-year-old traveling companion could barely keep up. At this rate, he knew it would take them at least six days to reach the settlements, so he cut their rations accordingly to keep from running out. But as the terrain grew steeper, the timber thicker, and the rain colder, the older man, Samuel Barlow, grew so discouraged he was ready to give up.

After they had gotten lost and had to retrace their steps, had trouble building a fire, and Barlow had suffered several bad falls, he dropped to the ground, exhausted. Rector later told how the older man said despondently:

> "Mr. Rector, if I should brake a leg in sum of these falls, what would you do with me?"
>
> "I wud eat you," was my reply. He said no more. I looked around at him and saw him shedding tears. "Why, Barlow, you old fool, I won't eat you. Neither will you brake a leg. We will get to the trail early tomorrow."

And they did.

After Barlow made a few improvements, he charged five dollars a wagon over his toll road, and he advertised that the crossing could be made in four days. But pioneers soon discovered that in places like Laurel Hill, the sixty percent grades were so steep that the rear wheels of the wagons needed logs chained to them to prevent their careening down the slope and smashing to smithereens. Many of the emigrants might have wished Barlow *had* broken his leg on the trail with Rector. In their hardship along his toll road, they might have even offered to eat Barlow themselves, if given the opportunity.

Steamboats on the River

Upstream from the Columbia River's mouth it ran wide and deep, and its negligible current made visible how the ocean tides caused its level to rise and fall up to 150 miles inland. But farther upriver, the character of the Columbia changed dramatically as it cut through the Cascade Mountains within the gorge. Steamboats absolutely could not navigate the six-mile stretch of white water called the lower, middle, and upper cascades. Beyond that point though, a fifty-mile stretch of relatively quiet water between the upper cascades and The Dalles could be negotiated by steamers built on and forever restricted to that part of the river. Above The Dalles, in a narrow, fourteen-mile stretch of river, the current raced at thirty miles an hour after dropping the twenty or so feet from Celilo Falls.

These two obstacles—the triple set of rapids and the swift water below Celilo Falls—divided the Columbia into three sectors, called the lower, middle, and upper river. Transporting freight and passengers from one portion to another required a laborious portage of six or fourteen miles.

The creation of Washington Territory in 1853 and subsequent treaties made with the Indians in 1855 caused unrest east of the Cascades. Until then, there was neither reason nor need for river transport to that side of the mountains. But as travel through the Columbia River Gorge by Willamette-bound emigrants increased, the Indians grew resentful and restless, so the U.S. Army established posts at The Dalles and the Cascades. To supply them, a small side-wheeler named the *Belle* ran the lower section of river between the lower cascades and Fort Vancouver, while two more side-wheelers, the *Mary* and the *Wasco*, ran the fifty-mile stretch between the two posts.

At first, portages on both sides of the river went along narrow trails cut into the rocky banks of the gorge via pack or saddle train. Then two enterprising brothers, Daniel and Putnam Bradford, built a six-mile-long rail line of wooden stringers topped by strap iron on which flatcars pulled by mules carried freight. On the Washington side of the river at the upper cascades, a small settlement called Bradfords' Store was built. Usually, the steamboat *Mary* docked there and its counterpart, the *Wasco*, tied up to the landing opposite on the Oregon shore.

On Tuesday, March 25, 1856, the *Mary* and the *Wasco* came downriver from The Dalles, running light, to pick up loads. For some months rumors circulated that the Yakima Indian Nation, a loose affiliation of fourteen related bands living north of the Columbia, were so unhappy with the terms of the treaty they had been forced to sign the previous summer that they were going to start a war against the whites. But few settlers took the threat seriously.

The *Mary* tied up by Bradfords' Store and put ashore her downriver cargo, while the *Wasco* did likewise on the south shore. During the the night, both boats lay at their docks, waiting for dawn when they would take on wood and freight, fire up, and head back upriver. Early the next morning, Captain Baughman and the mate of the *Mary* went ashore to supervise the loading of fuel and cargo. The cook, Dick Turpin, and his helper, John Chance, who had just finished serving breakfast to the crew, were clearing away the dishes.

Suddenly, a volley of bullets raked the landing. With wild yells, Indians charged the settlement. Caught in their cabin, an entire family was shot, scalped, dragged to the river, and dumped in. Men at the sawmill ran for the store. All but one made it. He was shot dead. Captain Baughman and the mate sprinted for the woods. Three members of the crew, running through crossfire, got to the boat and sprang aboard. In his book, *Sternwheelers up the Columbia*, Randall V. Mills tells what followed:

> On the boat, the crew grabbed whatever arms it could find and sallied out. Buckminster, the engineer, had a revolver. John Chance, the steward's helper, grabbed an old dragoon pistol. Dick Turpin, the cook, crazed with fear, seized the only useful gun aboard, a rifle, and jumped into the flatboat alongside. But the Indians were at the gangplank and already the fireman had been hit in the shoulder. In the flatboat, Dick Turpin took a bullet, screamed, and leaped into the river, drowning and carrying the rifle with him.

With the crew putting up a stiff defense of the boat, the Indians turned their attention to attacking the whites in Bradfords' Store. This gave the crew time to get a fire going beneath the boilers with the scant amount of fuel on hand. As soon as steam pressure began to mount, Hardin Chenoweth, the pilot, ran across the hurricane deck and into the pilot house. From ashore, the Indians raked the deck with a withering fire.

> Chenoweth dropped flat on the floor and held the wheel. Quickly the lines were chopped free, and someone began valving the engine. Once the side-wheels bit into the water, watchers shouted directions up to Chenoweth, who, still on his back, guided the boat into the stream. There was a chance that she would be caught in the current and swept into the rapids, but the wheels held and slowly she moved out of range.

Watching from shore, the besieged people in Bradfords' Store saw black smoke rising beyond the trees and thought that the Indians had set the steamboat on fire. But as she moved out and became visible in the river, Chenoweth stood up and pulled the whistle cord defiantly. The sound of his mechanical jeering at the Indians told the settlers that there was a chance for help. The whites cheered lustily. But the odds were still against the *Mary*.

> [The steamer] only had fuel enough aboard to raise steam, and not enough to move her very far. There were wounded aboard, too, who required attention. Chenoweth guided the boat in a wide turn and then angled her back to the bank around the settlement. There, a deserted clearing seemed free of Indians, and he nosed the boat to a landing. Desperately hurrying, the men rushed for what wood they could find—rails from a handy snake fence—and toted them down to the bank and threw them onto the deck as rapidly as they could. From beyond the bend, they heard shots and saw rising plumes of smoke as building after building at the settlement was set ablaze.

On the Oregon shore, the *Wasco*, also caught with cold boilers, worked frantically to build up a head of steam. When she did, she pulled out into the river and followed the *Mary*, heading for The Dalles and help from the military.

Meanwhile, the blockhouse at the middle cascades and the landing at the lower cascades also had been attacked by the Indians. Both were poorly defended, with the arsenal at the blockhouse consisting solely of a small cannon; the settlers at the lower landing had no guns at all. But the cannon, booming away at random, kept the hostiles at bay near the blockhouse while the settlers piled up bales of goods to shield against bullets. After darkness fell, the settlers scrambled into small keelboats and catboats at the landing, cut loose, and began drifting downriver toward Fort Vancouver.

When they and a friendly Indian runner who had raced ahead to carry news of the attack to the military post reached the fort, a young Army lieutenant named Phil Sheridan (the same one destined for national renown later during the Civil War) assembled a company of dragoons and twenty Portland volunteers, commandeered a pair of steamboats named the *Fashion* and the *Belle*, and headed upriver to the rescue.

At The Dalles, the *Mary* and the *Wasco* took on federal troops. The eager but underpowered *Mary* took a flatboat loaded with horses and men in tow, only to find that the river's current often pushed the flatboat ahead of the steamer. Although Colonel George Wright, leader of the troops from The Dalles, had hoped to trap the Indians between his force landing above them and another led by Lieutenant Sheridan landing below, his second in command, Lt. Colonel Edward Steptoe, spoiled the surprise by following the book of regulations too closely.

Suddenly, from his command, into the clear morning air rose the brassy blare of a bugle. The troops heard it and obeyed; the Indians, being sensitive about noises, also heard it. When Steptoe came up to Sheridan, not an Indian remained.

Though the hostiles had failed to overwhelm the defenders at the cascades, casualties among the whites had been heavy. Eleven civilians and three soldiers were dead, with three more mortally wounded. Twelve others had wounds, too, and a number of cabins, warehouses, and bales of freight awaiting shipment had been burned.

But the value of having steam-powered boats on the middle river had been proved beyond doubt. During the next two years of conflict with scattered bands of recalcitrant Indians living in eastern Oregon and Washington Territory, boat-building above The Dalles and Celilo Falls developed, assuring transportation up the Columbia as far as Canada and up the Snake into northern Idaho.

When the Indian wars finally ended and peace came to the interior country in 1858, settlers were drawn to the fertile land by its abundant sunshine and rich soil. At first, they came in trickles. But when gold was discovered in the Idaho mountains in 1860, the trickles became a flood. The quickest, easiest way to get to the diggings from western Oregon was by steamboat. Despite the formidable obstacles of portages, rapids, and navigational hazards, a colorful era of steamboat traffic lasting twenty-five years had begun, and a number of venturesome individuals were about to win and lose fortunes.

Stern-wheeler Glory Days

Perhaps the best way to describe what must be called "glory days on the river" is to embark on an imaginary trip from the mouth of the Columbia to Lewiston, Idaho Territory, at the height of the gold rush during the mid-1860s. The distance is 470 miles. People taking this trip cannot sleep late. Historian Randall Mills writes:

> The boats were good, but the passengers had to get up early to ride them. Those heading up the Columbia from Portland loaded all night; lines of drays strung out along Front Street for blocks waiting their turn to drive out on the big two-level company dock at Ash Street. By 4:30 in the morning the passengers began to arrive, and at a little before 5:00 the freight was stowed and the pilot climbed into the pilot house.
>
> The wheel was lazily turning, but now black smoke began to roll from the tall stack. Late passengers rushed up the landing stage, and the lines were cast off. The big wheel threshed the water, moving the prow of the boat away from the dock, and a pillar of steam shot from the tall escape pipe. Then with a flurry of white foam the long white

Columbia Gorge stern-wheeler, Cascade Locks.

vessel turned into the current, pointed downstream and slipped past the town. It was five o'clock in the morning. One hour later the downstream boat for Kalama and Astoria would pull away, and then the dock would be quiet until eleven, when the boat from the Cascades came in.

During the years when steamboat traffic flourished on the river, the whistles of more than two hundred boats echoed off the cliffs rising above either shore. Most children learned to identify each whistle lest they be ridiculed by their peers, especially the boys. Many small boys dreamed of growing up to be steamboat captains—and some of them did, earning such fabulous salaries as five hundred dollars a month for being the master of a boat that might pay for itself with one year's travel on the river, bringing cargoes of gold from Idaho worth a hundred thousand dollars.

As boat builders became more knowledgeable about the river, most of the steamboats plying the quiet, deep waters between Portland and Astoria were side-wheelers, while those running the middle river above the cascades and upriver from Celilo Falls were stern-wheelers. The docks downriver from Portland all had adjacent deep water, so the side-wheels never hit bottom. Upriver, though, the steamers usually had to nose the bow of the boat into the sandy shore, with the slowly churning stern-wheel holding the vessel against the bank as passengers and freight went ashore. Another advantage of the stern-wheeler was that if one of the slats in the paddle-wheel broke, it could be replaced quickly by the ship's carpenter, while fixing a damaged metal bucket on a side-wheeler was far more difficult.

Accommodations and amenities on the boats ranged from adequate to luxurious. Usually passengers took breakfast from tables in the main saloon, paying "two bits" for the meal at first, then later, up to twice that price—fifty cents. By the time Portland passengers had finished breakfast on the upriver trip, the boat had run out of the Willamette and into the Columbia, and had stopped briefly on the north shore at Vancouver. If the weather was decent, passengers gathered on deck to take in the spectacular scenery of the gorge: Beacon Rock, Rooster Rock, Multnomah Falls.

At first, the Oregon Steam Navigation Company, which soon gained a monopoly on river travel, was dead set against having bars aboard its boats. But because gentlemen in that place and time felt a great hardship traveling dry, bars were soon established and rented out to concessionaires. Their operations were so profitable that the company raised no objection when the steamboat's head barkeeper was elevated to the honorary title of "captain," even though he was not licensed to pilot the boat.

At eleven o'clock the boat docked at the lower cascades, where a train of the portage railroad waited. All the passengers went ashore. Because fast freight headed upriver had to be taken off the boat and transferred to railroad cars, a job that took an hour or so, there was no hurry. Once loaded, the small locomotive that had replaced mules tooted its whistle and began to move, with the passengers riding in elegant, light colored coaches.

At the upper cascades, the passengers got off the train and ate lunch at a hotel next to the landing. While they waited for the freight to be transferred to the boat destined to take them to The Dalles, they could watch the churning rapids, gawk at the remains of the blockhouse attacked by Indians in 1856, or go to the boat's bar for their second or third drink of the day.

In early afternoon, the stern-wheeler would pull out into the current, more noticeable here, and begin to chug the fifty-odd miles to The Dalles. During the four or five hours of this part of the trip the scenery changed dramatically. The lush greenery and thick evergreen forest of the rainy region west of the Cascade Mountains gave way to the bleak, open, basalt-covered dry country east of the Cascades. Sated with viewing scenery by now, the lady passengers looked forward to the comfort of a bed in a good hotel (which they hoped would not be cursed with the bane of travelers of that day, fleas, lice, and bedbugs) while the men anticipated a hearty meal, a few drinks in a friendly bar, and a bed in a room shared with not more than three strangers.

28

"They had a choice," writes Randall Mills. "The Cosmopolitan Hotel or the Umatilla House, the former being somewhat smaller and less gaudy, but still popular, having seventy-five rooms with such luxurious touches as a billiard room and a ladies' parlor, with piano. The Umatilla House was said to be the best outside of Portland, in spite of its notoriously friendly fleas and occasionally chummy bedbugs. Its fittings were elegant—the only word that seems appropriate to describe them."

The Umatilla House's 123 rooms and two baths, with a lavatory in the basement made it the most luxurious hotel east of the Cascades. Its dining room was large and a corps of cooks and waiters served the crowds that moved through the hotel every day. In any season, nights spent in The Dalles by travelers were short. Passengers heading downriver the next morning were called at 4 a.m. Those going upriver had to be aboard the portage train in front of the hotel at five o'clock. If the ever-present wind had not blown too much sand over the tracks, it took ninety minutes to reach Celilo Falls. Below the mouth of the Deschutes, John Day, and Umatilla rivers, tricky rapids challenged the river pilots.

The Mile-A-Minute Steamboat

Though most of the steamboats built for the middle and upper river were stern-wheelers, there were a few exceptions. The most magnificent example was the Oregon Steam Navigation Company's *Oneonta*, built in 1863 to serve on the run from the upper cascades to The Dalles. Designed like a Mississippi River steamboat, she had two tall stacks forward with the pilot house behind them and her side-wheels set well back from center. Her enclosed freight deck extended over the guards, as did her cabin deck, which stretched from stem to stern. She was big for her day—182 feet long—and expensive to operate.

The stern-wheeler Hassalo *shooting the rapids at the cascades.*
—Columbia River Maritime Museum

The sleek speedster Bailey Gatzert *negotiating the rapids in 1890.*
—Columbia River Maritime Museum

As revenue dwindled along the middle river, the *Oneonta*'s owners asked master pilot Captain John C. Ainsworth to bring her downriver through the six-mile stretch of wild rapids to the lower river, where there was more traffic. Ainsworth decided to wait until the river ran in full early summer flood, which smoothed out its hazards but picked up its flow to perhaps thirty miles an hour. To maintain steerageway, the boat needed to cruise faster than the river. Under a full head of steam, the *Oneonta* could do thirty; coupled with a current of the same speed, she'd be moving close to sixty miles an hour. Few railroad locomotives of the day could go that fast.

Captain Ainsworth brought the steamer through without so much as a scratch. Never mind that, after seven years of service in the lower river, the *Oneonta* was converted into a barge and ended her days ignominiously. But she had six minutes of glory as the first "mile-a-minute" steamboat to come booming through the gorge.

The Benevolent Monopoly

In that day of truly free enterprise, the Oregon Steam Navigation Company became sarcastically known as "the benevolent monopoly." True control of the river required control of the portages as well, since they represented bottlenecks in the flow of goods and services. Portage roads existed on both the Oregon and Washington sides of the river, so the O.S.N. paid the seller's price to buy one of the routes. It then immediately reduced rates to bring its competitor across the river to the verge of bankruptcy, buying it, too. Without surprise, the portage rates went back up. Applying the same strategy to competing steamboat lines, O.S.N. soon owned them also. Within a few years, there was not a boat landing, a steamboat, a portage train, or a single facility along the 470 miles of the Columbia and Snake rivers from Astoria to Lewiston that was not stenciled "Property of O.S.N."

The "benevolent" part of this monopoly did not an extend to commercial shippers, who screamed to high heaven over the rates they paid. For example, a ton of freight in this land of few scales was assumed to measure forty cubic feet. So, if a farmer from Walla Walla wanted to ship a wagon and a team of horses from Wallula Landing to Portland, the O.S.N. agent at Wallula measured the maximum length of the wagon with the team in harness, then measured the maximum height of the wagon unhitched from the team with its tongue raised vertically then multiplied these figures by the width to determine the cubic footage and divided that figure by forty. The calculated tonnage far exceeded real weight.

Of course, after the team and wagon were taken aboard, the horses would be housed in stalls below decks, the wheels and tongues of the wagons would be removed and stacked inside the beds, other wagons would be placed on top, and the load securely tied down. But the tonnage figure remained the same.

The benevolence applied to those folks down on their luck, such as an unsuccessful gold miner, who would be given passage and meals downriver "on the cuff"; or a cash-poor merchant or farmer, who could put freight charges "on account" and pay them when and if he became solvent. But when the traffic could bear it, the O.S.N. charged the users of its services to the limit.

Open River

As might have been expected, when Oregon became a part of the transcontinental railroad system in 1883, the Oregon Steam Navigation Company was on hand to establish a monopoly on this mode of transportation, too. Simply changing its name to Oregon Steam and Rail Navigation Company, it managed to manipulate rates between river and rail transport. The shipper still paid exorbitant fees to get his farm products downriver or his merchandise upriver to his stores.

What was needed, the shippers claimed, was an "open river"—that is, a water-level passageway free of obstacles from the upper Columbia River to the Pacific Ocean—which meant locks and canals. In a nation with a long tradition of the federal government providing free navigation of waterways to their users, this was a pressing need that could be ignored no longer.

In 1875, Army engineers surveyed the rapids at the Cascades and recommended construction of a canal around the upper stretch of white water. The next year Congress appropriated $90,000 to begin the work. For ten years, both the flow of federal money and the rate of ditch digging went slowly. When the railroad was completed in 1884, Oregon Steam and Rail Navigation brought most of its boats to the lower river, leaving shippers at the mercy of the railroads. Randall Mills writes:

> Great was the cry and impressive the reverberations while the wheat men of the high country demanded competition by steamboat. They shook Congress into action, and in 1893 it granted an appropriation of $1,239,653, which permitted completion of the canal. In November, 1896, it opened.

The 3,000-foot canal passed around the unnavigable upper cascades. At its lower end was a lock of two chambers, each 460 feet long, giving a lift of twenty-four feet at the low water stage, fourteen feet at high water. The cut ran through rock, and the canal had heavy masonry walls, with a controlling width of 90 feet and a water depth of eight feet, enough to handle any boat that might pass through.

For years the Cascade Locks were a tourist sight, with crowds coming from Portland by train or boat to spend a few hours enjoying a picnic in the O.R.N. park nearby, watching the water level in the locks rise and fall as a steamboat passed through. At last boats could travel from Portland to The Dalles without interruption.

The Bailey Gatzert *heading up the Cascade Locks.* —Columbia River Maritime Museum

Tug and barge heading downriver through the Cascade Locks.

Farther up the river, the obstruction from The Dalles to Celilo Falls was not so easily conquered. Of the several ingenious projects proposed, one from the Corps of Engineers called for a "boat-railroad." A steamboat would pull into a partially filled lock with flatcars parked below; draining the lock would lower the vessel onto the cars, which would then be towed by four locomotives pulling side by side to another lock above the rapids, where the process would be reversed. Though Congress appropriated $250,000 for planning and right-of-way purchase in 1896, only $30,000 had been spent by the end of the 1900 fiscal year. "By then, the folly of the scheme had become clear," writes river historian Fritz Timmen in his definitive book, *Blow for the Landing*. "Congress ordered all work halted while a study was made on the feasibility and cost of the canal. Back to the drawing board went the Corps."

We'll never know for sure if this idea would have worked.

An 1879 survey recommended a canal on the Washington side of the river at a cost of $7.6 million, but nothing came of it. In 1888, another plan called for one on the Oregon shore at a cost of $3.7 million. Again, the idea was shelved. By 1900 a new plan was ready, suggesting two locks and a 3,000-foot canal around Celilo Falls, a thirty-three-foot lift lock, a 9,000-foot canal around Five Mile Rapids, with a submerged dam at the head of these rapids, and navigational improvement at Three Mile Rapids. The whole project was estimated at $4 million. By fits and starts, work progressed as administrations and economic conditions changed from year to year, but it never completely stoppped. Finally, on May 3, 1915, the Celilo Falls Canal was dedicated.

Though a few impediments to navigation remained, such as the Deschutes and Umatilla rapids on the Columbia, and periodic low water or floating ice jams on the Snake, a skillful pilot in a powerful, shallow-draft stern-wheeler could overcome them with patience and luck. From the mouth of the Columbia to Lewiston, Idaho, the water-level passageway indeed now lay open and free of restrictive tolls.

The Gorge Highway

While river and rail had been the only two ways to ship goods to and from market, a new-fangled invention—the automobile—soon created a demand for paved roads. Only a farsighted genius could predict such a demand, let alone make filling it a reality. But just such a genius was waiting in the wings for his time onstage. His name was Sam Hill.

Even though their last names were the same, Samuel Hill and railroad magnate James J. Hill were not related. As an ambitious young attorney in Minneapolis, Sam Hill specialized in cases brought by farmers against railroads, and his favorite target during the 1880s was the Great Northern, of which James Hill was president. With his persuasive power over jurors, Sam Hill invariably won. Tired of paying off, James Hill sent for Sam Hill, and asked, "How would you like to go to work for me as an attorney for the railroad?"

"No, I won't work for you," Sam Hill answered. "But if you'll teach me the railroad business, I'll work with you."

The bargain was struck. Before long, Sam Hill knew as much about the railroad business as his mentor. He also courted and married James Hill's daughter, Mary. But she preferred to live in Philadelphia and he liked to roam, so they were soon estranged but never divorced because of Sam's close relationship with her father.

Sam Hill left his mark on Oregon by conceiving and building the most ambitious project of his time—the Columbia Gorge Highway.

In 1910, automobiles began changing the travel habits of Americans. But there were few suitable roads. During one of his trips to Europe, Sam Hill became fascinated with the hard-surfaced roadways, some of which had been built for Roman chariots. He hired an engineer named Samuel Lancaster, and they laid down an experimental stretch of macadam highway (layers of compacted broken stone) in the Columbia Gorge east of Portland. Ascending from river level to the bluff top 2,000 feet above on the Washington side, it was called the "Maryhill Loops" road in honor of his wife, whom he hoped to bring west.

The road was a marvel. Even though it led from noplace to nowhere, it was the kind of surface on which a daredevil driver could do sixty miles an hour—a speed few automobiles could achieve. With this feat of construction to his credit, Sam Hill approached the Washington State

Legislature with a bold proposal. For $65,000 he would have his engineer lay out a seventy-five mile stretch of highway through the Columbia River Gorge that would be the wonder of the world. Furthermore, he would save the taxpayers money by using convict labor. The legislature gave him cautious approval, and the project had barely gotten under way when trouble with his dynamite expert brought down a landslide of protest on Sam Hill's head.

At that time a radical union called the Industrial Workers of the World was attempting to dictate relationships between the interests Capital and Labor by setting off bombs on gateposts or doorsteps of officials who believed differently from I.W.W. The dynamite expert Sam Hill persuaded prison authorities to release for work on his highway just happened to be in prison because he tried to blow up a prominent public figure with whom the I.W.W. disagreed. The legislators felt that this was not the sort of man to be trusted with explosives.

When the state of Washington cut off his funds, Sam Hill told them, "If you don't want the highway on your side of the river, I'll take it across the Columbia to Oregon, where you can see it and regret your decision for the rest of your lives."

Oregon had no highway commission, though the recently organized Good Roads Association had tried to begin building a road through the gorge several times. When Sam Hill approached the state with his proposal in 1913, he was welcomed with open arms. The state highway commission organized within a matter of weeks, and Hill's use of convict labor was approved, so the project got under way.

Hill took Lancaster to Europe in 1908 to study the classic highways of France, Italy, Germany, and Switzerland. Lancaster was enchanted by what he saw. "When he remarked on stone retaining walls along the Rhine, Hill told him they had been built in the ninth century by Charlemagne and that one day such walls would line the banks of the Columbia," wrote *Oregonian* reporter Marylynn Wheeler.

If ever a highway could be called a work of art, the 73.8 miles of Columbia River Gorge Highway designed and built by Samuel Lancaster qualified. Lancaster loved nature and believed that it was good medicine for the ills of urban life. The gorge highway, he said, "Would enable tired men and women to enjoy the wild beauty of nature's gallery and recreate themselves." Dangling from rope slings along vertical cliff sides, wading knee-deep in ferns to find the most scenic views, plotting every curve of the the route to reveal new vistas, he designed every foot of the highway with the care of an artist.

Built to the most modern specifications, the highway was at least twenty-four feet wide, with a maximum grade of five percent, and a minimum curve radius of one hundred feet. A series of hairpin turns, modeled after alpine highways, allowed the road to climb steep hillsides

Multnomah Falls.

gradually. Unstable slopes were secured by long stretches of rock walls like those Lancaster admired in Europe. Seven viaducts skirted the edges of cliffs, some appearing to float on air, supported from beneath by concrete piers. Arched stone parapets marked roadside parks and viewpoints, inviting travelers to stop frequently. Its two dozen bridges gracefully framed their natural settings, giving views of lacy white waterfalls and distant snow-covered mountains. The most spectacular of its four rock tunnels was the 300-foot "Tunnel of Many Vistas" at Mitchell Point, its five massive arched windows echoing the Axenstrasse Highway of Switzerland.

It took 2,200 men two years to complete the first section of highway, using horses and bulldozers. Civic groups from Portland joined weekend road crews, united under the Good Roads Association slogan, "Let's Get Oregon Out of the Mud." President Woodrow Wilson officially dedicated the highway on June 7, 1916, by pressing an electric switch in the White

36

House that activated a circuit unfurling a flag over the Crown Point scenic overlook.

The Columbia River Gorge Highway was an immediate success. "Carloads of middle-class families set out east of Portland," writes Marylynn Wheeler, "gently negotiating 73.8 miles of cliff-hanging highway and stomach-wrenching switchback turns. They feasted on the magnificent scenery of the gorge, camping along the highway in rag-top Model Ts, warming canned food on radiators. They called themselves 'Thoreaus at 29 cents a gallon,' the price of gasoline."

For many years, the highway served as the only route through the gorge to Portland, but as traffic increased, its scenic beauty and engineering wonders became obscured by clouds of diesel smoke and the curses of motorists caught behind logging trucks crawling up twisting grades at fifteen miles an hour. After many demands for a straighter river-level highway, a shorter, faster road was completed in the late 1940s, making the scenic route obsolete.

When Interstate 84 opened in the 1960s, much of the scenic highway was abandoned and fell into disrepair. By 1980, only one-third of the highway remained intact; the rest had been abandoned or destroyed. But before this unique work of art could be completely obliterated, the state of Oregon initiated several restoration projects along the Columbia River Highway. Rock railings and walls were repaired, parts of bridges were remodeled and recast, and the observatory at Crown Point was refurbished. Sitting atop a bluff 720 feet above the river and offering a spectacular view toward Portland to the west and into the heart of the gorge to the east, this viewpoint can now be reached via the twenty-five

The view from Crown Point, looking east.

miles of old highway that has been restored. It is well worth the extra hour or two required to see it.

The old highway runs between I-84 exits 17 and 35, and between exits 69 and 76. The Barlow Road is discussed in greater detail in Part Four; to get to The Barlow Road, take US 26 south of Mount Hood.

A key part of the Columbia Gorge National Scenic Area Act passed by Congress in 1986, this portion of the historic highway reminds us of an earlier age, when craftsmanship—even in roadbuilding—mattered and was honored by a nation of travelers.

Dams, Power, and Fish

Since its beginning, the Columbia River flowed into the sea without a manmade obstacle to impede it. But, like the furry, flat-tailed rodent did by instinct, some human eager beaver dreamed a scheme to use the mighty river's water by building a dam to control its seasonal fluctuations.

The first step toward commercialization of the great river came in 1932, when the U.S. Army Corps of Engineers completed a survey of the system and recommended a series of dams to facilitate irrigation, navigation, and electrical generation. Public works projects were avidly sought and promoted during the depression years, and the suggestion to build a dam on the Columbia gained quick approval. They would call the first barrier Bonneville Dam, in honor of the Army officer whose

Fish wheels, such as this "McCord Wheel," caught immense quantities of salmon from the river and dumped them onto scows like this one. Bradford Island is in the background, 1910. —Columbia River Maritime Museum

Bonneville Lock and Dam, completed in 1938, looking south with Oregon on the far side of the river. —Corps of Engineers

mysterious mission to the Pacific Northwest one hundred years earlier played an important role in the Manifest Destiny of the Oregon country.

By 1938 the dam was operational. The massive concrete structure had three parts: Across the main channel a spillway regulated the height of the water in the reservoir behind it; across the chute between Bradford Island and the Oregon shore rose a powerhouse with penstocks and turbines; adjoining the powerhouse towered a navigation lock large enough to handle sea-going vessels up to 8,000 tons.

The 76-foot-wide 500-foot-long lock cut into the rock of the channel. Its lower gates were huge steel leaves 102 feet tall, making it possible to raise a vessel over 50 feet in a single lift. The first boat to use the lock was a cargo ship named the *Charles L. Wheeler*.

The taming of the Columbia had begun.

Cheap Electricity

During the long administration of Franklin Delano Roosevelt, projects aimed at putting men back to work were embraced enthusiastically. The bigger the project, the better. So, in 1933, just after work began on Bonneville, the biggest project ever conceived in the West—Grand Coulee Dam—received quick and hearty approval. At the time, no one knew what would be done with the massive amounts of electricity generated by the upper Columbia River dam or who would irrigate and farm the million acres of desert land around the storage pool, let alone where the market would be for the crops raised. But the project would put a lot of men back to work, so it must be built.

The dam was completed in 1939, but it took many years more to develop the irrigated desert land in the Grand Coulee area of eastern Washington. In 1943, though, the government found in Grand Coulee and the Columbia River Basin an ideal combination. They needed a huge supply of electricity, a large unoccupied space in a remote region, and a vast amount of water to cool reactors for the top-secret atomic bomb.

After World War II, the demand for housing, consumer goods, and manufactured products using new alloys that required large amounts of electricity to fabricate brought on a new era of dam building in the Pacific Northwest. The mighty Columbia and its husky tributary, the Snake, offered dam sites of unequalled potential for power generation.

In rapid succession, three more big dams were built between Bonneville and Grand Coulee: McNary Dam, near Umatilla, in 1952; The Dalles Dam, just upstream from The Dalles, in 1956; and John Day Dam, near the mouth of the Oregon river, in 1962. By the time these and other projects on the Snake River in eastern Oregon and central Idaho were completed, residents of the Pacific Northwest boasted that the electricity lighting their homes and fueling their economy was the cheapest in the nation. The region quickly developed a dependency on hydroelectric power for one hundred percent of its needs. Furthermore, it looked like production of cheap electricity would continue as plans emerged to turn the 1,200 mile Columbia and the 1,036 mile Snake into placid mill ponds to their sources.

Fish Passage Problems

Several unanticipated problems arose from this flurry of dam building. To assure fish passage around Bonneville Dam, a "ladder" was designed and built to provide white water pools resembling rapids like those the anadromous fish expected to negotiate during their once-in-a-lifetime return to spawn in the mountain stream beds of their birth. Eighty-five percent of the fish reaching the dam climbed a series of pools rising a foot at a time from the base of the dam to the quiet water above, with a concentrated stream of "attraction water" flowing at all times to draw the salmon toward the foot of the ladder. The fifteen percent that failed to climb the ladder would be replaced by a hatchery built just below Bonneville Dam. Salmon eggs collected and fertilized by icthyologists assured concerned sportsmen and Indians that "more fish than ever" would contine to make their spawning runs up the Columbia and its tributaries.

When McNary, The Dalles, and John Day dams were built, fish ladders also were included in their designs. There, too, fifteen percent of the fish reaching the foot of each dam failed to solve the ladder obstacle; but the experts overcame the loss by raising and releasing more hatchery fish.

But fish ladders are impractical if the height of a dam exceeds one hundred feet, so the 550-foot-high Grand Coulee has no such facilities. As a result, all anadromous fish runs upstream from it—including the entire upper Columbia River watershed in Canada—ended. But Canada did not protest. After all, it was a big country with many rivers filled with large numbers of fish.

The Indians who traditionally fished at Celilo Falls protested The Dalles Dam, though. This stretch of white water was being smoothed out forever, they knew, and they could not gaff or net salmon in still water. Back in 1855, the federal government had made treaties with all the Indian tribes in the Pacific Northwest, generally requiring them to give up most of their ancestral lands in exchange for relatively small amounts of money and goods, plus guarantees that the government would take care of them on designated reservations.

By white standards, the amount of land allocated to the Indians seemed generous. In addition, the government promised to build schools on each reservation, pay salaries to tribal leaders for a period of twenty years, teach the Indians how to read, write, farm, and work at trades— in other words, to Americanize them. That most of the Indians took pride in their racial and cultural heritage, and did not want to live like white men, never entered the minds of the federal representatives who laid out the terms of the treaties.

Though the white leaders talked of the treaties as having been "negotiated," the sad truth was they were "dictated" on a take-it-or-leave-it basis. Because they had no alternative, the Indian chiefs touched the end of the writing stick to signify that they had signed the treaties. But as soon became obvious, few of them understood the meaning of what they had signed.

Ironically, a century later, those very treaties became the strongest piece of evidence favoring Indian rights on such issues as fishing, hunting, land ownership, water, and sovereignty. The treaties ratified by the United States Senate and signed into law by the president became the law of the land, repealable only with a two-thirds approval of the U.S. Senate and signature of the President, which wasn't likely. In the many challenges to the conditions of the treaties, some of which have gone to the United States Supreme Court, the Indians have never lost a case.

To placate the natives thereafter restricted to reservations, the federal government had agreed to allow the Indians "to fish and take game in their usual and accustomed places."

The obliteration of Celilo Falls, the most important fishing place on the Columbia River for numerous Indian tribes, required monetary compensation for its loss. The Yakima Nation, the Nez Perce Tribe, the Umatilla Confederation, and the Warm Springs Tribe were awarded cash sums ranging from $3 million to $10 million, according to how much value could be placed on the loss of the Celilo fishery, with the Indians still retaining the right to fish in other "usual and accustomed places," wherever they might exist.

In all cases, the Indians invested these sums wisely: in sawmills, furniture or boat-building factories, cultural or visitor centers, or in tourist resorts that not only offer employment to tribal members but bring in present and future income.

Dam building continued. The term "multi-purpose dam" took on meaning. In addition to the great benefits of cheap power, flood control, and irrigation, navigation again became a popular cry. With huge locks installed in each dam, still water existed as far upriver as Pasco, Washington, 350 miles inland. Powerful diesel tugboats pushed or pulled barges so big that a single tug could move the freight of a hundred railroad cars. The old cry for an "open river" indeed had come true.

By 1970, a total of 161 dams held back waters on the Columbia River's greater watershed. Of these, 43 existed on the Snake River, also a fertile breeding region for salmon, steelhead, and sturgeon. Suddenly, in the early 1970s, fisheries specialists realized that some mysterious destroyer of fish was taking its toll.

Nitrogen Gas Poison

The killer, scientist soon learned, was nitrogen, "a colorless, tasteless, odorless gaseous chemical forming nearly four-fifths of the atmosphere and a component of all living things." In normal amounts, it is harmless. In excessive amounts, it is lethal.

Whether natural or manmade, all waterfalls pick up nitrogen from the air and carry it into the pools into which they plunge. The process causes the water in those pools to become "supersaturated" with up to half again the normal nitrogen level. When fish absorb excessive nitrogen into their bloodstream through respiration, they get sick and die. An increase of nitrogen by ten percent can eventually be fatal both to downriver-migrating smolts (young fish) and upriver-migrating adults.

Below a natural waterfall, riverwater gives up its nitrogen when it strikes shallows and rapids and resumes a normal balance of elements. But below each manmade dam on the Snake and Columbia, there is typically only a quarter mile or so of free-flowing river before another still, deep pool. In these pools, the nitrogen content reaches deadly levels.

To assure propagation of the species, at least 22,500 adult steelhead must pass through the counting station at Lower Granite Dam on the Snake River. It is the eighth dam (following Bonneville, The Dalles, John

Day, and McNary on the Columbia, Ice Harbor, Lower Monumental, and Little Goose on the Snake) they must swim through before reaching their spawning streams. The nitrogen supersaturation problem—added to the stress of negotiating eight sets of fish ladders—proved deadly to the fish runs.

In the autumn of 1974, only 10,000 steelhead made their way past Lower Granite Dam. Faced with the stark prospect that this sea-going trout most prized by fishermen would vanish forever from the upriver streams, the Fish and Game departments of Idaho, Washington, and Oregon closed the season to all sports fishermen in early October that year. For three years, the season remained closed, while fish experts and the Corps of Engineers took desperate measures to restore the runs.

Unfortunately, while Idaho and Washington classify the steelhead as a game fish, Oregon calls it a commercial fish, allowing gill-netters to take them from the lower Columbia. Another complication stemmed from the ruling of a federal judge in the state of Washington, which entitled the Indians (under the terms of the 1855 treaty) to catch half of the available anadromous fish in salt and fresh water. With the Indians and the commercial fishermen catching so many Idaho-spawned fish that it threatened survival of the species, Idaho prepared a case against the states of Oregon and Washington, which, if not compromised, eventually would have gone to the Supreme Court.

At the height of the dispute—which coincided with the low point in the steelhead run—sport fishermen claimed that commercial fishermen had five hundred nets strung across the Columbia River between its mouth and McNary Dam. Since the sport fishermen were the only group entirely cut off from fishing, they grew bitter and angry. "The commercial fishermen get half the fish, the Indians get the other half—and we get what's left!" was a typical complaint.

In truth, during an average season in the mid-1970s, the lower Columbia River and Pacific Ocean fishermen took a total of twelve million salmon and steelhead. Of this number, commercial fishermen caught ten million, sport fishermen one million, and Indians one million. But in the streams of the Snake River watershed, where most of these fish had been spawned, no anadromous fish at all were taken.

Since the major cause of nitrogen supersaturation is water pouring over dam spillways, where it falls a hundred or so feet, the Corps of Engineers experimented with several devices intended to reduce the amount of nitrogen absorbed by the falling water—perforated gates, flip-lips, and others—but none worked very well. Because the loss of a few adult fish could be tolerated, while the preservation of the young smolts was vital, the fish experts concentrated on saving the young fish, which would be the breeding stock of the future.

The Dworshak National Fish Hatchery in Idaho—which had been built at a cost of $8.5 million to mitigate the loss of 55 miles of the north fork of the Clearwater as a natural fish-spawning area—was raising 8-inch smolts in half the time it normally took Mother Nature. Released into the Clearwater at Ahsaka, the young smolts were destined to journey forty miles down the Clearwater to the Snake, 140 miles down that river to the Columbia, then 330 miles down the Columbia to the Pacific Ocean, where they would spend three or four years maturing before starting their return trip to their place of birth.

Unfortunately, most of these fish were dying from the slow poison of nitrogen in the eight downstream dam pools or were chopped up by the turbines into which they were sucked by the penstocks of those same eight dams. More misfortune came when nitrogen-contaminated water from behind Dworshak Dam was inadvertently turned into their hatchery beds, killing many.

A partially successful attempt was made to save the downstream-migrating smolts by installing moving screens at the intake level of the penstocks, which trapped the fish, transported them to a pipe down and around the turbines, and put them back into the river well below the dam. But the moving screens captured only about one percent of the smolts.

The urgency of saving the smolt led to several unique methods of transporting the young fish around the downstream hazards. A few made the trip down the Snake and Columbia in deluxe style—by air, in a specially equipped tanker plane. Others were transported around the dam pools by tanker trucks whose refrigerated, oxygen-enriched waters kept the fish in the best possible environment during the long ride from eastern Washington to western Oregon. Each of the four tanker trucks

Juvenile Fish Transportation truck. —Corps of Engineers

Juvenile Fish Transportation barge at the Lower Granite Collection Station, near Lewiston, Idaho.

— Corps of Engineers

in the Corps of Engineers' Save the Steelhead fleet could carry 30,000 smolts; during the crises of the first few seasons, the trucks were constantly on the move.

Soon after completion of Lower Granite Dam in 1975, another method of transporting smolt downstream was tried—hauling them by tug and barge. Since two million smolts can fit into a barge filled with specially conditioned water, this has proved to be the most efficient and successful of all the methods so far tried.

Which of the steelhead survival measures deserves the most credit for an increase in the upriver run, the experts cannot definitely say. But in September 1977, after three closed seasons, enough steelhead passed the counting station at Lower Granite Dam to persuade the Fish and Game departments in Idaho, Washington, and Oregon to permit a "barbless-hook-only, catch-and-release" pre-season on the Clearwater, Salmon, and Snake. The success of that program then led to a cautious "catch-and-keep" limit of one steelhead per day, with a total of not more than four in the season. By early October, some 45,000 steelhead had passed the Lower Granite counting station, and the fishermen begged for a more liberal limit, so Fish and Game departments of the three states upped the daily limit to two, the season total to six.

Since that time, the runs of steelhead and salmon up the Columbia and its tributaries have remained well above the levels needed for survival of the species; but the counts of each species are carefully monitored. Fifty years ago people commonly used the expression "so many fish you could walk across the stream on their backs." No more! As with so many of our natural resources, the word "unlimited" no longer applies.

45

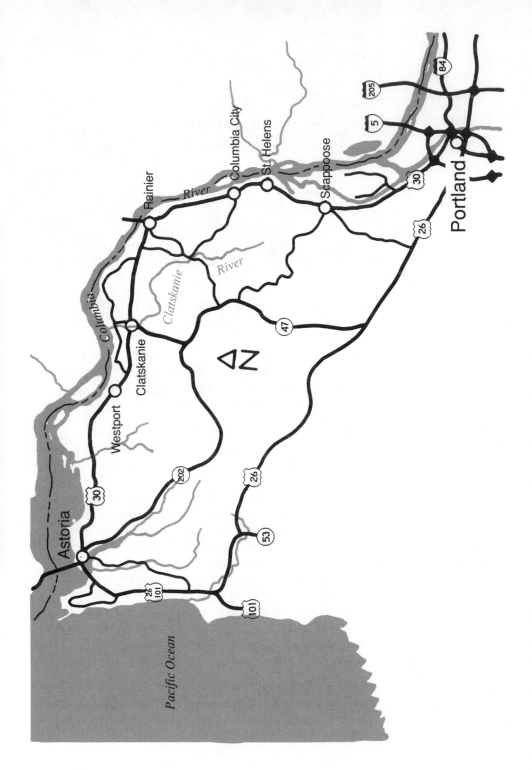

Gill-netters with a day's harvest of salmon at the mouth of the Columbia, around 1900. —Columbia River Maritime Museum

US 30
Portland—Astoria
100 miles

The Hidden River

One thing the Lewis and Clark party did not notice in the misty autumn fog on their way west was the mouth of a big river entering the Columbia from the south. Clark suspected its presence, however, for he wrote: "passed the lower point of the Island which is *nine* miles in length....the Indians make Signs that a village is Situated back of those Islands on the Lard. Side. and I believe that a chanel is Still on the Lrd. Side as a canoe passed in between the Small Islands, and made Signs that way, probably to traffick with some nativs liveing on another chanel." The oversight was corrected on the return trip upriver next spring.

As the party approached the nine-mile-long island noted on their journey downriver, they shrewdly deduced that the wide valley between the Coast Range and the Cascades must be drained by a sizable river. They were correct; Suavie Island, called Image Canoe Island by Clark, masked the mouth of a river called Multnomah by the Indians, Willamette by the whites. After passing it again, the two captains met a pair of local Indians who lived near the falls of the river and described it to them. Lewis wrote:

> we readily prevailed on them to give us a sketch of this river which they drew on a mat with a coal. it appeared that this river which they called the Mult-no-mâh discharged itself behind the Island which we

George Abernethy, first governor of Oregon Territory. —Oregon Historical Society

called the image canoe Island and as we had left this island to the S. both in ascending and decending the river we had never seen it. they informed us that it was a large river and run a considerable distance to the South between the mountains. Capt. Clark determined to return and examine this river accordingly he took a party of seven men and one of the perogues and set out ½ after 11 a.m., he hired one of the Cashhooks, for a birning glass, to pilot him to the entrance of the Multnomah river and took him on board with him.

Finding the river, from whose entrance he could see Mount Jefferson to the south, Mount Hood to the east, and Mount St. Helens and Mount Adams to the north, Clark judged it to be one-quarter the size of the Columbia and assumed that it drained a wide expanse of country as far south as Latitude 37 North, roughly San Francisco, which it did not quite do. He noted that its entrance was 142 miles up the Columbia from the Pacific Ocean, which was also an exaggeration, but quite forgivable since geographers' maps were blank until then.

The Astor Venture

The 1810 venture launched by German immigrant John Jacob Astor was so bold that it impressed even Thomas Jefferson, who tended to think big himself. He wanted to trade with all the natives of the Pacific, reaching north to Russian Alaska, south to Spanish California, and across the ocean to the East Asia. Annual supply ships sent out from New

York would sail on to the Sandwich Islands (Hawaii) and China, where prime furs, spices, and tea could net substantial profits in western-world markets. President Jefferson was so taken by the idea that he granted Astor what amounted to a monopoly charter in the fur trade of the Far West.

In forming his Pacific Fur Company, Astor planned to send forth two contingents: by sea, a ship laden with supplies and trade goods would sail around Cape Horn; by land, a strong, well-armed party would ascend the Missouri River to its headwaters, cross the Continental Divide, then follow the Clearwater, the Snake, and the Columbia to join the others. The seafaring party would arrive first and build a post at the mouth of the Columbia River, which should be operational by the time the overland group arrived.

Astor's intent was as epic in scope as the Lewis and Clark expedition had been a few years earlier. But unlike Jefferson's well-led Corps of Discovery, in which only one member of the party died during its two-and-a-half-year wilderness expedition, Astor's venture was ill-starred from beginning to end, leaving 63 dead by 1813. Blame lay on its leaders, who were as incompetent as Lewis and Clark were capable.

Seafaring Astorians, A Thorn in Astor's Side

In charge of the by-sea party on the three-hundred-ton, twelve-gun ship *Tonquin*, was a former naval officer, Captain Jonathan Thorn. A martinet by disposition and training, he brooked no challenge to his authority. Accustomed to such rigid discipline, Thorn's twenty-one man crew carried out their orders without question under risk of being flogged, keel-hauled, or worse. But of the thirty-three passengers, who included eleven clerks, thirteen Canadian voyageurs, and five mechanics, four of them—Alexander McKay, Duncan McDougal, and David and Robert Stuart—were full partners in the Pacific Fur Company; so far as they were concerned, the ship belonged to them, and the captain was their employee.

Everything his landlubber passengers did irritated Captain Thorn. Everything he did angered them. When the captain decreed that all lights must be extinguished by 8 p.m., the passengers insisted upon burning their lamps as late as they pleased; when Thorn reviled them for getting seasick and staying below decks, they retorted their right to deal with their illness as they pleased.

Upon reaching the Sandwich Islands on February 11, 1811, and dropping anchor in a small bay off the coast of the island of Hawaii, some of the crew deserted; they were captured, returned to the ship, and flogged. Moving to the island of Oahu, Captain Thorn ordered two more sailors flogged and put in irons for overstaying their leave by fifteen minutes; another, who had been absent all night, was beaten unconscious and thrown overboard, where he would surely have drowned had he not been rescued by some natives.

By the time the *Tonquin* again put out to sea and headed for the Columbia River, the members of the party were as heartily sick of the ship's captain as he was of them. When the weather turned cold and the passengers demanded that Thorn give them some warm clothing from the ample supply of goods with which the ship was stocked, he refused, driving them away with a pistol. Astor's cargo would not be touched, he declared, until it had been delivered to its destination.

They sighted Cape Disappointment on March 22; the tempestuous sandbar at the mouth of the great river raged with whitecaps. Under certain conditions of wind, tide, and current, the four-mile-wide entrance to the Columbia became a killer of ships and men; only a madman would attempt to force passage through it in this weather. But Captain Thorn did. Callously disregarding the advice of John Martin, an old seaman who had visited this coast before, Thorn ordered first mate Mr. Fox to take a whaleboat and scout a passage for the ship. Thorn also ordered four of the Canadian voyageurs to go along as crew. Fox asked that experienced sailors be sent along to man the oars, but the captain refused to spare them. "Voyageurs are supposed to be expert on water," he sneered. "Let them show me how skillful they are."

With a premonition that he was going to his death, Fox appealed to Astor's partners: "I am sent off without seamen to man my boat, in boisterous weather, on the most dangerous part of the northwest coast. My uncle was lost a few years ago on this same bar, and now I am going to lay my bones alongside his." Thorn called Fox a coward, disregarding a final plea from the partners. The longboat pushed off from the ship and the five men soon disappeared in the misty fog. They were never seen again.

Next morning, Captain Thorn dispatched a second boat, this time with volunteers Alexander McKay and David Stuart, who hoped to find some trace of the missing men. But the wind and tide set so fiercely against them that they nearly foundered and were forced to return at once. A third boat under the command of the second mate, Mr. Mumford, fared no better and nearly capsized before coming back to the ship. In exasperation, the stubborn captain sent out a fourth boat with a navigator named Aiken, sailmaker John Coles, armorer Stephen Weekes, and two Sandwich Islanders recruited at Oahu. It, too, disappeared.

During the night, a strong wind and a powerful ebb tide pulled the *Tonquin* closer to the rock-strewn beach, but by morning the weather improved and the wind changed to favor a landing. Finally, on the flood tide, the *Tonquin* crossed over the bar, scraping her keel several times but dodging further misfortune. Shore parties searched for the missing

Tonquin *crossing the bar at the entrance of the Columbia River, March 25, 1811.* —Penrose Library, Whitman College

men and found Weekes plus one badly injured Hawaiian. There was no trace of the other eight men.

Impatient to get his ship unloaded so that he could sail north to Nootka Sound and begin trading with Indians there, Captain Thorn gave the partners only three days to select a site for their trading post. Unable to find a very satisfactory location, they settled for a place on the south shore, where they erected a temporary shed to store their merchandise and equipment. After unloading building materials for the fort and the framework for a schooner to be used in the coastal trade, the *Tonquin* set sail for Vancouver Island.

The Tonquin Disaster

In a nearby bay the ship picked up an Indian named Lamazee, an interpreter who had traveled the northern coast twice before and knew something of the various tribal languages. "Steering to the north, Captain Thorn arrived in a few days at Vancouver's Island," Washington Irving wrote in his book *Astoria*, "and anchored in the harbor of Neweetee, very much against the advice of his Indian interpreter, who warned him against the perfidious character of the natives of this part of the coast. Numbers of canoes soon came off, bringing sea otter skins to sell."

In his dealings with the Indians Captain Thorn was every bit as impatient and tactless as he had been with the Astor party members during their voyage to the Northwest Coast. After quoting the shrewd old chief, Nookamis, a take-it-or-leave-it price for the furs he offered,

51

which the chief declined, the captain insulted him by rubbing a pelt contemptuously in his face, then dismissed him over the side of the ship; the rest of the natives of course followed.

Next morning twenty or so apparently unarmed Indians appeared alongside the ship and indicated that they were ready to trade on the captain's terms. Foolishly, he let them come aboard without limiting their number, which soon increased as they began to trade for the knives they so craved. Taking alarm at last, Captain Thorn ordered them off the ship. It was too late. Responding to a signal from their chief, the Indians threw back their blankets, and with knives and war clubs launched a murderous attack upon the captain and his crew.

After killing Thorn, Pacific Fur Company partner Alexander McKay, and many others, the natives were driven off the ship by four surviving crew members, who finally managed to break out and use the firearms. Mr. Lewis, the ship's clerk, was so badly wounded that when the other three proposed to take a small boat and escape the besieged vessel that night, he refused to go. Those three got only a few miles from the island before they were discovered, captured, and tortured to death by the vindictive Indians.

The final fate of the *Tonquin* can only be speculated upon, based primarily on a story later told at Fort Astoria by the native interpreter, Lamazee, whose life had been spared by his fellow Indians. On the morning after the attack, before the three escapees had been detected, some Indians cautiously approached the ship still at anchor in the bay, her sails loose and flapping in the wind. Lamazee was with them. As they paddled their canoes around the *Tonquin*, the seriously wounded Mr. Lewis came on deck and greeted them in a friendly fashion, waving an invitation to come on board. "Those who mounted to the deck met with no opposition," Irving wrote. "No one seemed to be on board, for Mr. Lewis, after inviting them, had disappeared. Other canoes now pressed forward to board the prize; the decks were soon crowded and the sides covered with the clambering savages, all intent on plunder. In the midst of their eagerness and exultation, the ship blew up with a terrific explosion."

The powder magazine of the *Tonquin* had apparently been ignited by Mr. Lewis, throwing Lamazee, who was in the main sheets, into the water unhurt. By his later account, arms, legs, and mutilated bodies were blown into the air, and dreadful havoc was made in the surrounding canoes. In relating the disaster to the partners at Fort Astoria months later, Lamazee estimated that perhaps one hundred Indians were killed.

Loss of the *Tonquin* greatly jeopardized Astor's enterprise. Not only did it ruin the initial trading run to Alaska, California, and China, but Captain Thorn's reprehensible actions seriously undermined the credibility of the traders who remained at the mouth of the Columbia and sought friendlier relations with the natives. The mere handful of men now stranded on the savage Northwest Coast faced potential hostility from local Indians, and there was no word yet from the overland party.

In need of leverage over the savages, partner Duncan McDougal abruptly halted rumors of a murderous conspiracy by threatening them with germ warfare. He called them within the walls of the fort and showed them a small bottle he carried in his pocket. Well aware of the Indians' extreme dread of smallpox, McDougal claimed the vial contained the highly infectious and deadly disease—safely corked, for now, but easily released should the need arise. Struck with horror and alarm, the chiefs implored him not to uncork the bottle. This advantage kept the natives friendly, or at least in check, until the Astorians could lessen their vulnerability.

By the end of September 1811, a substantial fort of stone and clay was built. The small schooner, *Dolly*, named after Astor's daughter, had been put together and launched. As soon as the overland party arrived, the fur-trading business could begin.

Overland Astorians, the Hunt for Oregon

Unable to hire a sufficient number of experienced Americans for the overland section of the party, Astor employed and took in as partners a number of French-Canadians, Scotsmen, Irishmen, and Englishmen whose loyalties inclined more toward the North West Company than toward his own fledgling Pacific Fur Company. One of these partners was former Nor'wester Donald MacKenzie, whom Alexander Ross describes as a big, powerful man weighing 312 pounds; another was fellow-American Wilson Price Hunt, whose loyalty to Astor was complete, but whose leadership decisions tended toward vacillation and weakness.

Hunt led the overland party of sixty-four, including a large quantity of trade goods, traps, ammunition, and baggage. Most of its members were seasoned frontiersmen. Originally planning to ascend the Missouri River, as Lewis and Clark had done, Hunt's fear of hostility from the Blackfeet induced him to abandon that route in the land of the Arikaras and cross the Rockies farther south. Taking a leisurely month to trade his boats and extra supplies for horses, his group traveled west through the Bighorn Mountains and the Wind River country, entering Jackson Hole by way of the Hoback River. Because of their slow pace, it was now late September, so Hunt detached four men to remain for the winter.

The party reached an abandoned trading post across the Tetons on Henry's Fork October 8, 1811. According to Hiram Chittenden, who has written the best history of this journey in his *American Fur Trade of the Far West*, it was here that Hunt "committed the great mistake of the expedition."

One hundred miles to the west over relatively easy terrain lay Lemhi Pass and the trail blazed earlier by Lewis and Clark. With 118 horses, in four days' time the well-mounted Hunt party could easily have reached the land of the Shoshones, who were friendly and would have gladly guided them across the Nez Perce Pass or Lolo Trail. And after the party reached the Clearwater and the even more hospitable Nez Perces, the rest of the journey would have been easy.

But, to the river-oriented French-Canadians, Henry's Fork looked very inviting. Hunt knew nothing about that country except that this southward-flowing river joined the Snake southwest of Jackson Hole, and that the Snake flowed west, then north, then west again until it joined the mighty Columbia. Local Indians warned him that the Snake was unnavigable, but these voyageurs were regarded as the finest rivermen in North America; what could the Indians know about navigating white water compared to such expertise? Furthermore, one of the partners was suffering "with an ailment that made riding a horse a torture." So, Hunt "yielded to the desires of the party, abandoned the horses, and decided to trust to the river the rest of the way. He at once set about manufacturing canoes, and this work was completed and the flotilla loaded within ten days."

Detaching four more trappers to winter in the vicinity plus partner Joseph Miller, who had grown so disgusted with the enterprise that he decided to give up his share and quit, the party left its horses in the care of two Snake Indians on October 19, and embarked in fifteen canoes on the strong, dark, rapid stream. Travel on the river went smoothly at first; they made good time and felt satisfied with choosing this route. But that soon changed.

As the river's true character revealed itself, the voyageurs changed its name from "Mad River," which they had first called it, to *La Maudite Rivière Enragée*, "The Accursed Mad River." In rock-strewn gorges and white water rapids expressively named the Devil's Scuttle Hole and Caldron Linn, a boat was wrecked and Antoine Clappine drowned. Belatedly, Hunt suspended further attempts at navigation until the downstream hazards could be appraised. His own inspection of a forty-mile stretch convinced him that the rapids could not be negotiated. But other members of the party thought differently until four more boats were lost.

Faced with the grim prospect of being set afoot in the midst of the bleak Snake River desert, probably in the vicinity of Twin Falls, Hunt called "a bewildered council," out of which came the desperate decision to split up into four smaller groups: the first stayed to dig caves in which to cache extra supplies; the second would head northwest toward the Nez Perce country; the third would return to Henry's Fork for the horses left there; and the fourth would proceed downriver. Where and when the groups might reunite in the desolate, unknown terrain ahead was left mostly to chance.

After three days, those sent back for horses declared their mission too risky, so they rejoined the men digging caches. Several days after that, the group continuing downriver returned, too, reporting the Snake's waters absolutely unnavigable. Now Hunt decided to travel afoot in two groups, one on each bank of the Snake. It was November 9, and winter had come.

The Nez Perce-bound group of Donald MacKenzie, Robert McClellan, and John Reed, was most fortunate of all; it made its way across the mountains to the Clearwater in twenty-one days. With help from the friendly Nez Perces, they floated down the Snake and Columbia without serious incident and reached Astoria Jaunary 18, 1812.

Hunt's pedestrian Snake River groups wandered, marching hither and yon and suffering greatly from cold, starvation, and illness. At Hells Canyon they found it impossible to follow the river's banks, so the two parties reunited. Near Farewell Bend on Snake River, they left behind a half dozen men too weak or ill to travel and the body of Baptiste Prevost, who had become so frenzied at the sight of food that he "danced in a delirum of joy" while in a canoe, upset it, and drowned; two others, hunter John Day and partner Ramsey Crooks, had gotten lost. The rest crossed the Blue Mountains in midwinter over what later became the Oregon Trail and reached the mouth of the Columbia on February 15.

The two lost men, Crooks and Day, were found wandering the west slope of the Blues by some friendly Umatilla Indians, who fed them and pointed them toward the Columbia. But the men proceeded too far west until they stumbled along a north-flowing river that was later named after John Day. They followed it to the Columbia, where they encountered a group of Wishram Indians who took their guns and clothes and left them to die of exposure. In May 1812, they were found naked, starving, and destitute by whites and taken to Astoria. Crooks quickly recovered, but John Day became mentally deranged and did not regain his health for many months.

Straggling into Astoria from ten to fourteen months after leaving St. Louis on March 12, 1811, the overland contingent of the Astor's Pacific Fur Company arrived only three months ahead of their competition—the British North West Company—which traveled overland from Montreal.

Astor Sells Out

The Nor'westers, disappointed at not being first on the lower Columbia, focused instead on the Snake, planting a flag and posting a sign at its mouth which laid claim to that country in the name of Great Britain. To avoid circumvention, the Astorians reached north to the Okanogan

Fort Astoria, as it was in 1813. —Penrose Library, Whitman College

and east along the Snake to establish trade with the inland Indians. But John Jacob Astor's plan to build a chain of trading posts throughout the Pacific Northwest was interrupted by the War of 1812 between England and the United States.

When news of the war reached the Astorians in early January 1813, they bickered amongst themselves about what to do. With the British navy controlling the high seas and a land route not yet established, there was no way the isolated trading post could get supplies and send its furs to market. They decided to sell out to their new rivals, the North West Company. After haggling for months over the price, they made the sale final November 12, 1813, so Donald MacKenzie headed east to tell Astor.

It appeared that the first American business enterprise in the Pacific Northwest had been an abject failure. The British even changed Astoria's name to Fort George. But by a fluke of fate, the enterprise ended on a happy, if slightly cockeyed, note. Shortly after the Nor'westers took over at Fort George, the British man-of-war *Raccoon* dropped anchor and its captain came ashore. Since a state of war existed between Great Britain and the United States, he told the traders his orders required him to take the post. He didn't appreciate that it was already British property; he seized it anyway.

But when the United States won the war, a condition of the peace treaty stipulated that all property seized by Great Britain must be returned to the U.S. Did sale or seizure take precedence? Seizure won out, and in a comic-opera scene, Fort Astoria—that is, Fort George—was solemnly given back to representatives of its former owners, the traders, who then, having gone to work for the British North West Company, reaffirmed its sale and ceremoniously turned it over again to the British. Thus, on a technicality, Astor managed to sell out and withdraw from the fur business in the Pacific Northwest without compromising his country's political claims to sovereignty in the region.

Under the terms of the 1818 Joint Occupancy Treaty, citizens of both Great Britain and the United States were allowed equal access to the Oregon country for ten-year renewable periods. This way, eventual ownership of the region would be decided by the people who lived there, which, for the time being at least, meant only those few wilderness souls who trapped and traded furs. In a world long used to settling territorial claims by force, the agreement was unique.

Steamers on the Columbia

Appropriately enough, the first steamboat to operate on the Columbia River was named the *Beaver*. Designed to work in the fur trade on the lower river for the Hudson's Bay Company, which had absorbed the British North West Company after a long and bitter battle, the *Beaver* was a small ship. It weighed a modest 187 tons, measured one hundred feet in length with a twenty foot beam and an eleven foot depth, and drew eight feet of water.

Brought over from England by the Hudson's Bay Company in 1836, the Beaver *was the first steamship to work on the lower Columbia and Northwest Coast.* —Columbia River Maritime Museum

Despite her size, the *Beaver* was built to last. Her keel, a solid piece of prime timber, was a foot square when laid in a Thames shipyard in 1834. "Good English oak went into her frames," writes marine historian Randall Mills, "and her planking was of oak, too, some English and some African. She was double planked—no doubt with a view to resisting the hard knocks she would receive in navigating that distant river—and she was copper fastened throughout. Copper sheathing completed the structure of the hull."

Though originally schooner-rigged with three masts, the *Beaver* was converted to a brigantine for the long trip to the Northwest Coast, which she made under sail. Once there, her two engines built by Boulton, Watt & Company propelled her with side-lever action. A side-wheeler with both thirteen-foot paddle wheels mounted well forward, her buckets measured six and one-half feet long. Her iron boilers, designed to supply low-pressure steam favored by early nineteenth-century builders, could turn the wheels thirty times a minute and send the ship along at a maximum nine miles an hour, though her usual pace was a plodding six. (While the speed of sea-going ships is measured in knots, river vessels are meted in miles per hour.) After completing her tests in the Thames to the satisfaction of Lloyd's, which pronounced her A-1, the *Beaver* had twenty tons of coal placed in her bunkers; then her paddle wheels were unshipped and stored on deck for the long trip to the Northwest.

Accompanied by the bark *Columbia*, her caretaker during the voyage, the *Beaver* cast off her lines and drifted out into the stream on August 31, 1835. Two months later the two ships rounded Cape Horn, then reached Honolulu in early February, where they stayed three weeks to resupply before setting out on the final leg of the voyage. At Fort Vancouver, one hundred miles up the Columbia, factor John McLoughlin grudgingly ordered a cannon fired to salute her arrival, even though he did not think much of such new-fangled inventions as steamboats.

> Fitting her for steam service did not take long. The wheels were swung overside and put in place, the engines cleaned and oiled, and the boilers filled. On her first run, her captain, David Home, took her a few miles downriver as a trial. Then he made a number of short jaunts to limber the machinery—to a sawmill, to a landing downstream where Indians reported that black stones would burn, then back to the sawmill, with the *Columbia* in tow, the first of a long series of towing jobs that she and her successors were to handle.

McLoughlin accurately predicted that the *Beaver* would be too expensive to operate profitably. Year after year, he reported that the ship's operating costs exceeded its income. Once its bunker of coal was exhausted, no local supply of the "black stones that burn" could be found, so the *Beaver*'s fuel switched to wood; and she consumed a fantastic amount of it. Wanting to get the smelly steamboat out of his sight, McLoughlin sent it up the coast to Puget Sound and Alaska. During one memorable trip to Sitka, the *Beaver* burned forty cords of wood a day, forcing the crew to alternately steam one day and chop wood the next. But its prestige and lasting impression on the local Indians far outweighed its exorbitant operating costs.

Though she occasionally paid brief visits to the Columbia River and Fort Vancouver, the *Beaver* spent most of her long working life cruising up and down the Northwest Coast picking up furs for the *Columbia* to take back to London. During British Columbia's Fraser River gold rush in the 1860s, her upper works were stripped down to an ugly cabin and a small pilot house. After her masts were removed, leaving her tall stacks rising awkwardly amidships, she went to work as a tug.

> Never a beauty, even in her prime, she became particularly unattractive in her new dress. But no one noticed as she plodded about the Sound, busy towing freighters. At last, in 1888, she slammed onto a rock at the entrance to the harbor at Vancouver, B.C., and refused to be dislodged. Spitefully, a newer, larger boat swept by and the wash from the paddle wheel rolled the old *Beaver* back onto the piercing ledge. It was all over, though her hull was still solid and undecayed, and her copper bolts and fittings as strong as ever.

The first American steamboat to enter the river came in May 1849, when the Army transport *Massachusetts* brought federal troops to subdue the Cayuse Indians east of the Cascades. Doubly a pioneer, the steamer built four years earlier in Boston was also one of the earliest screw-propelled vessels. Inspired by arrival of the *Massachusetts* and the booming California gold-rush trade, the citizens of Astoria decided to build a steamer of their own.

Finished and launched by July 1850, the new ninety-foot side-wheel *Columbia* was built double-ended, like a ferryboat. On her first trip upriver, with Captain Frost at the helm, two local Indian boys who were fishing on the river and claimed to know its channels were taken on as guides. The cautious captain settled for fifty miles the first day, pulling ashore and tying to a convenient tree when darkness came. Next day, he cast off and chugged upriver, coming abreast of Portland at three o'clock in the afternoon. It was the Fourth of July. The collective citizenry greeted her with pride and joy, and made no effort to keep the celebration quiet.

Diminishing the Deadly Sandbar

The first and most dangerous obstacle to navigation encountered by ships entering the Columbia was at the mouth of the river itself—the Columbia River sandbar. Contrary to what poets and creators of geographical legends had written, the Columbia was not a river that flowed "tranquilly into the Western Sea." As early seafaring explorers had learned, the four-mile-wide juncture of the mighty river with the even mightier ocean was one of nature's elemental battlegrounds, where currents, tides, and winds met in constant conflict.

Crossing the bar and entering the river had been a high-risk adventure during the age of sail. With the advent of steamboats, it became only slightly less dangerous. At low tide, the river meandered through channels cut in the constantly shifting sand. A pilot coming through deep water one day was never sure what he might find there the next.

"Two problems faced the engineers," writes Randall Mills. "To find a way to make the channel deep enough at low tide to permit ships of ordinary draft to enter, and to keep a channel open once it had been dredged." As early as 1875, the army engineers in charge of eliminating navigational hazards in rivers and harbors had been surveying and trying to improve Columbia shipping channels. In their search for a solution to the river's sandbar problem, the Corps of Engineers called on Colonel James Eads, who had faced the same problem at the mouth of the Mississippi.

> On first glance there seemed to be little similarity between the clear Columbia and the muddy Mississippi endlessly dumping silt into the Gulf, but the effect was the same. The ocean kept pushing sand up toward the mouth of the Columbia and building bars that the outflowing river had to cut through. Surveys in 1878 showed that an application of the methods Eads had used just below New Orleans would be effective, and in 1884 the first appropriation was passed for construction.

In principle, the solution was simple enough. The river mouth must be compressed between two dikes or jetties of stone. One would be built out from the north shore, Cape Disappointment, the other from the south, where there was a low projection called Clatsop Spit. The narrow

The Astoria Bridge to Washington is four miles long.

Stern-wheeler tugboat fleet at the Shaver Transportation Company in Portland. —Columbia River Maritime Museum

passage between the two jetties would naturally increase the river's velocity, constantly scouring the channel and maintaining a safe depth for ocean-going ships. Simple though the remedy was in principle, it was expensive to implement.

Railroad tracks were built atop jetties where pile drivers pounded timbers into the sands to form trestles for extending more rails toward the Columbia's central channel. Engines pushed strings of cars loaded with rocks to be dumped into the water. Gradually, as more and more rocks went into the sea beside the trestles, they packed and merged as long ridges or dams against which the waves piled sand to make the whole thing an extension of the spit or jetty itself. Where the bottom seemed unstable, trainloads of brush or small trees with their branches left on were dumped to form a mat that held the rock in place until the waves did their work of scooping sand.

Much of the rock came from a hundred miles upriver, transported there by a specially built stern-wheeler, the *Cascades*, a large vessel able to push or pull alongside five huge barges filled with tons of rock. By the time the engineers finished their work, the river had gouged out a thirty-foot deep channel.

> The jetties grew from the first thousand feet built in 1894 until the south jetty reached out seven miles from its beginnings at Fort Stevens. Toward it from Cape Disappointment the north jetty stretched four and one-half miles and gathered itself behind a shoal that enlarged Peacock Spit.

In truth, modifying the channel of a large river is a project that never ends. As long as water runs downhill, ocean tides ebb and rise, and winds move waves toward and away from shore, the river bottom will change and the depths of ship channels must be closely monitored, as they still are at the mouth of the Columbia River.

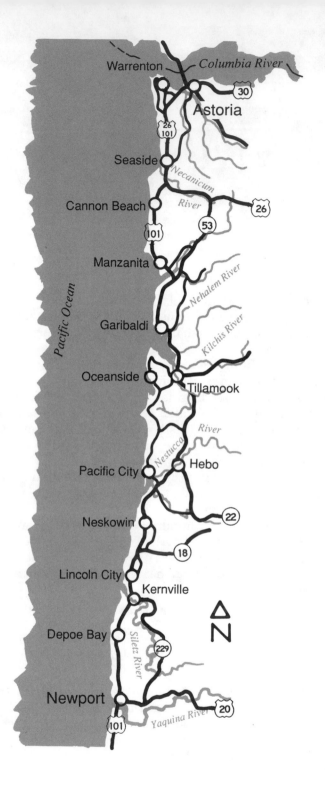

PART II

The Oregon Coast

US 101
Astoria—Tillamook
65 miles

Columbia River Bar

From the time of its discovery by Captain Robert Gray in 1792 to the present day, the Columbia River sandbar has been a graveyard for ships. The number of vessels lost or destroyed in the area—fishing boats, harbor craft, and seagoing ships—exceeds two thousand, marine historians estimate. Fifteen hundred lives have been claimed as a result of these wrecks.

Because winds and currents bring air and water of varying temperatures and velocities into constant conflict, the region's weather can be extreme. From April to August prevailing winds in the vicinity of Astoria blow from the northwest; for the rest of the year, southwesterly winds dominate. On the coast during the summer months, northwest winds become gales, which sometimes last for several days. In winter southerly winds may rage at any time, bringing with them heavy southwest swells. The wind velocity at the mouth of the river is usually high. United States Weather Bureau records show the average at fourteen miles an hour, increasing from ten in July and August to nineteen in December.

Fog most frequently shrouds the mouth of the Columbia River in July, August, and September, but it may roll in any time. Often the fog extends many miles out to sea, is very dense, and lasts for days. The average rainfall at Astoria is 77 inches a year.

The velocity of the current at the entrance to the river is two and a half knots at its peak. The range between high and low tide is seven and a half feet.

Lieutenant Charles Wilkes of the United States Navy made the first survey of the river's mouth in 1841. He found the bar's constantly shifting sands made it difficult to draw reliable charts. He dramatically demonstrated the dangers of the bar when a unit of his squadron, the USS *Peacock*, grounded on the north shore of the river entrance and became a total loss. He called the spot "Peacock Spit," a name it retains still.

Lieutenant Wilkes expressed puzzlement that so knowledgeable a navigator and explorer as George Vancouver had failed to discover the mouth of the River of the West. "I found breakers extending from Cape Disappointment to Point Adams in one unbroken line," he wrote in 1845. "I am at a loss to conceive how any doubt should have ever existed that here was the mouth of the mighty river, whose existence was reported so long."

From an early time, responsible ship captains accepted the necessity of employing local pilots with knowledge of the sandbar's changing channels before attempting to take their vessels into or out of the river. Impatient captains wishing to save money or time all too often took chances piloting themselves—and often regretted doing so. In 1849, for example, four ships wrecked on the bar: the *Aurora*, the *Morning Star*, the *Sylvia de Grasse*, and the *Josephine*. In 1852, five ships wrecked: the *Dolphin*, the *General Warren*, the *Machigone*, the *Marie*, and the *Potomac*.

Wrecks became less frequent with a growing knowledge of the bar and the establishment of pilot and tugboat service, according to marine historian James Gibbs. The first successful bar pilot association was begun by Captain George Flavel, who came west with the Gold Rush in 1849 and made his way to the Oregon country the following year, settling in Astoria. Once the state of Oregon began issuing licences to Columbia River pilots, Flavel was among the first to receive one.

"For almost twenty years, Flavel and his nervy pilots enjoyed a near monopoly of the towage and pilotage into the Columbia River. His rates were high, but his service was excellent. He never sent a man where he would not go himself," Gibbs writes.

George Flavel's Victorian style mansion in Astoria, from whose lofty cupola he once scanned the sea's horizon, is now owned by the Clatsop County Historical Society and open to the public.

"Near the turn of the century there was suddenly an amazing recurrence of wrecks," Gibbs points out. "Some nautical cynics surmise that this was a way of collecting insurance on hard-pressed sailing ships in the steam age. Besides, at ebb tide, the crew could walk from a ship grounded on certain graveyard beaches."

Navigational Aids

Recognizing the need for navigational aids at the mouth of the river, the government decided in 1853 to build a beacon on Cape Disappointment on the northern portal of the Columbia. Proof that it was badly needed came when the American bark *Oriole*, which carried supplies and a crew for construction of the signal light, wrecked near there in late September that year. Thanks to the skill of Pilot Flavel, no lives were lost, but because all the materials and equipment had to be replaced, the beacon was not completed until three years later.

Put into operation in 1856, the Cape Disappointment Lighthouse stood on a headland 220 feet above the water and shot its beam of 700,000 candlepower on the white flash and 160,000 candlepower on the red twenty-one miles out to sea. It is still in operation.

The Point Adams Lighthouse was built in 1875 at the river's southern entrance, but completion of the south jetty ended the need for it, so it was abandoned and eventually burned.

An increasing number of wrecks near the turn of the century resulted in the building of one of the most picturesque and powerful lighthouses on the Pacific Coast in 1898. Located on the extreme end of Cape Disappointment and only two miles away from that beacon, the North Head Lighthouse stands on a conical tower 194 feet high and sends out a beam of 3.5 million candlepower. More visible to ships approaching from the north than the Cape Disappointment beacon, it became automated in 1961.

*Point Adams
Lighthouse, 1878.*
—Columbia River Maritime
Museum

As a further aid to navigation beginning in 1892, lightships equipped with foghorns and lights were stationed about 5 miles southwest of the entrance to the Columbia River. Until outmoded by the universal use of radar in the 1960s, four lightships—known by their numbers 50, 88, 93, and 604—held the station continuously. Since these vessels were out of touch with land and endured extremes of wind, sea, and weather, and were stuck in a single spot for six-week stints without relief, serving aboard one of them was the worst kind of sea duty imaginable.

As any landlubber with a tendency to become seasick soon discovers on a deep-sea fishing trip once land is no longer in sight, the pitching and heaving of a small vessel in rough weather is magnified many times when the boat's wallowing from side to side is combined with its up and down motion. Add to that being confined in cramped quarters with several other people and nothing to do but keep a light shining and a foghorn blowing for 42 nights and days, and the term "stir-crazy" begins to take on new meaning. This describes the sort of duty lightship sailors had to withstand.

The fourth and last of these vessels, *Columbia River Lightship No. 604*, which went on station in the spring of 1950, was an all-steel vessel costing half a million dollars. The previous lightship had served forty years, since 1910. With a red hull and the word *Columbia* in large white letters on each side, the new vessel was 128 feet long, 618 tons, and

Moored next to the Columbia River Maritime Museum in Astoria, Columbia Lightship No. 604 *is open to visitors six days a week.*

The Columbia River Maritime Museum is one of the finest of its kind.

outfitted with the latest electronic gear, including a gyro compass, radar, and direction finder. The light shining from her foremast was 57 feet above the water and visible for thirteen miles; the radio beacon and fog signal were synchronized for distance-finding. Designed for the six-week vigils, she had an apparatus that made seawater potable and provided air-conditioned quarters for sixteen men.

Even with these amenities, duty on board her was hardly a luxury cruise. Curious visitors can see for themselves by taking a tour of the retired lightship moored next door to the Columbia River Maritime Museum in Astoria. If you desire a further glimpse into life afloat as a crew member of such a vessel, read the realistic novel, *Lightship*, by Archie Binns, originally published in 1934 by Reynal and Hitchcock. Binns had served aboard just such a ship only a few years earlier. He tells a particularly vivid story about a cook aboard the lightship who became so overwhelmed by the loneliness of his job that he kept threatening to "go over the side" and take a walk, even though the vessel was stationed several miles out to sea. Equally vivid is another novel by Archie Binns entitled *You Rolling River*, which is set in Astoria around the turn of the century and has a fictional bar pilot as its leading character; it tells of shipwrecks, storms, and crimps who, by doping drinks in waterfront bars, supplied sailors to captains desperate to fill out their crews.

Unexpected Storm

Not all of the lives lost in maritime accidents near the mouth of the Columbia River were in the wrecks of big ships. In his book *Oregon's Salty Coast*, James Gibbs tells of a day when small boats of the fishing fleet between the south entrance to the Columbia and Willapa Bay, 35 miles to the north, were caught in an unexpected storm with disastrous results.

On a typical spring morning May 4, 1880, virtually every fishing boat in the area was trolling for salmon or dragging for bottom fish. Unknown to the fishermen in perhaps 250 vessels, most of which were under sail, a phenomenal freak of weather was in the making.

> Without forewarning, a powerful wind of hurricane force suddenly came out of nowhere, changing the peaceful ocean waves into massive, seething billows. Showing no mercy, winds of more than 100 MPH contorted the sea's face and made playthings of the small fishboats. Pummelled, tossed, turned, capsized, and swamped, one by one they disappeared from view, the terrified fishermen thinking the end of the world had come. Thrown into the mass of liquid fury to fend for themselves, death to most came quickly.

The uncommon local squall, which roared in from the northwest, lasted only thirty minutes. By the time it ended more than 240 vessels had been destroyed and about 325 lives were lost. "Never before and never since," Gibbs writes, "has such a strange contingency of weather been witnessed off the Columbia River."

Great Republic Wreck

One of the most spectacular wrecks on the Columbia River sandbar was that of the *Great Republic* April 19, 1879, which killed eleven. Built in 1866 at Greenport, Long Island, New York, she had served in the China trade for several years, then in the late 1870s began carrying freight and passengers between San Francisco and Portland. She was a big side-wheeler measuring 378 feet and registered at 4,750 tons. She was also fast, once making the hundred-mile run from Portland to Astoria in five hours and fifteen minutes.

Departing San Francisco in the spring of 1879, she carried 896 passengers and over a hundred crew members when she arrived at the mouth of the Columbia at midnight April 18. The pilot boat was waiting for her and pulled alongside to put Pilot Thomas Doig aboard. He planned to wait until daylight before taking the ship across the bar, but changed his mind for some reason and set the vessel's course at 12:30 a.m. What happened then is best told in the words of the two men who testified in a special hearing held following the loss of the ship.

Stating that he had placed the vessel in charge of Pilot Thomas Doig at 12:30 a.m. on April 19, Captain James Carroll, the ship's master, gave this account of the disaster:

There was not a ripple on the water, and we came over the bar under a slow bell all the way, crossing safely and reaching the inside buoy. The first and third officers were on the lookout with me. I had a pair of glasses and was the first to discover Sand Island, and found the bearings all right. I reported to the pilot, who had as yet not seen it. We ran along probably two minutes, and I then told the pilot I thought we were getting too close to the island and that he had better haul her up. He replied, "I do not think we are in far enough." A minute later I said, "Port your helm and put it hard over, as I think you are getting too near the island." He made no reply, but ran along for about five minutes and then put the helm hard aport, and the vessel swung up, heading toward Astoria. But the ebb tide caught her on the starboard bow, and being so near the island, sent her on the spit.

She went on so lightly that few knew of the accident, but as the tide was falling we had no chance to get the vessel off that night. The next tide was a small one, and we could do nothing, and as the barometer was falling, indicating a storm, I sent Mr. Peck, the purser, to Fort Canby for assistance. The tugs *Benham* and *Canby* arrived, followed soon after by the *Shubrick* and the *Columbia* With the aid of small boats the passengers were transferred to the steamers and taken to Astoria, the *Benham* making two trips. The entire crew remained on board and I made arrangements with Captain Flavel to have three tugs there at high tide. In the meantime the crew was at work discharging coal in an effort to lighten the vessel. At 8 p.m. a southwest gale started in, making a heavy sea, chopping to the southeast about midnight. Up to this time the ship was lying easy and taking no water, but the heavy sea prevented the tugs from rendering assistance and also drove her higher on the spit, and shortly after midnight she began to work, breaking the steampipes and disabling engines. A few remaining passengers were put ashore on Sand Island at 6 a.m. on Sunday and were followed by the crew, the ship commencing to break up so that it was dangerous to remain aboard. The last boat left the ship at 10:30 a.m., and in getting away, the steering oar broke and the boat capsized, drowning eleven of the fourteen men it contained.

At about this time a heavy sea boarded the ship and carried away the staterooms on the starboard side, gutted the dining room, broke up the floor of the social hall, and carried away the piano. Several seas afterward boarded her forward and carried away the starboard guard, officers' room and steerage deck, also a number of horses. I remained aboard until 5 p.m., when the pilot and I lowered a lifeboat and came ashore.

At the time of the disaster, the *Great Republic* was insured for $50,000, and her cargo for an additional $25,000, Gibbs writes. She carried 1,059 tons of general freight valued at $75,000. Among the cargo were twenty-seven horses, only seven of which managed to reach shore after they were dumped overboard.

Pilot Thomas Doig gave his version of the wreck.

> I took charge of the ship at the automatic buoy at 12:30 a.m. I kept the lead going constantly from the time I took charge, and after crossing the bar, put the ship under a slow bell, and I ran her that way until she grounded. After crossing the bar I took my course for the middle of Sand Island with a bright lookout kept. Captain Carroll reported Sand Island to me, and I answered him and said, "That's all right." He then said, "Port your helm, Doig, she is getting too near the Island." I answered, "I don't think she is far enough in from two to four minutes." About that time I sighted Sand Island and put the helm hard over, she answering her helm and coming up on her course headed northeast; but immediately on getting her on course she brought up on the spit with her port bilge.
>
> On her starboard quarter I had five fathoms by the lead, and the only reason I can give for the disaster is that, when I took charge of the vessel, I did not figure in the ebb being so strong. I knew the tide had been ebbing for at least an hour and a half, but had no fear as to her not having water enough, as she was drawing but seventeen feet, and I knew there was plenty of water for that draught at that stage of the tide. The ship working under a slow bell, and the ebb tide striking her on the starboard quarter, had set her down for at least a quarter or a half mile from where I thought I was on my course. When she brought up on the spit, her headway was so slow that the jar was hardly noticeable by those who were standing on deck, and both the Captain and myself thought she would go off at the next high tide.

But the *Great Republic* was destined never to get off the bar intact. After the underwriters had settled with her owners, a salvage firm paid $3,780 for the stranded vessel and its cargo and went to work reclaiming what it could, which wasn't much. A month later the hull aft of the walking beam crumbled into the sea and the fore and aft mainmast went over the side. In another ten days the walking beam and the two large paddle wheels alone remained intact. Part of the wreckage could be seen at low tide as late as the turn of the century. The steamer's grave was marked on the charts thereafter as "Republic Spit."

Earlier, the decision of the marine inspectors' inquiry resulted in the suspension of Pilot Doig's license for one year and Captain Carroll's license for six months. Upon hearing the decision, Captain Carroll immediately appealed to the supervising inspector. Apparently agreeing with the passengers aboard the *Great Republic*, who commended the captain's actions, the inspector reversed the decision and cleared Captain Carroll of blame.

Scenic Coast Highway

According to the 1940 Federal Writers Project's guide to Oregon, *Oregon, End of the Trail* (WPA guide, for short), the distance from Astoria to the California border over Scenic Coast Highway 101 was 394.4 miles. Today the route is only 344 miles, fifty miles shorter. Neither the state nor the coastline has shrunk. But the highway's curves have been straightened, just as its ups and downs to visit scenic bluffs and sandy beaches have been bypassed to accommodate the demands of logging trucks, commercial overland shippers, and other hurried motorists who demand fewer curves and more level highways on which they can "make time."

Getting the fast-lane traffic off the scenic, crooked roads is all to the good, so far as the traveler interested in leisure and history is concerned. Today, the fifty miles of roadway saved by those in a hurry is preserved in the form of winding but easily driven secondary roads where "making time" is a low priority.

Part I of this book relates the difficulties encountered by early explorers in search of the Columbia River, the risks involved in crossing its dangerous sandbar, and finally the steps taken by the U.S. Army Corps of Engineers to lessen navigational hazards by extending jetties from the river's northern and southern banks, which acted to increase the stream's velocity and stabilize its constantly changing channels into a single deep shipping lane that could be marked and maintained. Visible evidence of that work begun a hundred years ago still exists in the form of rotting trestles that once supported a railroad carrying rock out to the end of the south jetty. To see it, a short detour is required northwest from Highway 101 to the small towns of Warrenton and Hammond, and Fort Stevens State Park. Here, the traveler gets a good look at the mouth of the Columbia and can imagine what crossing the bar has meant to seafaring men over the past two hundred years.

From atop the elevated end of South Jetty, the four-mile-wide mouth of the great river can be seen, extending to the headland mistakenly called Cape Disappointment looming in the distance above the Washington shore. Even from the low crest of the jetty, the speed of the current is visible by the choppiness of the water's surface. If an incoming tide is working against the current, the turbulence is intensified. If a southwesterly gale is blowing against the current and tide, the surface becomes a tossing, heaving boil of white water, against which pilots of even the largest of ships choose to wait for more favorable conditions before entering the river.

Governor Isaac Ingalls Stevens. —Penrose Library, Whitman College

Fort Stevens

Built in 1863 to protect the mouth of the Columbia River from any Confederate ship's attack during the Civil War, the fort now preserved as a state park was named in honor of the first governor of Washington Territory, Isaac Ingalls Stevens, who died while commanding a Union regiment in the Battle of Chantilly. Though the fort's long-range guns could have put up a stiff defense against any hostile ship's encroachment during the Civil War, the Spanish-American War, or the First World War, the guns of Fort Stevens never have fired a shot in the heat of battle.

The fort was once fired upon, though, during World War II when a Japanese submarine surfaced at extreme range under cover of darkness on June 21, 1942, lofted a few projectiles from its five-inch deck gun in the general direction of the fort, then submerged and ran. By then, all the coastal guns that could have reached the sub's position had been dismantled and shipped to Europe, where they seemed to be needed more urgently—except for a few that had been cut up and sold as scrap to the Japanese before the Second World War began. So, no answering shots were fired. Many years later, however, the commander of that Japanese submarine paid a visit to Oregon and reportedly apologized for the attack, pleased to learn that his shells left only a few shallow holes in the ground.

Early Shipwrecks

Legend has it that around the time Columbus discovered America in 1492, a Japanese sailor on a derelict junk made a landfall in the Nehalem Bay area, forty miles south of Astoria, where he was taken captive by the natives. Though his identity, exactly where he landed, and how he crossed the Pacific all are lost in the mists of time, he likely was a fisherman whose unwieldy junk with its awkward bamboo sails, which could not quarter close to the wind, got caught in a terrible, widespread storm that drove his ship so far in an easterly direction that it entered the Japanese Current. From time immemorial the current has pushed buoyant objects such as wood chips, fishing net floats, and small or large sailing vessels tenaciously across thousands of miles of ocean to come ashore on the Oregon Coast. How this lone fisherman survived the trip can only be guessed.

"He later gained his freedom through his talent for building small boats," James A. Gibbs tells us in his intriguing book *Shipwrecks of the Pacific Coast*. "Turning freebooter to exact tribute from the coastal tribes of Oregon, he organized a band of savages and pillaged villages from the Columbia River to Coos Bay via swift war canoes. He became a tyrannical figure among the Indians and one feared along the coast."

How much a Japanese sailor could teach the coastal Indians about building war canoes may be questioned, but in the world of legends one does not quibble over details. Inspired by the tale, Oregon poet Samuel A. Clarke immortalized the Japanese castaway in verse:

> There was an ocean potentate
> Who, all along the western shore
> With war canoes of hemlock made,
> Dashed through where noisy breakers pour
> And battles won with gleaming blade—
> With brazen gong made great uproar,
> And all the coast in tribute laid.

More solid evidence that ships from the Orient have drifted across the Pacific to wreck on the Oregon Coast is in the testimony of early white settlers in the Nehalem Bay area who found on the beach teakwood that showed considerable signs of wear. And another tale contends that a Chinese sailor landed on the coast of Mexico in the fifth century, then moved north as far as the Oregon Coast on an exploring expedition. In 1820 an Oriental junk wrecked at Point Adams; another washed ashore in 1833 at Cape Flattery, a few hundred miles to the north; a third is documented near Ocean Park, Washington, just north of the Columbia around 1900.

These prove that derelict vessels from the Orient have reached the American Northwest, with or without living crew members aboard. Better known is the tale of a white sailor who survived a shipwreck on the Nehalem coast around 1760. Said to be a Scotchman with fiery red hair and beard, he made such an impression on the local Clatsop Indians who rescued him that he was taken into the tribe and married a young maiden, who bore him several redheaded sons. One of these descendants is mentioned in the journals of Lewis and Clark, who built winter quarters on the Clatsop plains where they lived until late March 1806. A few years later, in 1813, Alexander Henry, a clerk with the North West Company, which had taken over Fort Astoria, told of seeing an old Clatsop chief who had with him "a man about 30 years old with dark red hair, supposedly the offspring of a white man shipwrecked near the mouth of the Nehalem River."

Beeswax Ship

Even more intriguing is Alexander Henry's statement that the local Indians regularly brought an odd sort of treasure to the fort to trade to the whites: "They bring us frequently lumps of beeswax fresh out of the sand, which they collect on the coast to the south, where a Spanish ship was cast away some years ago and the crew all murdered by the natives."

Though the timbers of the wrecked ship had long since rotted away or been buried under the shifting sands, such large quantities of beeswax were extracted near Nehalem Spit by the Indians that it seems likely more than one Spanish galleon met misfortune off the coast. Beeswax was an ordinary trade commodity carried by the Spanish between the Philippines, the Pacific Coast, and Spain since 1565. Excellent sailors though the Spaniards were, when tremendous southwest gales drove toward the North American mainland, a navigator aiming his ship toward San Francisco Bay sometimes found it driven ashore on the Oregon Coast. One very large piece of beeswax on display in Tillamook's Pioneer Museum bears the date 1679.

Among its many uses, beeswax often was shaped by the Catholic missions of the New World into candles, tapers, and holy images. Some of the wax cakes weighed several hundred pounds, though the average was about ten. Some were inscribed with the letters IHS, a Christian symbol for the name Jesus.

*Alex Walker on
Manzanita Beach,
holding a large piece of
Nehalem beeswax.*

—Burford Wilkerson, 1961,

Tillamook Pioneer Museum

Buried Treasure

Now and then over the years in the Yaquina Bay area, farther south along the coast near Newport, goblets of Spanish origin have been recovered from the bottom of the sea. Inevitably, these finds have generated tales of lost and buried treasure that might well inspire romantic novels in the vein of Robert Louis Stevenson's *Treasure Island*. As told and retold by generations of local Indians, the legends are complete with the usual blood, thunder, and mystery of such tales.

In the late 1600s, one story goes, a Spanish ship dropped anchor off the shores of Nehalem Bay. A boat was lowered and came ashore filled with men. After running the breakers, the craft was pulled above high tide, a large chest was carried ashore, and a procession of men climbed single file up the steep slopes of a bluff called Neah-kah-nie by the local Indians, some of whom were watching the bearded strangers.

> On the southwest side, the strangers began digging a deep hole and placed the chest inside. Before it was covered with earth again, a Negro, probably a slave, was slain with a cutlass and his body laid over the chest. The Spaniards knew that an Indian never disturbed

75

the burial place of a dead man. Their mission completed, the Spaniards returned to the beach.

From that point, the legend follows the formula prescribed for other tales of buried treasure. One version says the ship sailed away, never to be seen again; another relates that some of the ship's crew stayed behind but quarreled with the native men over women and got killed in a bloody fight—their secrets dying with them.

By the time permanent white settlements took root along this stretch of coast, many years had passed. Nehalem Indian descendants gave few details of where the treasure might be, but showed their white friends a few peculiarly marked stones, which some treasure hunters thought held clues to where the chest awaited discovery. During the next hundred years, one settler after another became obsessed with the story and spent months, years, or even a lifetime traipsing across the windswept, rainy blufftop, digging holes. One former Hudson's Bay Company employee, Thomas McKay, spent lots of time searching for the buried treasure, then suddenly quit and moved away, which aroused suspicion among his friends. Though he denied finding any treasure, years later "when he settled at French Prairie, he always had an abundance of money and freely passed it around, starting the rumor that he had unearthed the chest."

Still another tale relates that a black man showed up near The Dalles in the early 1800s, claiming that he had been present when the chest was buried and knew exactly where it was but dared not go back there because as a castaway he had been enslaved by a local Indian chief, who would kill him on sight if he returned. When a party of white men promised to protect him, he finally consented to return to the area and show them where the treasure was buried. Unfortunately, the man soon afterward contracted smallpox and died. So modern treasure hunters believe that the gold—if not yet secretly carried away or unwittingly scooped up in one of the numerous highway-straightening projects that have taken place along the coast—may still be there.

First American Landing

If Captain Robert Gray's 1792 discovery of the Columbia River had not solidified the United States' claim to the Oregon region, a landing made four years earlier at a bay sixty miles to the south might have been adequate. With the ink barely dry on the Constitution, Captain Kendrick sailed out of Boston Harbor on October 1, 1787, in command of two ships headed around Cape Horn for the Northwest Coast. Kendrick commanded the 212-ton *Columbia*, while Gray had charge of the 90-ton *Lady Washington*.

The merchants who backed the expedition hoped the captains, after trading with the coastal natives for furs, would exchange that cargo in the Orient for spices and teas, then sail on to England and finally back home to Boston. The two-year mission should have yielded a one thousand percent return on the backers' original investment of $50,000.

If new lands were discovered and claimed in the name of the fledgling nation, well and good; but profit motivated the enterprise. Fortunately, for posterity's sake, a meticulous, literate journal of this voyage was kept by nineteen-year-old Robert Haswell, second officer on the sloop *Lady Washington*.

While rounding Cape Horn during stormy weather the two ships lost sight of each other, so the *Lady Washington* was traveling alone when she made the first landfall on Oregon's coast August 14, 1788, ten-and-a-half months after setting sail from Boston. She dropped anchor one thousand yards off the entrance to a broad bay. Haswell estimated their location at 45 degrees, 27 minutes North latitude, and 122 degrees, 20 minutes West longitude. Since instruments of that day measured latitude more precisely than longitude, Haswell's latitudinal orientation of Tillamook Bay is almost exactly right; his longitude is off by a degree or two.

When a canoe full of natives paddled out and timidly approached the sloop, Captain Gray made friendly gestures and passed out some trinkets as gifts. Encouraged by their reception, the Indians soon returned with presents of berries and boiled crab, which were most welcome as a remedy for the curse of sailors during long voyages, scurvy, from which several of the crew suffered.

Next day, a brisk trade was carried on, with the natives swapping sea otter and other pelts for almost anything the white men chose to give them. Within a short time, over three hundred valuable pelts had been acquired. Although both whites and Indians kept their arms handy and were wary when trading with each other, Captain Gray felt relations friendly enough to risk sending a party ashore, beyond range of the ship's guns, to gather wood and fresh water.

After another day, on August 16, Gray weighed anchor at noon and started to sail out of the bay's entrance. But an incoming tide and an unfavorable breeze drove the sloop aground on a sandbar. Ordering two anchors dropped to hold the vessel in place until the next flood tide, Captain Gray permitted another party of men, consisting of the Second Officer Haswell, Chief Mate Coolidge, and five sailors to go ashore and cut grass for the livestock aboard. They armed themselves only with two muskets and a pair of pistols, besides their several cutlasses for gathering grass.

The Indians had been friendly enough until now, but they envied the white men's shiny metal tools and weapons. In the shore party was

Sea otter with pup. —Pacific Studio Photography

Marcus Lopius, Captain Gray's cabin attendant from Africa's Cape Verde Island. When an Indian snatched up and ran off with the cutlass Lopius had thrust in the ground, the young black man acted without thinking.

Shouting angrily at the Indian, Lopius followed the thief in hot pursuit. Aware of the danger to all in case of a physical encounter between the two men, Haswell and Coolidge gave chase to stop them. But Lopius had already caught the thief around the neck, and despite the crowd of natives pressing in around them, he tried to wrestle the cutlass out of the Indian's grasp, shouting for help as he fought. Before the two white men could interfere, Haswell was horrified to see several natives rescue their friend by plunging spears into the young black man's body. Badly wounded, Lopius fell to the ground, rose, then, as he staggered toward his mates, was struck by a flight of arrows fired into his back.

As the two officers retreated, Haswell shot one of the natives with his pistol and Coolidge fired at another. The shore party covered them with musket fire as they struggled through the surf to the long boat. Both men suffered superficial hand wounds, and another of their party collapsed unconscious after being hit in the chest with an arrow. As the shore party neared the sloop, the natives were turned back by fire from the swivel gun aboard the *Lady Washington*.

Although both Haswell and Gray later said the natives may have hatched a plot to attack the shore party and take over the ship, it is unlikely that anything so complicated was planned. More probably, the unfortunate incident was triggered by the impetuous reaction of the young cabin attendant to the theft of his grass-cutting tool, with predictable results. But it is ironic that the first contact between Americans and natives on the Oregon Coast resulted in the death of a black man from the Cape Verde Islands. In remembrance of the event, Haswell and Gray recorded the name of the bay as "Murderers' Harbor."

Tillamook Bay

But "Murders' Harbor" did not last long, and the inlet soon became known by the name of the local Indians, the Tillamook. At first, both Haswell and Gray speculated that Tillamook Bay might be the mouth of the great River of the West, for they noted that a large volume of fresh water flowed into it from the rugged range of coastal mountains. Later explorers learned that the bay was fed by five rivers now called the Tillamook, Kilchis, Trask, Miami, and Wilson, and by several smaller streams.

Curiously, the depth of the harbor, which Captain Gray measured in 1788 at seven fathoms (42 feet), has changed considerably; now it measures only ten to twenty feet. The reason is traceable to the great fire known as the Tillamook Burn in the summer of 1933. Salvageable timber was soon logged, and snags and debris were cleared from the hillsides. The bare slopes could do little to check erosion until the vegetation returned. But by then, so much silt and trash washed into the bay that it ended up less than half as deep as it was before the fire.

Fort Clatsop

When Lewis and Clark and their weary party reached the Pacific Coast and looked for a place to winter, comfort was relative; the cold, wet, ragged men needed only shelter, food, clothing, and salt. Unlike inland-dwelling vacationers today, who pay a premium for a view of the beach and fresh breezes off the sea, the members of this expedition had no desire to settle in a spot by the ocean. William Clark unabashedly said, "salt water I view as an evil in as much as it is not helthy." He also hated both its noise and its name. After a few weeks on the coast north of the Columbia River, he caustically wrote:

> the sea which is imedeately in front roars like a repeeted roling thunder and have rored in that way ever since our arrival in its borders which is now 24 days since we arrived in sight of the Great Western Ocian, I cant say Pasific as since I have seen it, it has been the reverse.

Wanting to find a more sheltered spot with plentiful game and timber, Lewis finally found a site south of the Columbia River "in a thick groth of pine ... on a rise about 30 feet higher than the high tides leavel." The party moved there on December 7, 1805, and commenced building Fort Clatsop. Though it rained every day, their quarters were completed by January 1, 1806.

With shelter now provided and skilled hunters such as George Drewyer prowling the woods for elk, deer, and beaver, the party now sought that dietary necessity from which they had been deprived—salt.

Salt Makers and Whales

The only source for salt was the ocean, so a salt-making party looked for a suitable site to boil seawater in kettles over fires twenty-four hours a day until they collected enough salt. After a five-day search they found a spot on the coast some fifteen miles southwest of Fort Clatsop, where they set up camp near a band of friendly Tillamook Indians. By constant labor and fire tending the salters found they could distill three or four quarts of excellent white salt a day.

While the salters worked, the Tillamooks brought them some whale blubber, which the white men relished—it was white, spongy, and somewhat like pork fat—a welcome change from what had become a monotonous diet of lean, tough elk meat. When the Indians informed them that the blubber came from the carcass of a dead whale that had washed ashore a few miles down the coast, the salters sent word back to Fort Clatsop. Captain Clark and a party of twelve set out in two canoes to see the beached monster and purchase some of its meat.

Sacajawea, the young Shoshone woman who had not yet seen the Pacific Ocean, lodged one of her few complaints recorded in the official "Journals": "the Indian woman was very importunate to be permited to go," Lewis wrote, "and was therefore indulged; she observed that she had traveled a long way with us to see the great waters, and now that this monstrous fish was also to be seen, she thought it very hard she should not be permitted to see either." So she went with Clark and the others to see the ocean and the bones that remained of the big "fish" on the beach below Tillamook Head.

Clark measured the skeleton's length at 105 feet. It probably was a gray whale, the largest of all living creatures. In late fall gray whales can still be seen spouting and flipping their tales a few miles off the Oregon Coast as they migrate south toward the warm waters of Baja California; in spring they pass by again heading north to the cooler Bering Sea. At elevations such as Tillamook Head, forty miles north of Tillamook Bay, whale watching has long been a great local attraction; people all along the coast spend hours sighting the cetaceans through binoculars and telescopes.

After trading for a few gallons of whale oil and three hundred pounds of blubber, Captain Clark, in a rare form, wrote: "I thank providence for directing the whale to us; and think him much more kind to us than he was to Jonah, having sent this Monster to be swallowed by us instead of swallowing us as Jonah's did."

The camp of the salt-making crew had been set up a hundred yards from the beach just below Tillamook Head. Though all vestiges of the original camp have disappeared, a replica has been constructed and may be seen in the town of Seaside, a popular resort for inlanders yearning to breathe fresh coastal air.

Following the construction of Fort Clatsop, the main section of the Lewis and Clark party spent three long, dreary months there; the leaders updated their journals, maps, and descriptions of the flora and fauna of the country, while the men hunted, made clothes and footgear, and prepared for the expedition's return journey.

Captain Lewis found proof that English-speaking white men had spent time on this part of the coast by several words the Indians knew, such as "muskit, powder, shot, knife, file, damn rascal, and sun of a bitch, &c." Lewis, the naturalist of the party, was awed by the size of the trees growing in the surrounding forest. He wrote:

> There are several species of fir in this neighbourhood which I shall describe as well as my slender botanical skil wil enable me.... [One is] a species which grows to immence size; very commonly 27 feet in the girth six feet above the surface of the earth, and in several instances we have found them as much as 36 feet in girth or 12 feet diameter perfectly solid and entire. they frequently rise to the hight of 230 feet, and one hundred and twenty or 30 of that hight without a limb.

This species has since been identified as the magnificent Sitka spruce. A second tree which he describes as being four to six feet in diameter and one hundred sixty to eighty feet tall is recognized as the mountain hemlock.

On Sunday, March 23, 1806, the Lewis and Clark party said farewell to their winter quarters with no regret and began the long journey home. Clark wrote:

> . . . we loaded our canoes & at 1 p.m. left Fort Clatsop on our homeward bound journey. at this place we had wintered and re-mained from the 7th of Decr. 1805 to this day and have lived as well as we had any right to expect, and we can say that we were never one day without three meals of some kind a day either pore Elk meat or roots, notwithstanding the repeated fall of rain which has fallen almost constantly since we passed the long narrows.

Visitors Center

To get a good impression of how and where the Lewis and Clark party spent that winter almost two centuries ago, visit Fort Clatsop National Historical Memorial a few miles south of Astoria and just east of US 101. Located on a 125-acre site of primitive forest that includes the spot where the original winter quarters were built, it has an excellent visitor center where the history of the expedition is graphically explained. Well concealed from the parking lot is a faithful reconstruction of the original fort based on the floor plan sketched by Captain William Clark.

As he designed it, the 50-foot square compound comprised three connected huts on one side facing four connected huts on the other; palisades joined the two rows of huts and in the center was a parade ground measuring 48 by 20 feet. Because trees of all sizes grew nearby, obtaining materials was no problem. Using the same kind of logs cut the same way, the modern reconstruction looks, feels, and smells as it must have then.

Adding to the authenticity of the illusion, park interpreters bring history alive for several months each summer. Dressed in period costumes, they demonstrate such frontier skills as curing skins, working with wood, and making fires by flint and steel; they also show wilderness survival techniques common in the early 1800s.

The centerpiece of the visitor center is the dramatic, life-size bronze sculpture titled "Arrival" by its creator, Stanley Wanlass, an internationally renowned artist who has lived in Astoria many years. It depicts an imaginary scene in which Meriwether Lewis, standing with his arms outstretched, beholds the Pacific Ocean with excitement and thankfulness. Kneeling in a position of stabilty and supplication, Willam Clark records the event in his journal. An unnamed Clatsop Indian, representing native assistance through the course of the journey, holds a starry flounder for documentation in the journals. Included in the group is Lewis's Newfoundland dog, Scannon, the most famous and well-traveled dog in the nation's history.

Scenic Side Roads

As noted earlier, by staying on US 101 you shorten your journey along the Oregon Coast by fifty miles. But if you take a side road west to the beach now and then, that is where you can see the best scenic views; the shortened highway's designers put it a few miles inland to straighten it, often beyond sight of the sea.

Side roads leading to lighthouses, whale-watching viewpoints, state parks, and national recreation areas nearer the coast are not usually marked. Though winding and hilly, most of them are hard-surfaced and easy to drive if you don't hurry. Taking such roads may lead to adventure, but along the entire three hundred and sixty miles of coastline there is one thing you won't find at the end: a sign reading *Private Beach, No Trespassing.*

In the early 1900s a wise Oregon governor named Oswald West decreed that the Oregon's coastline belongs only to its people, and their right to use it must never be infringed. So from Astoria on the north to Brookings on the south, any portion of the beach may be walked upon at any time; other uses, such as camping, picnicking, crabbing, clam-digging, scavenging for flotsam and jetsam, and the use of vehicles, are subject to reasonable regulation. But visitors may walk anywhere, anytime.

But use caution—riptides and currents along the coast can be dangerous. Coves backed by steep cliffs should be avoided so you can head for higher ground when the tide changes or if storm-driven winds stir up the sea. Swimming and surfboarding are reserved for the few hardy souls who can brave cold, but there are no lifeguards.

Shipwrecks on a Lee Shore

The best authenticated account of beeswax-laden shipwrecks on the Oregon Coast is in the 1895 book *Marine History of the Pacific Northwest.* It tells us a ship from Spain's Oriental fleet, laden with beeswax and Chinese bric-a-brac, was blown too far north while crossing the Pacific from China and wrecked near the mouth of the Columbia River. Throughout the nineteenth century, most historical writers placed this wreck north of the Columbia, but *Marine History* authors Lewis and Dryden contend a strong possibility that the wreck occurred near the mouth of the Nehalem River, where large quantities of beeswax were still found washing ashore in the late 1800s.

The authors say Adam, an intelligent Tillamook chief who lived a full century before he spoke with them, told them that his father witnessed the wreck as a young man. He said the entire crew drowned. Conjecture led them to conclude that the Spanish beeswax ship blown north in 1772 was indeed the one Adam's father saw wrecked near Nehalem Bay.

Modern-day historian James Gibbs sheds more light on the beeswax mystery by telling us the prized Ghedda beeswax came from India and was valued for its higher melting temperature and slower burning rate than European or North American beeswax. Spanish ships usually carried it by the ton from India. And probably there was an even more precious cargo of gold, silver, and gems aboard the galleon *San Francisco Xavier*, which left Manila in 1603:

As she was about to sail, the Chinese and Filipinos were engaged in a massive revolt. With her destination as Acapulco, the ship became the sanctuary of several wealthy families of influential Spanish officials who sought safety and protection in the New World. With them went fabulous amounts of personal treasures—millions of dollars in uncut stones, jewelry, cash, gold and silver bullion. It is claimed that the vessel departed Manila with more riches than any other galleon in the two and a half centuries of the Pacific trade.... It is not impossible that the ship, which went missing without a trace, lies moldering off the Oregon Coast, and not in California waters as some have suspected. The truth may never be known.

What is known is that at least sixty derelict Oriental junks wrecked along the Oregon Coast before 1875, with no survivors aboard and no written records to tell their origin or details of their fate. Among the Clatsop Indians, a persistent legend identifies one of the first white men known to them as Konapee, the Iron-Maker, whose ship wrecked just south of the Columbia's mouth. First published over a hundred years ago in William D. Lyman's classic history, *The Columbia River*, the tale begins:

An old woman living near the ancient Indian village of Ne-ahk-stow went to the seaside and walked along the shore toward Clatsop Spit. While on the way she saw something very strange. At first it seemed like a whale, but, when the old woman came close, she saw it had two trees standing upright in it. She said, "This is no whale; it is a monster."

Closer inspection by the old woman revealed that the outer side of the strange object was covered with a bright metal, which she later learned to be copper. Ropes were tied all over the trees, and the inside of the thing was full of iron.

While she gazed in wonder, a being that looked like a bear but had a human face with hair all over it came out of the Thing. Badly frightened, the old woman hurried home and told her people what she had just seen. Seizing their bows and arrows, the male warriors of the tribe hurried to the spot.

Now there were two creatures standing on the Thing. Whether they were bears or people, the Clatsops did not know, though the Indians were beginning to realize that the Thing with two trees growing out of it was an immense canoe which had become stranded on the beach. Climbing down out of the big canoe with kettles in their hands, the two hairy-faced creatures then did something very strange.

As the bewildered Indians watched them, they started a fire and put corn into the kettles. Very soon it began to pop and fly up and down with great rapidity. The popcorn, the nature of which the Clatsops did not understand, struck them with more surprise than anything else—and this is the one part of the story preserved in every version.

The sight of a pair of shipwrecked sailors from a distant land popping corn on a rainy Oregon beach as their first act upon coming ashore would seem as odd to us now as it did to the natives then. The two bearded strangers made signs that they wanted drinking water; this, plus an examination of the strangers' hands—which the Indians found to be the same as their own—convinced the Clatsop chief who was in charge of the greeting party that the creatures were indeed men. Since they seemed to be friendly, the Clatsops gave them a hospitable welcome, calling them Tle-hon-nipts, "those who drift ashore."

As word of the white men's arrival spread up and down the coast, a great rivalry arose among the various tribes vying for the honor of entertaining them. Finally it was decided that one of the bearded strangers should go live with the Willapa Indians some miles north of the great river, and the other would remain with the Clatsops, near the spot where the ship had washed ashore. After all the metal parts had been salvaged from their wrecked ship, he showed the Indians what marvelous weapons and tools could be fashioned from copper and iron; he is remembered as "Konapee, the Iron-Maker."

By the time traders and explorers arrived on the Northwest Coast, they reported the Indians there used some metal tools and weapons, and were apparently accustomed to having them for some time.

Final Voyage of the Shark

In 1846, expansionists shouted "54-40 or Fight!" in support of setting the United States' western north boundary at that latitude, roughly the southern end of Alaska; Great Britain insisted on putting the border at 46 degrees, or the Columbia River. To monitor the situation, the U.S. Navy sent its schooner *Shark*, commanded by Captain Schenck. Approaching the Columbia River sandbar with little knowledge and poor charts, the schooner was hailed by a lone black man in a small canoe, who offered his services as a pilot. His only qualification was surviving the wreck of the Navy brig *Peacock* five years earlier at the spot dubbed "Peacock Spit" on the north entrance to the river. What he did not tell the captain was that he had been a cook, not a sailor, aboard that vessel, and he deserted from service in the Navy as soon as he got safely ashore. Captain Schenck reluctantly hired him.

If the black man had been as poor a cook as he proved to be a pilot, he would have poisoned every sailor he fed; he grounded the *Shark* on a sandbar, where it stuck fast. Captain Schenck fired the man, then worked the vessel off the bar and anchored it in calm water. At last a competent pilot and local pioneer, John Lattie, came aboard and brought the vessel through the tricky, shifting channels into the lower river, where it began its work.

Because of the the friction engendered by the boundary dispute, belligerent Americans and nervous Britishers living in the area suspected the *Shark*'s real mission was less obvious than the surveys it conducted. Since the three-masted schooner was armed with twelve cannons, she might quickly become a man-of-war to blast forts George and Vancouver into submission; their small ceremonial cannons could offer little defense.

But going to war was the last thing on the captain's mind. After long months at sea, his weary, underpaid sailors were deserting en masse, with no replacements available. Hastily completing his survey of the lower river, Schenck weighed anchor and set sail on September 10, 1846, without waiting for the services of a pilot or a favorable tide to cross the bar.

This time, the captain's luck ran out. Striking a shoal at the south entrance, the schooner stuck hard and fast. Soon heavy breakers began pounding it forcefully. To lighten the load and float free Captain Schenck ordered the three masts cut down and the twelve cannons jettisoned, but the schooner refused to budge. As the *Shark* started breaking up, the captain gave the order to abandon ship; the crew launched boats and all rowed safely ashore, leaving the vessel to its fate. In the winds and storm that raged that night the *Shark* went to pieces. A large portion of the hull floated over the bar and came ashore a few miles south at Arch Cape.

Apparently the crew had failed to jettison all the cannon, for enough deck planks remained to keep one cannon afloat until it washed shore. That spot was appropriately named Cannon Beach, and a town grew up there. The old weapon, the ship's capstan, and a few links of chain have been preserved as a monument.

Some eight years after the wreck, enterprising settlers living in the Tillamook Bay area decided to build a boat of their own but needed iron and steel for bolts and fittings. Local Indians told them about the wreck of the *Shark*, so they went to the site and salvaged enough metal to finish their ship. Christening their new schooner *Morning Star*, the ingenious pioneers gave quiet thanks for the gift from the sea that had washed ashore for their benefit.

City of Dublin Wreck

When wind alone was the motive power for a ship, it was more at the mercy of adverse currents and tides than steam-powered vessels. Because the age of sail continued long after steam-driven vessels began to ply the high seas, crossing the Columbia River Bar remained a chancy business for windjammers well into the 1900s, particularly for ships that refused the assistance of skilled pilots and tugs. Such was the case with the British sailing ship *City of Dublin* in the autumn of 1878.

As the ship neared the mouth of the Columbia, her master, Captain Stevens, who was unfamiliar with the bar, brought her in too close against the stiff offshore breeze, which suddenly died. In an attempt to keep the vessel off Clatsop Spit, he ordered the bow and stern anchors dropped. They did not hold. Breaking out an auxiliary anchor, he ordered it lowered. But against the adverse wind and tide, even three anchors could not keep the ship from going aground. When the cables attached to the anchors parted one by one, the ship became a helpless derelict, driven remorselessly through the breakers.

When the *City of Dublin* began taking on water and breaking up, Captain Stevens ordered it abandoned; then he and the crew took to the boats and made their way to the safety of the harbor. Insured for $40,000, the vessel was written off as a total loss and relinquished to salvagers. Within two weeks the ship fell apart and yielded nothing of value.

Local legend contends that the figurehead carried on the bow of the ship, a striking carving of an Indian chief wearing a full headdress, drifted ashore in Baker Bay soon after the wreck, and was mounted on a local resident's barn. When the barn eventually rotted and collapsed, the owner is said to have buried the carving so he could install it on his new barn someday.

Unfortunately, he died first without telling anybody where he had buried the striking figurehead. So, as with the treasure interred under the dead man's corpse on the slopes of Neah-Kan-Nie Mountain, the figurehead must still be there, somewhere.

Of the many shipwrecks along the northern Oregon Coast, two of the more spectacular were those of the *Peter Iredale* in 1906 and the *Glenesslin* in 1913. Both were big, handsome British sailing ships built of steel—the pride of the grain fleet carrying sacked wheat from the fertile fields of the Pacific Northwest to the people of a hungry world.

Peter Iredale Wreck

With a gross capacity of 2,075 tons, a length of 287 feet, and a beam of forty feet, the *Peter Iredale,* built in Maryport, England, in 1890, was known as a large, dependable sailer, ruggedly constructed with steel plates over iron frames, a partial iron deck, and steel masts. Twenty-eight days out of Salina Cruz, on the west coast of Mexico, the ship made good time heading north on October 25, 1906, when she went ashore at 6 a.m. a few miles south of the jetty on Clatsop Beach. Her captain, H. Lawrence, planned a fast run about fifty miles off the coast, and promised a bonus to the crew if they could cut five days off their usual sailing time. He recalled later:

> I picked up Tillamook Light at 2 a.m. and immediately called all
> hands to set all sails, intending to stand off the mouth of the

Columbia and pick up a pilot by day. A heavy southwest wind blew and a strong current prevailed. Before the vessel could be veered around, she was in the breakers and all efforts to keep her off were unavailing.

The first shock sent the mizzen top hamper overboard, and when she struck again, parts of the other masts snapped like pipestems. It was a miracle that none of the crew was killed by the falling masts as the ship pounded in the surf. After the crew had escaped the danger of the falling debris, all hands were summoned aft as the vessel ran up on the shelving sands with little violence. I told them to abandon ship. The Point Adams surfboat was soon alongside and took all hands safely ashore.

Whatever his qualities as master of a ship may have been, Captain Lawrence was a gentleman and a sport. When he came ashore, he carried three objects he had saved: the ship's log, a sextant, and a bottle of whiskey. After thanking his rescuers, he stood at attention for a moment and gazed silently at the stranded *Peter Iredale*. Saluting the ship, he said fervently: "May God bless you, and may your bones bleach in the sands." Then he picked up his bottle and passed it around to each member of the crew.

Following an investigation, the insurance company paid off the owners. Salvage attempts were undertaken, but they all proved to be futile as whipping gales and heavy seas covered the tilted carcass of the ship ever deeper into the shifting sands. Year after year the metal frame

The Peter Iredale *shortly after the wreck in 1906.* —Columbia River Maritime Museum

The remains of the Peter Iredale *in 1956, 50 years after it wrecked.*
—Columbia River Maritime Museum

of the *Peter Iredale* lay on Clatsop Beach; it became a great tourist attraction and is still one of the most photographed relics along the Oregon Coast.

Once in 1942 a Japanese submarine took a bearing on Tillamook Light on a dark night, and lobbed a few shells in the direction of Fort Stevens, some of which landed near the remains of the *Peter Iredale*. For the remainder of the Second World War, rolls of barbed wire kept people away from the wreck; when peacetime returned, the beach, too, was returned to the clam diggers and photographers.

Glenesslin Wreck

If ever a ship lived past its time, it was the *Glenesslin*. Built in Liverpool in 1888, this full-rigged steel sailing ship of 1,645 registered tons operated at a time when sails were being replaced by steam. But manned by a crew of old salts skilled in their trade, the *Glenessin* could outsail any commercial ship afloat on the high seas.

In 1901 she won a transoceanic sweepstakes over a field of eight square-riggers by seventeen days. In 1902, she covered one thousand miles in four days running time. In a voyage never equalled by any other sailing ship, she made the run from Portland, Oregon, to Port Elizabeth, South Africa, in 74 days. But along with the second decade of the 1900s came bad times for the windjammers. Basil Lubbock, a British maritime writer, explains:

> In the last half dozen years before World War I, it was heart-breaking work for the masters of British sailing ships, and many of them left

89

their old love, the square-rigger, for steam, simply because they could not get competent officers or men. Those who hung on usually had to put up with an old "has-been" as a mate, who either drank or was such a poor sailorman that he either lost his ship in disgraceful circumstances or had never been trusted with one. And for second mate, the windjammer "old man" had to be satisfied with a boy just out of his teens. More than three-quarters of the crew, also, were likely to be useless steamboat men or crooks and invalids, who were of no use aloft.

In such conditions sail could not be carried safely, for the skipper was certain to be let down by his watch officers or his crew at the first emergency. The former could only handle the ship in the clumsiest fashion and the latter could not take in sail in any wind. There were, of course, any number of good men afloat, but they preferred the easier conditions and greater opportunities of steam. Thus in her old age we find the *Glenesslin* sailing without her royal yards and with two boys as mates.

Leaving Santos, Brazil, May 28, 1913, bound for Portland with 850 tons of rubble ballast and a crew of 23 men, the ship drew thirteen feet. According to a later court of inquiry, about 8 p.m. September 30, they saw the light at Tillamook Bay. At 1:30 a.m. the ship moved offshore until 8 a.m., when it came back inshore. Sights were taken at 8:30 and land was sighted about 11. It was very hazy, and their latitude at noon was 45 degrees, 38 minutes North, and 124 degrees, 26 minutes West.

At about 30 minutes to one the master went to the chart house to lie down, leaving the second mate in charge of the vessel, with instructions to hold the course set and to call the master at 2 p.m. At five minutes before two the second mate states that he called the master, as the vessel was getting close to the shore, and again called him at five minutes after two, and was told by the master to call him again at 2:30.

The second mate then called the first mate, who came on deck, looked at the shore and went back to his room. In two or three minutes the second mate called the first mate again, and the first mate then went to the master, who came on deck and ordered the crew to wear ship, but before this could be done she struck and immediately began to fill with water.

Viewers on the Nehalem shore were puzzled by the ship's behavior: it was a beautiful fall day, the ocean was calm, and the sky was flecked with light clouds. Visibility was almost perfect and the gentle breeze should have been the delight of any sailor. Suddenly, for no understandable reason, the vessel pointed its bow directly for the base of Neah-Kah-Nie Mountain, five miles north of the mouth of the Nehalem River. Historian James Gibbs writes:

Those who observed the strange antics of the ship thought they were seeing an apparition. But this was no *Flying Dutchman*; it was a staunch iron ship with a crew of live men. All sails were set and she was coming in fast. At precisely 2:30 p.m. an underwater ledge ripped a hole in her bottom and the ship crashed head on against the precipitous base of the 1600-foot mountain.

Soon after the vessel struck, its master, Captain Owen Williams, shot a line to the rocks ashore, where landsmen made it fast. All the officers and crew made it to safety without difficulty. But none was answering questions about how the wreck happened. After examining the officers and crew, the court of inquiry ruled Captain Williams and his second mate negligent, suspending each for three and six months, respectively; the first mate received a reprimand.

As usually happens in such cases, there were rumors that the *Glenessin* had been deliberately wrecked to collect the insurance, or that her captain had been drunk. Modern historians discount these allegations by pointing out that if the wreck had been deliberate, the local agent for Lloyd's of London would not have recommended settling the claim. But he did.

The 1913 wreck of the Glenesslin, *a total loss.* —Columbia River Maritime Museum

Tillamook Rock Light

Although professional pilots in Astoria began guiding ships across the Columbia River Bar as early as 1850, they didn't start using lighthouses until Congress finally appropriated $50,000 for a warning beacon on June 20, 1878. It was built on Tillamook Rock, just a mile offshore. Dubbed "Terrible Tilly" by its tenders and the coastal communities of Seaside and Cannon Beach, this station became known as one of the most desolate lighthouses in the world.

Tillamook Rock, an igneous formation, is surrounded by depths ranging from 96 to 240 feet, making it extremely difficult to build on. Even small craft could land only at great risk from the pounding ocean waves. Early landing parties had to leap from their boats onto the rock when wave and current combined to present an opportune moment.

The *Thomas Corwin*, a U.S. Revenue Cutter, landed the first construction party on the rock in October 1879. A breeches buoy rigged by a rope between the vessel and the rock became the standard method of transit. Fifty square feet of the rock's summit had to be blasted away for the lighthouse foundation. The structure was then constructed of imported stone blocks. Finally, on January 21, 1881, Tillamook Rock Light Station shot a beam eighteen miles to sea at a cost of $123,493.

Tragically, the light came on just a few weeks too late for one ship. On the cold, stormy night of January 3, the construction superintendent came into his crew's living quarters with the startling news that he'd seen the running lights of a ship just a short distance from Tillamook Rock. The crew followed him outside, climbed to the highest vantage

"Terrible Tilly," built atop 120-foot-high Tillamook Rock, was completed in 1881. —Columbia River Maritime Museum

point, and stared out into the darkness. There was no mistaking the eerie glow of port and starboard lanterns. Over the roar of breaking seas, they heard a voice shout: "Hard aport!" Immediately following this command came the creaking and rattling of rigging and turning yardarms, indicating that the order had been promptly obeyed.

The light was not yet able to shine and warn the ship of danger, so the construction crew did the next best thing: they built a large bonfire on the seaward side of the lighthouse and placed lanterns where they could be seen. Soon, the running lights of the ship disappeared, leaving the contruction crew hopeful that their warning had been in time.

The gray dawn a few hours later revealed a terrible sight. Breaking the surface of the sea just below the steep cliff walls of Tillamook Head was the mizzen topmast of a ship, the only evidence of a hull sunk under the heaving water, which was two hundred feet deep at that spot. The ship turned out to be the British bark *Lupatia*, inbound for the Columbia River from Japan. The only survivor was a dog, a bedraggled Australian shepherd pup found limping along the beach, whining with thirst and hunger. His human companions were gone.

The thirteen hundred ton square-rigger *Lupatia* was skippered by First Officer B.H. Raven at the time of the tragedy. His brother, Captain Irvine Raven, the vessel's commander, had died nine days out of Antwerp. Departing Hioga, Japan, in ballast, the *Lupatia* was part of the grain fleet coming to the Columbia for a load of wheat. According to historian Gibbs, she was in every sense a splendid commercial sailing vessel. Twelve of her sixteen-man crew washed ashore, and burial was little more than covering them with sand and rocks. The dog went to live in Astoria with a friend of the Raven brothers. Three weeks later, Tillamook Light came on for the first time.

Located as it was in open water and exposed to the full force of the Pacific, the light station was the target of nature's devastation through its long existence. During the early stages of construction, a derrick with a long boom transferred personnel and supplies to the rock. An article in the *Quarterdeck Review* says heavy seas periodically ripped out this apparatus and tossed it uselessly into the water below. Over the years, repairs to the station far exceeded its original cost. And when only a year old, the light's dome was inundated by sea green water 150 feet above its normal level.

In 1890 crews laid an underwater communications cable from the mainland to the rock. Wind-lashed seas severed the cable for the first of many times just a year later. In an 1894 storm lantern panes shattered, pitching rocks, seaweed, and fish into the lantern room. The iron roofs could not withstand such damage and had to be replaced by others reinforced with concrete. In 1912, a gigantic chunk of rock weighing several tons was swept away by the ferocious sea.

Perhaps the most savage storm of all occurred in October, 1934. Winds reached 110 miles an hour. Huge waves lashed the light tower with unbelievable fury. Rocks weighing up to 150 pounds were hurled against the structure. One hundred thirty feet above the surface of the sea sixteen panels of glass were smashed and the lantern room was flooded. The four lighthouse keepers, struggling to clear out the debris, were submerged up to their shoulders. One of the keepers, Hugo Hansen, had his hand torn open by the broken glass. The lens was badly cracked; the light did not shine that night.

When the seas abated the next day, the keepers were able to survey the damage. The place was a shambles: the foghorn trumpets were choked so tightly with rocks and debris that only crowbars could unclog them; railings were battered, pipelines uprooted, and concrete footings cracked; the entire landing apparatus was torn out and carried away, including the three-foot iron bolt anchorages embedded in solid rock. Isolated from the outside world, the keepers were able to send for help only through the ingenuity of Henry Jenkins, who rigged up a short-wave radio device. Six days after the storm began, the tender *Manzanita* finally could approach the rock and deliver much-needed supplies. The storm inflicted over $12,000 in damages, and the station was not back in top operating condition for months.

Soon afterwards, an 80,000 candlepower all-electric light replaced the original oil vapor lamp and Fresnel lens. Fitted around the exterior of the lantern was a heavy steel cable to ward off flying fragments. Other innovations lessened the storm damage, but the elements still wreaked havoc on the station.

Visits to the Tillamook Rock Light Station made terrifying experiences for landlubbers. Recording the details of his trip after returning to solid ground in Astoria on April 4, 1937, A.J. Tittlinger, who conducted a survey for the federal archives with photographer David H. Ellis, concluded his report with these words: "This ought to be good for a medal of honor—or at least a national archives medal."

After a bleak trip over the Columbia River's sandbar and down the coast, the *Manzanita* finally arrived at its destination a quarter mile from the rock. Tittlinger writes:

> At this position, somebody wrapped me up in a life preserver, Mr. Ellis, too, and hustled us into a lifeboat. Before we knew what had happened we were adrift in the Pacific Ocean between the good ship *Manzanita* and Tillamook Rock, wolfish waves licking at our lifeboat and jagged rocks beckoning our frail craft to destruction. However, under the skilled guidance of the second mate of the *Manzanita* and its gallant boat crew, we managed to avoid both evils; but more was in store for us.
>
> A few feet from the rock where billowing waves surged madly into foamy spray, a crate was lowered from the boom on the lighthouse

onto the bow of the boat. Expert oar work by the men and surprisingly skillful timing by the second mate kept both boat and crate together. This crate is about three feet square and two feet high, sides and bottom latticed to allow draining. Into this contraption Mr. Ellis and I were hustled by experienced hands, who knew the timing to a nicety.

While contemplating my present predicament with great misgivings, and daring a look at Ellis (whose countenance verified what I feared: the worst is yet to come), devilish waves reached up through the latticed floor trying to wet our feet. It was only a matter of seconds before we dangled over a hundred feet high between the sea and the sky. The good keeper of Tillamook Light did as is his custom: let us dangle for what seemed an interminable time, evidently to enjoy the three elements of nature—land, sea, and air—from a vantage point such as we had in that suspended crate.

Being ignorant at the time of his good intentions, and apprehensive lest the cable break, besides being unable to enjoy and appreciate the spectacle from that position in the sky, I tried to convince our host above the roar of the ocean and the fury of the gale, biting cold, and fusilade of rain, that of the elements we were beholding, we were most beholden to only one: land.

Still the boom did not move landward; and finally in desperation and in agony of fear I yelled uncomplimentary remarks about his ancestry. This had the desired effect, for immediately understanding dawned on his face as he nodded affirmatively and swung the boom inland, lowering us carefully and gently on the concrete landing base. After climbing something like eighty steps, we reached the feudal castle-like shelter of the lighthouse. Warmed by a cheery fire and a steaming hot cup of coffee, we proceeded on our missions, Mr. Ellis to his and I to mine.

The keepers who served on Tillamook Rock have included many real characters whose personalities were well suited to the unique conditions in which they lived and worked. Old timers remember Bob Gerloff as the "Grand Old Man of Tillamook Rock." He came to respect and admire the light station so fervently that he actually expressed displeasure at having to go ashore. Reportedly, he once did a five-year stretch on the rock without any relief.

After he retired from the service, Gerloff asked if he could remain at the light station as a "paying guest." The government refused both this request and his final wish that his ashes be dropped into the ocean from Tillamook Rock after he passed away.

Some, like writer James Gibbs, who also spent time tending the beacon on the rock, remember Roy Dibb as Tillamook Light's resident golfer. He tied a cotton ball to a long string attached to a rail stanchion so he could tee off on the shortest course in the world. With scores commonly in the seventies, his effort paid off.

Reflecting on his own period of service, James Gibbs graphically related his experiences in his book *Tillamook Light*. Behavior deserving of a court martial while serving in the Coast Guard during the Second World War netted Gibbs a tour of duty on Tillamook Rock. He went through periods of fear, hate, and finally fascination with the most unique lighthouse ever to exist in the United States, if not in the entire world. Just before the Coast Guard decommissioned the station on September 10, 1957, Gibbs wrote a final entry for its log:

> Farewell, Tillamook Light Station. I return thee to the elements. You, one of the most notorious and yet most fascinating of the sea-swept sentinels in the world. For 77 years you have beamed your light across desolate acres of ocean. Keepers have come and gone; men have lived and died; but you were faithful to the end. May your sunset years be good years. Your purpose is now only a symbol, but the lives you have saved and the service you have rendered are worthy of the highest respect.

Since her light ceased to shine, "Terrible Tilly" has been sadly neglected. But, the lighthouse has continued to live up to her reputation for individuality. One group of owners tried to establish a gambling casino on the rock; another purchased it as a summer home, but spent only a few days there; a third proposed to dismantle the structure stone by stone and erect it again in California as a restaurant. Its last known use, reported in 1980 by the *Quarterdeck Review*, was as a columbarium— a permanent storage facility for cremated remains.

US 26, US 101, OR 6
Portland—Seaside—Tillamook

In the 47 miles between Seaside and Tillamook, there are more scenic viewpoints overlooking the ocean, and more state parks along the beach, than in any similar stretch of highway along the Oregon Coast. The sometimes crooked roads leading to state parks are hard-surfaced and well marked, but sightseers should inquire locally before taking dirt or graveled roads to such spots as Tillmook Head.

US 26 crosses the low, rolling heights of the Coast Range from Portland before joining US 101 four miles south of Seaside and five miles north of Cannon Beach; this route is popular on weekends as city dwellers escape to the resort towns. Oregon 6 crosses the Coast Range farther south, and provides the best access to the popular salmon-fishing towns of Garibaldi, Bay City, and Tillamook.

Both highways go through the huge, beautiful Tillamook State Forest, where some of the largest and finest trees in the Pacific Northwest once grew. Much of this old growth forest succumbed in the disastrous fire called the Tillamook Burn in 1933, or in the succeeding fires that oddly occurred every six-years for some time. Attempts at reforestation eventually took hold and most of the scars left by the fires are now concealed, though a weathered, bleached, leafless old snag standing high on a hilltop may still be seen here and there. The drama and aftermath of the Tillamook Burn are detailed in the next section of this book.

Oswald West Memorial

A few miles south of Cannon Beach, the highway climbs to a high point of land just above Oswald West State Park. Here, overlooking endless miles of the Pacific Ocean, stands a turnout and a plaque embedded in the rock wall—a fitting monument to the governor who preserved the Oregon Coast for the public. The plaque reads:

> If sight of sand and sea has given respite from your daily cares then pause to thank Oswald West, former Governor of Oregon 1911-15. By his foresight nearly 400 miles of shore was set aside for public use from the Columbia River on the north to the California border on the south. This marker is erected by the grateful citizens of Oregon to commemorate this outstanding achievment in conservation of the natural resources.

Governor Oswald West (center) visits a rescue crew in Newport, June 23, 1912. —Pacific Studio Photography

US 101 stays inland for forty miles south of Tillamook, well beyond sight of the sea. The highway crosses low, relatively open country patched by green fields where dairy cattle graze and produce milk for one of Tillamook's main industries: cheese. But a few miles to the west winds a network of blacktop roads that lead out to a series of capes, scenic lookouts, and state parks.

South of its junction with Oregon 18, US 101 returns nearer the coast again, and opportunities to view the ocean occur frequently along the thirty miles to Newport. For the past hundred years this stretch of coast has been the domain of a hardy, venturesome breed called "summer people" by the year-round residents. No matter how much local industries might fluctuate, "summer people" could be depended upon to flee urban congestion and heat in the Willamette Valley to seek rest and recreation in the bracing salt air.

Because this stretch of the Oregon Coast lacked rail lines, decent roads, and regular steamboat service from Portland or San Francisco, getting to it was a problem. But the "summer people" came in ever-increasing hordes once they discovered the delights of the coast; they still

Early map of the Tillamook Bay area. —Tillamook County Pioneer Museum

In 1911 Tillamook was a resort town—complete with gondolier.

do. Along this thirty miles of scenic coastline are accommodations to suit all tastes and pocketbooks—from $200-a-day luxury condominiums to modest motels and trailer parks to Spartan camps where you pitch your own tent.

Wreck of the Juliet

Like many sites along the Oregon Coast, Yaquina Bay first received attention because of a shipwreck. In time, the town of Newport was built around this lovely inlet. Back on January 28, 1852, following the wreck of his schooner *Juliet*, Captain J. Collins reported:

> A fine river, navigable for vessels drawing six or eight feet of water a distance of twenty miles...but from the appearance I deemed the inlet to be a bad one. The river abounds with oysters, clams, and fish of all kinds. The land around is level and highly productive. The timber has been nearly all destroyed by fire. None of the land in the vicinity is claimed yet.

Neither Hudson's Bay Company trappers, who visited Yaquina Bay in the 1820s, nor the detachment of U.S. Army troops there in 1849 under Lieutenant Theodore Talbot left any record of what they saw. The local Indians, called Yaquinas, were southern representatives of the Chinook group, though they spoke a different language. They lived on salmon,

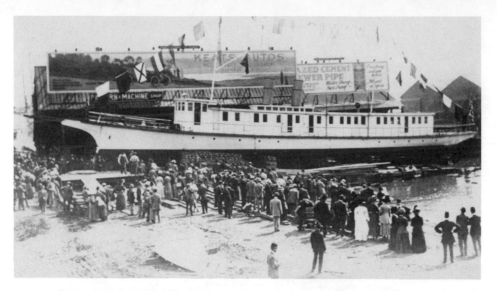

Launched in 1911, the Bayocean *was a luxurious steam-powered yacht. Weekly trips were made to Astoria to pick up the train passengers from Portland.* —Tillamook County Pioneer Museum

shellfish, roots, berries, and game. Newport historian Richard L. Price says the Indians sometimes used fire either to drive game or to attract it by improving the cover, and that this practice "occasionally resulted in large forest fires that devastated large areas."

White men brought diseases to western Oregon, just as they had all across America—diseases for which the Indians had no immunity. Various disorders killed them off in large numbers. To protect the Indians from the whites, and vice versa, four thousand natives from the central Oregon Coast were put on reservations established on the Yamhill River at Grande Ronde and at Siletz on the Yachats River. One suspicious historical account tells of Lieutenant Phil Sheridan leaving Fort Yamhill in 1856 for Yaqina Bay "to quiet the Indians."

Lieutenant Phil Sheridan

In his autobiography dictated many years later, Sheridan said that he had to succor the besieged local Indian agent, after which he located a site to build a blockhouse for the agent's protection.

> Nearly all around the bay the land rose up from the beach very abruptly. The only good site that could be found was some level ground used as the burial place of the Yaquina Indians. Their dead were buried in canoes, which rested in the crotches of forked sticks a few feet above ground.

I made known to the Indians that we would have to take this piece of ground for the blockhouse. They demurred, for there is nothing more painful to an Indian than disturbing the dead. But at last they gave in.

It was agreed that on the following day at twelve o'clock, when the tide was going out, I should take my men and place the canoes in the bay, and let them float out across the ocean to the happy hunting grounds.

This piece of history is suspect for several reasons: the area has plenty of level ground on which to build a blockhouse without disturbing the Indian burial site; furthermore, no physical evidence of the remains of a blockhouse has ever been found; finally, Sheridan's reminiscences were published many years later, after he had retired as one of the top military leaders in the country, so they were quite possibly colored a bit to enhance his illustrious career.

Verifiable is the fact that Phil Sheridan spent several years at Fort Yamhill, near the small town later named after him to honor his Civil War record. In June each year, the town's 2,249 residents still celebrate Phil Sheridan Day. The young lieutenant, affectionately known as "Little Phil," was sent to the new post from Fort Vancouver in the summer of 1856. He was not happy with the assignment.

According to Sheridan, "In those days, the Government did not provide very liberally for sheltering its soldiers. This post was no exception. I was kept busily employed in supervising matters, both as

Fort Yamhill Blockhouse, originally built on the Grande Ronde Indian Reservation in 1856, was moved to Dayton, Oregon, in 1910.

commandant and quartermaster, until July, when Captain D.A. Russell took command and I was relieved from the first part of my duties." But Captain Russell was called east to the Civil War early in 1861. Sheridan again took command of the post, though he yearned for a summons to the greater conflict raging a continent away.

Finally, in September 1861 his wish came true, and he announced: "I am going into this war to win my captain's spurs, or die with my boots on. Goodbye, boys. I may never see you again." He not only won captain's spurs, he quickly achieved the rank of general during the war, then led Indian campaigns in the West during their bloodiest years; and in 1884 he became commander of the U.S. Army.

In 1911 the town of Dayton, Oregon, twenty-five miles east of Sheridan on Oregon 18, relocated the old Fort Yamhill blockhouse to its City Park and dedicated it to the town's founder, Joel Palmer, who was the first superintendent of Indian affairs in Oregon Territory.

Yaquina Bay

Soon after the outbreak of the Civil War in 1861, regular army troops stationed at Fort Yamhill, Fort Hoskins, and the Siletz Indian Agency were withdrawn and replaced by volunteers from the the Fourth California Infantry. Most of these amateur soldiers were '49ers who had hoped to strike it rich in the California gold fields; but their dreams faded in the dozen years since.

The three years they served in Oregon were quiet: the local Indians remained peaceful and no Rebel raiders attacked the Oregon Coast.

Summer people in Newport on July 4, some time after 1911.
—Pacific Studio Photography

Though her name was Anne Rocco, this local Indian woman was known to many early-day Newport residents as the "Rock Oyster Queen."
—Pacific Studio Photography

Many of the soldiers grew so fond of the area that when the Yaquina Bay section was opened to white settlement in 1865, they were the first to file claims.

The natural oyster beds mentioned by Captain Collins in 1852 were rediscovered in 1862. The San Francisco firm of Winant & Company obtained a lease from the Indian agent to harvest the beds, and by 1864 a lucrative trade had developed. The company's headquarters was established at Oysterville, about four miles from the coast. Soon the Willamette Valley settlers and soldiers from Fort Hoskins were making regular trips to satisfy their growing taste for these delicious mollusks.

Corvallis, a thriving city in the heart of the fertile farmlands of the Willamette Valley, lay sixty miles to the east. The low, rolling hills of the Coast Range offered no great obstacle to travel in fair weather, even though roads were few. Summer days in the Willamette Valley could be hot, dry, and dusty, while temperatures on the coast remained pleasant. Although getting there was sometimes a problem, the bracing salt air and remarkably different environment made the effort worthwhile.

An enterprising man from Maine named Samuel Case, a former '49er, found a more dependable source of riches near Yaquina Bay. Staking a claim on the north shore in 1866, near the mouth of the Yaquina River, he advertised in the Corvallis newspaper his intention to build a big

The small schooner Wilhelmina, *called the "Beer Ship," brings liquid refreshment to the citizens of Newport.* —Pacific Studio Photography

resort hotel called the "Ocean House." He remembered the success of a similar venture in 1840, when a hotel of the same name had been built in Newport, Rhode Island, to accommodate summer visitors. The same potential existed at Yaquina Bay, he thought, so he borrowed the hotel's name, and later proposed Newport as a name for the town that would be built around it. Wasting no time, Case and his associate, J.R. Bayley, opened for business in August 1866.

Early Days of Newport

In the fall of 1868 government engineers completed their survey of the harbor. It showed a depth of seventeen feet at high tide—deeper than expected. This raised hopes for the eventual development of Yaquina Bay as a major seaport. Based on these hopes and optimistic talk of a railroad through to Corvallis and points east, civic boosters predicted that Newport soon would become "The San Francisco of the Northwest." It never achieved that goal. But in 1885, when the rail line from Corvallis to Yaquina Bay was finally completed, the local leaders gratefully settled for that.

Daily passenger service between Corvallis and Yaquina City began in 1885, and steamers offered connections to San Francisco. Traveling overland from Portland to Corvallis, then to Yaquina City, cut forty hours from the usual three-and-a-half-day's travel time from Portland to San Francisco.

Summer people on Nye Beach in 1912. —Pacific Studio Photography

Unfortunately, two of the steamers serving Yaquina wrecked in the late 1880s and were not replaced. And the badly managed railroad changed owners and names several times before it became the Corvallis and Eastern in 1897, and was no longer in the running for a transcontinental link; its purpose became simply to haul timber from the coast to mills in the Willamette Valley. By that time, Newport residents conceded that their greatest resource was "summer people." And it's been that way ever since.

Before the turn of the century, local citizens were exploring such seaside curiosities as the "Devil's Punch Bowl" near Otter Rock. —Pacific Studio Photography

In 1918, surfers made their own boards. —Pacific Studio Photography

Summer People

As Newport grew beyond the area along the bay front, many cottages and cabins sprung up around Nye Creek, northwest of the bay on the ocean side of the peninsula. The creek was a favorite spot for campers; and in 1891 the city built a sidewalk to connect it with the bay front. A couple of years later city streets connected Front Street with Nye Creek to accommodate the increased traffic. Historian Richard Price writes:

> The owners of the cottages in the area found that they could rent them easily for any length of time during the summer months, if they didn't occupy them themselves. Many families began spending the entire summer season at the beach in these cottages. The working husband or father would join the family on weekends by taking advantage of the low three-day excursion fare offered by the raiload explicitly for this purpose. These round trip weekend fares from Corvallis were $2.75 as opposed to the regular $3.50. From Portland the fare was $3.00 for a weekend ticket compared to $6.00 for the normal round trip season ticket.

In 1909, Newport entered the modern age in grand style. The newly completed local light company began generating electricity for a few hours each day; starting with 57 customers, the list grew daily. A year later, a group of citizens presented a petition to the city council requesting that during the winter months electricity be generated every morning from 5 to 7:30, and evenings from 4 to midnight: "On dance nights the dancers would take up a collection to pay the engineer to continue generating after midnight."

As in all coastal cities with navigable rivers and harbors, repairs to the jetties and dredging the harbor and channels required constant help from the government. But it paid off. Ships called regularly for loads of lumber; the fishing fleet grew steadily; and in 1924 the first shipment of fish bound for East Coast markets went out in refrigerated boxcars on the Southern Pacific. By 1930, 125 halibut and salmon fishing boats were registered in Newport. Both commercial and charter boat fishing have played important roles in the local economy ever since.

Automobiles, like summer people, showed up in steadily rising numbers around Newport throughout the 1910s. Every spring someone would set a new record by navigating the muddy roads from Corvallis a little earlier than the year before. At most, the road was driveable only about five months out of the year. The 1920 Fourth of July festivities drew over four hundred cars and trucks to Newport. Talk in 1919 of good roads connecting Newport with the rest of the state inspired one newspaper editor to remark: "Think of getting up some morning, and eating dinner in Portland and coming back home the same day."

Roosevelt Military Highway

All over Oregon, other motorists were having the same dream. A statewide bond issue passed in 1919 provided funds to construct a road the full length of Oregon's coast. The Roosevelt Military Highway would replace the spotty, primitive wagon road system that in places traveled along the beach and was regulated by the tides. A Newport area resident

Yaquina Bay Bridge under construction in 1935. —Pacific Studio Photography

worried that "an invasion of the Willamette Valley through Yaquina Bay would completely nullify the fortifications at the mouth of the Columbia."

To access the Roosevelt Military Highway from points east, another highway was built connecting Newport with Corvallis. By 1924, three buses ran daily each way over this road. The Fourth of July celebration in Newport that year brought an estimated 4,500 cars over the Corvallis highway, more than ten times the number from four years earlier.

By the late 1920s the Roosevelt Highway reached south along the coast to Siletz Bay, eighteen miles north of Newport. A few years later it stretched on down to the California border and points south. Imperceptibly, the era of the "summer people" blended more into one of "tourists," who could travel any time of the year, thanks to cars and good roads, no matter what the weather.

Along the thirty miles from Newport to the northern limits of Lincoln City, a coastal community grew and flourished with businesses, homes, and tourist accommodations strung out in a long, narrow settlement lying within sight and sound of the sea.

Farther north, along the forty miles between Oregon 18 and Tillamook, tourism, fishing, and dairies contributed much to the local economy; but the mainstay was timber. In the vast forests of the Coast Range grew some of the oldest, biggest, and finest trees found in North America.

Fire in the woods had long been an accepted fact of life all over the Pacific Northwest since commercial logging began. But the idea that a substantial portion of what many called an "inexhaustible resource" could be destroyed in a matter of hours was so ridiculous that no reasonable person even considered it. On a hot August afternoon in 1933, the inconceivable happened. It was called "The Tillamook Burn."

Yaquina Head Lighthouse in the early 1900s. —Pacific Studio Photography

OR 6, US 26
Tillamook—Portland
74 miles

US 101, OR 22
Tillamook—Willamina
44 miles

The Tillamook Burn

In his book *Burning an Empire*, Stewart Holbrook, the dean of writers about the timber industry, graphically opens one of the chapters with these words:

> The Tillamook Fire took all the life out of twelve and one-half billion feet of fine old timber, a figure probably never reached before or since by any fire within the memory of white men. I saw it burn, and I never expect to see another sight like it.

As Lewis and Clark noted in 1805-06, some of the trees growing in the area were ten to twelve feet in diameter and more than two hundred feet tall. This mature, varied forest of Douglas fir, cedar, hemlock, and Sitka spruce milled into the finest top-grade lumber. Douglas fir trees reach maturity at four hundred and fifty years; some of the trees standing in the early 1900s were close to a thousand years old. Yet, in a brief twenty-hour holocaust, 87 percent of this ancient forest was reduced to piles of black ashes and bare snags—scars that lasted many years on the face of once beautiful country.

How The Fire Began

The summer of 1933 on the Oregon Coast was hot and dry. The relative humidity—that is, the amount of moisture in the air compared to what the atmosphere can hold at that temperature—fell below thirty percent. Prudence and area foresters suggested that all logging activity in the woods cease because of the fire danger. But there was no law requiring loggers to obey.

Temperatures soared into the nineties on August 14, and by noon the relative humidity dropped into the twenties. Most logging operations stopped under these conditions. But the owner of a small outfit camped in Gales Creek Canyon, forty miles east of Tillamook, sent his crew back into the woods after one o'clock to drag out just a few more big trees.

As other loggers would have done, had they been working, this crew set a choker around the butt of a big Douglas fir and dragged it through the thick undergrowth and old rotting wood debris using a steel cable attached to a steam-powered donkey engine. At some point along the way, the big log scraped across a pile of tinder dry punk, which burst into flames from the intense heat generated by friction.

A dry wind blew from the northeast as the men tried to extinguish the growing blaze. A hundred men from the logging crew fought the fire; but it continued to grow in size and intensity. By mid-afternoon fire lookouts reported sighting new smoke south of the Wilson River road several miles away.

Truckloads of men from sawmills, logging camps, and the Civilian Conservation Corps hurried to the fires to hold them at bay with hand tools. Much of the area had no roads. Trees grew so thick that passage through the forest was difficult; the forest floor was strewn with highly combustible debris accumulated over many years. The situation was grim.

Though they worked well when told what to do, most of the CCC boys were from big cities like New York, Detroit, and Atlanta. The Great Depression-inspired Civilian Conservation Corps was the federal government's way of teaching a work ethic through training, experience, and wages to needy young men; they helped the Forest Service, the National Park Service, and other land managers to build trails in parks and wilderness areas during those times of severe budget restraints. Before coming to Oregon and other western states, few of these young men had ever seen such large trees, and most had no knowledge of the woods.

Each CCC camp housed two hundred young men regardless of race or background; the only qualifications were being unemployed and willing

A logging railroad chugs across a high trestle built of timber.

—Tillamook County Pioneer Museum

Logging crew around 1900.
—Tillamook County Pioneer Museum

to work. They received room, board, medical attention, a modest amount of military discipline, and thirty dollars a month, half of which usually went to their families back home. Working under the supervision of government career experts in their fields, the CCC was one of the better projects undertaken by the federal government in the 1930s.

Over the ten days following the outbreak of fire in the woods, the firefighting force grew from hundreds to thousands. Though not yet under control, the fragmented fire was being checked on many fronts. By the eleventh day, August 24, nearly 40,000 acres of fine timber had been burned over, but prospects for containing the fire looked good. The humidity was rising. The wind had died down. Then disaster struck.

Teams of oxen hauling huge logs on skid roads.
—Tillamook County Pioneer Museum

The Blowup

In his book *Epitaph for the Giants*, J. Larry Kemp gives a vivid description of what happened.

> The fire blew up! It blew forty thousand feet straight up! A great orange wall of flame eighteen miles across the front of the fire exploded out of the treetops. All the fires became one enormous inferno, belching smoke and flaming up, up, up into the heavens. A cloud forty miles wide mushroomed into the sky, to hang dull red, angry, and ominous over the blaze.

Hot coals and ashes scattered far out over the ocean; ships five hundred miles at sea were pelted with smoldering rubbish rained down from the sky. When the debris washed back to the shore, black drifts piled two feet deep along miles of beach.

> The fire created its own hurricane. The hot air rushing up was replaced by fresh air, bringing more oxygen to the flames. The wind created by the inversion was frightening, its roar fantastic, its force incredible. It swooped on the burning trees, plucking out firs two

The centuries-old Tillamook forest in 1926, seven years before the Burn.
—Oregon Department of Forestry

112

The Tillamook Burn in progress. —Oregon Department of Forestry

Damage after 1951's North Fork fire. —Oregon Department of Forestry

hundred and fifty feet tall as though they were seedlings, swirling them through the air, throwing them back into the conflagration.

Incredibly, considering the scope and intensity of the fire, only one life was lost. Frank Palmer, a CCC tree ranger from Marseilles, Illinois, was crushed to death by a huge tree uprooted by the hurricane and then thrown back upon him.

Endless numbers of narrow-escape stories were eventually told: A forest lookout left his post just a few moments before it went up in flames; people camped or living deep in the woods barely escaped the encroaching fire before it destroyed their shelters; women and children clung to careening flatcars across burning railroad trestles, while the engineers driving the locomotives found the throttle controls too hot to touch.

> In Tillamook, and other coastal towns, the sun was blotted out completely by the cloud of smoke, and noon seemed to be midnight. Old-timers called it the darkest day in history, Black Thursday. At mid-day chickens went to roost and birds were silent in the forest. Cars drove with their lights on.

Incalculable numbers of wildlife died.

The worst of the damage occurred in the blowup on August 24, but the fire continued to burn in spite of the thousands of men brought in to combat it. Relief finally came on September 5, 1933, when a hard, pelting rain cleansed the air and drenched the ground for several days. Only then could the cost of the Tillamook Burn be calculated. The totals were incredible.

Cost of the Fire

The damage spread across thirteen and a half townships, or 486 square miles; 311,000 acres of old-growth timber had been burned, 270,000 of which went up during those twenty terrible hours on August 24-25. Nearly thirteen billion board feet of prime timber was gone; its estimated value in 1933 stood at $275 million. Had those trees lived to be cut, they would have kept 14,000 loggers and sawyers working forty hours a week for sixty years, and their wages would have totaled $3 billion.

The burned forest is believed to have been 82 percent Douglas fir, 15 percent western hemlock, and 2 percent red cedar, according to a study made by the Pacific Northwest Forest Experiment Station. "All of the sawmills, lath mills, shingle mills, and pulpwood mills in the forty-eight states, working together," concludes author Stewart Holbrook, "used approximately twelve and one-half billion feet of timber in 1932, the amount killed in the Tillamook Fire."

Logging the Burn

Devastation after the fire appeared so great that the area might never recover, but experienced foresters knew two important facts also borne out in Stewart Holbrook's writings: First, fire does not kill growing timber; and second, dead timber is soon attacked by hole-boring insects that quickly render it worthless as lumber. The salvage effort could overlook live trees that were merely scorched, but the dead ones must be logged, hauled to a mill, and cut into lumber before the insects ruined them.

But before any salvage work could begin, timber transportation facilities needed to be replaced; all railroads, sawmills, and logging equipment in the burned area were destroyed. Timber owners and mill operators lost more than a million dollars in equipment. The operating capital of many companies working in the Tillmook region dissipated with the smoke, for only a few giants in the industry could absorb financial loss on this scale.

Tillamook County faced bankruptcy if logging companies couldn't pay their taxes, which totaled $400,000 annually. In a unique merger between private owners and government officials at the county, state, and federal levels, collective resources were combined to form the Consolidated Timber Company, which led the salvage operation. The first order of business for logging boss Lloyd Cosby was putting men to work falling salvagable trees and reconstructing rail and truck roads to haul the timber out. Before a single log could be moved, $1.5 million was spent on railroad construction, $1.25 million on locomotives and rolling stock, and $800,000 on truck roads.

Early in the summer of 1934 the salvage operation began in earnest. Loggers took only number one timber; snags 8-10 feet around and 150-200 feet tall went first; no trees less than twenty-four inches in diameter were cut. Buckers sawed logs into lengths of 70-90 feet, and steam donkeys dragged them to the landings. Once at the mill, sawyers removed up to six inches of scorched bark and outer wood to find the inner timber as sound and pure as if the trees had never been burned. The charred outer surface actually protected the trees from destructive insects. Both Consolidated and independent companies logged over one hundred million board feet of useable timber.

But, as if to show that the fire menace could strike any time, on August 1, 1939—just six years after the devastating blaze—the cry again was heard: "Fire in Gales Creek Canyon!" Apparently ignited by a careless contractor, this fire started near the same spot as the earlier one. Before it could be subdued, it reburned two hundred thousand acres of the 1933 fire, plus an additional twenty thousand acres of green timber.

A single piece of Douglas fir is a truckload. —Tillamook County Historical Museum

Again logging companies lost lumber, equipment, and roadways. But as soon early autumn rains killed the fire, logging operations resumed; this time with renewed intensity and purpose. War had broken out in Europe, and the United States began building shipyards in Portland and elsewhere on the Pacific Coast to produce minesweepers, destroyers, freighters, and other ships to assist and support our allies, lest we use them ourselves. Two years later, that would be the case.

After we entered the war, sugar, like many other items, became a precious commodity and was rationed. Honey filled some of the void, and Tillamook produced its share. Fireweed pioneered regrowth of the ground cover on the thousands of acres that burned; bees ran by apiarists converted the fireweed pollen into thousands of pounds of distinctive wild-tasting honey.

By 1943 approximately 3.5 billion feet of salvaged timber had come off the burn, Consolidated boss Lloyd Crosby estimated. He told Stewart Holbrook that by 1945 his loggers would have saved all the trees possible. Neither man foresaw the lumber shortages during the post-war housing boom, in which small-time "gypo" outfits sawed and sold almost every tree that could make a useable two-by-four. But while the salvage operation and World War II continued full-tilt in the summer of 1942, the Japanese High Command, desperate to injure the American war effort in any way, undertook a unique bombing mission against Pacific Northwest forests.

Bombs in the Woods

J. Larry Kemp writes:

> In August, 1942, the submarine I-25 left Yokohama harbor bound for the coast of Oregon. Beneath her steel deckplates was a disassembled Zero float plane. During the inky blackness of night on September 8, the I-25 surfaced silently off Cape Blanco, where the crew assembled the Zero and loaded it with incendiary bombs. The mission of the Zero's pilot was to drop incendiaries on the forest of the Oregon coast, let his plane with the Rising Sun markings be seen, and, if possible, escape to sea and the I-25.

His mission succeeded, but its purpose failed. The blaze started by the bombs was quickly extinguished by alert foresters. Some people saw the plane, but no one realized it was a hostile bomber until bomb fragments with Japanese markings were found later; and even then they didn't believe the plane they had seen was Japanese.

> Ten days later the submarine surfaced again off the Oregon coast, and the plane roared into the early morning sky. This time the bombs fell on the Siuslaw National Forest, just south of the Tillamook Burn. The bombs did no appreciable damage, but the pilot, on his return home, was promoted for his daring and heroism.

The Japanese also tried a more ambitious and potentially more dangerous attack on the woods of the Pacific Northwest. They constructed and released thousands of balloons thirty to forty feet in diameter, which they packed with fragmentation and incendiary bombs designed to start devastating fires and panic the coastal population. The wax-covered rice paper balloons were programmed to float about fifty hours, enough time to cross the Pacific Ocean in the perpetually east-flowing jet stream, then deflate, drop, and explode.

> By December, 1944, Project V-1 was ready to execute. Nine thousand balloons were sent up from Tokyo and another sixty thousand reportedly were released from Formosa and the Kurile Islands during the next several months. Of these, only about one thousand reached the United States, and only a few were known to have exploded.

Twelve counties in Oregon reported balloon landings, another came down near Seattle, several others come down in northern California, and one landed in the Mare Island Naval Complex in San Francisco Bay. As an attempt to destroy trees and panic people, the V-1 Project was not very cost effective. After spending the equivalent of $200 million over a two-year period, the Japanese gave it up shortly before the war ended.

Replanting the Tillamook Burn. —Oregon Department of Forestry

The Six-Year Jinx

Following the Tillamook Burn in 1933 and another bad fire in the same area in 1939, the six-year curse struck again on July 10, 1945, and also in July 1951. The 1945 fire scorched more than two hundred thousand acres of the old burn and thirty thousand new acres of green timber. People began to wonder if the Tillamook forest would ever turn green again, and each time fire struck meant that much longer until the new trees could mature into logging timber.

Renewing the Burn

The citizens of Oregon decided to help restore and protect the forest. Newspaper editorials in 1945 prompted Governor Earl Snell to appoint a committee to determine what could be done; a few months later, the state legislature submitted a $10.5 million forest rehabilitation measure to the voters. In 1948 the amendment passed, and the following summer Governor Douglas McKay signed the bond program into law while sitting on a stump. Charged with implementing the program, the Oregon State Department of Forestry had no precedent to follow for a projects of this size.

A booklet published by the department on the Tillamook Burn explains that foresters:

> . . . viewed vast stretches of snags and remembered the repeated fires
> that ran uncontrollably through the midst of those ghostly giants.

118

Despite the two thousand men available on the 1945 fire, and the virtually unlimited supply of bulldozers, pumpers and fire fighting tools, control was impossible among the snags.

The forestry department acquired some 250,000 acres of the Burn, mostly from counties seeking someone to manage the tax-foreclosed timber land. Fireproofing the forest was not feasible; but with improved fire detection capabilities, more access roads, well-managed firefighting crews, and, above all, snag-free fire breaks, the agency felt that the Tillamook Burn area could be reasonably safeguarded. Surveys determined the placement for access roads, areas for natural renewal, and reforestation details such as seed sources, cover types, and soil conditions. One and a half million snags were felled by independent contractors, state crews, and prison inmates, and over 220 miles of snag-free firebreaks were constructed.

More than half of the fire-killed timber—seven billion board feet of Douglas fir—was salvaged. Seventeen years after the original Tillamook fire, useable timber continued to come from the burned area. The great demand for lumber following World War II increased the number of area logging companies from fifty to two hundred. But all efforts to renew the forest by either natural or artificial were hopeless as long as the "six-year jinx" returned. And it did.

Devastating fires swept the Tillamook region with deadly regularity: the 1939 fire occurred six years after the first one hit, another came in 1945, and another in 1951. Each time newly planted trees grew for five years, then burned. Some people believed the forest was cursed, destined

Young volunteers planting trees. —Oregon Department of Forestry

By 1974 young trees were showing up among the snags on King Mountain.—Oregon Department of Forestry

forever to remain a charred desert. But in 1951, the fire wardens were ready. Kemp writes:

> The alarm had barely sounded when crews with bulldozers and other heavy equipment moved over the fire roads into the path of the inferno. On July 24 the fire had been trailed and by the next day it was under control. It had burned over twenty thousand acres in those few days; fortunately, almost all of the territory afire was within the boundaries of the previous burns.

In the central area of the 1933 blowup, where fire had raged most intensely for twenty hours on August 24 and August 25, the ash-covered earth was so badly scorched that no seeds survived and no natural reforestation could be expected. So a cooperative effort to replant by hand on a scale never known in forest lands before began. Garden clubs, school children, scout troops, civic and social groups, and people from all walks of life donated time and energy to planting trees as directed by professional foresters.

The New Tillamook Forest

The Tillamook Burn changed gradually. Old white snags and blackened stumps gave way to young, green forests. On July 18, 1973, exactly twenty-four years after the reforestation bond program began, Governor Tom McCall dedicated the the former burn as the Tillamook State Forest. Rehabilitation costs on 364,000 acres of state-owned lands in the area stood at $13 million. The first commercial thinning took place in 1983 to allow the other trees to grow faster until they are logged.

Blimp Hangars

A few miles south of Tillamook on the east side of US 101 stands a pair of immense wooden buildings listed in *The Guiness Book of World Records* as the largest structures of their kind. These two blimp hangars are relics of the Second World War, when eight U.S. Navy blimps patrolled the Pacific skies in search of Japanese submarines. Built in 1942, each hangar is 195 feet high, 1,080 feet long, and 300 feet wide. The blimps stationed there measured 251 feet long and 79 feet high.

One of five stations on the West Coast, the Tillamook blimp guard scanned the waters from northern California to British Columbia and escorted ships into the Columbia River and Puget Sound. The Navy admits the downing of one airship off Eureka, California, another was destroyed by winds at the base, and a third crashed into Tillamook Bay with no fatalities; but whether they ever dropped a bomb on an enemy, or were fired at, never has been revealed.

Dense fog sometimes obscured the crane operator's view while the hangars were being built, so some nimble, sure-footed worker high above on the catwalk telephoned directions to get the large arched trusses properly placed. Because of the wartime shortage of steel, ten million board feet of lumber from the Tillamook Burn were used.

Years later, after a long period of little or no use, blimps returned to the hangars when not in use as "sky-hooks" for loggers working on steep mountain slopes, where it is either impractical or ecologically damaging for ground vehicles to go. Flying stunts have sometimes been popular at these hangars; one such event was filmed here for a James Bond movie.

Each of the two wooden blimp hangars near Tillamook can house eight blimps with room to spare. —Tillamook County Pioneer Museum

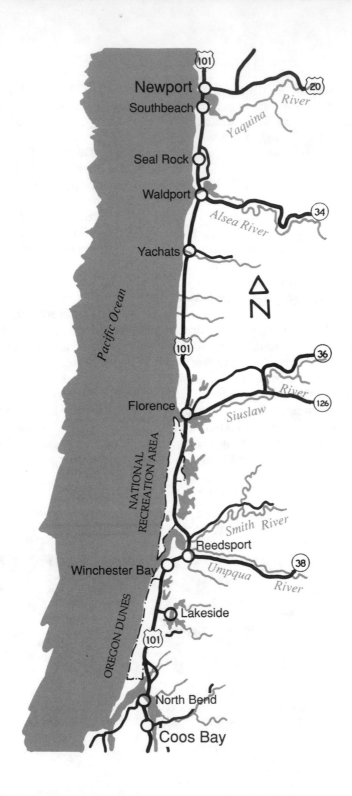

Just as the original Columbia River Gorge Highway has been described as a work of art, so may the many graceful bridges spanning inlets and bays along the Coast Highway be classed as structures whose beauty rivals their utility. Certainly the high, arched bridge just south of Newport ranks at the top of the list. East of the highway on the bay is the Marine Science Center; run by Oregon State University and established under the sponsorship of Senator Mark Hatfield, it is well worth an hour or two.

Spectacular Coast

To say that one stretch of the Oregon Coast is more scenic than another is pointless; all of it is beautiful. But for variety, the ninety-eight miles between Newport and Coos Bay are hard to equal. In places, the mountains crowd so close to the sea that the highway is forced to climb a thousand feet or more, winding across mist-shrouded headlands.

Rocks offshore are covered with basking seals, and caves house noisy sea lions. Sea otters, perhaps the most wonderful fur-bearing mammal of all, once abounded in these waters—until they were hunted into oblivion; as a threatened species, they are now protected. All efforts to reestablish the otter along this coast have failed, but it flourishes still in Alaskan waters farther north.

Three rivers beloved by sports fishermen and boaters—the Smith, the Umpqua, and the Coquille—rush to the sea from the steep slopes of the mountains to the east. For fifty-three miles between Florence and Coos Bay, the Oregon Dunes push the highway inland. These crests of scrub evergreen and grass grow five hundred feet high. This area's history is full of tales of shipwrecks and bloody battles with the natives. The record begins with an encounter between the American fur trapper Jedediah S. Smith and the Umpqua Indians.

Jedediah Smith

Among mountain men roaming the West in the 1820s, Jedediah Smith was unique in that he did not drink, smoke, or swear. His Christian ethic and piety preceded his reputation as a good leader while still in his early twenties; that and his sound judgement earned him financial backing for a fur expedition to Spanish California.

Starting here with 1914, this sequence of photographs shows the effect of erosion on Jump Off Joe Rock at Nye Beach, Newport.—Pacific Studio Photography

Jump Off Joe Rock in 1924.

Jump Off Joe Rock in 1982.

But the Spaniards weren't so charmed. They confiscated his furs and jailed him to teach a lesson, then they released him with the stern warning to get out of Spanish territory and never return. Professing Christian though he was, the only lesson his arrest and incarceration taught him was not to get caught next time.

Making his way north from the San Francisco Bay area into southern Oregon, he and his eighteen-man party had reaccumulated furs worth several thousand dollars, plus about three hundred horses, when they made camp near the mouth of the Umpqua River in July 1828. The details of what happened then are sketchy since Jed Smith, perhaps feeling partially at fault, never elaborated on it. But the Umpqua Indians attacked and killed fourteen of his men, took their horses and furs, and left the handful of survivors in desperate circumstances.

Somehow they made it to Fort Vancouver, the Hudson's Bay Company post where Dr. John McLoughlin led the British effort to prove title to the Oregon country over the claims of the United States. McLoughlin took Smith and the others into his fort and sent a force of Hudson's Bay Company employees south to the Umpqua. They "punished" the Indians and recovered Smith's furs and most of his horses. The HBC party warned the Indians that the "White Eagle," McLoughlin, would not tolerate attacks on white men, even if they were Americans.

McLoughlin offered to buy the furs from Jedediah Smith, deducting only the cost of wages for his employees sent to recover them, and Smith accepted. Impressed by the British factor's gracious action, he promised never to trespass or trap in the Oregon country again. And he never did.

Sand Dunes

According to William S. Cooper, a Minnesota botanist who began studying the Oregon Coast sand dunes in the early 1920s, they are unique. Extending from Coos Bay north to Sea Lion Point—a distance of fifty-three miles—the dunes reach inland as much as three miles and pile as high as five hundred feet. In *A Century of Coos and Curry*, Cooper writes: "There are few things in nature that can match a dune in grace of curve and contour and in play of light and shadow. In Oregon the great forest adds variety to the dune landscape, and in the background are sea and surf."

Three elements combine in the creation of a dune: sand, water, and wind. Rivers eroding slopes inland bring sand down to the sea. Wave action erodes cliffs and throws sand against the shore. Wind, constantly shifting in direction and force, deposits the sand in piles and drifts that may creep inshore or move laterally along the beach. Consequently, a sand dune is a like a living thing that always moves and changes.

Sand dunes near Florence.

"On the coast of Oregon the winds of summer and winter differ greatly," Cooper writes. "In summer, ... they blow from the northwest, often attaining a velocity of forty miles an hour. In winter, direction is inconsistent, but the important ones for the dunes are the frequent gales from the southwest."

Summer winds account for very definite dune patterns—a system of low ridges spaced at regular intervals lying transverse to wind direction. Each ridge slopes gently windward, while the leeward angle grows as steep as the sand will allow. "Sand is constantly removed from the windward slope and dumped over the crest; the ridge itself is thus in constant motion."

The growth of vegetation, such as grass, stabilizes a dune. A battle constantly occurs between sand and vegetation, changing the appearance of the landscape from year to year. Cooper writes:

> Beach grasses like to be buried, binding the sand into a coherent mass. Farther inland, where the winds are weak, plants take hold and gradually gain the upper hand, first herbs, mosses, and creeping shrubs like kinnikinnick, then tall shrubs—blueberry, huckleberry, salal, manzanita—and finally trees. In many places dunes once in active motion bear dense forests of pine, spruce, and Douglas fir. Many of the trees are several feet in thickness, and on one stabilized dune I found a Douglas fir five centuries old.

126

Oregon Dunes National Recreation Area

Following its long tradition of preserving the coast for the people, Oregon State established a 47-mile stretch from Florence to North Bend as a national recreation area. Averaging two miles in width, the area is managed by the Siuslaw National Forest and has become a sand dunes playground for people of all ages and tastes.

Viewpoints, boat-launching ramps, hiking and riding trails, and beach facilities enhance recreation in these 32,000 acres. Fifteen diverse campgrounds include some designed for off-road vehicles and others catering exclusively to hikers. Headquarters for the Oregon Dunes National Recreation Area is where US 101 intersects with Oregon 38 in Reedsport.

Local Indians

Though Lewis and Clark did not visit the natives living around Coos Bay, they estimated their population at fifteen hundred. The name Coos means "lake" or "lagoon." Unlike tribes along the lower Columbia River, these people did not practice head-flattening, although their northern neighbors, the Alseas, at Yachats, supposedly did.

The Coquille Indians to the southeast, studied in 1890 by anthropologist Owen Dorsey, lived in 32 scattered villages. They were known variously as "people at big rocks," "people at big dam," "good grass people," and "village on the dark side of a canyon"; the names undoubtedly lost something in translation. Farther south are the "Rogue," or "Rascal" Indians, whose name for themselves was *Tutini*.

White Settlers

Emigrants to Oregon from the East Coast often expected to find country similar to what they left behind. William P. Mast and his family fit that category when they joined sixty-six of their neighbors from the hills of North Carolina and journeyed west in 1872. Learning that the Coos Bay Wagon Road opened up into timbered hill country much like that back home, Mast decided to settle there, even though the spot he chose required four-miles of travel over a rough mountain trail from the main road. His son, Reuben Mast, later recalled how they transported trunks, boxes, cook stoves, chicken crates, and the essentials of a blacksmith shop by horseback.

In this land of heavy timber and swift, deep, unfordable streams, the newcomers had to build their own bridges. Often little more than a tree felled across a stream with the top side leveled, these served settlers until they could build better roadways. Trees were cut and burned so enough sunlight could penetrate the earth to grow a garden.

Soon the Mast family was settled in a twelve-by-fourteen foot board shanty, which Reuben Mast recalled as "surrounded by tall fir timber on the north and east, and on the south by a stretch of ten acres of black logs which had been cut down in the early summer and burned over in the fall. All through the long winter we toiled in those black logs, cutting, rolling, burning, and grubbing, day in and day out and often till ten o'clock at night, so that when the June roses blushed and nodded in the sun, ten acres were raising as fine a crop of grain and grass as ever grew."

Another emigrant remembered his daily job as a boy to "clink up" the fires, some of which burned for fifteen years in order to clear off the land. But the settlers competed with more than the forest for their gardens; they also had to combat animal rivals. To keep deer and elk from raiding the crops, settlers erected split-rail fences higher than a deer could jump.

Animals could end up on either side of the food issue, as these recollections of a pioneer woman show. "John found a bee tree," she wrote. "He chopped it down and carried home the honey, placing it on a high log beside the house. That night we didn't get much sleep, as bears came prowling. A couple of them got into a fight. John went out and shot at them in the dark. They jumped off a log into the brush. The next morning all the honey was gone."

Charlie, the first horse John bought, used to carry eggs, blackberries, dressed chickens, and other trade goods loaded in a pair of kerosene cases from the farm to Myrtle Point. "One day Charlie was in a playful mood and when John tried to catch him, he kicked up his heels, tossed his head, and galloped away. As he bounded along he stepped in a hole, fell, and broke his neck. John cut Charlie's head off and used it to bait a bear trap. The next day he had a big black bear in the trap. We ate the bear meat."

Wreck of the Tug Fearless

With inlets at Waldport, Florence, Reedsport, and Coos Bay, into which ships often tried to make their way against tricky currents and tides, maritime disasters now and then happened. A few were never explained.

On November 20, 1889, Captain James Hill drifted his steam tug *Fearless* onto the north spit of the Umpqua River entrance en route from Astoria to Coos Bay. The tug had been sighted earlier steaming down the coast just outside the fringe of the breakers. The sea was rough and she was under a slow bell. At 6 p.m. her whistle sounded off the mouth of the Umpqua. Forty-five minutes later she gave three blasts in succession—a signal of extreme distress. No more was seen or heard of the vessel until

Wreck of the Tillamook *near Bandon, 1910.* —Pacific Studio Photography

her broken pilothouse, the stern section, one side of the hull, and numerous pieces of wreckage came floating up the river with the incoming tide.

She may have sprung a leak and broke up in the river's current. Captain Hill, who commanded the tug for fifteen years, would not have entered the Umpqua on an ebbing tide without good cause. Those lost forever included the captain, the engineer, two deckhands, and a Chinese cook. The body of a passenger, George Marshall, who had been proprietor of the local Empire City Cannery, washed up later on the beach clad in a life preserver. Since it lay several feet above the high tide line, he may have landed alive and died from exposure before being found.

Wreck of the Marconi, *Cape Arago, 1909.* —Pacific Studio Photography

Cranberry Culture

The "Father of Pacific Coast Cranberry Culture," Charles Dexter McFarlin, raised cranberries in South Carver, Massachusetts, before he came west. Noting rainfall and climate in Coos County similar to that back east, he determined that cranberries would flourish there. To prove it, he built the first cranberry bog on the entire Pacific Coast in 1885 with wild vines from a natural bog on Cape Cod. The "McFarlin" berry soon became the most prominent variety in the United States.

Before heading west, Dexter had arranged with his brother, Thomas, to send him some of these vines. He searched from Humboldt Bay in California to the Columbia River before deciding on North Inlet as the ideal spot to establish his berries. With an ox team and some hired men, he turned a piece of extremely rough, stump-infested swamp into one of the finest cranberry bogs on the Pacific Coast. In December 1898, he wrote:

> I have been cultivating cranberries in Coos County for thirteen years. I have about five acres from which I gathered 687 pounds in 1898. I have gathered as high as 400 bushels from a single acre. At no time have I gathered less than 565 bushels from my five acres. One year my crop was 940 bushels, and it would have reached 1,200 but for a heavy frost. There is money in a well managed cranberry bog.

As might be expected during that era, such a get-rich-quick statement brought a mad rush of inexperienced and uniformed individuals into the business in hopes of making a killing. Those who tended their bogs and were content with modest returns did well. In 1906 McFarlin wrote: "To plant a berry marsh and go off and leave it for three or four years to mature won't do. The vines want constant care, the same as other farm crops. Keep the weeds out and in three or four years the marsh that is properly planted and cared for will produce 150 bushels per acre per annum for an indefinite time."

By 1951, seventy-five percent of Coos County's 350 acres of cranberries were of the McFarlin variety.

Coos Bay Coal Mines

Infected with the '49er mania for striking it rich, a number of prospectors in the Coos Bay area thought they had found their bonanza in veins of coal. As early as 1854, a consignment of 200 tons mined and shipped to San Francisco paid two brothers well for their winter spent digging the black gold. Prices fell sharply the following year, when Captain Park Butler, whose actual cost per ton of coal laid down in San Francisco was $14, found that the best price he could get was $7.50. Even so, coal mining continued for a number of years, leaving scars across the twenty-mile peninsula between Coos Bay and the Coquille River.

Like hardrock gold or silver mining, which required the sale of stock to finance, some of the coal mines made more profit for the stock salesmen than the investors. The Henryville mine opening in 1874 was the Coos Bay district's most elaborate, a reflection of the $5 million invested by San Francisco capitalists. The project got off to an ambitious start with buildings and wharves for the town and tunnels sunk several hundred feet down for the mine. But the beginning was all that was propitious: the vein was lost, and after less than two years the mine closed and the town folded. For forty years the town's sole inhabitant was the company watchman who watched the wharves and buildings fall to ruin.

But in at least two respects coal mining was a leading factor in the pioneer development of agriculture and farm life in Coos County. First, the mines provided a market for farm products—butter, cheese, eggs, beef, pork, potatoes, apples, and vegetables. In some cases these were transported all the way from the farm to the market by boat. Second, many of the leading Coos farm homes were started by part-time coal miners. Mining was somewhat seasonal, with a brisk fall and winter market and a lagging market in spring and summer. Out-of-work miners established homesteads in the summer, setting up their families with gardens and some livestock before returning to coal in the winter.

One temporarily successful mine called the Newport Coal Company (not to be confused with the town of Newport 98 miles up the coast) managed to produce 40,000 tons of coal a month, shipping most of it to San Francisco. But this was a fickle market; ships hauling wheat from California's fertile fields often arrived at port with cheap coal from abroad as ballast, which they were only too glad to get rid of for whatever the buyers would pay.

Unfortunately, when the interior valleys of California suffered a drought and there was a complete crop failure, few ships arrived with coal ballast. As a result, there was a coal famine in San Francisco and the price went sky-high. That year the mine made $300,000. But the next year, crops were good, coal ballast filled the ships, and the price of Coos Bay coal again dropped below the cost of production. By the early 1900s, when oil and natural gas became available, coal mining was no longer profitable.

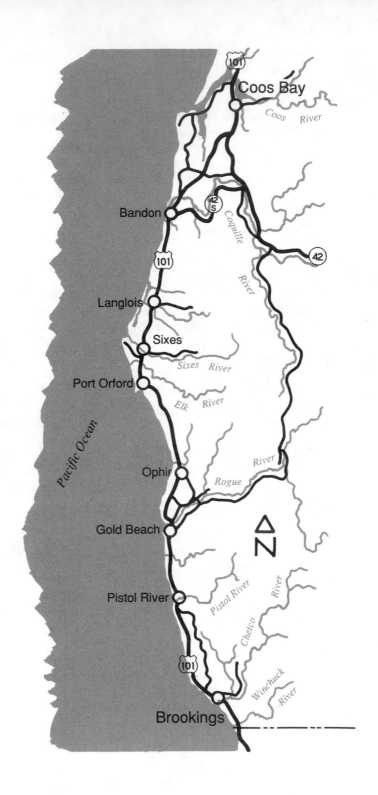

Battle Rock

Though the southernmost stretch of Oregon Coast between Coos Bay and the California state line has such a mild, pleasant climate that it often is called the "banana belt," this region—like so many others in the Pacific Northwest—began its recorded history with an act of mindless violence. On June 9, 1851, the *Sea Gull*, a small steam schooner from Portland, landed nine men led by Captain J.M. Kirkpatrick on the coast a few miles south of Cape Blanco apparently to establish a settlement. They had not bothered to check with the local Indians about land ownership.

"We lost no time in making our camp on what was to be called 'Battle Rock,'" Kirkpatrick later wrote. "There were a few Indians in sight who appeared to be friendly but I could see they did not like to have us there."

Their camp was protected on three sides by sheer cliffs dropping off into water a hundred feet below, while a four or five pound cannon set up to keep potential hostiles at bay shielded the narrow passage on its fourth side. "We put in a two-pound sack of powder and on top of that about half an old cotton shirt and as much bar lead cut into pieces from one to two inches long as I could hold in my two hands," Kirkpatrick wrote. "We then primed the gun with some fine rifle powder and trained it so as to rake the narrow ridge in front of the muzzle and the gun was ready for business."

Kirkpatrick didn't say whether any effort was made to talk with the Indians. But it's clear from the natives' behavior that they wanted to talk, not fight. They had no idea of what havoc a cannon could wreak when fired into their unprotected bodies at point-blank range.

"I stood by the gun holding a piece of tarred rope with one end in the fire as the Indians crowded in front of the cannon. When a red-shirted fellow in the lead was not more than eight feet from the muzzle of the gun, I applied the fiery end of the rope to the priming. At least twelve or thirteen Indians were killed outright, and such a tumbling of scared Indians I never saw."

Though Kirkpatrick called the encounter a "fight" or "battle," the only arms the Indians had were bows and arrows, and knives, none of which were used against the whites. "After the fight was all over, probably an hour, an Indian chief came up on the beach within hailing distance, laid down his bow, arrows and knife and then made signs that he wanted to come into our camp. I went down and met him."

By means of signs, the chief made it clear that he wanted to carry away the Indian dead. Kirkpatrick allowed him one assitant, so he called for a strong, muscular man who appeared to weigh at least two hundred pounds. In eight trips they had carried away all the dead except the man in the red shirt. "I tried to get the big chief to carry him off, but he shook his head, stooped down and tore his shirt in two, then gave him a kick with his foot and turned and walked away."

Forced to bury the red-shirted man themselves, Captain Kirkpatrick's party noticed that "he was very white for an Indian; he had yellow hair and a freckled face. He turned out to be a white man who had been with the Indians for many years" after being saved by them from the wreck of a Russian ship.

Kirpatrick managed to make the chief understand that a ship would return for his party in fourteen days. The chief granted the white men peace for two weeks. "But on the morning of the fifteenth day the Indians were there in force. We had lied to them, they said. We could not make them understand why the steamer did not come.

"The big chief was now their leader. He had his warriors all drawn up around him about 250 yards from us. He made a speech to them so loud that we could hear every word he said above the roar of the surf. When he got about 100 yards from us, I raised my rifle to my shoulder and said, 'Fire!' Had a hundred thunderbolts dropped among his warriors they could not have stopped them as suddenly as the killing of their big chief. They gathered around his body with a groan that was terrible, picked him up and carried him away."

When another Indian leader rallied his people and tried to mount an attack, the whites killed him, too. "This ended all efforts of the Indians to rush upon us. Now was our chance. We left everything we had in camp. With nothing but our guns, an ax, and all the small ropes we had, with two or three seabiscuits apiece, we bid farewell to our old camp on Battle Rock, and started on our fearful retreat through an unknown country...."

Port Orford Begun

The *Sea Gull* had been delayed for repairs at San Francisco, but the man behind establishing the colony, William Tichenor, did not abandon his plans. In the autumn of 1851, he returned to the area with sixty-five new recruits. He had acquired title to a square mile of land under the Donation Claims Land Act, platted a town site, and offered city lots to the public.

Stirred to action by the recent bloodshed, federal agents came to make peace with the Indians; troops arrived to "protect" the white settlers; blockhouses and log cabins were built. When gold was discovered on the beaches and in the nearby creeks, the town boomed. Hotels, stores, and saloons lined the streets, and for a few years business flourished.

"Adjoining the military reservation of this fort," wrote Dr. Rodney Glisan, chief medical officer at Fort Orford in 1856, "is a small village called Port Orford. It was laid out during the mania for townsites along the coast. Having the best port between San Francisco and the Columbia River, it was thought to be an admirable site for a large city, but like many similar attempts, it has proven a failure.

"It has a good summer harbor, as the wind during this season is from the northwest; but in the autumn, winter and early spring it is generally very dangerous for a vessel to attempt to lie to in the harbor, or even to enter it, as the prevailing winds are then from the south, southwest or southeast."

Though the gold boom petered out and traffic in the Port Orford harbor never did make it the busiest city north of San Francisco, its sawmills, fisheries, and, in later years, its dairy industry, kept it alive and a pleasant place in which to live, negating the libel against it written by the irascible historian Hubert H. Bancroft, who said, "Port Orford is a little hamlet on the wrong side of the mountain with no reason on earth for being there."

Irish Settlers

Just as hill people from North Carolina looked for the countryside in Oregon they were used to back home, so did foreigners from overseas look for their kind of country when they migrated here. Americans moving west are called "emigrants" because, although they left the land they knew, they remained within the country; the Irish and other Europeans are "immigrants" because their act was one of coming into another country. Either way, their motivation was the same: free land.

At mid-century in Ireland, the opportunity to claim and hold a square mile of land that never had known the bite of an ax or the share of the plough simply did not exist. So they came to Oregon. Typical of Irish immigrants in 1869 were Dennis Collins and his wife, Honora, who, with their four children and several other Irish families, took up land near Gold Beach, just thirty-five miles north of the California border. Debarking from the small schooner that brought them to the mouth of the Rogue River, they found that their claim could not be reached by wagon, for there was no road.

"Horses were hired to take them in with such of their goods as they could manage. Honora and the smaller children remained with the goods, while Dennis and Jimmy took the horses back for a second pack load. Even the cook stove had to be taken apart and packed in on horseback over the trail."

While clearing land for a garden, pasture, and orchard, they lived in a one room cabin and bought cattle and sheep. The yearly wool crop was their main source of income for many years. With two adults and four children living in the cabin, it was crowded. The boys shared the loft while the girls and the parents slept downstairs. Even so, it was not nearly so crowded as Dennis and Honora might have wished; the last child to bless their marriage—a girl born in 1872—was their thirteenth birth but only their fifth child. Eight earlier infants had died one by one— typical mortality at that time.

The nearest school was in the small town of Ellensburg, several miles away. For several winters, Honora lived in the town with the children so they could attend. The cook stove went to town with them, while at the home place back in the woods, the father and the older boys used the fireplace to cook, as men living alone in the the Old Country frequently did.

Compared to the relative poverty Dennis and Honara had known as tenants in Ireland, life on a square mile of their own land in Oregon was luxurious, despite all the hard work. When the boat came in from "The City"—which in this remote region meant San Francisco—it brought such exotic fruits as oranges, peaches, and bananas, if the family wanted to splurge on a rare treat. But mainly they relied on their own garden products—potatoes, cabbage and kraut, root vegetables, and fruits raised in their orchard.

Strawberries, blackberries, and huckleberries grew wild on the hills, and luscious salmonberries grew thick along the creeks. The river abounded with salmon, and there was no wealthy landowner to arrest them for poaching. The going price for a four-foot salmon, if a person wanted to buy or sell one, was two bits. Rock oysters and mussels from the ocean, just over the hill, could be bought from the Indians for ten cents a bushel. Venison and bear meat were plentiful. Hogs allowed to run loose in the woods grew fat on acorns, then were shot, butchered, and cured as hams and bacon. The hills were full of bee-trees.

Devout Catholic that she was, Honora missed formal church services, but, in addition to making all the clothes for her and her family, she somehow bought enough black silk to make herself a dress, which she wore to services whenever a priest made the long ride out to the coast from Roseburg.

She missed friendly visits with neighbors, too. Soon after she and Dennis made camp and started building their cabin, he showed her smoke from the chimney of a house hidden by the trees. "It was a cheering thought to her," wrote Ann Truman Connel, who recorded the life of the Collins family many years later, "and she visioned the comfort of another woman dropping in to borrow odds and ends, and to trade recipes. We can but imagine the shock it was to her when she met her neighbor and found out that she was an Indian!" Whatever mental picture of wild savages Honora may have held, she did not avoid her neighbor, who she found to be kind, good, and cleanliness itself. "Married to a man of German descent, the Indian woman and her children spoke English with his broken accent. He had a long white beard, of which his wife was very proud, and she kept his denim clothing bleached almost white to match it. No floors in the community were sanded so white as hers. Her sons taught young Jerry Collins many bits of wood lore, and they often went hunting together."

Zane Grey Country

From 1910 until 1935 the most popular writer of Westerns in the world was Zane Grey. Best known for colorful action novels set in the high desert country of the Southwest, he was an avid fisherman. His favorite fish was the sea-going rainbow trout known as steelhead. His favorite fishing stream was the Rogue River, whose tumbling white rapids and shadowed deep pools he guarded so zealously that he resented even the local natives who fished there.

Then, as now, the controversy between commercial and sports fishermen was so heated and bitter that at times the parties resorted to blows or bullets. One of Zane Grey's less well-known novels, *Rogue River Feud*, published around 1935, was based on that rivalry. As in so many of his books, his description of scenery is superior to his characterization, plotting, or writing, which reads as if composed by a man impatient to finish his daily stint of words so that he can go fishing. But it does give the reader a good feel for the country.

US 101
Gold Beach—California Line
35 miles

Early Day Butchery

In their book *A Century of Coos and Curry*, local historians Emil R. Peterson and Alfred Powers state that this corner of Oregon probably boasted more game birds and animals per square acre than any other region in the Pacific Northwest: "Had someone ventured to remark in those days that some time in the future there would be legislation for the protection of those animals, he would have been laughed at."

Deer and elk were killed by the score simply for their hides. "In the case of elk, their two ivory teeth were taken along with their hides, both bringing fair prices in the market. Five hunters who took pack animals into the Eden Valley country during the early pioneer days returned a couple of weeks later with 300 deer hides and not even a mess of venison." On the lower Coquille River, three hunters killed 85 elk in three days, taking only the hides and teeth. A Curry County resident killed every single elk in a herd of twenty-four, not even bothering to skin the elk and removing only one ham.

Bears and cougars also were once plentiful in the area. The greatest bear hunter in the Rogue River Country was a man named Jake Fry, who began hunting bears when he was eleven years old and continued to hunt them for fifty years. "During that period he owned one hundred bear dogs. Eight years was the ordinary life of the bloodhounds and beagles he used. Jake Fry remembered the heroic services of dogs that had been dead over forty years. During retrospective evenings the ghosts of the hundred dogs he had owned came back to him, eager for the hunt, nimble of foot, musical of voice." Jake Fry sometimes killed as many as ten bears a day. He thought he averaged about twenty-five a year, so his lifetime total would have been approximately 1,250.

Even the ocean did not prevent men from declaring war on native creatures. For a quarter century along the southern Oregon Coast, bounty hunters butchered thousands of sea lions, a slaughter initiated by complaints from commercial fishermen and enacted by the Oregon State Legislature in 1900, which authorized $2.50 paid for each sea lion scalp. Later the bounty was increased to $5.00, then $10.00. Finally, in 1926, the bounty dropped to fifty cents, which discouraged hunters so much they all but ceased pursuing the animals.

The sea lions ate the fleshy middles from the salmon, biting into the profits of the fishermen. Sharpshooters made good money. "One June day in 1923, U.S. Game Warden Ray C. Steele visited the Cape Blanco rocks. With him was W.M. Hunter, a state-employed sharpshooter. A good marksman, he looked 106 times along the sights of his rifle barrel. Each time he fired at an animal sunning itself on the rocks, he killed it." In addition to rifles, dynamite was used. In 1917, on the Rogue River Reefs and at Cape Blanco, the crews of gasoline-powered boats were killing three or four hundred sea lions a month.

Well-Traveled Doctor

Not all of the residents of the southern Oregon Coast lived in the woods or spent their time killing animals. Dr. Walter Haydon, a skilled surgeon and world traveler, came to the Coos Bay area in 1903 and practiced medicine there until his death in 1932. The dean of writers for

Portland's prestigious *Oregon Journal*, Fred Lockley, once wrote: "Dr. Haydon's headquarters was a gathering place for intellectuals, for scientists and for prominent visitors who sought particular information of the Southwestern Oregon country."

Born in England in 1854, Haydon learned to cook while studying medicine in London; his specialty was preparing food for invalids. He wanted to see Europe, Russia, and the Far North, so he put in a year studying diets and also took lessons in carpentry and metal work to learn things that might come in handy during his travels. "After I had received my degree," he told Lockley, "I put in a year in Russia and elsewhere in Europe. I then made a trip as surgeon aboard the *Hope* on a voyage to the Arctic. We had a crew of about eighty men. We were gone a year. I collected specimens as well as taking care of the health of the crew."

For six years Dr. Haydon was employed by the Hudson's Bay Company at Moose Factory, in the Northwest Territories, traveling over the region by dog team, snowshoe, or canoe. "While there I made a collection of butterflies and plants for Darwin, who was anxious to study the variations in animal and plant life due to climatic conditions."

In addition to his other interests, he was a first-rate photographer. "In those days I prepared my own wet plates and made many of my own chemicals. In 1922 a fire swept the lower part of Front Street in Marshfield and destroyed all my collections, including the photographic plates. A few years later my brother ran across in a second hand store in London a book of photographic views that I had printed and sent to a friend in England and that had been sold after his death. My brother bought the book and sent it to me, and you can imagine how much pleasure I had in looking over the photography I had made nearly fifty years before."

Gorse-Killing Time in Bandon

If a stranger to southwestern Oregon had stopped in the small coastal town of Bandon in the summer of 1950, he might have been befuddled to read this headline in the local paper: "All Out Drive on Gorse Scheduled for Sunday."

The first sentence of the article would not have cleared his state of confusion in the least: " 'Gorse Riddance is Good Riddance' will be the battle cry this Sunday, when every Bandon family is urged to join in a communitywide attack on the area's worst menace—gorse."

Was a gorse some kind of fierce wild animal? No, it was a shrub. But it was fierce. Not too many years earlier it had destroyed the town, taking several lives in the process. Now it was threatening to do the same thing again. So the gorse must be killed without mercy.

When a new frontier is opened by migrating people, they all too often recall a plant, animal, or fish that thrived and enriched their lives in the Old Country and should do the same in the new land. In Australia, some nameless sportsmen from England introduced the rabbit so that he could have a spot of good hunting. In the high mountain lakes of Idaho, a newcomer from the Plains states introduced catfish and carp. In the Bandon area, an early resident known as Lord George Bennett, who came from Ireland and was homesick for the Olde Sod, brought in an ornamental roadside shrub that reminded him of home—gorse.

In each case, the result was ecological disaster.

"I can recall back to May, 1894," a Bandon resident wrote many years later, "when I saw two rows of gorse approximately twelve feet long and two feet high at Lord Bennett's place. He stated to me that he had brought the seed from Ireland."

The initial spread of gorse is slow. Its seed may lie in the ground for twenty-five years before it germinates. But once it begins to grow, it is nearly impossible to kill. Fire may destroy many of the plant crowns, but it hastens seed germination. Gorse seedlings have appeared in fields many years after the original stands were destroyed. Any system of control, therefore, must recognize that the seeds can endure an extended period of dormancy.

"It grows especially well on sand dunes, gravel bars, fence rows, on logged-off and burned over forest lands, and in other areas where it is not disturbed by tillage. Once established, it excludes all other vegetation. Under normal conditions the oily plant grows from the center outward, leaving a mass of dead, dry matter in the center. When the plant is fired, this center burns to form a chimney or draft which rises in increasing intensity of fire."

By 1936 the shrub had long since gone wild along the southern Oregon coast. "It lined the streets of Bandon," Stewart Holbrook writes. "It infested the second-growth timber around town, it hedged highways north and south. At times the Oregon legislature had been moved to consider its eradication, but nothing was ever done."

In 1936, Bandon's main industries were fish, lumber, and summer people. Every day the local sawmill produced over one hundred thousand feet of the beautiful Port Orford, or white, cedar. In the summertime, the town's population of eighteen hundred was doubled by the influx of visitors who came to enjoy the finest weather on the coast.

The morning of September 26, 1936, was unusually hot for a coastal town; the temperature climbed into the seventies long before noon. Even more unusual, the relative humidity had dropped to eight percent, which meant that there was almost no moisture in the air. Slash fires had been burning south and east of town for several days, but, since most of the trees had been logged off the hills, the fires seemed harmless. Twice before noon the city's fire department dispatched trucks to put out small blazes in shrubbery near the high school. At noon a more serious fire just outside the city limits threatened the town's main water line, so Fire Chief Woomer moved quickly to extingush it. Later in the afternoon, an extremely dry easterly wind came up, blowing smoke, ashes, and sparks toward Bandon from a slash fire on Bear Creek.

Around dark, the sound of what people first took to be an explosion blasted the southeast part of town. "Probably it was an explosion," Holbrook writes, "for that is about the only way to describe what happens when fire gets into a good clump of gorse."

Never in all their experience, the Bandon firemen declared later, had they faced a fire so hot as those flaming clumps of gorse. "They cursed the memory of Lord George Bennett. The fire raced quickly along the south side of East Eleventh, shooting up tongues of flame fifty to one hundred feet, spitting off oily gobs that turned into balls of fire and went whirling away over the town roofs. A hose full of water burned in two as though it were made of paper."

Soon it became clear that the fire was out of control. Sometime between eight and nine o'clock Chief Woomer went to the Hartman movie theater, stopped the show, and asked that all able-bodied men report to help fight the fire. Ironically, the feature that night was titled "Thirty-six Hours to Live."

"The fire department was now making a sort of last stand to keep the fire from getting down into the business section. They found they were up against something few fire departments had ever seen. A stray spark would fall in a green clump of gorse near a house. An instant later the gorse was flaming higher than the house. In another instant the house was wholly on fire. Time and again it happened. Many homes were all but surrounded with gorse, hedges of it, and these fairly exploded." More men and equipment hurried to help from the nearby towns of Myrtle Point, Coquille, and Marshfield. But nothing could stop the flames. The town was doomed.

By eleven o'clock that night, with no water and no way to fight the fire Chief Woomer and the U.S. Coast Guard decided to evacuate the town. "A roaring wall of flame threw itself with dreadful fury down the draw that led from the bluff to the heart of Bandon's business life," Holbrook writes. "Here the flames boomed like cannon, and reddened the faces of hundreds of citizens.

"It was a stirring if ghastly scene. The single street crammed full of automobiles and people on foot, folks bent with bundles and boxes, and wide-eyed children lugging dogs and cats and birds in cages."

There were only three ways to leave town: across the Coquille River to the sand dunes; down to the jetty on the town side of the river; or along the road to Coquille, which was still open but hot and blazing all the way.

The Coast Guard's *Rose*, the Port of Bandon's tug, and tugs from the Moore Mill & Lumber Company made repeated trips from the burning side of the river over to the sand dunes. But many people wanted to save their most precious possession, their automobile. So, even with the fire on top of them, there was a traffic jam along First Street as a line of cars moved out toward the jetty.

"Soon the jetty was swarming, and the refugees were to find that the rocks within the jetty walls already were warm. Red embers beat them with a hail of fire; overhead, carried by the strange, strong wind, went flaming pieces of boards, even whole sections of roofs."

The eighteen miles of road to Coquille were filled with refugees, in cars and afoot. The fire burned right down to the sides of the highway. On the jetty, it was so hot that the refugees had to throw sand and gravel on the logs behind which they sought shelter from the flames. People prayed that the buildings in the city of Bandon would soon burn to the ground so that the terrible heat would cease.

Aftermath of the Fire

Like the Tillamook Burn three years earlier, the damage done by the Bandon Fire took place during an incredibly short period of time. The entire business district was lost in only an hour; eleven people died; property loss totaled $3 million, half of which was in Bandon itself.

"Since the fire," Stewart Holbrook wrote seven years later, "efforts have been made in the Oregon Legislature to get an appropriation to eradicate the gorse or at least limit its spread. Leo Isaac of the Pacific Northwest Forest Experiment Station, who knows as much about Oregon vegetation as any man, says the gorse continues to spread rapidly. It often crowds out all other vegetation from an area. But the legislative efforts have come to nothing."

Unique Trees

Of the many species of trees that grow along the southern Oregon coast, the two noted here—red alder and myrtle—are remarkable for contrasting reasons: red alder because it is so common; myrtle because it is so rare.

Red alder is a pioneer species of tree. It is among the first to take root in logged off areas and it shields less hardy plants and trees from the glaring sun, allowing them to grow in its shade. In time and with protection from the alder, the other varieties grow strong, eventually overshadowing and crowding out the alder.

Many good qualities of red alder are not visible to the eye. Settlers did not seek garden spots in groves of firs, hemlocks, or cedars; their fruits and vegetables grew better in soils where alders had stood. And worms—indicators and assistants of fertile soil—like alder groves. Still another virtue of red alder was that it made very good fuel for the fireplace or cook stove, giving off a pleasant odor when it burned. Humble and common though it appeared, brief as its lifespan was compared to the mighty Douglas fir and soaring Sitka spruce, it served the pioneer who knew its virtues very well.

Myrtle trees, on the other hand, are so limited in their range and valued so highly for the beauty of their wood that they rightly may be called the "diamonds of the forest." They are also the source of a great deal of misinformation.

A persistent myth is that myrtle trees grow only along the southern coast of Oregon and in the Holy Land. In truth, these *Unbellularia californica* trees do not grow in the Holy Land, but they do grow also in northern California.

One claim, however, can remain undisputed: myrtle wood, when finished, is the most beautiful natural wood in the world. And most of it is found along the southern Oregon coast. There are three varieties of myrtle wood—black, white, and yellow. Whatever its color, the grain of this wood is as unique as human fingerprints.

Some years ago one of the sons of J.H. Oerding, who manufactured myrtle wood products in Coquille, came home to find the famous novelist Jack London sitting on his doorstep. London had come there to order a special piece of polished myrtle wood for his dream house, Wolf Lodge, which he was building near Santa Rosa, California, in the Valley of the Moon. The Oerdings once furnished covers for a collector's edition of an Oregon book. It was bound in myrtle wood with a red Moroccan back. Myrtle wood novelties are widely sold today.

Brookings and Bulbs

It may truthfully be said that the twin towns of Brookings and Harbor, Oregon, which are only a mile apart and a scant eight miles north of the California state line, escaped being part of California by only the narrowest of margins. They owe their existence largely to a sawmill worker named Tony Olsen, who grew flowers as a hobby.

Brookings' post office was established in June 1913. It primarily served the Brookings Lumber Company, which operated a large sawmill there for lumber from the redwood forest of northern California and a few miles along the southern Oregon Coast. The depressed lumber market following World War I brought an end to the mill's operation, and Brookings seemed destined to become a ghost town, despite a faithful few who clung to the hope of its renewal. But Brookings held its reputation as a beautiful and pleasant place to live.

143

Long before coming to work at the Brookings sawmill, Tony Olsen had been interested in flowers. At his home on the Chetko River, near Harbor, he had planted some flowers along with his vegetables. Blessed with a green thumb, he watched them flourish and grow as they responded to the rich soil, perfect climate, and his loving care. Not having the heart to throw the bulbs away, he gave them to neighbors and friends, then planted more.

"He can't eat them," said a neighbor woman, "he can't feed them to stock, he can't sell them. What better evidence do you want to prove he's crazy?" Crazy or not, Tony persisted. He found some distant markets and managed to sell a few of his bulbs. By the 1950s, Olsen's business was well known and highly regarded.

Croft Easter Lily

Before World War II, the United States imported over 25 million lily bulbs from Japan, with Holland and Bermuda also contributing, according to a May 1946 article in *Northwest Science Magazine*. American production was less than 1.5 million bulbs. But the war cut off imports from both Japan and Holland, providing a high-priced market for American raised Easter lily bulbs. Curry County's sandy loam soil, old beach terraces, and mild climate created an ideal combination for the production of bulbs.

Sidney Croft came to Oregon from Michigan in 1939. He knew about growing bulbs and established some fields near Brookings. At first, without much of a market, he sold bulbs for a nickel apiece; the war-time market soon drove the price up to a dollar, making his bulbs famous. He did not live long after that, but Croft bulbs are still the leaders in Oregon.

In Curry County, the bulb business boomed. In 1944, one grower reported the sale of $6,000 worth of Croft bulbs from a crop produced on a corner lot. Land values skyrocketed, with suitable lily land selling for as much as $2,000 an acre. Within a few years time, there were nearly a thousand lily growers in the Brookings area. Profits from bulbs grown on an acre of ground were reported to run from ten to twenty thousand dollars.

Today, there are fewer bulb growers; the "banana belt" economy has diversified, but its newer industries of tourism and retirement still rely on the wonderful climate.

Oregon State Parks

No account of the Oregon Coast would be complete without favorable mention of the Oregon State Parks system, which, since 1929, has helped preserve the state's quality of life. Though not a heavily populated state,

Oregon ranks among the top ten in the number of people using its parks. Many are visitors, of course, but Oregonians frequent the two hundred parks in the state system, too.

From the time when a farsighted governor, Oswald West, determined that the seashore belonged to the people, Oregon residents have treated their coastline with special care. Once each year—usually a Saturday in early October—a cleanup day brings thousands of volunteers along each of Oregon's 325 miles of shoreline. The coast is divided into a dozen or so sections and the state Department of Fish and Wildlife furnishes litterbags. Through their efforts, the "Keep Oregon Green" slogan might well be lengthened to read: "...and Clean."

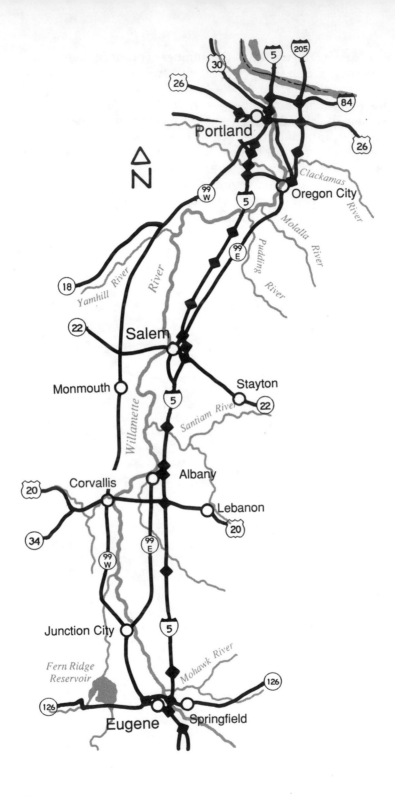

PART III

The Willamette Valley

I-15
Portland—Salem
47 miles

OR 99E
Portland—Aurora
19 miles

Fort Vancouver

The history of the Willamette Valley began on the north side of the Columbia River in what is now Washington State. Before seeing Portland and points south, the I-5 traveler should first cross the interstate bridge to Vancouver, Washington, and spend an hour or two seeing the beautiful grounds and well-preserved buildings of Fort Vancouver National Historic Site.

As noted earlier, British explorer George Vancouver sent Lieutenant William Broughton to the mouth of the Columbia in 1792 to check out Captain Robert Gray's claim that he had discovered and sailed twenty-five miles up the long-sought River of the West. Finding that the river indeed existed, Lieutenant Broughton ascended it one hundred miles, then claimed it and all the adjacent country in the name of "His Brittanic Majesty, having every reason to believe that the subjects of no other civilized nation or state had ever entered the river before...."

Following the sale of Fort Astoria to the English, it was renamed Fort George and served as headquarters for the Hudson's Bay Company in the Pacific Northwest until 1824. With the Joint Occupancy Treaty taking effect in 1818, the British felt they could establish a strong claim to the Oregon country if they built a post in the center of this area accessible by sea, land, and river, so they built Fort Vancouver to control the interior valleys where the citizens of both nations would eventually settle.

The man put in charge of the post was Dr. John McLoughlin. For twenty-two years, he ruled as chief factor of the Hudson's Bay Company in the Pacific Northwest, wielding tremendous power over employees, Americans, and Indians. To his eternal credit, he never once abused that power, even though he later suffered grievously from people he had befriended.

"Within two years McLoughlin and his employees had constructed a stockade of fir posts, forty log buildings and a powder magazine made of stone," states the WPA guide to Oregon. They had "cleared a considerable area, established a sawmill, a forge, and were grazing seven hundred head of cattle on the adjacent lands." Today, visitors can tour an authentic reconstruction of the fort and many of its buildings, which are furnished just as they were in the heydey of the post in the 1830s.

Dr. John McLoughlin around 1851. —National Park Service

L to R: Priest's House, Chief Factor's House, Bachelor Quarters, Fort Vancouver, 1860. —National Park Service

From the front steps of Dr. John McLoughlin's home, which sits on a rise of land in the center of the expansive grounds, the visitor gets a magnificent view of the Columbia River to the south. More than a mile wide here and so deep that ocean-going ships can negotiate its slow-moving current, it once was a port of call for vessels engaged in worldwide commerce. Inside McLoughlin's home gentlemen dressed as formally as they might have in London, sat long at a table laden with fine foods and wines, and engaged in wide-ranging, intelligent conversation while being served discreetly by Indian women married to company employees.

Dr. John McLoughlin married an Indian woman, as did several employees of the Hudson's Bay Company. Except for rare visits by

Chief Factor's House, Fort Vancouver, May 1860. —National Park Service

missionaries, such as Marcus and Narcissa Whitman and Henry and Eliza Spalding, women did not dine at the table; they ate in a separate room, but were otherwise treated as equals. Legend relates that the fine orchards now famous in the Pacific Northwest got their start here from the Indian women who planted apple seeds left on the dinner plates of McLoughlin's gentlemen guests.

Military Post Years of Fort Vancouver

After the northern boundary of the United States was established at the 49th Parallel in 1846, Fort Vancouver became an American military post. A number of officers who were (or would yet become) nationally famous served there. The first was Colonel Bonneville, who, a few years earlier, had unsuccessfully competed with the monolithic Hudson's Bay Company. Another was Lieutenant Phil Sheridan, who took part in Indian campaigns at the Cascades of the Columbia and along the central Oregon Coast.

But the most famous soldier of all to serve at Fort Vancouver was Ulysses S. Grant, eighteenth president of the United States. As a lowly captain, Grant tried to add a few dollars to his scant army pay by planting a patch of potatoes on the grounds. In his "Memoirs," written many years later, he tells wryly of his endeavor. In 1852, following an extremely bad year, potatoes were selling for the fabulous price of $45 per hundred pounds. So Grant—and many other people—got into potatoes in a big way the following spring. "Luckily for us, the Columbia River rose to a great height from the melting of the snow in the mountains in June, and overflowed, killing most of our crop. This saved digging it up, for everybody on the Pacific Coast seemed to have come to the conclusion at the same time that agriculture would be profitable. In 1853 more than three-quarters of the potatoes raised were permitted to rot in the ground or were thrown away."

Traveling Fruit Orchard

Back on the south side of the Columbia River, the villages that sprang up following the first large American emigration in 1843 often were named after cities "back home." Two merchants from New England flipped a coin to choose the name of the stump-filled settlement where the Willamette River meets the Columbia. The merchant from Maine won, so the village was named Portland; if the man from Massachusetts had won, the new town would have been called Boston.

Twelve miles up the Willamette, a village called Milwaukie was founded in 1848, continuing to spell its name differently than Milwaukee, Wisconsin, even after the error was pointed out. For a time, it rivaled

Portland as a commercial center, but after building and launching the first and finest steamboat of its place and time, the *Lot Whitcomb*, it stopped competing and became content as a suburb of the larger municipality.

It did make a name for itself, however, by establishing the first fruit tree nursery in Oregon. Iowa emigrant Henderson Luelling brought a traveling nursery of seven hundred fruit trees across the plains in 1847, watering and caring for them for four long months across two thousand miles. "He planted the first Royal Anne cherry tree in the state, and in the 1860s originated the Black Republican and Bing cherries. The Black Republican was so named for political groups of the day, and the Bing for his Manchurian gardener."

Father of Oregon Memorial

Though Dr. John McLouglin's orders from Sir George Simpson, director of operations for the Hudson's Bay Company, were to discourage American settlement in the Oregon country by all means short of violence, McLoughlin's personal humanitarian standards inhibited him from turning down any emigrant in need, regardless of nationality. Time and again he supplied food, clothing, and other necessities of life to Americans, very few of whom bothered to thank or repay him.

When the missionaries Jason Lee and Marcus Whitman arrived in the mid-1830s, McLoughlin tried to get them to settle in the Willamette Valley, south of the Columbia. He hoped that the eventual boundary settlement between the United States and Great Britain would grant England everything north of the river, leaving the Americans content with the area to its south. But in the 1840s the United States was in an expansionist mood. Led by such men as President James K. Polk, who boldly ran on a platform "54-40 or Fight!", the westering Americans were not to be contained.

Unable to appease his company's stockholders, Dr. McLoughlin was forced to resign in 1845. When it became clear in 1846 that Oregon would go to the U.S. instead of England, the autocratic McLoughlin made the soul-wrenching decision to renounce his British citizenship and become an American. Filing a claim in Oregon City, nineteen miles up the Willamette River from its mouth, he lived out his years trying to be as good an American as he had been a Britisher.

Rightly called the "Father of Oregon," John McLoughlin is honored by a plaque on a bridge spanning the Clackamas River, and his home in Oregon City is preserved as a National Historic Site. His house was moved intact some years ago from its location on 99E near the Falls of the Willamette to a spot higher up the hill. The falls were raised eleven feet by a concrete dam to increase their power potential; you can see them from a viewpoint on the 99E, nine blocks south of the McLoughlin home.

Another Englishman, Rudyard Kipling, immortalized the Clackamas River after catching a fish there. In his travel book, *American Notes*, the famous author wrote: "I have lived! The American Continent may now sink under the sea, for I have taken the best that it yields, and the best was neither dollars, love, nor real estate." With an eight-ounce rod he had spent thirty-seven minutes fighting and landing a ten-pound salmon. "That hour," he wrote, "I sat among crowned heads greater than all! How shall I tell the glories of that day?"

French Prairie and Champoeg

Because many employees of both American and British fur companies were French-Canadians, it is not surprising that many towns, rivers, and landmarks bear French names, such as Gervais, Galice, Grande Ronde, and The Dalles. But few of these names are pronounced here as they would be in France or eastern Canada, for early day westering Americans, who knew little and cared less about French pronunciation, often committed linguistic mayhem on foreign words.

The distinction of being the first permanent white settler in the Oregon country belongs to a French-Canadian named Joseph Gervais, who came west with the Astor overland party in 1811. Staying on with the North West Company when it took over Fort George, then continuing with the Hudson's Bay Company, he liked the Willamette Valley so much that he wanted to end his days in it.

He settled along the Willamette River around 1828 in an area known as French Prairie near the town later named for him, as did a several other former employees of the Hudson's Bay Company. According to the WPA guide to Oregon, "Dr. McLoughlin gave seed-wheat to the settlers on the promise that they would return the same amount to him after the harvest." Some years later, Gervais and his neighbors began the "Wolf Meetings" at his house, which soon evolved into discussion about a new "American" form of local government.

With the Joint Occupancy Treaty still in effect, former Hudson's Bay Company employees were content to obey whatever edicts Dr. McLoughlin issued, for they knew him to be a fair man. But many American citizens refused to accept McLoughlin's rulings because he represented the long-hated British crown.

Upon the death in 1841 of an American ex-trapper named Ewing Young, who owned considerable property and a large herd of cattle, his compatriots were troubled by the fact that he had left neither a will nor an heir. "A meeting was finally called and an executor to the estate was appointed," says the WPA guide. "Meanwhile Young's stock ran wild in the Chehalem Valley and wolves and panthers were soon attracted by the easy prey. The settlers finally had what was called a 'Wolf Meeting.' On February 2, 1843, it was agreed that each person present should be assessed $5 to pay bounties on all wolves, lynxes, bears, and panthers killed."

Some claimed that the "Wolf Meetings" concealed a secret purpose, which was political and probably illegal. At the second meeting on March 6, the real intent of many men present—both Americans and French-Canadians—was revealed: "A resolution was unanimously adopted for the appointment of a committtee of twelve to take into consideration the propriety of taking measures for civil and military protection of this colony."

The meeting that swayed the destiny of Oregon was held two months later, May 2, 1843, in the corner of a Hudson's Bay Company warehouse at Champoeg. Whether the name of this town derived from the French *champ* (field) or from the local Indian word *champooick* is open to question; regardless, local pronunciation then and now is "ShamPOOegg."

Many of the British subjects thought this was merely another "Wolf Meeting" to further organize protection against predatory animals. "As

This marker in Champoeg State Park marks the site where the 52-50 vote to go American was taken in 1843.

soon as they became aware of the true purpose, most of the French-Canadians withdrew. Employees of the company were indignant over the use of the warehouse for what they considered seditious purposes." But the Americans present were determined to continue the meeting, even if it had to be held in a nearby field.

There was much talk of inalienable rights to self-government. Some of the Americans were grateful to Dr. John McLoughlin and the Hudson's Bay Company for all the help they had received. But Joe Meek, a big, outspoken-by-no-one ex-trapper, ended the discussion when he shouted enthusiastically: "Who's for a divide? All in favor of the report and an organization follow me!"

Legend holds that when the milling ceased, fifty men were on Meek's side of the field, and fifty were on the other. Two men were undecided: Etienne Lucier and his friend F.X. Matthieu, both French-Canadians. "Lucier hesitated because someone had told him that should the United States Government come into control here it would tax the windows in his house. Matthieu, who lived with Lucier, argued convincingly otherwise. In the end the pair took their position with those favoring organization."

Provisional Government

So, by a skinny 52-50 vote, the men decided to set up an American-run government. The report of the committee was then disposed of article by article and a number of officers were chosen. A committee of nine Americans was named to draw up a program.

"When the legislative committee made its first report at a mass meeting at Willamette Falls (Oregon City) on July 5, it created four legislative districts. One of them was called 'Champooick,' and included the settlment of Champoeg as its judicial center." No doubt Joe Meek, who liked to think big, was in on the district's planning, for its eastern boundary was set at the crest of the Rocky Mountains and took in what later became Idaho and parts of Montana and Wyoming.

For a time, the town of Champoeg thrived as center of both government and commerce. Oregon Territory was organized in 1848. Sure that the next step would be statehood, the citizens of Champoeg held a glorious Fourth of July celebration in 1854. "In the forenoon a procession formed in the town's center and marched to the house of Ed Dupuis, where Dr. Edward Shiel read the Declaration of Independence. Later, the celebrants enjoyed a sumptuous dinner given beneath the roof where the first laws were enacted. After dinner the guests proceeded on a pleasure excursion, three miles up the river, on board the steamer *Fenix*."

Leonard White, an original thinker who had built the steamer and pioneered steamboating on the Willamette River, believed words should be spelled exactly as they sounded. Thus the boat's name: *Fenix*.

Despite its promising start as a thriving settlement and its well-deserved place in history as the birthplace of Oregon, in 1861 Champoeg literally was swept away in a matter of hours. Heavy rains fell across the whole Willamette Valley in November; in December the river flooded the lowlands. The waters rose so fast that many of the residents suddenly became trapped in their homes and stores and had to be rescued by men in rowboats. Gradually even the heavy hewn timbers of the warehouse loosened and were swept away.

"The Willamette River rose to terrifying heights," writes historian J. A. Hussey in his book, *Champoeg*. "On December 2 it broke over its banks. At Salem it swelled into the town and ran through the streets in a current four feet deep and a quarter of a mile wide." Farther downstream, at Champoeg, the lowlands were seven feet underwater by December 6, at the crest of the flood. "The current was so rapid that no structure could stand against it." Of the forty buildings in the town, only three survived, and eventually these too crumbled into dust.

Because of the location's importance to Oregon history, the state legislature in 1901 designated 107 acres in the area as a park. Today Champoeg State Park, which now covers over 600 acres of beautiful hill country, lies a few miles west of I-5 just south of Wilsonville. Its visitor center is excellent.

As an interesting historical footnote, on May 2, 1901, upon the dedication of a monument to the 52 men who had voted in favor of the United States on May 2, 1843, the only survivor present at the ceremony was F. X. Matthieu, the former French-Canadian who had persuaded his friend, Etienne Lucier, to change his vote.

McLoughlin House

In her biography of Dr. John McLoughlin, *Royal Family of the Columbia*, historian Alberta Brooks Fogdall does not speak kindly of either the early-day Methodist missionaries, who came to the Willamette Valley in the 1830s, or the greedy American settlers who followed them in the mid-1840s. She points out that one reason they treated Dr. McLoughlin shabbily was not because they lacked respect for him, but because they hated England so much.

As early as 1829, the Hudson's Bay Company had been told by the British government to establish claims south of the Columbia River as future bargaining points in securing the territory England especially wanted north of the river. So when Dr. McLoughlin took possession of a prime site at the Falls of the Willamette, which he and Governor

Simpson chose on a visit there, it was not clear whether he was making the claim in his own name or in the name of the company. In building a gristmill, a sawmill, and two houses, he exceeded the minimum construction necessary to hold his claim.

Though the Methodist missionaries first came to the Willamette Valley "to convert and civilize the heathen natives," they soon gave that up, turning instead to acquiring real estate and dabbling in politics. With McLoughlin's permission and his help supplying lumber, a member of the Lee mission built a store on the McLoughin claim, though he made it clear that he owned the land.

When the new Provisional Government was proposed in 1843, the Hudson's Bay Company told Dr. McLoughlin to support it, "both for the security of the Company's property and the protection of its rights." To demonstrate support of the Provisional Government, the company contributed $226.65 to its treasury. And since the new government set the Columbia River as the northern boundary of its domain, the company felt assured that it recognized the area north of the Columbia as British.

"The new government provided legal machinery to aid the Company in collecting $30,000 in debts owed by American settlers in the Willamette Valley and in respecting Company (or McLoughlin) land claims. Ruffians, lawless elements, and desperate characters from Missouri could be controlled more easily when responsible to a legal authority, especially since the Americans outnumbered the British."

In January 1846, Dr. McLoughlin completed and moved into his beautiful new home overlooking the Falls of the Willamette in Oregon City, and prepared to embark on his life as a good American citizen. At the age of sixty-one, he was still energetic and vigorous, though at times he was described as being disillusioned, bitter, and discouraged.

Falls of the Willamette in Oregon City.

McLoughlin House, Oregon City.

"Too, he was pictured as having difficulty in curbing his anger if he met one of the settlers who had borrowed money and goods from him in past years and who consistently refused to repay him, even though able to do so. He would begin instinctively to bring up his famous gold-headed cane, then, catching himself, would stop and mutter 'God forgive me,' and hurry on.

"His granddaughter Louisa Rae told how he would sit for hours sorting his numerous papers into categories according to probability of payment, entering them in his books of different colors, and, finally, wearily fall asleep over them."

Samuel Thurston, Oregon Territory's representative in Congress, who was described by some of his contemporaries as having "both eyes and both ears open for the main chance," coveted McLoughlin's Oregon City property. In a blatant piece of chicanery, he managed to get a rider included in the Donation Claims Land Act of 1850 that, in effect, defrauded McLoughlin of most of his property.

But among the American settlers, McLoughlin had many friends who remembered the help he had given them when they needed it so badly. On May 30, 1849, he made his oath of allegiance to the United States. On September 5, 1851, he became a full citizen. Shortly thereafter he was elected mayor of Oregon City, receiving forty-four of the sixty-six votes cast.

Although title to his land and his home was taken away from him, he was "permitted" to live in the house he had built until his death in 1857. A month before he died, a young politician named L.F. Grover, who later became governor of Oregon and a U.S. senator, visited him. Dr. McLoughlin quietly told him:

> I became a citizen of the United States in good faith. I planted all I had here, and the government confiscated my property. Now what I want to ask of you is that you will use your influence after I am dead to have this property go to my children. I have earned it as other settlers have earned theirs, and it ought to be mine and my heirs.

Five years after his death, a measure of justice finally came to Dr. John McLoughlin on October 11, 1862. On the final day of its session, the Oregon Legislature "did try a righteous act by restoring to the heirs of the late Dr. McLoughlin his land claim." Though not all of the property taken from him during his lifetime was restored, partial restitution was better than none at all.

In 1905, during the centennial celebration of the Lewis and Clark Expedition, "McLoughlin Day" was observed by the Oregon Historical Society. In 1907 the Oregon Legislature designated him officially as "Father of Oregon."

When each state was asked to name two outstanding citizens to represent it in the National Hall of Fame, Dr. McLoughlin was one of those chosen from Oregon. On February 14, 1952, Leslie M. Scott, whose father had been editor of the Portland *Oregonian*, dedicated the statue of Dr. John McLoughlin in Statuary Hall in the Capitol in Washington D.C.

Old Aurora Colony

One of the greatest virtues of the interstate highway system is that it takes the fast-moving passenger and truck traffic off the lesser roads, making travel on them once again a pleasure for the tourist interested in scenery and history. Certainly this is true in the Willamette Valley, where, without exception, following the well-maintained state and federal roads is the best way to see and enjoy the country.

More than most states in the West, Oregon has—from its earliest times—preserved its history through town, county, and regional museums, which began as "pioneer societies." Travelers interested in history may visit at least fifty county historical societies and seventy-five museums while touring the state. Lists of these societies and museums may be obtained from the granddaddy of them all, the Oregon State Historical Society in Portland, which has long been known as one of the best in the nation.

Old Aurora Colony Museum.

After seeing Fort Vancouver, the McLoughlin House, and Champoeg State Park, visit the Old Aurora Colony on 99E thirty miles south of Portland. Established a few years ago as the first National Historic District in the state—that is, having at least five buildings worthy of historic preservation—Aurora was founded in 1857 by a German immigrant, Dr. Wilhelm, or William, Keil. So obsessed was he with the vision of an ideal communal society that he placed the body of his recently deceased son in the lead wagon of the train to Oregon as a symbolic guide to the Promised Land.

According to an article published in the *Oregon Historical Quarterly* in 1935, William Keil was born in Prussia, Germany, in 1811. A tailor by trade, he took interest in many other pursuits as well. "This man Wilhelm Keil," wrote historian John E. Simon, "was a tailor, doctor, preacher, pioneer, dictator, mystic, and fanatic."

Possessed of a vivid imagination, he was attracted to the theater and also became deeply interested in religion. He began searching for the so-called stone of the wise, a panacea for all diseases. From a woman known for her home cures he obtained secret remedies, "under the condition that he would migrate and not make use of them at home. He seems to have dealt in magnetism. He had a fair knowledge of botany; and he knew how to prepare good, wholesome medicines."

Soon after marrying in Germany, he resolved to migrate to America and arrived in New York City in 1835 or 1836. For a short time he worked as a tailor, but the trade did not satisfy him. He delved deeper into mysticism, theosophy, alchemy, magnetism, and botany. Moving to Pittsburg, he opened a drug store and assumed the title "Doctor." As a result of some of the strange cures he performed, some referred to him as "Hexendoctor," or witch doctor.

About this time he formulated his philosophy for a communal society:

> Every man and woman must be a brother or sister to every other man and woman in our family under the fatherhood of God. No man owns anything individually but every man owns everything as a full partner and with an equal voice in its use and its increase and the profits accruing from it. But in no other way do we differ from our neighbors. As a community we are one family.

Seeking a place where he could establish a new colony, Dr. Keil moved to Bethel, Shelby County, Missouri, a hundred miles northwest of St. Louis. During the twelve years that he and his followers lived there, they acquired six thousand acres on which they developed a prosperous community of homes, mills, and shops, supporting several hundred families, living by the rule that ran through their law of love: "From every man according to his capacity, to every man according to his needs."

Though the commune's only radical belief was the sharing of property, by 1854 Dr. Keil decided to relocate in Oregon because of the local unrest over Mormons temporarily settled in Missouri, the slavery question, and other regional conflicts that soon would lead to civil war. At that time and place, malaria ravaged the country, killing many people, offering yet another reason to move to a healthier climate. Though the properous Bethel colony numbered over seven hundred, Keil had suffered a severe bout of malaria and was sick of the country. "The regional fevers had not been able to conquer him," wrote John E. Simon, "but now the Oregon fever did."

A colony delegation sent west in the spring of 1854 selected a reportedly ideal location on Willapa Bay in Washington Territory, one hundred and twenty-five miles northwest of Portland. Preparations for the journey began at once. According to one of his contemporaries, Dr. Keil livened up the work by directing the most effective curses in his vocabulary against Missouri. Topping his scorn for Missouri now was the loss of his eldest son, William, to malaria. "Nothing could have kept him at Bethel from now on; he had to get out of the 'damned dog-world' in which not one member should remain."

> Keil had promised his now deceased son that he would take him along to the west. Finding in this an opportunity to impress the sanctity of a promise upon his people, he secured a metal coffin for

Dr. William Keil. —Old
Aurora Colony Museum

his son, and in order to preserve the body, he had it filled with alcohol. Thus preserved, the body was placed on one of the wagons, which was put at the head of the train.

Obtaining a sufficient quantity of alcohol was no problem, for the Bethel colony habitually turned its surplus grain into whiskey, which sold for as little as nineteen cents a gallon along the Misssissippi.

The train of twenty-four wagons left Bethel in early May 1855, a bad year so far as Indian disturbances were concerned; despite its small size, the wagon train encountered no hostility. Keil's secret for getting along with the Indians was simple: instead of fighting them, he fed them.

In the Grande Ronde Valley of eastern Oregon the Keil train made camp just half a mile from a large band of Cayuses, the Indians who several years earlier had massacred fourteen people at the Whitman Mission near Walla Walla. "These Indians, too, were very friendly," Dr. Keil later wrote. "There were four chiefs among them, who, with the rest, visited us daily. I proclaimed to the four chiefs that they would dine with me every day I was with them; they were very happy about this." The chiefs were so happy, in fact, that they urged Dr. Keil to settle in their country, and were deeply disappointed that he did not—even after they tried to win his good will by giving ponies to each of his three boys, Augustus, Elias, and Fred. "Chief Camaspallo wept as he said farewell. I took him to my wagon and gave him a last cut of pie."

Disappointment at Willapa Valley

Bypassing the Willamette and reaching the Willapa Valley on the coast of Washington Territory in early autumn, Dr. Keil soon realized that his advance party had fallen victim to a fraudulent developer whose rosy promises of a "Paradise on the Pacific" were mostly pipe dreams. Dr. Elijah White, an early-day emigrant to the Willamette Valley with a long record of duping gullible people, had promised a city, a park, school-houses, and handsome residences. But the "city" did not exist, the "park" had only wild deer, the "schoolhouses" were those built by nature, and the "handsome residences" belonged to birds in the trees and game in the thick underbrush.

The area was so heavily timbered and the rainfall so constant that no grass grew and nothing ever dried out. Though there were lots of oysters in nearby Shoalwater Bay, the nearest market of any size was San Francisco, whose ships seldom sought cargoes on this rain-drenched coast. Food and shelter were scarce. Prices were high. A barrel of flour here sold for $15 to $20, while in Portland it cost only $3.50.

Determined to go back to Oregon and seek a more suitable site in the Willamette Valley, Dr. Keil lingered in the Willapa area only long enough to complete one sad duty—the interment of his son on November 26.

Aurora Mills

Plenty of trees grew on the foothills of the Willamette Valley, but there were many open prairies, too. The Kalapuya Indians occasionally cleared trees and brush by setting fires in the valley during late summer; game preferred the grasses that soon grew, and this made good hunting for the Indians.

The prairies looked good to Dr. Keil, who had been practicing medicine in Portland until he could find a place to establish a colony; he finally settled in Marion County, twenty-nine miles south of Portland on Pudding River, a few miles east of Champoeg. To the German mystico-theosophists, the word aurora, which meant "dawn," had a special significance—it was also the name of one of Keil's daughters.

The original settlement, called "Aurora Mills," was a mile or two away from the present town, but for a number of reasons it was destined to prosper under any name. States the WPA guide to Oregon:

> Aurora's location was in its favor. It was situated about midway between Salem and Portland and on the main road east of the Willamette. It was an ideal place for a hotel and restaurant. After the stagecoach came into its own, Aurora became an independent depot. By 1863, the Oregon Telegraph Company's line was in operation, and by 1870, the "iron horse" ran from East Portland to Waconda, one station below Aurora.

Shops and small factories of all kinds blossomed: tannery, sawmill, gristmill, carding machinery, looms, blackmiths, wagon makers, cabinetmakers, tin makers, tailors, shoemakers, and carpenters. The needs of the community came first, the surplus was sold to whoever would buy it. A ready market existed for quality goods.

Farming, the colony's main industry, supplied most of its income. In addition to common farm products, fruit from the extensive orchards soon became known as the finest in the state. Apples sold very well in San Francisco, while apple butter and cider gained renown throughout Oregon.

Before long, Aurora's fine hotel offered such excellent accommodations that people traveled from Portland to vacation there and enjoy its delectable treats. Citing one satisfied customer, the WPA guide to Oregon quotes:

> Aurora fried potatoes surpass all other fried potatoes. Aurora home-baked bread is without a peer in the broad land. Aurora pig sausage has a secret that, if captured, would make a fortune for an enterprising packer.

Old Aurora Colony Hotel, 1880.
—Aurora Colony Historical Society

Why did trains stop for meals at Aurora when the Portland terminal was only twenty-nine miles away? Because the trainmen wanted the better meals they could get at Aurora—better meats, better vegetables, better pies and puddings.

End of Aurora

As time went on, Dr. Keil became more and more dictatorial. His will was supreme, and those who did not bow to it soon left the colony.

Keil discouraged marriage, from what seems to have been selfish motives. Celibacy was to the advantage of the economic life at Aurora. Unmarried men and women could be boarded and lodged at much less expense than it would cost to furnish homes for the young married couples. Then, too, spinsters and bachelors left no heirs; hence their share of the property would revert to the colony, and the colony was Keil. However, Keil's own children were not discouraged from marrying.

At the time of his death of a stroke December 13, 1877, dissatisfaction had been rife in the colony for some time. As always happens on the breakup of a communal society, there were many disputes over how the property should be divided. Including the holdings left back in Missouri, the total value came to just under $110,000.

Old Aurora Colony Today

Of all the dreams Dr. Keil and his followers held when the colony was first established in 1857, what remains today are five preserved or restored buildings filled with their tools, materials, and instruments of everyday living. The uses and operation of the sausage-making machine, the loom, the spinning wheel, and the shake splitter are skillfully demonstrated by the director of the historic district or its staff. He tells visitors, "On one occasion we had some of the members of the Portland Symphony play a few period musical numbers on the instruments we have preserved. Though they made good music, the clarinetist complained that no matter how hard she tried she still got a squeak now and then, which made her cringe."

The ingenuity and inventive genius of the members of the colony are shown in many ways. For instance, the stone chimeny for the big fireplace in the Wash House, where much of the cooking was done, was completely enclosed within the house walls so that its heat would warm the room before it went up the chimney. On the spinning wheel, an arm that moved out and back as the spinner worked made a sit-down job out of one that usually required constant movement. The only spinning wheel of its kind, its nameless inventor never bothered to patent the improvement.

164

Portland—the First Hundred Years

Condensing the history of a city the size of Portland into one or two dozen pages of a book is obviously an impossible task; instead, I shall simply relate three key events that vitally affected the destiny of this modern metropolis of half a million residents. The two common elements shared by these three events are that each drastically changed the course of Oregon's history, and no physical evidence remains of them today in the form of a monument, statue, or plaque. The first event occurred in 1850:

Joe Meek Administers Justice

Black Measles

Ever since he gave up his life as a trapper in 1840 and decided to settle down in the Willamette Valley, Joe Meek had managed to get involved in the development of the Oregon country. With his Rocky Mountain trapping partner and friend Robert "Doc" Newell, Meek brought the first wheeled vehicles ever to roll on the Oregon Trail, first crossing the Snake River Desert from Fort Hall to Fort Boise, then over the Blue Mountains to the Whitman Mission, finally following the Columbia River to The Dalles.

Arriving at the Whitman Mission in early October, Joe Meek went hat in hand to Narcissa Whitman and begged a special favor. He wanted to leave his three-year-old daughter, Helen Mar, at the mission.

"Truth is, Missus Whitman, I don't know beans about raisin' little girls," Joe Meek said humbly. "So I was thinkin' ... I was wonderin' ..."

"If I would take her in?"

"That's the idea, yes ma'am. I know she don't look like much. But she's bright as a button and minds purty good, if you're firm with her. And she sure does need a good home."

"All right, you can leave her here for a while," Narcissa said reluctantly. "Come, child. We'll give you a bath, cut your hair, and put you into some decent clothes."

Meek's Shoshone Indian companion and mother of his child, Mountain Lamb, had returned to live with her people, leaving Joe to care for Helen Mar, whose name he'd taken from a character in the novel *Scottish Chiefs*. In the novel, he explained to Mrs. Whitman, the heroine had been a lovely, ethereal girl, and since the baby was "so purty" he had given her that name.

Meek knew that the Whitmans' only child, Alice Clarissa, had drowned in the Walla Walla River at the age of two. Narcissa could not bear more children of her own, but she loved them and never refused any who needed care.

The Cayuse Indians, on whose land the Whitmans established their mission in 1836, were never a large tribe. By 1847 the four hundred or so Cayuses not yet killed by disease or the enemy were bewildered and overwhelmed by the thousands of Americans traveling through their country to the Willamette Valley.

Rabble-rousers of mixed blood, who bore bitter grudges against the whites, told them that the Whitman Mission should pay them rent for their land; that the medicines used by Dr. Whitman cured whites only; and that the doctor intended to poison them so that he could steal their property. In support, the dissidents recalled the story handed down about the Astorian trader, Duncan McDougal, who many years earlier showed coastal Indians a corked bottle containing deadly smallpox, claiming it would kill them all if he chose to pull the stopper. Dr. Whitman had corked bottles of the same kind, the dissidents said. Sooner or later he would pull a cork and they all would die.

In early November 1847, an emigrant train stopped at the Whitman Mission for a couple of days so that worried parents could ask the doctor to identify and prescribe a remedy for an epidemic affecting children in the train. After examining the children, he diagosed the the sickness as black measles.

"It's relatively harmless," Dr. Whitman said reassuringly. "Keep the children quiet and clean, give them plenty of fluids and a light diet, and they will recover in a few days with no ill effects."

For the white children born with natural immunities, this proved true. But after the wagon train moved on and the local Indian children caught the disease, its effect was deadly. In a matter of weeks nearly half of the Cayuse tribe died—198 Indians, mostly children.

So the stunned, desperate Indians took their desperate revenge....

Ambassador in Buckskin

At the time of the Whitman Massacre, November 29, 1847, Narcissa had eleven children of white or mixed blood under her care, including ten-year-old Helen Mar Meek and eleven-year-old Mary Ann Bridger, daughter of a Ute woman and the famous mountain man, Jim Bridger. Both girls had been ill with black measles and, though neither was attacked by the Cayuses, they both died soon afterward from improper care. The Cayuses responsible for the attack held fifty-seven hostages until Peter Skene Ogden ransomed them in January 1848. The Provisional Government of Oregon declared war against the Indians and looked to the federal government for help.

By unanimous agreement, the messenger chosen to cross the continent and make an appeal to President James Polk and Congress was ex-mountain man Joe Meek. "Just happens President Polk is a shirt-tail relative of mine," Meek said. "Second or third cousin by marriage—somethin' like that. Anyways, you kin be sure when I get to Washington City he'll listen to what I got to tell him about Oregon."

After arriving in the nation's capital in the spring of 1848, Joe Meek was lionized by the press, Congress, and his "shirt-tail relative" President Polk. Even though Polk had made Oregon part of the United States by abrogating the Joint Occupancy Treaty in 1846 and setting the northern boundary at the 49th Parallel, Congress stubbornly refused to spend any money organizing it as a territory and accepting its Code of Laws established by the Provisional Government.

But news of the Whitman Massacre brought to Washington in such a colorful way by the buckskin-clad "Man From Oregon" soon turned neglect into action. In short order Congress passed an Enabling Act organizing Oregon Territory; then federal troops were dispatched to whip the dissident Indians into submission, and Joe Meek was appointed U.S. marshal for the new territory.

A Father's Right

With the power of the federal government added to that of the Oregon Volunteers, what was known as the "Cayuse War" soon reached its inevitable conclusion. Faced with the grim choice between surrender or extermination, the few Cayuse leaders who remained asked Oregon officials what they must do to end this hopeless war. The reply: turn over the instigators of the massacre for trial and accept whatever punishment the white men deemed appropriate.

Early in 1850, five Cayuse braves known to have taken part in the killings were surrendered by their tribal leaders. Taken to Oregon City, they were tried, found guilty, and sentenced to death. When asked why he and the others had surrendered, Tiloukait replied: "Did not your missionaries teach us that Christ died to save his people? So we die to save our people."

The hangings took place June 3, 1850, with United States Marshal Joe Meek officiating. Though the five doomed Cayuses were brave men resigned to their fate, they abhorred being hanged. They begged Marshal Meek to shoot them and let them die like men. Regretfully, he told them he could not change the sentence of the court. Then, according to legend dramatized as history by more than one regional writer, he made them a promise that eased their minds. As related by his old friend "Doc" Newell, this was what happened:

> After passing the priest, who murmured consolation and a prayer for each man, the five Cayuses walked by Joe Meek, who was standing just beyond. As they did so, Meek touched each Indian on the arm to get his attention, made a quick series of hand signs, and said something in a voice so low that his words could not be heard two paces away.
>
> As a result, a curious thing happened. Each Cayuse straightened, stood tall, looked proud, and walked with a firm, manly step to the

scaffold platform, where he stood unflinching on the trapdoor as the noose was adjusted around his neck.

Promptly at 2 p.m., Joe Meek cut the rope controlling the trapdoors. Five Cayuse souls recently baptized as Andrew, Peter, John, Paul, and James entered eternity. Peace came at last to the upriver country.

Later that afternooon, the legend continues, Doc Newell and Joe Meek shared a few drinks in a riverfront tavern. "One question, Joe," Doc said. "What was it you told those poor devils that put such iron in their backs?"

"Why, I just told 'em," Meek said quietly, "that they'd murdered my daughter, Helen Mar. For that, I told 'em, I was taking blood vengeance, as any father has a right to do."

"About what I'd guessed," Doc Newell murmured, nodding. "If anybody could understand a father taking revenge for the loss of a child, they would...."

Lewis and Clark Exposition

The Great Extravaganza

Lewis and Clark missed seeing the future site of Portland on their trip down the Columbia in the fall of 1805, and would have again passed it by on their return trip the next spring if local Indians had not told them about the mouth of the Willamette. But residents of the city in 1905 did not intend to let the rest of the United States overlook Portland on its one hundredth birthday.

Plans for "The Great Extravaganza," as the celebration came to be called, began before the turn of the century. In his book of the same name, historian Carl Abbott noted that by then world's fairs were widely accepted as "schools of progress," attracting investors and newcomers to the host city. It would be, boosters proclaimed, the greatest exposition ever staged on the West Coast, one that would put the city of Portland on the national map once and for all, asserting that if one of the two cities bearing that name should be called a backwoods hamlet, it must be the one in Maine.

Americans flocked to the Centennial Exposition at Philadelphia in 1876, the Columbian Exposition at Chicago in 1893, and Omaha's Trans-Mississippi Exposition in 1898. Since St. Louis planned a real humdinger for its Louisiana Purchase Exposition in 1904—celebrating the centennial of the beginning of the Lewis and Clark journey west—would it not be eminently fitting, proper, and rewarding for the great state of Oregon, and for Portland in particular, to tell the nation and the world about the Promised Land at the end of Lewis and Clark's trail?

Upon its first proposal in 1895, the idea met with little enthusiasm; a national depression was two years old and hanging on. Since federal assistance would be required to stage the show, Portland businessmen preferred that any funds appropriated by Congress be spent improving navigation across the bar at the mouth of the Columbia. But by 1900 the mood of of the community leaders had turned more optimistic. A committee began exploring the possibilities of putting on the tentatively named "Lewis and Clark Centennial and American Pacific Exposition and Oriental Fair."

Though Portland's population was barely 100,000, the city's movers and shakers thought big. Businessmen were asked to put up $300,000 to get the project rolling. Within ten days the pledges were oversubscribed. "The decision to stage the Lewis and Clark Exposition put Portlanders into the mainstream of American boosterism. During 1903 the corporation dispatched five special agents to stalk the corridors of western capitols and cadge votes in the nearby barrooms."

By the end of the year sixteen states came through with appropriations for exhibits; ten would construct special buildings. Prompted by the fact that the exposition would promote and benefit the entire state, the legislature authorized $450,000 for exhibits emphasizing "the development of our material resources and manufacturing interests."

In lobbying for money in Washington, D.C., the Portland promoters soon found out that nobody in Congress cared about historical heroes and their 2,000-mile trek. But they did share the same vision of Pacific trade that had motivated the exploration and settlement of the Oregon country. "Oregonians learned quickly in the winter of 1903-04 to cut the references to Lewis and Clark and to hammer home the idea that the Portland fair was an undertaking of national interest and importance."

With congressional delegations from California and Washington supporting the claim that the exposition was a Pacific Coast enterprise endorsed by chambers of commerce from San Diego to Spokane, it was not difficult to sell the slogan: "The railroads have opened the door and

Boardwalk and pool at "The Great of Extravaganza" of 1905.
—Penrose Library, Whitman College

laid the region's resources open for development. The only remaining need is for enough people to break the soil and fell the trees." The perfect complement to the resouces of the Northwest, said the lobbyists, was the huge potential market of the Orient; for example: "If all the wheat raised west of the Mississippi River were ground into flour for the Chinese trade and made into pancakes, the consumption per Chinaman would not exceed one pancake per month."

The final step was to settle on a location for the fairgrounds. President Theodore Roosevelt strongly supported the exposition from the beginning. But even with his help, a thrifty Congress reduced the requested allocation of $2 million to $475,000. So the site finally chosen was in northwest Portland between the Willamette and the Columbia rivers, an area which contained a grove of trees, 180 acres of pasture, and 220 acres of waist-deep stagnant water. Still thinking big, the fair commissioners hired Massachusetts landscape architect John Olmstead, whose father had designed New York City's Central Park, to lay out a design for the exposition's grounds.

Largest Log Cabin in the World

The agreed-upon style of architecture for the buildings on the exposition grounds was Spanish Renaissance, which leaned heavily to domes, cupolas, arched doorways, and roofs covered with red tile or paint. The notable exception, which stood as a reminder of the fair well into the 1960s, long after the rest of the structures were gone and forgotten, was the Forestry Building, an example of pure Oregon Gothic. Carl Abbott writes:

> Standing out like a logger at a tony party, scrubbed and shaved but still wearing a wool jacket in a room of tails and starched shirts, it was a huge log cabin of the sort no pioneer had ever built.

In February 1904, lumberman Simon Benson, the leading timber magnate in the Pacific Northwest, signed a contract for materials that specified "sound live timber with bark in perfect condition." The fir logs were to be cut "before the sap runs." Any damaged bark was to be repaired before being put into the building.

> The building itself stretched 105 by 209 feet, fronted by a portico of natural tree trunks. The interior copied the nave of a church, with marching columns of tree trunks supporting the high ceiling and setting off the exhibition galleries and balconies along the sides. The largest foundation logs weighed thirty-two tons and measured fifty-four feet in length by five feet across.

The New York *Review of Reviews* offered statistics on the building of "two miles of five-foot and six-foot fir logs, eight miles of poles, and many tons of shakes and cedar shingles."

170

Forestry Building, Expo 1905. —Penrose Library, Whitman College

The promotional campaign preceding the exposition began two years in advance and, despite the modest size of its budget, was awesome in its scope. "The Division of Exploitation helped to secure more than 250,000 columns of newspaper space. There were 10,000 papers on the mailing list by the mid-point of the Fair; more than 6,000 received a weekly packet of features and photographs on western history."

One of the best chunks of money spent on publicity was the $50,000 appropriated by the Oregon Legislature in 1903 for the state's participation in the St. Louis Lewis and Clark Centennial Exposition in 1904. Among many other Oregon products donated, displayed, or given away at St. Louis were six tons—a freight car load—of Oregon prunes.

The Wonderful Summer

From the moment the exposition opened June 1, 1905, to the day it closed October 15, it was clear that Portland was a rare specimen—an exposition city equipped to handle its visitors. Despite the fact that it was the smallest city ever to put on a world's fair, its advance planning had been superb.

From the central business district, fairgoers could catch the Portland Railway streetcars for a twenty-minute ride for a nickel. For a dime they could board a steamer for a ride down the Willamette to the U.S. government building on the fair grounds.

Twenty-one nations had exhibits at the fair. Backing up Portland's claim that it was the Gateway to the Orient, the million dollar Japanese pavilion was the most impressive foreign building on the grounds.

The most elaborate concession was the Carnival of Venice, whose performance required a 400-foot stage and a cast of hundreds. As the press release described the show: "Gondolas float between the audience and the stage, and the entertainment consists of dances, choruses, solos, marches, specialties, and tableaux, with a touch of comedy running through the performance."

After an hour-long enjoyment of Venice, the fairgoer probably was more than ready for Professor Barne's Educated Horse and Diving Elk. The two elk dove off a forty-foot high ramp into a tank of water. Trixie the horse demonstrated her mastery of arithmetic and English. "These elk are an example of what can be accomplished with wild animals through the kind and rational methods of training pursued by Professor Barnes," wrote the *Lewis and Clark Journal*. "Princess Trixie demonstrates to the most skeptical that the noble horse can be taught the English language and can think and reason the same as any human being."

On the Map

In 1904, a year before the fair, publicist Jefferson Myers had predicted a total attendance of one million people. In January 1905, the *Oregonian* raised that prediction to 1,370,000. From the opening day, June 1, through the offical closing day, October 15, 1905, the gatekeepers counted 1,588,000 paid admissions. Free passes to reporters, workmen, officials, and others accounted for another 966,000 visits. Further analysis reported in the newspaper showed that thirty-four percent of the attendees came from Portland, forty percent from elsewhere in Oregon and Washington, sixteen percent from California and the mountain states, and ten percent from east of the Rockies.

In all, the fair made a modest profit of $84,461. Thanks to good planning and alert police work, there had been very little price-gouging, few complaints about pickpockets, and the city's sizable Chinese population had neither kidnapped children nor made opium addicts of any visitors. Portland accomplished exactly what it hoped, which was to put the city, the state, and the West Coast on the map as an economic region worthy of recognition as the Gateway to the Orient. In one fell swoop, Oregon put its past behind it and its future before it.

The Vanport Disaster

Kaiser's Plan

"During the early part of World War II," wrote historian Manly Maben in his book *Vanport*, "this city, the largest housing project in the United States and probably in the world, was conceived, designed and completed in the space of one year's time. Five-and-a-half years later it was dead." Vanport and its incredible shipbuilding industry brought Portland more publicity than it had seen since the 1905 Lewis and Clark Expostion. In its sudden, dramatic end, it achieved the maximum exposure reserved for major disasters—the kind of publicity Portland neither wanted nor needed, but over which it had no control.

As war clouds gathered and it became evident that the United States would fight, the federal goverment made a strong effort to increase ship production in the Portland area, which already had a history in that business. On September 27, 1941, more than two months before the Japanese attack on Pearl Harbor, the first Oregon-built Liberty ship was launched. Soon Oregon was leading the nation in the production of the Liberty-class ship, a workhorse of a freighter in the 10,000 ton range.

One year and 76 ships later, a new shipbuilding record had been set with the *Joseph N. Teal*, which took slightly less than fourteen days from start to finish. President Franklin D. Roosevelt secrotly attended the

Kaiser shipyards in Vanport during the 1940s. —Oregon Historical Society

launching, later boasting the deed to Winston Churchill, to which the English statesman remarked, "almost unbelievable."

But in those times, the unbelievable happened every day in Portland. So many shipyard workers were poured into the city that restaurants appealed to people with homes to stay home to eat. The *Oregonian* newspaper encouraged "out-migration" to those not working in "essential activities," to leave the city for smaller communities east of the mountains like Enterprise and La Grande, to rent or sell their homes to people engaged in war work.

Henry J. Kaiser, a master at planning and getting things done in a hurry, knew that the workers needed housing, so he bought 650 acres of slough, pasture, and truck-farm land along the Oregon side of the Columbia River. High dikes surrounded the area, which lay below the level of the river. In February 1942, Kaiser announced that 10,000 more homes were needed within walking distance of the Oregon Shipbuilding Corporation. Calling the current proposals inadequate, he went to the United States Maritime Commission with his own spectacular plan for a wartime housing project. With a minimum of red tape and delay, they approved Kaiser's plan for a $26 million dollar community of housing units called Kaiserville at first, then Vanport City, and finally simply Vanport.

Wartime Box

To build the new community in the shortest possible time, labor recruiters scouted all over the West to round up skilled workmen. Of the 13,000 men and women who eventually worked on the project, only about 5,000 were employed at any one time. Any question about whether women could handle such back-breaking labor as ditch-digging was quickly put to rest by the fact that one-third of the working force was women, who handled their jobs just as well as the men did.

Even though native Portlanders admit that it rains during the fall, winter, and spring, what they fondly describe as "Oregon mist" broke all records that season: fourteen inches in November; heavy rain mixed with snow in December; then, on January 21, 1943, an incredible fifteen inches of snow fell. Workmen labored on the housing project in a sea of mud so deep that materials and tools had to be hauled around the site on sleds pulled by tractors.

Still, for most of the people recruited to work in the shipyards, many of whom were migrants from the Dust Bowl of western Oklahoma, Kansas, and the Texas Panhandle earning the highest wages ever in their lives, the housing was a miracle come true. As one weary young "Okie" housewife said: "It sure beats living in a tourist court."

Architectually, the design of the housing units was Wartime Box. Each two-story building measured 38' by 108', and contained fourteen

Vanport in earlier years.
—Oregon Historical Society

apartments, each with a living-room/kitchen area in front, a bathroom with a shower stall, a closet, and a bedroom in the rear. The walls were thin; insulation, non-existent; coal-heating furnaces, poor; and all other amenities, the bare minimum. Zoning and local housing laws posed no problem at all; the city of Portland, the county of Multnomah, and the state of Oregon were never consulted on any phase of Vanport's construction.

By mid-August 1943, the last of the community's 9,942 units was completed and furnished. Thirty tons of grass seed and 68,000 shrubs were used to landscape the project. An administration center, a post office, five grade schools, six nursery schools, three fire stations, a library, a 130-bed infirmary, and a number of other service buildings were finished and ready to serve the city of 39,000 to 42,000 people, depending on how many people would live in each unit.

"Two characteristics of Vanport's population soon became apparent," historian Maben points out. "Residents were young and they did not stay long."

Room Without A View

Because the shipyards worked twenty-four hours a day, the constant noise level in the community of twenty-foot distant apartment buildings with thin walls and high-paid, hard-drinking, party-any-time single residents made living there stressful, almost unreal. Since the government owned everything and the tenants nothing, the residents cared little for upkeep of the property.

175

Under such intense use, the units quickly aged; furnaces, refrigerators, and hot water heaters stopped working. The complaint department in the complex went on a twenty-four basis, but because of red tape and a shortage of skilled repairmen more and more time was required to fix less and less. The danger of fire became so serious that a number of residents moved out. Pests became a problem, especially bedbugs; but the exterminating company regularly went after fleas, roaches, mice, and rats, sometimes fumigating units with cyanide.

The psychological effects of living on the bottom of a relatively small area, diked on all sides to a height of 15 to 25 feet, Maben writes, was vaguely disturbing. "It was almost impossible to get a view of the horizon from anywhere in Vanport, at least on the ground or in the lower level apartments." In those days, of course, any complaint about living conditions, working hours, or shortages of goods and services, was answered with a shrug and the comment: "Well, there's a war on."

Veterans' Village

Everyone assumed that Vanport and its increasingly bothersome problems would cease to exist when the war ended. Surprisingly, this did not happen. The Housing Authority of Portland (HAP) at first approved selling and moving some of the vacant units to other areas where housing was needed. But unexpected events forced the agency to revise its decision.

The war workers did not leave Portland, yet veterans and those engaged in war work elsewhere returned. Housing remained a shortage. And if Vanport were to exist much longer, the disposal of sewage needed redressing, since all wastes were pumped, untreated, over the dike into the Columbia River. By March 1947, the number of occupied housing units in Vanport stabilized at about two-thirds capacity.

The returning veterans, mostly married and raising children, began to change the nature of the community; they wanted an education, a home, and a decent neighborhood. Pressure from these serious-minded veterans helped establish Vanport City College, which eventually became Oregon's major urban collegiate institution, Portland State University. Gradually, Vanport's identity changed from a company town of shipyard workers to a colony proudly calling itself Veterans' Village.

When the federal government withdrew its school support and discontinued the summer school program, seventy adults volunteered as recreation supervisors, and the community raised its own money for recreation supplies and equipment. Though some conservative politicians and writers accused HAP of encouraging socialism in its management of Vanport, it was successfully managing fifty percent more low-cost housing than any urban area in the United States, with even New York City a distant second.

Don't Get Excited

Warm weather in the spring of 1948 began melting the exceptionally heavy snowfall that had accumulated in the mountains of the seven states and one Canadian province that comprised the Columbia River's drainage area. Even though Vanport lay fifteen feet lower than the Columbia, there had never been any real concern for its safety. So-called impervious dikes surrounded the entire project. At that time, only two dams—Bonneville and Grand Coulee—existed on the river, and their function was generating electricity, not controlling floods.

In May 1948, nearly six thousand families lived in Vanport, an estimated total of 18,700 people. A combination of unusually high temperature and rainfall during the month of May made the experts predict that the most water since 1894 would flow past Portland to the mouth of the Columbia River that summer; it appeared that the crest would come very early. But no one was worried.

On Tuesday, May 25, routine patrols of the north and south dikes went on twenty-four hours a day. Two men in an automobile equipped with a spotlight drove the roads at the base of the dikes looking for seepage, boils, or blisters. Two years earlier, when the water reached a relatively high level, the auto patrols increased, another man watched the west dike (which was railroad fill), and a foot patrol was added; but, no problems had occurred. This time, Housing Authority officials had decided to rely on the advice of the U.S. Army Corps of Engineers, who had completed the diking system and had previous experience in flood control; they assured HAP that they had nothing to worry about.

Continuing its rapid rise, the river now appeared more ominous. The possibility of evacuation was discussed, but the problems involved in housing and feeding 18,000 people, added to the difficulties in moving them, made postponing a decision for a day or two seem the logical thing to do—particularly when there appeared to be no imminent danger.

Memorial Day dawned fair and clear, with a promise of more sunny, warm weather. At 4 a.m. that Sunday morning a sheet of paper bearing a message from HAP was shoved under each door by the furnace firemen. It stated:

> "...the flood situation has not changed ... barring unforseen developments Vanport is safe. However, if it should become necessary to evacuate, the Housing Authority will give warning at the earliest possible moment."

A siren and air horn would blow, the message promised, and sound trucks would broadcast instructions. If the warning came, residents were told to not panic, to pack personal goods and a change of clothes, to turn off lights and stoves, close windows, and lock doors. Sick, elderly, or disabled persons were encouraged to leave for a few days. The message concluded:

REMEMBER: THE DIKES ARE SAFE AT PRESENT; YOU WILL BE WARNED IF NECESSARY; YOU WILL HAVE TIME TO LEAVE; DON'T GET EXCITED!

At 4 p.m. that afternoon, the river gauge on the north bank at Vancouver read 28.3 feet, 13 feet above flood stage. Near what was regarded as the strongest link in the chain of dikes protecting Vanport—the railroad fill to the west—the water level was still seventeen feet below the top. This dike, 125 feet wide at its base and 75 feet wide at its top, was considered indestructible. But deep within its seemingly solid exterior lay a hidden, fatal weak spot.

At 4:17 p.m., without warning, the railroad fill gave way. Calvin Hulbert, who was flying a seaplane above the tracks when the roadbed washed out, saw it happen. Suddenly the break was six feet, then sixty, then 500. A ten-foot wall of water flattened some buildings, others crumpled or split open.

As the surging waves first moved in, they quickly hit the many sloughs. One report described showers of spray fifty feet high upon impact with the slough water. Then, for thirty-five to forty minutes, a creeping inundation took over the sloughs. After they were filled and a sheet of water had spread over Vanport, the waves began to roll again.

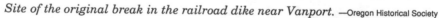
Site of the original break in the railroad dike near Vanport. —Oregon Historical Society

Vanport, a few hours after the break. —Oregon Historical Society

Cars were sent careening, houses wrenched apart. The water reached the high part of the project near Denver Avenue, and all vehicular traffic was quickly flooded out. Now the water level rose rapidly. All electric power went off at 4:50 P.M. Buildings floated like slow-moving giants, sometimes turning in the whirlpools being created.

The water surrounded the two KGW towers and the station left the air at 5:21. At 5:50 p.m. a floating apartment crashed into one of the towers and toppled it. The American flag on top of the project's flagpole survived until 5:44, when it was hit by a house and gently dipped into the water. Some abandoned cars with closed windows floated for a short period of time before sinking.

The fact that the area flooded on a warm Sunday afternoon greatly reduced the fatalities from drowning that would have surely occurred if the dike had broken during the night as people slept in their beds. Despite the promise made that morning in the bulletin, the warning siren either sounded too late, could not be heard, or did not sound at all.

The sheriff issued an emergency call for boats, which brought quick responses. People crawled through windows to get into boats; later they waited on rooftops. The compactness of the project and its proximity to Denver Avenue proved invaluable so far as rescue efforts were concerned. Buses, taxis, ambulances, and private cars lined the streets to help the victims; sightseers lined the surrounding roads.

Vanport, the day after the flood. —Oregon Historical Society

Rotten Timbers

The sudden flood made headlines in newspapers and magazines all over the United States as the worst disaster of its kind since the Johnstown flood May 31,1899. It took months to compile the official death toll. Over 2,000 names were on the missing list. Sheriff Martin T. Pratt predicted the death count would total no more than twenty-five persons; he proved right. Though only eighteen bodies were found and identified, seven others known to have been living in Vanport at the time of the flood remained lost and unaccounted for, so were assumed to be victims.

From the day of the disaster it was clear that the question of liability was going to be important and difficult. The lack of warning and poor evacuation plan upset many people. No one seemed to know why the city of 40,000 had only one exit. Most residents felt that either HAP or the Corps of Engineers should be accountable. HAP looked to the Corps, and the Corps recounted the history of diking in the area. The railroad fill had survived a similar situation in 1933. In 1941, the whole system was completed and turned over to Peninsula Diking District Number 1. One likely theory suggests that the fill was dumped around an existing trestle and, as the covered timbers rotted they left the roadbed weak, and this is where the dike broke.

The lawsuits soon reached the state courts, then the federal courts. Congress set an August 1950 deadline for filing suits. By then there were over seven hundred cases involving 2,993 claimants and 91 attorneys.

All claimants had to stipulate that they would abide by the decision rendered for a typical 20-case selection. Finally, in August 1952, the court decided that an honest mistake had been made, freeing both HAP and the Corps of Engineers from responsibility. By then, the former Vanporters had either left the area or found other housing. Vanport disappeared into oblivion.

"Could a rampaging Columbia River again inundate its diked plain?" asks historian Manley Maben. The U.S. Army Corps of Engineers says it cannot. There are no other buried trestles and no other dikes have ever broken. Also, the Columbia River now has a dozen more dams. Still, industries and flood insurance companies remained reluctant to build in the area. When it became clear that nobody else wanted it, the city of Portland decided to turn Vanport into a recreational park. Writes Maben:

> The city built a sports car track, drag strip, and sold bonds for a golf course. The race track has been upgraded to accommodate India-napolis-type cars. Bass and perch were planted in the lakes and sloughs. The golf course, situated close to the railroad fill, was designed by famed golf architect Robert Trent Jones. Governor Tom McCall officially opened the course by hitting the first drive on April 29, 1971.
>
> As long as the disaster had to happen, perhaps it was best that both federal agencies and profit-making industries turned away, so that, after the passage of time, in an era of open space recreation, the land remained for these important uses. It provides a pleasant prospect, giving the viewer a sense of peace and tranquility that was never present in Vanport City.

State Capital in Salem

Lee's Mission

Much of impetus that made people emigrate from the eastern states to the Oregon country was fueled by religious zeal. Coming west in 1834 to minister to the Flatheads and Nez Perces of the interior Northwest, Methodist Jason Lee decided instead to go on to the lower Columbia River region, where the natives might be more receptive to religious instruction.

At Fort Vancouver, Lee took the advice of Dr. John McLoughlin to travel a few miles up the beautiful, fertile Willamette Valley, and settle among the Kalapuya Indians near French Prairie. There he planned to "teach them first to cultivate the ground and live more comfortably than they could do by hunting, and, as they do this, teach them religion." Unfortunately, this mission did not succeed; the "great sickness," small-pox, wiped out about four-fifths of the Indians in Reverend Lee's flock.

On June 1, 1840, he began a second mission at what he hoped would be a more healthful site a few miles farther south. Soon after building a house and a mill, the missionaries decided to establish a literary and religious institute of learning. To finance this Oregon Institute, they laid out a town and sold lots. The new town needed a new name; someone suggested *"Chemetaka,"* a Kalapuya Indian word meaning "place of rest." But the missionaries preferred a Biblical word with a similar meaning, so they chose Salem.

Following the great emigration of 1845, the Oregon Institute turned its emphasis from Indians to the education of white children and became the forerunner of Willamette University, which was chartered in 1853.

Religion was the bedrock upon which the character of Oregon's pioneers was built. Differences could and did exist between French-Canadian Catholics, strait-laced Methodists, and the communal-types such as Dr. William Keil and his followers at the Old Aurora Colony—but so long as people sincerely believed in some kind of religion, they were tolerated. That's why the open-minded representatives of Oregon's new state legislature resigned themselves to suffer in patient silence while a fire-and-brimstone "hardshell Baptist" preacher named Joab Powell gave the invocation to open its deliberations, no matter how long the prayer might take.

"Uncle Joab" Powell, as he was known to his neighbors throughout the hills and hollows of the Santiam Valley east of Salem, was a remarkable man. Though less than average height, he was "two axe handles broad," weighed a muscular three hundred pounds, and had an appetite that was legendary in a place and time of hearty eaters. Born in Tennessee, he converted to simplistic religious beliefs while still in his teens, migrating first to Missouri and then to Oregon. Uncle Joab preached whenever the mood came on him, which was often. Once started, he was good for two or three hours a session morning, afternoon, and night, with time out only for meals. His voice was as big as his body and his appetite.

"When he's outside, like he is today," one of his parishioners told a stranger who wondered what the roaring noise in the distance was all about, "you can hear him a mile and a half away. We tried him out one day last summer. He lambasts sinners like the devil beatin' tanbark."

So, when the Oregon State legislators settled down to hear Joab Powell proclaim the invocation, they knew they were in for it. And they got it. Not what they expected perhaps; but probably what they deserved. After a reverent hush had fallen and all heads were bowed, Joab Powell raised his eyes to heaven and said in what was for him a extremely quiet tone of voice: "Father, forgive them, for they know not what they do. Amen."

Land of the Willamette

One of the chief attractions of the Willamette Valley was its many open prairies with deep, fertile soil needing only to be plowed and planted to produce bountiful crops. In contrast to the heavily timbered regions along the coast, where huge trees had to be cut down and burned before the sunlight could dry out and warm the land for grass and grain, this 60-by-180-mile valley—from French Prairie to the Siskiyous north and south, and from the Cascades to the Coast Range east and west—had seemingly natural grassy clearings.

What the white settlers did not know but soon found out was that the clearings were not natural at all. The Kalapuya Indians learned long ago to set fires in late summer, killing the brush but encouraging growth of the lush wild grass; the game thrived on the grass, and the Indians thrived on the game.

In a spring 1981 article in the *Lane County Historian*, Professor Henry W. Lawrence, who taught landscape history at the University of Oregon, states:

> The effect within the present area of Eugene of periodic fires set by the Indians was to keep almost all of the flat valley floor and many of the hillsides an open grassland, devoid of trees. In lower wet areas

of the prairie grew the camas, the lily-like perennial whose sweet bulbous root was a staple of the Kalapuya diet.

Dotting the higher and dryer stretches of prairie and many of the grassy hillsides were the two native oaks, California Black Oak and Oregon White Oak. The oak species both have a thick corky bark which resisted the flames of the fast-moving grass fires. They occurred usually as isolated individuals or in open loose groupings termed "oak openings" by the early settlers.

Botanist David Douglas

A Magnificient Tree

Although neither William Clark nor Meriwether Lewis was an expert botanist, the plant specimens they collected and brought back were remarkably diverse and new to the civilized world. If preserved as President Thomas Jefferson had intended, their display would have added greatly to scientific knowledge. But when the young British botanist, David Douglas, visited the collection at the University of Pennsylvania in 1823, he found very few plants of that irreplaceable

Tree ready for falling, 1909. —Lane County Historical Museum

treasure in evidence. William Morwood tells us in *Traveler in a Vanished Landscape, the Life and Times of David Douglas*:

> The bulk of it had been spirited away through neglect and larceny. Benjamin Smith Barton, professor of botany at the university, had provided the neglect in generous quantities. It was to Barton that Thomas Jefferson entrusted the amazing flora of the Columbia River for classification and description. Incredibly, Barton postponed the the work for years.
>
> When he finally got around to it, it was too late. Most of the collection had been purloined by his former assistant, Frederick Pursh, who had long since departed for his native Germany. With the publication of *Flora Americae Septentrionalis*, a work largely based on the Columbia material, Pursh secured for himself the international botanical reputation Benjamin Smith Barton might have had—and also, perhaps, a niche in the pantheon of infamy.

Wandering over the hills of upstate New York, David Douglas was awed by the size and number of hardwood trees found in its virgin forest, many of them so tall and lacking in lower branches that they could not be climbed. While his American host hunted wild game on the forest floor, Douglas sharpened his marksmanship by shooting down leaves and acorns as specimens off branches he could not reach—a skill that later came in handy bringing down pine cones in the Oregon country, where the Indians questioned the sanity of a white man who would do such a thing.

Douglas had been sent to America by the Horticultural Society of London. His first trip to the East Coast had been so fruitful that the society arranged for a second trip, this time to the Pacific Northwest, in 1824, where the Hudson's Bay Company promised to transport, house, and protect the collector for an indefinite stay on the Columbia River, though warning that he might find "the fare of the country rather coarse and be subject to some privations."

Before the Hudson's Bay Company ship *William and Mary* sailed from England in the summer of 1824, Douglas intensely studied the only three texts that existed on the almost completely unbotanized Pacific Northwest. *The Genera of North American Plants* was by the highly respected botanist Thomas Nuttall, whom Douglas had met and liked; *The North American Sylva*, by a man named Michaux, was an authoritative book on the conifers that predominated in the Columbia River region—but neither author had been in the Pacific Northwest. *Flora Americae Septentrionalis*, by German botanist Frederick Pursh, who had stolen the material from Lewis and Clark, was the closest thing Douglas could find to first-hand observation.

Soon after the *William and Mary* dropped anchor in the lower Columbia in April 1825, Douglas went ashore and began exploring the rain

185

Willamette River log drive, 1896. —Lane County Historical Museum

forest. His description of the Douglas fir, the magnificent tree that bears his name, is worth noting:

> The trees which are interspersed in groups or standing solitary in dry upland are thickly clad to the very ground with widespread pendant branches, and from the gigantic size which they attain form one of the most striking and truly graceful objects in nature. Those which are in the dense, gloomy forests are destitute of branches to the height of 100 to 140 feet, having a magnitude exceeded by few if any trees in the world.

One of the fallen giants he measured at 227 feet long, 48 feet around, and 15 feet thick.

Sweet Pine

David Douglas made a number of exploring trips over the next few years from Fort Vancouver, collecting and classifying as he traveled. The Indians he encountered in the Willamette Valley grew increasingly curious about him. They were used to trappers. But his occupation baffled them. Douglas biographer Morwood writes:

> They could understand what the other King George men were doing on their river—beaver skins had a value to them, too. But that a young chief should be sent all this way to collect twigs and flowers, didn't make sense. Finally they concluded that King George was mad and that Douglas was collecting novelties to amuse him. They called Douglas the "Grass Man" and treated him with deference because of his connection with an unhinged mind.

186

On a trip to the upper Columbia in what is now northeast Washington, he catalogued a huge pine tree with bark cracked like an alligator's hide, which turned out to be the western yellow pine, commonly called "Ponderosa"—a tree whose value as timber is second only to the Douglas fir. On another journey into the Blue Mountains of northeast Oregon, he found and classified the only peony ever discovered on the North American continent—a flower with a purple and yellow bloom which he named *Paeonia brownii*, in honor of Robert Brown, one of the greatest English botanists of the day.

In the mountains of the Umpqua region in the upper Willamette Valley, he found a unique species of pine tree with cones measuring sixteen and a half inches long. Even more astonishing, unlike the bitter or bland resin of most pines, the taste of these cones was sweet, yet only broadleaf trees such as maples, magnolias, and willows were known to exude sap with a sugar content. "Trees of this *pinus*," he wrote, "produce a substance which, I am almost afraid to say, is sugar."

His method of obtaining cones to measure and taste—shooting them down with a rifle—proved to be extremely risky when the local Indians failed to understand what he was doing. He had seen the pine cones in clusters far above him, he wrote, hanging from the branches "like small sugar loaves in a grocer's shop." With one shot he managed to bring down three big cones. But the sound attracted a band of eight Indians "painted with red earth, armed with bows, arrows and spears," who barged into

Parson Creek flume, 1890. —Lane County Historical Museum

the clearing and surrounded him as he reloaded. After a bit of explaining and bargaining, he agreed to pay them with gifts of tobacco for any pine cones they shot down; so peace was made.

The mysterious sweet tree he had discovered was the sugar pine. Back home, the tallest Scotch pines grew only to 75 feet. As he measured a wind-felled monster, he must have wondered if the homefolk would believe the dimensions of this tree: 57 feet 9 inches around—large enough to contain an elephant, and 215 feet long—twice the height of a factory chimney.

During his exploratory journeys in the Pacific Northwest, David Douglas discovered and named seven of the seventeen presently known species of pine on the Pacific Coast. The fact that he was not a university-trained botanist (few explorers in the field at that time were) but a mere "horticultural gatherer," makes his finds even more impressive, as does his youth. Unfortunately, he was killed in a tragic accident in the Hawaiian Islands at the age of thirty-five. But the results of his work in the Oregon country live after him.

Where There's Smoke

On one of his trips through the upper Willamette Valley, a fire recently set by Indians had blackened the tree trunks and destroyed the undergrowth so thoroughly that he had to give up his botanizing in that area. Apparently, it was not the first time that fire—whether from Indians or lightning—had gotten away and raged uncontrolled. Historian William Morwood noted tree-ring evidence that indicates a fire about 1690 that burned half a million acres.

Today, in the region from Salem to Eugene, where grass seed production is a major industry, fire is still a matter of grave concern. To produce the highest yields, seed growers torch their fields in late summer each year. Though they are permitted to burn only when favorable wind and air conditions are predicted, sometimes fires don't cooperate fully and highway motorists may experience blinding smoke. The problem has yet to be solved.

A Valley Worth Seeing

At 60 miles wide and 180 miles long, the Willamette Valley comprises only eleven percent of the state, yet it contains seventy-five percent of Oregon's population. Even so, once you leave the metropolis of Portland, get off Interstate I-5, and follows less-traveled secondary highways such as 99E and 99W, the rural community seems quiet, uncluttered, and prosperous.

Salem, despite being the state capital, is uncrowded and rich in parks and open spaces; the office buildings of state bureaus and agencies are spread over a wide area of the city, which borders the beautiful Willamette River. Salem is bisected by several small, swift-flowing streams, which once supplied water power for gristmills and early-day manufacturers. Still in operation today and under the management of the Marion County Historical Society on the site of the Thomas McKay Woolen Mill, the water-powered mill and museum at 1313 Mill Street is well worth seeing.

Another unique structure is the State Forestry Building at State and 24th streets, which is a living museum of rare Oregon building materials. Designed by the same architect who drew up the plans for Timberline Lodge on Mount Hood and constructed during the WPA (Works Progress Administration) period of the mid-1930s at a time when now-precious woods were cheap in Oregon, the building is a well-maintained landmark of a bygone era.

I-5, OR 99E and 99W
Albany—Eugene
44 miles

On Interstate 5 between Albany and Eugene, neither scenery nor historic sites will distract the traveler in a hurry. However, scenic and historically interesting routes on 99E and 99W, which go west from Salem, offer a choice of routes if you prefer a relaxed drive through one of the loveliest sections of the Willamette Valley. Corvallis, on 99W, is the site of Oregon State University, while Eugene, 43 miles to the south, is the site of the University of Oregon.

River Runners

If stern-wheelers still operated on the Willamette River, rival sports teams from the two universities could travel by boat from one school to the other, since both are situated along the river. During pioneer days from the 1850s well into the 1870s, river boats were the main means of transportation up and down the valley, especially in winter and spring when rains turned the few roads and trails into muddy swamps.

Some of the boats that navigated the often shallow waters of the upper rivers, such as the Willamette in western Oregon and the Snake through Hells Canyon in eastern Oregon, were as remarkable as their masters. Stern-wheelers needed water only a foot or so deep to propel themselves with the current and just slightly deeper water to make progress against the current. One boat in Hells Canyon a hundred feet long could carry one hundred tons of freight, yet drew only eighteen inches of water when fully loaded. Smaller boats plying the Willamette could just about run "on a light dew."

Captain Leonard White, one of the best pilots and boat builders, was not only a master of rivers but something of a character as well. An advocate of spelling words exactly as they sounded, he made misspelling a science in the letters he wrote to newspapers on matters of navigation. This excerpt from an 1855 letter is typical:

> I anticipat that navigashun will be opened az far az Ujen Siti [Eugene City] the cuming winter, if the good inhabitants wil alou us to Bush-hwak above Korvalis ... the smal timber that groz along the ej wil be ov yus for Bush-hwaking....

This odd use of the word *bushwhacking* goes back to one of its lesser-known meanings: "to propel a boat by pulling on bushes along the bank." In the early 1800s, the speaking style of a politician who sawed the air with his hands also was called bushwhacking by country folk.

Albany was founded in 1848 by two brothers, Walter and Thomas Monteith, who had come to Oregon from New York and named the settlement after the city in their home state. Each of them filed a land claim on adjacent sites, then built a cabin whose single room exactly straddled the two claims, so that each brother could honestly say he "lived on his own land."

Enlarged in 1849 and finished in 1850, the cabin became the civic and social center of the new settlement, sheltering the first religious service in Albany, and serving as the first store. Although remodeled in 1918, it retained the original architectual lines and has been well maintained up to the present day. It is now open to visitors as a private museum.

To Oregon by Ox Team in 1852

Typical of the tragedy and triumph of emigrations to the Willamette Valley is the story of John J. Abbott, who set out at the age of eleven with his family and survived to tell his story fifty-nine years later. The following excerpts are taken from an account published in the *Oregon Journal* in 1911:

> Friends and neighbors of my parents had emigrated to the Oregon Country in 1846. They gave highly colored descriptions of Oregon, stating that the climate was unexcelled and that the soil would produce all crops that could be grown in Missouri. They added that stock of all kinds could "winter" on the range and come off fat in the spring.

His parents and grandparents were so excited by the flattering reports of Oregon that they sold their farms in Missouri, bought oxen and wagons, and prepared to emigrate. The party of ten families set out from Osage County, Missouri, April 11, 1852.

The Cholera Belt

Young, active, and fond of horseback riding, John Abbott was given the job of driving the party's forty head of loose stock. At Westport, the jumping-off place for the long journey across the plains, other emigrant families joined the group. In all, the train now consisted of forty wagons and sixty able-bodied, well-armed men.

> The men called a meeting to consider their protection and organized by electing my maternal grandfather, John Geabhart, Captain. He was a veteran of the war of 1812 and had fought Indians on the frontier under General Jackson. He was cool and considerate and a man of good judgment.

In Nebraska, a band of Indians threatened to attack the train, but changed their minds at the sight of the strong force of armed, disciplined emigrants waiting for them.

A few days later tragedy struck when an epidemic of cholera hit the train. "My father was the first victim. He lived only a few hours. We laid him to rest where the Old Emigrant Road left the Little Blue River. The next day we arrived at Fort Kearney." Cholera was raging there; people died at a fearful rate in tents lining the banks of the Platte River.

Panic prevailed for several days.

> You could see men and women on their bended knees asking God to show mercy on their loved ones. The road was lined with dead cattle and horses. Many emigrants were compelled to lighten their loads. You could see all kinds of wagons from prairie schooners to one-horse buggies standing by the roadside.

Frantic travelers cast away carpenter and blacksmith tools, bedding, clothing, and valuable books.

At least thirty percent of the men, women and children died before the wagon train reached Fort Laramie, John Abbott estimated. West of Fort Laramie, which appeared to be the limit of the cholera belt, the disease disappeared; noted in the diaries of many Oregon-bound emigrants, this phenomenon has never been satisfactorily explained, but time and again it did happen.

Near Salt Lake, where the Mormons had settled, a friendly "Saint" who had established a trading post sold the emigrants a number of articles they needed at reasonable prices. He also offered to exchange liberal quantities of silver for their gold. "By way of accommodation, some of our people let him have sixty dollars in gold for quite a bit more than that in raw silver bullion." Indeed, it was raw. The emigrants soon learned that what the Saint so generously traded was really lead thinly coated with silver. "Four young men in the party returned to interview the trader. In two days, they overtook us again and had the gold."

On to Portland

With the cholera belt far behind them by the time the emigrants crossed South Pass and headed across the Snake River desert, another ailment, "mountain fever," appeared. Apparently a form of pneumonia made worse by dust, exposure, and exhaustion, it frequently put its victims in the grave.

"On Snake River my mother was taken ill with the mountain fever," John Abbott recalled. "She died and was buried on the banks of the Powder River, a few miles below where Baker City now stands. My brothers and sisters and myself were left in the care of our grandparents."

A week or so later near the juncture of the John Day River with the Columbia, his grandfather, John Geabhart, captain of the wagon train, also came down with mountain fever. Knowing that he could not handle the oxen and wagon any more, he sold the entire outfit to a cattle buyer with the understanding that the man would haul him and his family as far as The Dalles, where they would embark on scows for their journey through the Columbia Gorge.

By the time the emigrants took passage on the scows, many members of the Missouri party were ill with mountain fever. Traveling down the river in the cold rain, the sick and weary emigrants sought what shelter and warmth they could find ashore each night, then resumed their journey the next day.

> The first night out there was a young man delirious with fever, who walked out into the river and drowned. The screams of his mother awakened the entire camp. The men procured torch lights and searched for the body until daylight. The next day my Grandfather Geabhart died. He was buried on the north side of the river a few miles above the falls.

Arriving in Portland in October 1852, eleven year old John Abbott had lost his father, mother, and maternal grandfather during the grueling trip west. His paternal grandparents raised his two brothers, two sisters, and John.

Of how they survived, he says simply: "Most of the emigrants of that year landed in Portland without money, but they found friends..."

192

Bohemia Johnson's "Dust"

From the time of the first discovery of gold in California in 1849, prospectors prowled the mountains of the Oregon in hopes of striking bonanzas. Now and then they did. For the most part, Oregon gold strikes occurred in remote areas of the Siskiyous, the Cascades, and the Blue Mountains.

During the 1850s, Willamette Valley towns such as Portland, Salem, Albany, and Eugene lost so many young men "gone to California" that there was a shortage of sailors to man the ships, farmers to till the fields, and skilled craftsmen needed to develop towns. Few of them struck it rich in California. Those who did soon discovered that after exhausting the easily obtained placer gold of the lower river bars, the veins ran into hardrock requiring expensive stamp mills and refining plants. It was hard work, too.

Sluicing in the Bohemia Mining District, 1930.
—Lane County Historical Museum

Cabin in the Bohemias, 1890. —Lane County Historical Museum

The overwhelming majority who did not find gold reluctantly returned to Oregon and went back to work at their former jobs, while those who had become affluent also came home to establish businesses that they hoped would keep them wealthy. But whether losers or winners, they both had been infected with "gold fever," so all it took to make them head for the hills and try again was a show of color in a prospector's pan.

Cottage Grove, at the head of the Willamette Valley thirty miles south of Salem, calls itself the Covered Bridge Capital of Oregon. Of the half dozen covered bridges in the area, one is still in use. Before seeing the bridges, travelers should consider visiting the excellent small museum in Cottage Grove to obtain a pamphlet showing their locations. Housed in a building that was once a Catholic church, the museum features a stained-glass window, working models of a stamp mill and sawmill, and, in the yard outside, a five-stamp mill once used by the Bohemia Mining District thirty-two miles southeast of the town for crushing quartz to extract its gold.

Spanning the ridge between the Willamette and the Umpqua rivers, the Bohemia Mining District covers 225 square miles of mountainous country heavily timbered with fir, spruce, and hemlock. The WPA guide to Oregon describes: "Turbulent mountain streams fighting their way through gorges, wooded scarps, and jagged peaks, [that] make this a region of great natural beauty. Deer, elk, cougars, bears and other game are found here in abundance."

The district was named for "Bohemia" Johnson, a prospector who discovered gold-bearing quartz in 1863. An immigrant from Bohemia, Johnson is said to have killed an Indian, hiding out in the mountains to avoid capture. Later, he brought out gold to the "great excitement" of settlements in the valley. But, when settlers found out that his "dust" had to be extracted by machinery from the quartz ledges rather than simply plucked or panned from streambeds, the excitement quickly died down.

> Until 1891, only intermittent attempts were made to mine the region. However, in that year, Dr. W.W. Oglesby located and opened the Champion and Noonday mills at Music Ledge. The height of activity in the district came in 1900 after assays had demonstrated the richness of the strike.

Before 1910 the Bohemia district yielded between $500,000 and $1 million in gold. When the free milling ledges were exhausted and the cost of working the lower grade ore became prohibitive, miners gradually abandoned the region. Some mining activity continues still.

This covered bridge built in 1920, located a few miles east of Cottage Grove, is still in use today.

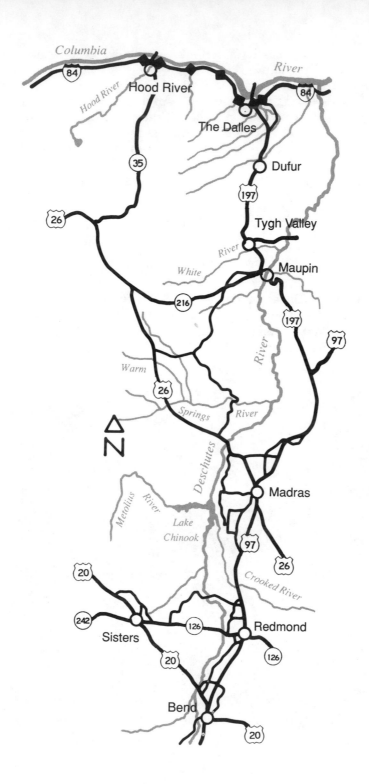

PART IV

The Cascade Mountains

OR 35, US 26
Hood River—Madras
104 miles

Volcanic Splendor

The Cascade Mountains form part of the eastern edge of the Pacific Rim, also known as the "Ring of Fire." More violent volcanic activity has occurred here in the relative present and recent geologic past than any region in the Western Hemisphere. In his book *Fire and Ice, the Cascade Volcanoes*, geologist Stephen L. Harris calls the Cascades "potentially the most dangerous mountains in the country."

Within view from Portland, Mount St. Helens in southwest Washington erupted dramatically in 1980. A hundred miles south of the Oregon border, Mount Lassen in northern California spewed ash and molten lava intermittently from 1914 to 1935. Since the coming of the white man, no volcanic activity among the peaks in Oregon's Cascades have been as cataclysmic as the explosion of the legendary Mount Mazama, which formed Crater Lake and devastated many square miles countryside 6,600 years ago.

The main spine of the Cascade mountain range through Oregon averages 5,000 feet in elevation, with nine peaks topping 9,000 feet. Some of them, like Mount Hood, which is the highest at 11,235 feet, are symmetrical and forested to the timberline, then topped with glaciers and snow. Others, like the Sisters and Three Fingered Jack, have slopes so steep and barren that they have been used as lunar training grounds for astronauts.

The Pacific Crest Trail, beloved by hikers and backpackers, extends four hundred miles north and south through the Oregon high country. It rewards wilderness lovers rugged enough to endure its challenge with spectacular views of primitive peaks and valleys. For those less inclined to hike, yet willing to leave the main highways and follow curving but safe mountain roads, there is still a rich vista of beautiful scenery available from border to border.

Mountains Named After Rapids

Part One of this book mentioned the series of Columbia River rapids called the lower, middle, and upper cascades. Though the naming of individual peaks in the mountains causing those rapids followed no particular pattern, explorers and mapmakers appear to have commonly consented that the range should be called simply "Cascades."

For a few years during the 1830s, New England promoter Hall J. Kelley tried to sell the idea of calling the Cascades the "Presidents Range." Pointing out that Lewis and Clark already had named one Oregon peak Mount Jefferson, he wanted to throw out the foreign names such as Mount Rainier and Mount Hood and give all the peaks from Canada to California patriotic American names. Though he talked what may have been a good idea, nothing came of it.

Three peaks in the Cascade range were named after presidents. In Washington, broad-shouldered Mount Adams, at 12,276 feet, carries the name of the nation's second president, John Adams. In Oregon, Mount Washington, at 7,802 feet, bears the name of the first president, with Mount Jefferson, at 10,495 feet, honoring the third president.

Eight other Cascade peaks in Oregon rise above 9,000 feet. North of Mount Jefferson is Mount Hood, at 11,235 feet. South of Mount Jefferson are: North Sister, at 10,085 feet; Middle Sister, at 10,047 feet; South Sister, at 10,358 feet; Broken Top, at 9,152 feet; Bachelor Butte, at 9,060 feet; Mount Thielsen, at 9,178 feet; and Mount McLoughlin, at 9,493 feet.

The Scenic Road South

With the lower Columbia River near Portland only a few feet above sea level, Mount Hood's rise to 11,245 feet just forty miles away is dramatic. To the British sea captain, William R. Broughton, who first saw and named it from Point Vancouver in October 1792, Mount Hood must have looked even more impressive, for he estimated its altitude at 25,000 feet.

It is understandable that Lt. William Broughton should name the most impressive mountain peak he had ever seen after Lord Samuel Hood, for as vice-admiral of the British navy he had signed the original instructions for Vancouver's voyage. Enlisting in the Royal Navy as a

Mount Hood from the south. —Penrose Library, Whitman College

captain's servant in 1741, he rose steadily in rank until at the end of the Revolution, in 1783, he was second in command of the fleet in American waters. In 1796 he became Viscount Hood in the peerage of Great Britain. He died January 27, 1816, at the age of 92. Of him, Lewis McArthur writes in *Oregon Geographic Names*: "Mount Hood is an unusual mountain, and none can say but that it was named for an unusual man."

To get the best view of the mountain, start from the heart of the Columbia River Gorge, Hood River. Following a hungry time in the 1850s when stranded emigrants sometimes resorted to eating their pets, this settlement was called Dog River. But one of its first permanent residents, a strong-minded woman named Mrs. Nathaniel Coe, declared she would accept no mail sent to a town by that name, so the settlers changed its name in 1856.

Half a mile south of Hood River on Oregon 35, a road turns left and rises a thousand feet or so to a small park called Panorama Point. From here visitors get a magnificent view of Mount Hood to the southwest and the extensive fruit orchards of the Hood River Valley, which are especially lovely in the spring bloom. A plaque in the park explains the previous property owners' desire to share this vista with others.

At Parkdale, thirty miles south of Hood River, the right-hand fork in the road takes you to Cloud Cap Inn, the oldest mountain resort in Oregon. Built in 1889 at the 6,000-foot level on the north slope of the mountain, people from Portland favored it for holidays, traveling by boat up the Columbia, then continuing by buggy or stage. To withstand the tremendous wind of winter storms, it was anchored to the ground with cables. It is now used by mountaineers and a rescue group.

Twenty-five miles farther south, Oregon 35 joins US 26. A mile west of there, another road turns right and climbs five miles to Timberline Lodge. Here the trees open up to reveal a spectacular panorama of Mount Hood in all its glory. The lodge, built in the heyday of the WPA in 1937 at the 6,000-foot level on the mountain's south side, uses native materials on a massive scale. The handicrafted Indian and wildlife motifs contribute to this unique, picturesque structure.

From the lodge, sightseers can ride comfortably in a Snow Cat to the 9,000-foot level, or skiers can ride lifts to the tops of several runs. With year-round snow on some slopes, the mountain hosts an international summer ski school and competition. According to geologist Stephen Harris, Mount Hood is second only to Japan's Fujiyama as the world's most climbed snowpeak.

Climbers often smell sulphur up to a mile from its source at Crater Rock, reaffirming the mountain's volcanic nature. The lodge frequently receives calls from anxious Portlanders who think they see a new eruption on the horizon. The "smoke" often visible around the mountian top forms from condensed clouds of vapor and gas and does not seem to indicate any increased volcanic activity, or hasn't anyway since 1907. But it reminds us that "Mount Hood's fires are not extinguished," as Harris says. "This volcano, in fact, is the only one in Oregon for which we have a well authenticated record of observed eruptions."

Shortly before Lewis and Clark passed through the region, Mount Hood exploded violently, despositing a layer of ash six inches thick at timberline on the southwest side. In 1835, the American missionary, Samuel Parker, wrote that he had heard Indian reports of "smoke and fire" on the mountain. In 1853, '54, '59, and '65, activity was reported by local newspapers. Though he did not write down his experience until some years later, an Oregon pioneer named W.F. Courtney recalled that in September 1859:

> We were camped on Tie Ridge about thirty-five miles from Mount Hood. It was about 1:30 in the morning when suddenly the heavens lit up and from the dark there shot up a column of fire. With a flash that illuminated the whole mountainside with a pinkish glare, the flame danced from the crater. For two hours, as we watched, the mountain continued to blaze at irregular intervals, and when morning came Mt. Hood presented a peculiar sight. Its sides, where the day before there was snow, were blackened as if cinders and ashes had been thrown out.

Historical Landmarks

A few miles west of Timberline Lodge on US 26 are several sites of historical interest, all relating to this overland route. Emigrants from the east and soldiers from the west thought any trail on land preferable to risking the wild waters of Columbia through the gorge. Barlow Monument honors Samuel K. Barlow, who in 1845 declared that "God never made a mountain without some place to go over it."

Barlow applied to the Provisional Government for a permit to build and operate a toll road over the route he claimed he had laid out. Granted the franchise, he charged toll and did enough road improvement to keep the permit, but the road was far from perfect. According to the WPA guide to Oregon, one traveler later recalled:

> Some men's hearts died within them and some of our women sat down by the roadside and cried, saying they had abandoned all hope of ever reaching the promised land. I saw women with babies but a week old, toiling up the mountains in the burning sun, on foot, because our jaded teams were not able to haul them.
>
> We went down mountains so steep that we had to let our wagons down with ropes. My wife and I carried our children up muddy mountains in the Cascades, half a mile high, and then carried the loadings of our wagons by piecemeal, as our cattle were so reduced that they were hardly able to haul up our empty wagon.

Just down the road from Barlow Monument is Government Camp, so named for a detachment of soldiers sent overland in 1849 to keep peace in the newly acquired Oregon Territory. Like the first emigrants, they found it impossible to take their wagons any further, so abandoned them here, leaving a warning sign: "Government Property—do not touch."

Also nearby is the infamous Laurel Hill, a hazardous descent of two miles with only three level spots large enough for the oxen to rest. "We went down Laurel Hill like shot off a shovel," wrote William Barlow, a son of the road-builder. Another emigrant observed in 1853:

> The road on this hill is something terrible. It is worn down into the soil from five to seven feet, leaving steep banks on both sides, and so narrow that it is almost impossible to walk alongside of the cattle for any distance without leaning against the oxen. The emigrants cut down a small tree about ten inches in diameter and about forty feet long, and the more limbs it has on the better. This tree they fastened to the rear axle with chains or ropes, top end foremost, making an excellent brake.

The lower tollgate, where Samuel Barlow collected his fee of $5.00 for each wagon and $1.00 for each head of stock, was located ten miles down the road. "Many a settler arrived at the gates unable to pay," says the WPA guide. "But Mr. Barlow would accept a note. He always permitted widows to pass without payment."

Mount Jefferson

Forty miles directly south of Mount Hood looms the second highest peak in the Cascades, Mount Jefferson, sometimes called "Guardian of the Wilderness" because of the vast untamed areas around it. Vistas appear from US 26, which crosses the Warm Springs Indian Reservation to the north, and from US 97 in the Madras area to the east, but most of the region surrounding it is accessible only by hiking trails and an occasional rugged logging road.

With a sharp, pointed summit rising 10,495 feet, it is covered by a number of glaciers. This is the peak seen and named by Lewis and Clark for the financier of their Corps of Discovery. Though the peak is obviously of volcanic origin, the last pyroclastic activity took place about 6,500 years ago, according to geologist Stephen Harris, who cautiously adds, "Jefferson does not seem to be a prime candidate for the honor of being the next Cascade volcano to erupt."

Mount Jefferson from Smith Rock State Park. —Deschutes County Historical Society

Ogden and Fremont

After Lewis and Clark, whose routes west and east kept close to the Columbia River, the first white man to lead a party south along the eastern slope of the Cascades was Peter Skene Ogden in 1825-26. Under orders from the Hudson's Bay Company to determine if beaver were plentiful east of the mountains, and, if so, to reduce their numbers so that American fur traders would not bother coming into the region, Ogden led parties south from The Dalles up the John Day, Deschutes, and Crooked rivers, and along the Klamath and other streams well into northern California, which then belonged to Spain. He was the first English-speaking man to see and name 14,162-foot Mount Shasta in northern California, the second highest peak in the entire Cascade Range. Ogden's party did trap some beaver, but the pickings were slim compared to the Rocky Mountains, so he doubted the Americans would ever show any interest in the region.

A few years later, in 1843-44, the "Great American Pathfinder," Captain John C. Fremont, traveled Ogden's route south from The Dalles, searching not for beaver but for geographic knowledge and to determine whether the land held promise for the expansionist-minded American nation, welcoming whatever measure of personal glory he might pick up along the way to aid his military and political career. The fact that veteran scout and former mountain man Kit Carson pointed out the trail to the "pathfinder" took nothing away from his accomplishments as an explorer, for, while Carson could read the lay of the land, he could not set his knowledge down on paper, so the two made a good team.

The Confederated Tribes

The Indians who had lived in the area for thousands of years also were unable to write, and thus record their claims to the land in any form acceptable in a white man's court. So, as had been done in the East since the day of the Pilgrims, the question of Indian rights to land the whites wanted begged settlement. Upon the establishment of Oregon and Washington territories, pressure mounted to "settle" the Indian question once and for all.

Newly appointed Governor Isaac Ingalls Stevens spoke for Washington Territory, while General Joel Palmer, the new superintendent of Indian Affairs, negotiated with the native Americans for Oregon Territory. Because the two white officials admittedly sought to "extinguish" Indian title to the land, *negotiate* is hardly descriptive of the process. But they were men in a hurry to accomplish what their government had ordered them to do, so they did it by the most direct means possible.

Reduced to its simplest element, the difference between the white man and the Indian on this land question was that the white man felt he had a basic right to *own* a piece of land, while the Indian felt his basic right was only to *use* a piece of land. Ask a white man where he lived and he would name a section, township, and state; if necessary, he could produce a deed asserting ownership of the land. Ask an Indian where he lived and he would say with his people, wherever they slept according to the season, the food supply, and their activity; sometimes in the valley, sometimes in the mountains.

In 1855 the white leaders tried to define certain areas for the Indians and other areas for the whites, separating the two races to minimize contact (or conflict) between them. The Warm Springs Indian Reservation, covering roughly a thousand square miles and with boundaries today very close to those established then, is a good example of how the process worked. Bound on the west by the eastern slope of the Cascades, on the north by the Columbia River, and on south and east by the high desert country, the Confederated Tribes of the Warm Springs Reservation of Oregon (as their official designation became) traditionally had roamed across 15,000 square miles.

The Indians of this reservation represented three different cultures: Chinookan, a water-oriented, fishing nation extending along the Lower Columbia from Celilo Falls to the Pacific; Sahaptin, the horse tribes from the eastern hills and mountains of the Columbia Plateau; and Shoshonean, a pedestrian, desert people from the northern reaches of the Great Basin. As drawn by Superintendent Palmer and agreed to with considerable reluctance by the Indians, the reservation restricted them to a fraction of their former range. To mollify this vast reduction, the government granted the native Americans a right "to fish and hunt in the usual and accustomed places" in perpetuity.

Since the 1850s, many choices have been offered the Indians by the federal government, some of which were designed not to benefit them but to eliminate their treaty rights with offers of money or land. In some cases, tribes dissolved when members voted to sell their assets. In others, a parcel of land was distributed on a per capita basis to each member of the tribe, with the rest of the original reservation sold to the highest bidder and the cash then doled out to individuals. But, from the beginning, the people living on the Warm Springs Reservation have voted time and again to govern themselves, to keep their land intact, to live on it, and to use any funds collected to develop it for the benefit of the people.

The confederated tribes' present government began in 1938. The Tribal Council is the central governing body; of its eleven elected members, eight serve three-year terms and three serve for life. Though the council delegates much of its authority to an administrator who oversees all tribal endeavors, the elected body regulates the development and use of reservation lands and resources.

Most of the 2,300 people living on the reservation are members of the confederated tribes. Ninety percent of the tribe's members live on the reservation, and, unlike other Indian reservations in the Pacific Northwest where many parcels are owned by non-Indians, all the lands within the boundaries of the Warm Springs Reservation are owned by the Indians themselves.

Typical of the Warm Springs Indians was their decision in 1957 to accept $4 million from the federal government to settle the loss of their traditional fishing grounds at Celilo Falls. They, like the other Columbia River Indians who had caught fish there for thousands of years, did not want the government to build The Dalles Dam, realizing its backwaters would permanently flood this ancient site. But the government proved unshakable, so the Indians sought the best cash settlement they could get for this "usual and accustomed" place to fish.

They could have insisted that this sum of money be paid out on a per capita basis to each tribal member. But they did not. Instead, for a small sum, they hired Oregon State University to study the reservation's resource and economic development potential. Encouraged by what they learned, they invested most of the remaining money in projects that would benefit the entire reservation. Since the higher elevations of the reservation are covered with prime Douglas fir and Ponderosa pine, the tribe developed its own forest products manufacturing plant, which recently paid most of a $2,400 dividend to each member from its profits. In addition to timber, the tribes invested in a recreation facility. The Metolius and Deschutes rivers had become popular for fishing and rafting, so they built a unique resort called Kah-Nee-Ta, which attracts many vacationers and conventioneers.

Built around a natural hot springs in an area where the mountains meet the desert, the Kah-Nee-Ta Village at first contained cottages, campgrounds, a swimming pool, and mineral baths. Its original cost was $1 million. In the early 1970s the tribe spent $5.7 million to build the lodge and related facilities, and in 1979 they remodeled and refurbished everything with another $1.5 million. Ten years later, Kah-Nee-Ta had an annual payroll of $1.5 million and 255 employees. Open year-round to all visitors, the resort is ten miles north of the town of Warm Springs. Like shareholders in a corporation, tribal members benefit from the economic success of the confederated tribes.

Edge of the Desert

Eleven miles southeast of the Warm Springs Reservation is Madras, a blend of mountains and desert. Here US 26 meets US 97, the main artery of travel and the route followed by Peter Skene Ogden and Captain Fremont so many years ago. With mountains looming to the west and rolling desert of sagebrush and juniper to the east, north, and south, this is big country of long vistas.

In a land of low rainfall, Madras has an abundance of water from the many rivers flowing out of the nearby mountains. Before the advent of sprinkler irrigation, only an occasional farmer tried to raise grain in this dry cattle and sheep country. But now wheat is raised along with hay to feed the livestock during the sometimes bitterly cold months of winter.

US 97
Madras—Bend
42 miles

Crooked River Gorge

Fifteen miles south of Madras, US 97 crosses a bridge over an unexpected and fantastic gorge of the Crooked River. With no advance warning that a river even exists in this flat, sagebrush-covered plain, the sudden canyon is narrow and drops eight hundred feet straight down. On the west side of the highway is a small park called the Ogden Scenic Wayside. Though high stone walls shield sightseers from the frightening descent, parents are warned to keep control of their children.

Peter Skene Ogden

A plaque in the park explains that the site is named for Peter Skene Ogden, and tells about his travels through this area. While this brief summary of his life is true as far as it goes, he deserves more than can be inscribed on a bronze plaque. Like Dr. John McLoughlin, he was not born an American citizen; unlike McLoughlin, he never became one. But few men in the history of the Oregon country did so much for the cause of westering Americans.

Peter Ogden could have been an American had the Revolutionary War not occurred, for his family lived in New Jersey at the time. But his father was a loyalist Tory, faithful to the crown and unable to agree with the American rebels, so the family moved to eastern Canada during the war and it was there that Peter was born.

In another place and time, young Peter might have been called a rebel without a cause, a juvenile delinquent, or just a plain hell-raiser, for he would not stay in school or behave in ways that did not suit him, and he would fight any person who crossed him. Instead of locking him up, the authorities turned him into a trapper and sent him into the wilderness. Too mean and ornery for others to handle, he quickly advanced to brigade leader.

A short, stocky, powerful man, he was a veteran of Canada's bitter fur company wars and capable of drubbing any three men in his employ. Of himself, he wrote at the age of twenty-three: "My legal primer says that necessity has no laws." One of his associates wrote: "We bid adieu to the humorous, honest, eccentric, law-defying Peter Ogden, the terror of the Indians, and the delight of all gay fellows...."

Whatever Ogden's good or bad qualities, his loyalty to the Hudson's Bay Company was complete. Even when he detested tasks assigned to him by his superior, Sir George Simpson—who instructed him to trap the country bare in violation of common sense conservation—the thought of failing to execute the orders never entered his head. Year after year he took trapping parties east and south from interior posts such as Spokane House, Flathead Post, and Fort Walla Walla on expeditions that left few beaver alive, making sure that the regions would hold no reward in furs for the Americans.

As the plaque at Ogden Scenic Wayside states, Peter Skene Ogden played a pivotal role in rescuing the survivors of the Whitman Massacre. No other man then living in the Pacific Northwest could have accomplished that feat, for no other man was so respected by the Indians. And

Hanks Lake, Mount Jefferson Wilderness Area. —Deschutes County Historical Society

the incredible thing about this event was that he had not the slightest vestige of authority to support his action—other than his name.

The Prince of Good Fellows

The Whitman Massacre took place November 29, 1847. Besides those killed that day, over fifty women and children were taken hostage by the irate Cayuses. A year earlier the Joint Occupancy Treaty ended, officially ceding all the country south of the forty-ninth parallel (the present U.S.-Canada border) to the United States. Since then, the Hudson's Bay Company factors, of which Ogden was one, had devoted their energies to winding up business affairs. Conflict between Indians and Americans in the region was not their concern. But to their eternal credit, the British reacted to this tragedy with the cool-headedness that had long marked their dealings with Indians.

Soon after word of the massacre and hostages reached Fort Walla Walla twenty-three miles away, Factor William McBean dispatched a courier with a secret, urgent message to the only man he knew of capable to negotiate release of the captives—Peter Skene Ogden—who was then the factor at Fort Vancouver.

Two decades had passed since the former "prince of good fellows and terror of all Indians" had made his grueling treks across the Oregon country. And the years had taken their toll. Now white-haired, pudgy, and full of an old man's aches and pains, Ogden could have said this was not his problem, sent Oregon Governor Abernethy a sympathetic note, and gone back to his paperwork. But Peter Skene Ogden did no such thing. Instead, he ordered two bateaux filled with trade goods drawn from Hudson's Bay stores, stating that if the company so wished, the goods could be charged to his personal account; he sent a brief note to the governor requesting that he make no move that would jeopardize ransom negotiations; then he stepped into the lead bateau and headed upriver.

His protective force, if such it could be called, consisted of sixteen French-Canadian paddlers—men notorious for their lack of enthusiasm when it came to fighting Indians—and his own well earned reputation for never making a promise he did not keep.

His mission succeeded. After negotiating a ransom for the fifty-four hostages, he paid off the Indians with the goods he had brought with him, and then escorted the freed captives to safety downriver.

The Hudson's Bay Company never billed the Americans for the ransom goods nor did the Americans ever offer payment. Governor Abernethy did write Ogden a note of thanks, but, for the rest of his life, Ogden shrugged off whatever scant showers of gratitude came his way by saying he simply had done what any other man in his situation would have done.

Julia of the Salish

Less well known is the courtship, marriage, and long years of domestic life Ogden shared with Julia. Few British fur traders who ranked in the gentlemen class ever talked or wrote about the Indian women with whom they lived, though it was common knowledge that most of them did so. In his detailed journals, Ogden never so much as mentions either the first or second Indian woman with whom he lived and fathered children. Yet, he never tried to conceal the relationships from his peers.

In a biography of Peter Skene Ogden, Archie Binns states that as a young man Ogden lived with a Cree woman who bore him two sons. Sarah, Peter's mother then living in England, knew about the union and accepted that a man in the wilderness needed a woman, but she could not bear the thought of her son giving his name to an Indian woman. She asked Peter to vow never to legalize the relationship. He gave her his promise. The Cree woman died in 1823. Leaving the two children with their mother's family, Peter journeyed west to Spokane House. This was a pleasant post among some of the most enlightened and reasonable of western Indians, the Salish, or Flatheads. There, he met and became attracted to Julia, a Salish woman a few years older and somewhat taller than he, but beautiful, intelligent, and widowed.

After a courtship—during which she made him adhere to every rule, including the dowry of fifty horses to her father—Julia and Peter were married according to Flathead custom. He sent for his half-Cree children, whom Julia raised as her own in a mutually loving relationship. Of this remarkable woman, Binns notes: "Peter loved her increasingly and never considered having any other wife; in time, he even learned to be faithful to her."

Within a year of their marriage, Julia bore Peter a son, the first of their eight or ten children (the record is inconsistent) despite the fact that she was in her thirties when they met. She accompanied him on five of the six expeditions he led, usually carrying an infant and caring for the rest of her brood, who always came along. The only reason she missed going on one trip, the fifth, was that Sir George Simpson ordered Peter Ogden to leave her behind. But on the sixth trip, she defied both Sir George and her husband and went along anyway. Her right to go wherever her husband went was never questioned by either man again.

When urged by his old friend, Dr. John McLoughlin, to marry Julia in a Christian ceremony, Peter Ogden refused, saying: "What more, in God's name, could make it a marriage than a lifetime of living together?"

Ogden died after a brief illness September 27, 1854. Julia moved to Lake la Hache, British Columbia, to live out her years with her daughters, a son-in-law, and grandchildren; many Ogdens live there still. Julia died in 1886 at the age of ninety-eight.

Clusters of Volcanoes

Between Redmond and Bend, mountain peaks, sleeping volcanoes, and rugged wilderness regions lie west of US 97. None of the volcanoes are currently active, but a brief geological hiatus may last from a few thousand to a million years. The fire in the mountains may be considered banked, but not extinguished, for some of the fumaroles along the upper slopes still give off enough heat to melt the surface ice and snow.

Mount Washington and Three Fingered Jack are farthest north. Bachelor Butte, at 9,065 feet, and Broken Top, at 9,175 feet, both show signs of historic volcanic activity. Says geologist Stephen Harris: "The well preserved state of Bachelor Butte suggests that it may now be resting between outbursts. Its Holocene activity possibly indicates that it is still in the cone-building stage and may eventually grow significantly in size and height."

In recent years, a number of popular year-round resorts have been developed in the Bend and Sisters area, with dude ranches, golf courses, and campgrounds in the relatively dry ponderosa pine country of the lower regions, while skiing and wilderness hikes await tourists on the higher slopes. Many peaks, like The Sisters, which top 10,000 feet, are snow-covered year-round. South and west of The Sisters, the adjacent wilderness area contains thirty-seven alpine lakes and 240 miles of hiking trails. Much of the appeal of the area is its remoteness from city traffic and the dryness of its climate compared to the western, rainy side of the mountains.

The Family Mountains

Though history buffs may deplore that theme names in what might have been the Presidents Range stopped with Mounts Washington, Jefferson, and Adams (in southern Washington State), there is a down-to-earth charm in the fact that a trio of the highest, most impressive peaks in the central Oregon Cascades are called the Three Sisters. If a romantic Indian legend inspired the name, I have not found it, nor did the author of *Oregon Geographic Names*, Lewis A. McArthur. He wrote:

> The town of Sisters is just east of the summit of the Cascade Range and is named for the imposing nearby peaks, the Three Sisters. There was previously a post office at Camp Polk, about three miles away, and in 1888 it was found advisable to move the office, and as a result of the move the name was changed, as Camp Polk was no longer significant. It is said that Jacob N. Quilberg selected the new name.

This tells us nothing about the origin of the Three Sisters' names—other than the comfort in seeing that the new postmaster was not vain enough to call them North, Middle, and South Quilberg.

210

Smith Rock State Park near Redmond. —Deschutes County Historical Society

The family theme is carried on in the names of lesser nearby peaks such as Little Brother, The Husband, The Wife, and Bachelor Butte, though The Sphinx is inexplicable. Together, this group of peaks rightly is called "Oregon's volcanic playground." By taking the Cascade Lakes Highway southwest from Bend, you can see lava overflows, mountain meadows, glacial lakes, and an impressive view of snow-covered peaks.

Three Sisters

The North Sister, 10,085 feet, is the oldest mountain in the area, according to geologist Harris, and it is considered the most difficult to climb because its summit consists of almost sheer cliffs of disintegrating rock.

> With a base 15 to 20 miles in diameter, the North Sister was once one of the mightiest volcanoes in the Oregon Cascades, at least 11,000 feet high. During its late stages of activity, it apparently erupted from numerous secondary vents bordering its summit area....
>
> Finally, a massive steep-sided plug of brown-crusted, greenish lava welled up into the main conduit, thrusting aside and displacing many of the earlier dikes and fragmental deposits. Completely filling the volcano's throat, the 300-yard wide plug now forms the the two summit pinnacles, known as the Middle and South Horns.

Other peaks in the area, such as the Middle and South Sisters and The Husband, are lesser replicas of the larger peak. Says Harris:

> The Husband is also remarkable for its two enormous summit plugs. The southern plug measures 600 by 200 yards; the northern one is

Three Sisters viewed from Broken Top. —Deschutes County Historical Society

three quarters of a mile along its major axis and 300 yards along its minor and stands 800 feet high.

Broken Top, 9,175 feet, is one of the largest volcanoes in the Three Sisters constellation. Its summit cone once was much higher than its present peak. Like the North Sister and the inner walls of Crater Lake, Broken Top provides superb "inside views" of how a large volcano is put together, Harris says.

> In its interior, one can see layers of pumice, ash, bombs, basalt blocks, and lava flows. As at Crater Lake, the stratas are brilliantly colored, showing bands of red, purple, and black scoria alternating with yellow, brown, and orange tuffs. A conspicuous stratum of white pumice is strikingly interbedded with chunks of black basalt.

Middle Sister, the smallest of the trio at 10,047 feet, has neither a crater nor an impressive peak, but it does have three sizable glaciers, the Hayden, Diller, and Collier. The Collier Glacier, which is on the north shoulder, seems to have recently stabilized after several decades of shrinking, but it may advance again if the present cooling trend continues.

South Sister, at 10,358 feet, is the highest and best preserved of the three peaks, Harris says, with an almost perfect circular summit crater. He finds it strange that there are no reports of recent activity here, considering the fresh volcanic evidence in the peak's summit area. It's probably because of the relatively short time that people likely to report such things have lived in the area: the town of Bend dates only to 1900.

Before anyone was around to see such cataclysms, Broken Top once erupted in what must have been spectacular fashion, burying the nearby area with twenty to fifty feet of incandescent flows of hot lava, pumice, and ash. "If a comparable eruption were to occur today, many lives would be endangered," Harris warns, adding that "Bend's expanding suburbs, as well as several other towns and villages, are built atop glowing avalanche deposits...."

High Desert Museum

Before such a disaster takes place, you may wish to pay a visit to the High Desert Museum, three miles south of Bend on the east side of US 97. Relatively new, this truly living museum uses the latest eye-catching techniques in its exhibits. Nature trails wind through its rocks and woods, and trained professionals are on hand to introduce such live animals as "Spike," the porcupine, whose twenty thousand quills make him a prickly but lovable character.

Despite its name, the museum includes as much mountain-and-forest-related flora and fauna as desert life. With a forestry building well concealed in timbered country, its logging exhibits include a set of ten-foot wheels used to haul big sections of felled trees out of the forest. For supposedly dry country, a surprising amount of water exists in the form of springs, streams, and pools in which fish spawn, beaver work, and otter play. But always the plants show that in this land of transition between mountain and desert, water must be conserved, not wasted, and they do this in a number of ingenious ways demonstrated by a variety of examples along the museum's nature trails.

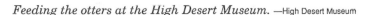

Feeding the otters at the High Desert Museum. —High Desert Museum

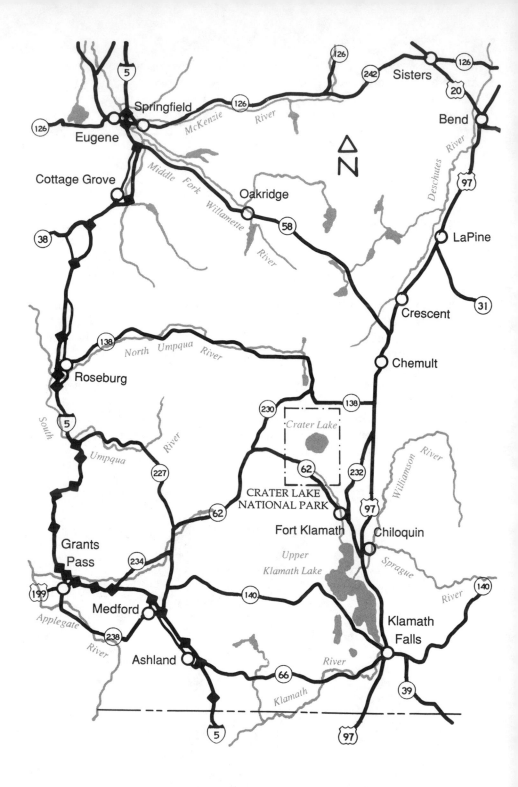

Crater Lake

US 97 angles southwest from Bend for fifty-seven miles at approximately four thousand feet in elevation through mostly national forest land. Skinny lodgepole pine dots the lower plateau, while larger trees such as ponderosa pine and Douglas fir cover the higher slopes of the mountains, which are always in sight both west and east of the highway. Where Oregon 58 intersects the highway from the northwest, having crossed the Cascades through beautiful, scenic lake country from Eugene at the head of the Willamette Valley over the 5,128-foot Willamette Pass, US 97 heads directly south toward the Klamath region.

To visit Crater Lake from Bend or other points north of the lake on US 97, you should turn west on Oregon 138, which intersects with the road leading into the north entrance of Crater Lake National Park after fifteen miles. This road is closed in winter because of heavy snows,

Benham Falls,
southwest of Bend.
—Deschutes County Historical
Society

sometimes as much as fifty feet. But during more clement seasons, the circuit drive around the rim of the lake offers some fantastic views and eventually winds up at Crater Lake Lodge, which is on the south side of the lake.

If you are coming from Klamath Falls area on US 97, turn northwest on Oregon 62 just beyond Klamath Lake to enter the park. Since this road goes on across the Cascades to Medford, it is kept open year-round, as is the entrance to Crater Lake Lodge.

Lightning Rod of the Cascades

A few miles north of Crater Lake and clearly visible from Oregon 138 looms Mount Thielsen. This jagged, Matterhorn-type peak has been struck by lightning so often that it is known as the "lightning rod of the Cascades."

It last erupted perhaps 100,000 years ago, and originally rose a thousand feet higher than its current height of 9,182, says geologist Stephen Harris. The countless lightning strikes to its summit have fused the surface rock particles into "fulgurite," which looks like carrot-shaped tubes of brownish-green glass.

The Bluest Lake

The first white men to view Crater Lake were searching not for a scenic gem but for gold. Following a strike in the Jacksonville area of southern Oregon (near present-day Medford) in the early 1850s, small parties of prospectors fanned out through every remote creek and valley in search of what they hoped would be new bonanzas. On June 12, 1853,

Crater Lake. —Penrose Library, Whitman College

1870s' settler's cabin exhibit at High Desert Museum. —High Desert Museum

three men—John Hillman, Isaac Skeeters, and Henry Klippel—crossed a high ridge and beheld one of the scenic wonders of the world.

Calling it the bluest lake he had ever seen, John Hillman commemorated their discovery by writing "Deep Blue Lake" on a page torn out of a notebook he carried, fastened it to a stick placed in the ground at Discovery Point on the rim of the canyon. Finding no gold in the vicinity, the party quickly moved on.

Nearly ten years later, in 1862, a group of miners returning to Jacksonville from the John Day country, visited the spot again. They described it as "Blue Lake" to a newspaper editor, whose brief article in Jacksonville's *Oregon Sentinel* first acknowledged the lake's existence in print. Three years later the editor mentioned it again following a visit by two soldiers from Fort Klamath, who stumbled across it in 1865; they had renamed it "Lake Majesty." Later still, another Jacksonville newspaper editor visited the site and speculated on how the lake was formed. Concluding that it must be the crater of an extinct volcano, he used the term "Crater Lake," giving it the name it has since retained.

Local Klamath and Modoc Indians had several legends relating the formation of the lake. Because their ancestors were probably around during the cataclysmic event that formed the crater, the legends likely were based on eyewitness accounts and passed down through the generations by word of mouth with surprising accuracy. But because the

Crater Lake's Phantom Ship. —Penrose Library, Whitman College

native Americans regarded such natural wonders as creations of the spirit gods, they felt that they would be punished by the gods if they talked about or visited such sacred places too often, so they were reluctant to tell white men about them.

The Father of Crater Lake

"The person most intimately associated with Crater Lake was William G. Steel," writes K. R. Cranson, a geologist and ranger at Crater Lake National Park for seven years, and author of *Crater Lake, Gem of the Cascades*. From the moment he first saw the stupendous crater and the incredible blue waters of the lake in August 1885, William Gladstone Steel knew that this scenic marvel must be preserved for the enjoyment of everyone. He spent the rest of his life achieving that goal and, finally, in 1902, Congress inducted Crater Lake as the fifth national park in the United States.

"The first official soundings of Crater Lake were made by the Geological Survey party of July 1886," writes Stanton C. Lapham in his intriguing book *The Enchanted Lake*. "Will G. Steel had been appointed by the government to prepare boats and equipment for the soundings and to have charge of the work. Three boats were built in Portland, and shipped to Ashland by rail, and then hauled one hundred miles by wagon to the Lake."

The Deepest Lake

In an earlier attempt to check the depth of the lake, a man using a six hundred foot line had found no bottom. No one in Steel's party believed that the lake could be that deep. Getting into a boat and pulling out a short distance from shore, the Steel party cast the lead attached to their sounding line, which passed over a pulley in the back of the boat. With intense interest, they watched it sink.

> The line recorded the six hundred foot mark, and then eight hundred and nine hundred. Still, the lead went down. Something must be wrong with the sounding apparatus, they thought. The machine was stopped and when it was ascertained that it was working properly the lead was again sent on its way plumbing the unknown cerulean depths.
> The line reached a thousand feet, and then one hundred, two hundred feet more, and at one thousand two hundred and ten feet it rested on the bottom.

Still deeper spots were found later. Crater Lake is the deepest lake in the United States, plunging 1,932 feet. Since the average rim of the crater is two thousand feet above the surface of the lake, the drop from the rim to the lake's bottom is nearly four thousand feet.

Because of its great depth, Crater Lake maintains an extraordinarily constant temperature at about 39 degrees. Some say it never freezes; occasionally in bitter cold weather a skim of ice may form, but it doesn't last long. Those brave enough to try a swim during the blazing heat of summer can attest that long hours of sunshine also do not affect the water temperature.

Almost all the water in Crater Lake fell directly from the sky. Its watershed for surface runoff is very small and erosion is minimal. The water is as pure as water can be. Its clarity is remarkable.

A Bucket Full of Minnows

Though I have not been able to verify Lapham's statement that: "They are the hardest fighting trout in the world!" I will convey the statement he made in 1931 that a nameless fisherman "equipped with light tackle, spinners and flies, held up four Crater Lake trout, deep-bodied, thick through, measuring from 16 to 28 inches in length, totalling fifteen and a half pounds. And the biggest one—36 inches long."

If such rainbow and black-spotted trout were being caught at Crater Lake in 1931, the person to be thanked for planting their ancestors was William Steel, for at the time of its discovery there apparently were no fish in the lake and no natural way for them to get there.

Stanton Lapham tells a story in *The Enchanted Lake* about William Steel heading to Crater Lake in 1888 and stopping over at a friend's home on the Rogue River, forty-nine miles from the lake. Steel decided to take along some minnows from the river, so his friend's sons caught some for him. Steel told the boys he would pay them ten cents for every minnow they provided. Next morning, as he was about to leave, the boys delivered hundreds of trout minnows in an old wooden tub. Not at all sure that he could afford to pay the price he had offered, he asked the two boys how much they would take for the tub full. The older boy said four-bits—fifty cents—would be about right. Considerably relieved, he gave them each a silver dollar.

> He dipped out a bucket full of water and fish, estimating that it contained six hundred fingerlings. Tying mosquito netting over the top, he placed the bucket in the wagon, but at the first lurch the water began splashing out. He jumped from the wagon, refilled the bucket and started out ahead, walking the entire forty-nine miles to Crater Lake, bucket in hand. At each mountain stream along the way he stopped, dug a hole in the sand or gravel and placed the bucket in the water so fresh water would flow in.

When he reached the lake toward evening of the second day, he noticed that in spite of his efforts to keep their water fresh, many of the fingerlings were going belly-up. Before making camp, he picked his way down two thousand feet of rocky slope to the shore of the lake, where he plunged the bucket into the water.

> Removing the mosquito netting, he awaited results. Gradually a few fish revived and swam over the edge of the bucket. He counted them, and the first planting of fish in Crater Lake numbered thirty-seven Rainbow trout.
>
> Over a period of ten years, no fish were seen in the lake. Then a few were taken, one of which measured thirty inches in length.

Ten Townships Set Aside for Park

In the mid-1880s the idea of setting aside unique areas because of their scenery, beauty, or natural wonders was relatively new in the United States. Oregon Territory's 1850 Donation Land Act and the federal Homestead Act of 1862 allowed people to claim land and secure ownership with minimal or no financial investment, which was great for individuals. But the idea that national park areas should be set aside for the future use and benefit of all the people seemed to many citizens a mighty radical notion.

Yellowstone, the first national park, was established in 1872. But for years it remained a wilderness known to and visited by very few people, for Congress refused to appropriate funds for its development. In California a nature-lover named John Muir, who certainly was a radical for his day, made such a fuss about preserving some big trees, cliffs, and waterfalls in the Sierras that the federal government created the second, third, and fourth national parks—Yosemite, Sequoia, and Kings Canyon—in 1890.

At the same time, William Steel clamored to preserve Crater Lake, but the only action he could get out of President Grover Cleveland in the late 1880s was a withdrawl of ten townships—360 square miles—from the Homestead Act while the pros and cons about making the area into a national park could be threshed out.

The Vanished Mountain

Local Indian legends told fanciful tales about a tall mountain that had once existed and of an epic battle between a spirit god of the sky and a spirit god of the depths over the love of a beautiful maiden. At the height of the battle, the tall mountain exploded and vanished, leaving behind an immense crater which eventually filled with water.

Geologists in the 1880s could see clearly enough that a high peak once had existed on the spot, that an explosion had taken place, and that a large lake now filled the crater. As late as 1931, when writer Stanton Lapham speculated that a mountain 17,000 or 18,000 feet high must have occupied the area, more knowledgeable geologists felt that his figures were exaggerated. The vanished peak probably was no more than 12,000 feet high, they said. But they were unable to answer the perplexing question: If such a big mountain exploded, where did the pieces go? Certainly there was not enough lava rock rubble, ash, or pumice in the area to account for such a peak, let alone for the immense crater left behind.

The Mazamas

Meanwhile, William Steel occupied himself with what he considered a more important matter—organizing a group of people to support the preservation of Crater Lake as a national park. Steel's favorite pastime, climbing mountains, put him frequently on the slopes of Mount Hood, not far from his Portland home. He belonged to several mountain-climbing groups, but these independent-minded people resisted his efforts to organize into an influential unit. Finally, he managed to form the Oregon Alpine Club.

Conceived and launched in 1887, the Oregon Alpine Club included not only mountain-climbers as members but also took in campers and other outdoors enthusiasts. Because of their diverse interests, the members did not stick together very well. So, Steel decided to create a more exclusive group called "the Mazamas."

Open only to those who had reached the 11,235-foot summit of Mount Hood, charter membership in the Mazama Club would be restricted to those who participated in a mass climb of that peak on July 19, 1894. In spite of a sudden storm and other unexpected adversities, 155 men and 38 women reached the top of Mount Hood that day. These charter members were declared the most unique mountain-climbing group in the United States—the Mazama Club.

Mount Mazama

In the Indian tongue, Mazama means "mountain goat." As president of the Mazama Club, in which the membership soon included a number of scientists, educators, politicians, and people who knew how to make themselves heard in high places, William Steel frequently visited Washington, D.C., where he continued to press for the establishment of Crater Lake National Park. In his report for the year 1895, he recommended that the Mazamas make their next annual expedition to Crater Lake early in August.

That next summer several hundred people, including a number of Indians from the nearby Fort Klamath Reservation, gathered at Crater Lake. The meeting of the executive council of the Mazamas was held in the Witches' Cauldron, the crater atop Wizard Island, eight hundred feet above the surface of the lake. Prominent experts attended the meeting and the subsequent campfire lectures on biology, rocks, volcanism, and mystery of how the crater and the lake formed. Their presence not only assured that Congress would notice the efforts to preserve the area as a national park, but this meeting also initiated a scientific examination of this scenic wonder.

Thirty-five years later, Stanton Lapham wrote:

> The crowning accomplishment of this historic gathering of Mazamas at Crater Lake was the inauguration of Mazama Day, August 21st, 1896. There was enacted on that occasion one of the most unique ceremonies relative to geological fact and fancy ever witnessed in the naming and christening of a great ice-clasped, fiery volcano, once among the mightiest, consumed and falling within the gulf containing Crater Lake....

Obtaining a bottle of water at Wizard Island, Fay Fuller, the first historian of the Mazamas, carried it up to the rim of the crater above the lake, shattered it against a rock, and declared: "I dedicate thee Mount Mazama."

The task to which the scientists now had to apply their skills was reconstructing the vanished mountain and putting together a reasonable explanation of what had happened to it.

A Giant Stirs

The basin occupied by Crater Lake covers an oval area measuring five by six miles. To explore its mysteries, visitors can descend a trail to the water's edge and take a launch tour of the lake, getting a spectacular view from water level of the inner shell of a now-quiet volcano. Friendly and informative park rangers advise that the lake is newly formed, geologically speaking, for it has been there only 6,600 years. At its maximum height, Mount Mazama probably towered 12,000 feet and the buildup to the series of eruptions preceding its final cataclysmic explosion was probably relatively short—a mere million years.

"As it approached full stature, it may have resembled Sicily's Mt. Etna," geologist Stephen Harris writes, "which is also a vast complex of superimposed cones. Like Etna, Mt. Mazama was probably a broad, gently sloping dome, bristling with subsidiary vents."

Over a period of many years, thirteen cinder domes inside the park boundary and eleven more beyond erupted on a minor scale. During quiet interludes, glaciers advanced, retreated, then advanced again. Finally, as a prelude to the final cataclysm, a series of violently explosive eruptions began. Harris describes the scene:

> First, immense quantities of dacite pumice were blown high into the air from vents on the north slope. Mixed with this coarse pumice were angular chunks of old rock—andesite fragments ripped from the mountain itself. Thick layers of pumice and boulders were deposited all over the mountain, but chiefly on the north and east side, where they now lie 50 to 100 feet deep. Afterward, glowing avalanches rushed down the northeast flank of the volcano, leaving a thick stratum of welded tuff.

The Final Eruption

Geologists can only reconstruct the climactic explosion in terms of similar eruptions that have been seen and recorded. In modern times, only two caldera-forming eruptions similar to that of Mount Mazama have taken place. The first was the Sumatra volcano, Krakatoa, in 1883; the other is Mount St. Helens, in 1980. While those who witnessed the St. Helens explosion firsthand or by means of pictures were awed by its power, it was modest compared to that of Krakatoa, which was the most violent eruption in recorded history. Like Mazama, Krakatoa's peak collapsed into the cavity created by the expulsion of its magma.

223

The Mazama eruption began rather mildly, with a west wind carrying ash and small lumps of pumice east into the desert of central Oregon. But, as the explosions increased in intensity, the wind veered to the northeast, transporting ash over hundreds of thousands of square miles. Near the base of the volcano, ash covered the land with a blanket twenty feet deep, while seventy miles northeast of Mazama the initial ashfall measured a foot deep.

Harris writes:

> In 1883, Krakatoa's explosion clouds soared an estimated 20 miles into the stratosphere, where high winds swept them around the globe. It is possible that Mazama's cauliflower clouds rose even higher, for fine powdery ash drifted over an area of incredible extent: most of Oregon, Washington, Idaho, northern Nevada, western Montana, part of Wyoming, southern British Columbia, Alberta, and even Saskatchewan. The ash wafting through the stratosphere must have produced brilliant sunsets throughout the whole northern hemisphere. Ancestors of the Druids in England and Gaul may have observed this atmospheric phenomenon and wondered what it portended.

On the ground, avalanches of incandescent particles raced down the slopes, following the valley of the Rogue River for forty miles, incinerating thick stands of timber. Other branches ran north to Diamond Lake and the valley of the North Umpqua, leaving deposits of pumice up to thirty feet thick.

Following the loss of its inner supporting material, Mount Mazama's peak collapsed, leaving the huge, gaping hole that would become Crater Lake. The canyons extending into the earth must have resembled a "Valley of Ten Thousand Smokes." Harris sums up the lingering dilemma:

> Where a snow-capped peak once towered, there was now only a colossal depression, five to six miles wide and nearly 4000 feet deep. The dust-smeared Indian of 6600 years ago must have asked himself the same question that scientists still endeavor to answer: where did Mt. Mazama go? Was it blown apart by the earth-shaking explosions? Or did it subside into a subterranean pit of its own making?

Everywhere, Nowhere

Geologists seem to agree that the mystery of what happened to a big piece of Mount Mazama may never be solved. In their *Roadside Geology of Oregon*, David Alt and Donald Hyndman write:

> As it happens, only a small part of the debris blanket surrounding Mount Mazama consists of chunks of old volcanic rock. Most of it is freshly-erupted pumice and ash. So Mount Mazama could not have

blown itself apart and must have simply subsided as the eruption withdrew magma from beneath it.

The eruption surely included some mighty explosions but they blew fresh pumice, not volcanic rock, all over the landscape.

Geologists estimate that approximately ten to twelve cubic miles of rock erupted from Mount Mazama during its last great outburst, and that fifteen to seventeen cubic miles of mountain disappeared. Alt and Hyndman add: "Both estimates are difficult to make and obviously are subject to all sorts of uncertainties. But the difference between them is still too large to be ignored. No one is quite sure how to account for it."

A Rare Gem

Experts and laymen are certain, however, that Crater Lake is a treasure worth preserving. As finally established in 1902, Crater Lake National Park covers 286 square miles. Since its only drainage is by slow seepage through the lake's bottom almost two thousand feet down, if it ever becomes polluted it will be a long time cleansing itself, geologists warn. Crater Lake represents a closed, extremely fragile system. It would be extremely difficult, if not altogether impossible, to renew the water in Crater Lake.

Recently, scientists have begun to explore the bottom of the lake with a small submarine equipped with an underwater camera, in hopes of solving such mysteries as its drainage system and what might happen if deep wells were drilled in the area outside the park. They agree that the lake is too rare a gem to risk any venture that might alter its delicate balance.

OR 62, US 97
Crater Lake—Klamath Falls
60 miles

From Crater Lake Lodge to Klamath Falls the route along Oregon 62 and US 97 drops three thousand feet from heavily timbered mountain slopes to the marshy, open country of Agency Lake and Upper Klamath Lake, the largest body of fresh water in the state. Though these extensive shallow lakes long have been a haven for migrating birds, they never contained many of the prized beaver so fiercely competed for by the British and American fur trappers during the Joint Occupancy period of 1818-46.

In August 1825, Finan McDonald and Thomas McKay led a party of Hudson's Bay Company trappers from Fort Vancouver on a mission to search out a legendary lake thought to feed the headwaters of the fabled Buenaventura River, and travel downstream through Spanish territory to the Pacific Ocean. If they ran into any American trappers, they were to "discourage" them by any means short of violence, which meant trapping the country bare so the Americans would have no reason to ever come back. Quickly discouraged themselves by a lack of beaver and threat of hostile Indians, the party never made it beyond the southern Cascades.

Born into a prominent Scottish family in 1782, Finan McDonald began his trapping career with the North West Company in 1804, later transferring his allegiance to Hudson's Bay Company when the two enterprises merged. Highly respected by both Indians and whites, and married to a Spokane Indian woman, the red-haired, bearded McDonald stood six-feet four and feared neither man nor beast. Although he usually spoke English with a Gaelic accent, the *History of Klamath County* tells us that McDonald could let loose a "patois of Gaelic, English, French, and a half-dozen Indian languages" when angered.

Tom McKay, McDonald's junior by fifteen or so years, was the son of a Cree woman and a Scotchman named Alexander McKay, who had been one of John Jacob Astor's partners killed in the 1811 *Tonquin* massacre. Though never given his rightful position of leadership in the Hudson's Bay Company because of Sir George Simpson's bias against any person of Indian blood, Tom McKay had further solidified his relations with the Indians by marrying the eldest daughter of the Chinooks' Chief Concomly. Well regarded by all who met him, McKay earned high praise from the great biologist J.K. Townsend, who once wrote: "I am much pleased with this gentleman. He unites the free, frank and open manners of the mountain man with the grace and affability of the Frenchman."

Crossing the Cascades over what would become Santiam Pass, the Hudson's Bay party traveled south up the Deschutes River into the unexplored Klamath country, trapping as they went. The thirty-two seasoned mountain men in the brigade got poor results for their hard work, bringing back only 460 pelts from the region. Though the Klamaths were friendly enough, they warned the white men that the Indians farther south were both numerous and hostile.

With beaver scarce and hostiles plentiful, McDonald recalled a brutal trip a year or so earlier to the Snake River. His party got four thousand pelts, but six white men and sixty-eight Indians died. He said: "I got safe home from the Snake Cuntre, thank God, and when that Cuntre will see me again the beaver will have Goulde skin." This time he decided he'd rather turn back, so the party made canoes and descended the Deschutes River. When they got to the mouth of Crooked River, they met Peter

Skene Ogden, who enlisted McKay as his second in command with the intention of returning to the Klamath country the following spring.

Finan McDonald continued on to his wife and children at Fort Vancouver, then headed back east to Ontario for a well-deserved rest after twenty years in the wilderness. But Peter Skene Ogden and Thomas McKay were still young, energetic, and eager to explore and conquer new country in the name of the company and the crown.

Ogden's well-equipped party of fifty men, some with Indian wives and children, one hundred horses, and servants camped near the Link River before heading south. But game was scarce and they didn't want to kill any of their horses because the animals were needed to transport their baggage, so the party purchased dogs to eat from the Indians—172 on one occasion, 48 on another, which pretty well wiped out the local canine population. It is interesting to note that the Klamath Indians would never eat their dogs, no matter how hungry they got.

Calling what later became Klamath Lake "Dog Lake," and Dry Lake "New Years Lake" because they spent the first day of the year there, the Ogden party reached the headwaters of the Klamath River on January 13, 1827. In his journal, Ogden wrote:

> The river here is a fine large stream one-quarter mile wide, deep and lined with willows, taking as far as the eye can see a southern course.... This is certainly a strange country, in no direction can we possible travel without seeing lakes....
>
> Hot and boiling springs are numerous in this quarter. No less than four in a short distance from our camp....

The hot springs are indeed numerous and in use today to heat homes and supply geothermal electrical power. Mount Mazama's inner fires keep its furnace fueled six thousand years and counting since its last eruption.

Paiute exhibit.
—High Desert Museum

The poor results of Ogden's expedition into the Klamath country kept the Hudson's Bay Company from building a trading post in the area. Trappers mostly avoided the region until 1843, when a party of Americans led by Old Bill Williams returned. At the age of fifty-six and having survived as a mountain man in Indian country for thirty years, the red-haired, gaunt Williams was as tough as a hickory knot and full of wilderness wisdom. He and his party of forty-two free trappers got along well with the good-natured Klamath Indians, who traded, hunted, camped, and shared food with the Americans. But the Modocs, who lived just south of the Klamaths, refused to smoke the peace pipe when it was offered to them, then arrogantly demanded horses, hides, weapons, and anything else of value the trappers had.

Old Bill Defies the Modocs

Old Bill Williams knew of the Modocs' reputation as deadly fighters, so he and his party holed up in a patch of trees with a good spring six miles east of Lost River and braced to wait for contact. Besides their muzzle-loading pistols and rifles, which could fire only four rounds a minute at best, the mountain men had revolvers and double-barreled shotguns and the usual assortment of knives and axes.

"Wrapping themselves in water-soaked blacktail deerskins for protection against the Modocs' legendary poisonous arrows," says the Klamath County Historical Society's *Klamath County History*, "they were thoroughly prepared for an assault by daybreak the following morning."

Soon after eight o'clock, two hundred Modocs approached the trappers' fort. Holding up their hands to signify their peaceful intentions, two chiefs met Old Bill Williams in a clearing between the opposing forces. In sign language, which he understood perfectly, they again demanded the property of the mountain men. In graphic sign language, he refused. The two chiefs then contemptuously rubbed one hand over the other, which clearly indicated to Old Bill that they intended to rub out the intruders. He signed in reply an acceptance to their challenge.

Both parties walked backward as they separated, warily eyeing each other. The Modocs outnumbered the trappers five to one. But the mountain men were fortified and better armed. Half of the Indians dismounted and charged on foot, while the other half attacked on horseback.

The first skirmish ended with losses for both sides: fifteen Modocs fell dead a short distance from the breastwork, and three of the trappers died. A brief truce allowed the Modoc women to haul away the dead warriors. In subsequent assaults it became clear that the whites had the upper hand, so the Modocs withdrew and stayed clear of the mountain men. But conflict intensified their hatred for Americans.

Fremont and Kit Carson

Though never proved, it probably was Modocs who once attacked a party led by the explorer Captain John C. Fremont, who came through the Klamath country at least twice between 1844 and 1846. Fremont later ran for president as the "Great American Pathfinder," a term he never would have called himself, for he knew his role more as that of a "pathmarker." Serving as guides during all of Fremont's expeditions were mountain men such as Kit Carson, Thomas Fitzpatrick, and Old Bill Williams—men who had prowled the streams and valleys across the West and had indelibly etched in their memories the lay of the land and how to get from here to there. But while their maps resided only in their heads, Fremont had the skills, tools, and government cartographers to set their knowledge down on paper so that it could be readily used by others.

While traveling through the Klamath country in late December 1845, the Fremont party recorded a strange experience:

> The air was dark with falling snow which everywhere weighed down the trees. The depths of the forest were profoundly still, and below we scarcely felt a breath of the wind which whirled the snow through their branches.
>
> Toward noon, we found ourselves on the verge of a vertical and rocky wall of the mountain. At our feet, more than a thousand feet below, we looked into a green prairie country in which a beautiful lake was spread along the foot of the mountain, its shores bordered with green grass. Just then the sun broke out among the clouds and illuminated the country below while around us the storm raged fiercely.
>
> Shivering in snow three feet deep and stiffening in a cold north wind, we exclaimed at once that the names of Summer Lake and Winter Ridge should be applied to these two proximate places of sudden and violent contrast.

Near Klamath Lake, Indians attacked Fremont's party and killed three of its members. Though the Indians probably were Modocs bearing a grudge from the lost battle with Old Bill Williams, Kit Carson took ten men and brashly retaliated on the nearest native village, which happened to be a band of Klamaths almost certainly innocent of any wrongdoing. No matter. To Carson and his ilk, an Indian was an Indian.

Southern Emigrant Road

By 1846, settlers in the upper reaches of the Willamette Valley sensed a need to encourage development of an emigrant road to bring people directly into their part of Oregon Territory, bypassing both the dreadful water passage through the Columbia River Gorge and the alternative horrible route over the Cascades on the infamous Barlow Toll Road. Asked which was worse, most travelers said: "Whichever route you take, you'll wish you'd taken the other."

In early June 1846, Jesse and Lindsay Applegate and a dozen other men went to see Levi Scott on his claim near the small settlement of Yoncalla (between Roseburg and Eugene) and asked him to join their effort to open a new route across southern Oregon. Fifteen strong, they rode south into the Siskiyou Mountains, ferried across Rogue River near present-day Grants Pass, struck Bear Creek near Medford, then traveled in an easterly direction toward Lower Klamath and Tule Lake in northern California. They crossed rugged country of steep mountain slopes covered with big trees, which were regarded in those days not as treasured assets but as a nuisance to trail-building and farming. Lindsay Applegate described their relief at the sight finally before them:

> After noon we moved down through an immense forest ... when all at once we came out in full view of the Klamath country, extending eastward as far as the eye could reach. It was an exciting moment, after many days spent in the dense forests and among the mountains, and the whole party broke forth in cheer after cheer.

A band of Modocs near Tule Lake fled at the sight of the white men, leaving only one old woman "shaking and trembling as though she were dying with fright." She made peaceful overtures to the white strangers by presenting them a stick of dried fish, which failed to whet their appetites. They handed it back to her and rode on. Soon smoke signals rising from distant hilltops announced the aliens' intrusion to all the "digger" Indians—a catch-all term applying especially to Paiutes but also to other desert-dwelling bands that dug for roots in treeless reaches of the northern Great Basin.

This part of the great interior basin was a strange, forbidding country. Rivers had no outlets to the ocean, sometimes vanishing from sight below lava fields, other times turning into disappearing pools; water in the stagnant lakes simply sat there until it evaporated, leaving behind brackish, salt-encrusted marshes and flats useful only to waterfowl and some varieties of fish but worthless for drinking or irrigation.

Passing near Clear Lake and Goose Lake, the proposed route then angled northeast across the high desert country of southern Oregon toward the existing Oregon Trail near Fort Hall at the juncture of the Portneuf with the Snake River. Here, the Scott-Applegate party met a wagon train from Missouri, which it persuaded to try the new route.

The Pringle Party

Virgil K. Pringle, his wife Pheona, daughters Virgilia, Sarelia, and Emma, sons Clark, Alero, and Octavius, along with his mother-in-law, Tabitha Moffet Brown, had left Hickory Grove in Warren County, Missouri, on April 15, 1846. By the time they reached Fort Hall, the emigrants had traveled 1,400 miles, and as the first to try the new Southern Oregon Wagon Road they certainly qualified as pioneers. But the most unique member of their party and a woman long to be remembered in Oregon was the mother, Tabitha Brown.

Even though sixty-six years old and a widow, she drove her own ox teams and handled her own wagon, assisted only, says the WPA guide to Oregon, "by an aged relative." The truly remarkable quality about her was not just that she survived the grueling trip in good health, but that she had enough energy and spirit when she finally reached Oregon to remedy its pressing need for schools and teachers.

Hardships on the Trail

But such civilized triumphs lay far in the future, for the most pressing matter in 1846 was survival. In the Tule Lake area, the hostile and aggressive Indians moved the emigrants to name "Hopeless Pass" and "Bloody Point" as hurdles to cross before they could reach their goal. Indians scattered the cattle at Tule Lake: it took a full day to round them back up; ten head never were found.

Crossing Lost River on a natural bridge, the fifty-wagon party camped on the shore of Lower Klamath Lake early in October. By the time it moved on into the Rogue River Valley, illness, breakdowns, exhaustion, and worsening weather began to take their toll. Mr. Crowley's fourteen-year-old daughter died and was buried as the emigrants struggled through the Umpquas on a road described as nearly impassable.

One emigrant wrote:

> Started through on Monday morning and reached the opposite plain on Friday night after a series of hardships, breakdowns and being constantly wet and laboring hard and very little to eat, the provisions being exhausted in the whole company. We ate our last meal the evening we got through.
>
> The wet season commenced the second day after we started through the mountains and continued until the first of November, which was a partially fair day. The distance through, 16 miles. There is a great loss of property and suffering, no bread, live entirely on beef, leave one wagon.

1890s' emigrants in the Bend area. —Deschutes County Historical Society

Tabitha Brown later wrote:

> The canyon was strewn with dead cattle, broken wagons, beds, clothing, and everything but provisions, of which latter we were nearly all destitute. Some people were in the canyon two or three weeks before they could get through.

Recognizing the seriousness of their situation, Pringle sent his fourteen-year-old son, Octavius, across the Calapooyas for provisions. The oxen became so weak that the women and girls had to walk.

"Had nothing to eat yesterday for supper," Pringle wrote. "A beef killed in camp and we got the paunch and upper part of head, which did us till Monday for breakfast. Rains all day. 1 mile."

After eating the last of the beef tripe, they headed on and were happy to run into some Indians who sold them six venison hams. They were even happier when Octavius returned with half a bushel of peas and forty pounds of flour.

Despite its difficulties, between 450 and 500 settlers came out to Oregon by way of the Applegate Trail in 1846. At the end of her long and arduous journey, Tabitha Brown recalled: "On Christmas day, at 2 p.m. I entered the house of the Methodist minister, the first house I had set my feet in for nine months."

Tabitha Brown's School

Though she was practically penniless when she reached the Willamette Valley, Tabitha Brown possessed a wealth of energy and ideas. On a visit to Tualatin Plains, the idea of a boarding school for orphans occurred to her. Less than a year after arriving in Oregon she began conducting classes in a log church. The settlers quickly embraced her goals and started sending their children to her.

Eventually, the institution she established became one of the most prestigious places of learning in Oregon. Located in Forest Grove, Tualatin Academy was just twenty-three miles southwest of Portland. American educators Henry Ward Beecher, Edward Everett Hale, and Samuel B. Morse were among those who offered time and money to keep the academy going. Harvey Scott, editor of the *Oregonian* for fifty years, was a student in its first graduating class in 1863.

The Tragic Year

Though a large migration used the Applegate Trail in 1852, it was a summer marked by violence and death. At Bloody Point on Tule Lake hostile Indians killed seven of eight packers in late July. On August 1 at the same spot, a pair of guides who got too far ahead of the two wagon trains for which they were scouting also were killed. The first train, made up of thirty men, a woman, and a boy, was besieged by Indians for eighteen hours until joined by the second group. Meanwhile, the sole survivor of the original assault on the packers had made his way to Yreka in northern California, where a man named Ben Wright put together a force of twenty-seven men to go to the aid of the emigrants. In a bloody fight with the Indians, Wright's band killed thirty hostiles, but afterward counted the bodies of thirty-two white emigrants.

Another company of volunteers from Jacksonville, Oregon, found an additional fourteen bodies, which brought the total number of white people killed at Tule Lake in 1852 to fifty-five. Warned before reaching the area, subsequent wagon trains were combined into larger parties east of Clear Lake and given heavier guards to forestall further attacks.

Despite its hazards, the Applegate Trail was used by more than a thousand emigrants in 1853, traveling in over 250 wagons and bringing in large herds of livestock. Because of the influx of whites and the increasing hostility of the Indians, it became apparent to the regional and federal governments that some sort of treaties must be made defining the lands on which the Indians could live and the whites could settle—which meant keeping the two races as far apart as possible. In the meantime, military posts would be built in suitable locations where soldiers could be posted to enforce the peace. One of these was Fort Klamath.

Fort Klamath

Having crossed the country in the great migration of 1843 with his brothers Jesse and Charles, Lindsay Applegate, who became a member of the Oregon State Legislature, long had felt that the Indians should be dealt with firmly but justly. He had served as a captain of a company of mounted volunteers during the bitter, bloody Rogue River Indian War in 1855 and knew that violence solved little. As a member of the legislature, he secured passage of a resolution calling for the establishment of a military post in the Klamath country.

"About 1861, the Rogue River settlements were plagued by an influx of Klamath, Modoc, and Paiute Indians," writes Theodore Stern in his excellent ethnic history, *The Klamath Tribe*, "who were soon supporting themselves by trading with the whites, by theft, and by prostitution of their women. They expressed themselves as eager to sell their lands."

In 1863 a new military post was authorized, to be built in the heart of Klamath country beteen Fort Creek and Wood River. Lindsay Applegate, by then a private citizen since his office lapsed for "lack of authorized pay," bitterly opposed its location at first, certain that it could not accomplish its mission. But before it could be built anywhere, the long-standing warfare waged by the Klamath and Modoc against the Shasta and Pit River tribes must be ended before it embroiled white people living in the area.

It was a common misconception among white people in those days that Indians living in the same contiguous area should get along with one another when placed on the same reservation. But, as with some European nations in hotbeds such as the Balkan countries, where hatreds running back many generations made conflict inevitable every time they met, some tribes of Indians whose members looked alike, spoke the same tongue, and lived just over the hill or across the river from one another hated their neighbors bitterly.

Frequently, bands of Indians on poor terms with each other—such as the Klamaths and Modocs—would put aside their differences long enough to ally against an enemy they hated more than each other, such as the Shasta and Pit River tribes. Suspecting some of the white settlers of having sided with the Shastas, who had killed several Klamath and Modoc warriors, Captain George, accepted by both the Klamaths and the Modocs as their war chief, began stealing cattle, robbing travelers, inciting rumors of impending war.

In response to a citizen petition, Colonel Charles S. Drew promptly arrested Captain George and a "troublesome colleague named Skookum Jack" and summarily hanged them both, ending that source of conflict before it got out of hand. The Indians, not surprisingly, found these measures profoundly unsettling, and sought out their friend, Lindsay Applegate, who wrote:

> They complain bitterly of these things, but say they do not want war with the whites. If the bill before Congress proposing to make treaties with these Indians passes, we will be saved in all probability from an Indian war, for the course that Drew is pursuing toward them will, I think, if not counteracted in some way, certainly lead to war.

A Modoc chief named Schonchin expressed the anguish, frustration, and resignation of his people when he said:

> I thought if we killed all the white men we saw, that no more would come. We killed all we could; but they came more and more like new grass in the spring. I looked around and saw that many of our young men were dead and could not come back to fight. My heart was sick. My people were few. I threw down my gun. I said, "I will not fight again." I made friends with the white man.

FORT KLAMATH INDIAN RESERVATION

Treaty of 1864

Signed willingly in December 1869 by twenty-one Klamath leaders and reluctantly by three Modocs and two Paiutes, the treaty ratified by Congress on February 17, 1864, writes historian Theodore Stern, marked "the passage of the Indians—who came to be designated the Klamath tribe—from a stage of sovereign independence to a place under the government of the United States, and more directly under the supervision of an Agent."

To live unmolested by the whites proved so important to the 710 Klamaths, 339 Modocs, and 22 Paiutes that even though forced onto a reservation by the Indian commissioners, they consented to live in peace and friendship with one another and to give up to the soldiers any person who violated this principle. The Indians also agreed to permit whites free passage through their country, charging them only ferry passage across rivers or for guiding services.

Imposing some of the settlers' concerns, the treaty also forbade the Indians from getting drunk in the settlements or white camps; being in these areas at night; stealing—even from the Chinese miners; selling children; or selling women, unless the buyer married her first under authority of a judge.

As with all Indian tribes throughout the West, the government's extensive program of policies and treaties sought to change these hunting and gathering people into American-style farmers in less than a generation. Writes Stern:

It was even envisaged that [the Indians] should at some time privately own the land they tilled, though without the power to alienate it. The terms of the payment make it very probable that both parties to the treaty thought the Indians would be able to attain self-sufficiency by the end of twenty years.

"Fort Klamath! The most beautiful Frontier post that any soldier was permitted to occupy!"

This seemed to be the consensus of opinion regarding the beautiful Wood River Valley in which the fort was established, says *Klamath County History*, though no testimony by any of the enlisted men who served there has been entered into the record. That it is a place of abundant water, timber, grass, and scenic beauty is as evident today as it was then.

The original garrison, Troop C of the First Oregon Cavalry, under the command of Captain William Kelley, arrived in the fall of 1863. During their first winter, the men lived in tents. With winter temperatures sometimes below zero and heavy snowfalls common, being "permitted to occupy" the post must have been a dubious honor for the troops.

The first order of business the following spring was to build a sawmill for turning the many trees growing nearby into lumber, an industry that proved a substantial benefit to both Indians and whites who lived in the area. During the post's twenty-seven years and sixteen commanders between 1863 and 1890, the pinnacle of its existence came during the Modoc War.

Captain Jack

During the time the treaties were being negotiated, the Modocs were led by an aggressive chief named Captain Jack. Of him, one historian wrote: "Captain Jack had become contaminated by association with the Whites about Yreka, where he had learned all their vices and none of their virtues."

Even though he signed the treaty which committed his people to live on the Klamath Reservation, he so hated the conditions there that he led rebellious groups of Modocs back to their homeland, which was neither extensive nor particularly picturesque, but the land near the mouth of Tule Lake is where they had lived from time immemorial. Finding increasing numbers of white people settling there, he harassed them by destroying their fences, stealing their hay, and threatening their lives.

Fort Klamath's Major Jackson forwarded affadavits from the settlers of Captain Jack's depredations to headquarters in Portland, where the documents were studied, then returned with a request for further information in "a specimen of red-tape that would have done credit to an older and better organized department than that then existing in Oregon."

According to *Klamath County History*, "what the Modoc Indians really wanted was the Lost River system," which flowed ninety miles from its source at Clear Lake to the non-draining sump called Tule Lake.

While it might be claimed that the Modocs had ceded title to their homeland by the Treaty of 1864, white settlers had begun squatting there without legal right several years earlier. Jesse Applegate had suggested that the Modocs be granted a township-sized reservation—six miles square—where the Lost River joined Tule Lake. But neither the federal nor state government would tolerate such a "waste" of public lands. So the commandant of Fort Klamath was ordered to return Captain Jack and the others to the reservation—"peacefully if you can but forcibly if you must!"

Thus, the Modoc War—one of the most expensive Indian wars in the history of the country—began.

Battle of the Lava Beds

The first shots rang out in November 1872, when Lieutenant Frazier Boutelle exchanged bullets with a Modoc named Scarface Charley. Several soldiers and Indians died in the ensuing skirmish. Provoked by a surprise attack from a cavalry troop on a band of Indians near Tule Lake, the Indians retaliated in kind on a party of white men and boys nearby, killing eighteen.

Captain Jack and about sixty warriors took familiar shelter in the lava beds, where an endless number of caves and tunnels gave them a defensive advantage. Lt. Col. Frank Wheaton assembled all the available men and mounted a bold attack on the stronghold from two directions on January 17, 1873, despite the fact that the area was covered with a pea-soup fog in which the soldiers could not possibly see their targets. *Klamath County History* recalls the event:

> Men were shot at. Men were wounded. Men were killed. Men were hauled off in stretchers, blankets, and on saddle horses. The Army retreated way back to Lone Pine Ford on Lost River. If any Modoc was killed or wounded no one knew of it.

During the Civil War, the press began routinely sending correspondents to cover all the battles. Detailed stories of the action, avidly absorbed by readers nationwide, brought celebrity status to the best reporters. Since the most colorful stories gained the widest readership, the correspondents often personalized their stories. One sure-fire device for an exciting tale called for the writer to champion a hero, with whom the reader could identify, and then to clarify or set up a villain. Then, as now, depicting the army as an inept, bumbling force uncapable of defeating even a small band of unlettered Indians held great appeal to the readers.

Captain Jack soon became a popular hero. As the historian Fairfax Downey wrote in his book *Indian Fighting Army*, a bit of doggerel soon was being widely recited:

> I'm Captain Jack of the Lava Beds,
> I'm cock o' the walk and chief of the reds,
> I kin lift the hair and scalp the heads,
> Of the whole United States Army.

Hoping to end the war before more blood was shed, the federal government appointed a peace commission to treat with the Modocs, while a force of five hundred soldiers kept the Indians "surrounded and contained" in an area where they wanted to remain anyhow. Quite comfortable in the caves and tunnels normally used for shelter during the winter, the Indians were in no hurry to talk. But the five hundred soldiers, who were living on field rations in canvas tents during a bitter-cold high country winter, suffered through three months of misery and boredom.

When the Indians finally agreed to talk, the three commissioners—General Edward R. S. Canby, Lieutenant William Sherwood, and a civilian, Reverend Eleazer Thomas—went into the Modoc stronghold under a white flag. Exactly what happened next has never been fully explained or justified. The Modocs killed all three men.

> Accordingly, on April 15, 16, and 17 Col. Alvan C. Gillem lashed out at the Modoc Stronghold from both east and west with a tenacity not felt before by the Modocs. His battle plan was almost identical to the scheme of Wheaton in January except that this time the numbers were about triple, and four little snub-nosed Coehorn mortars incessantly pounded the inner circle of defense every quarter hour....
>
> Modocs nor anyone else could long withstand the brutal pounding of the little cannon that "fired twice" (once at the muzzle and the second time as the shell burst). That early morning of 17 April 1873 was the last time that a Coehorn was fired in military action.

Though the Indians had been flushed out of their stronghold, they were far from defeated. Retreating into the seemingly endless lava beds to the south, Captain Jack and his band of hostiles fought the increasingly formidable forces brought against them time and again over a large area, winning every battle but the last. Even then, he would have continued to fight if he had not been betrayed by some of his fellow tribesmen who had grown weary of the conflict.

He finally laid down his arms and surrendered on June 1, 1873.

"Of course, to assuage both a vocal press and blustering citizenry, somebody had to hang," concludes the *Klamath County History*. "Captain Jack, Black Jim, John Schonchin, Boston Charley, Slolux and Barncho were tried by a hastily formed and completely biased military commission. The first four named were hanged on 3 October 1873 and the latter two were sentenced to life imprisonment at Alcatraz."

Ironically, what was left of the Modoc tribe did get a reservation of its own. But instead of being in the lava beds of southern Oregon, or even on the Klamath Reservation, this piece of land was half a continent away in what was then called "Indian Territory" by the whites and "Hot Country" by Pacific Northwest Indians exiled there. We know it now as Oklahoma.

Like Chief Joseph's band of Nez Perces, who joined the Modocs and many other tribes after their gallant resistance to the white soldiers in 1877, a generation would pass and most of the former warriors would die before the Modocs would be permitted to return to Oregon after 1900.

Fort Klamath Closes

With the Indian wars over and civilization well entrenched in the area, the federal government decided to begin closing unnecessary military posts to save expenses. So, in 1881, the Secretary of War reduced the Klamath post and hay reserve to one thousand acres, releasing the excess to the Department of Interior for sale. On May 4, 1886, the order came out from Washington, D.C., to abandon the post. But the local citizenry and the Klamath Indians, both of whom had come to depend on the fort for income and protection, raised such an outcry that the closure was postponed until July 20, 1889, when the Secretary of War wrote the Secretary of Interior: "The time has come. Please designate an agent from your department as custodian."

On August 9, 1889, says *Klamath County History*, "The entire staff, officers and enlisted men, stood at attention as the Flag of thirty-eight stars was lowered for the last time. Fort Klamath was abandoned!" A skeleton crew remained through the winter to take care of the post. Despite their efforts to keep the heavy snow cleared off the roofs of the buildings, it piled up five feet deep and some collapsed under the weight. In the summer of 1890 the crew was transferred to Vancouver Barracks, leaving a lone man, John Loosley, as caretaker of the decaying post.

Every Fourth of July for a number of years, white settlers and Indians living in the area got together for a celebration of the old days. Eventually, the land went to the state of Oregon, which in turn sold it to private individuals. The proprietors in 1973, Mr. and Mrs. William Zumbrach, donated a parcel of land containing the grave sites and the location of the flagpole to Klamath County for the purpose of establishing a public park and museum.

A replica of the guardhouse was built on the site of the original one, which now houses the museum. Where the flagpole originally stood is a brass marker, which marks the origination of all land surveys in the valley. A new flagpole stands six feet west of there. Worth visiting are the graves of Captain Jack and three of his compatriots who were all tried, convicted, and executed here.

Klamath Indian Reservation

As originally laid out, the Klamath Indian Reservation covered nearly 1,800 square miles. Unlike its Warm Springs counterpart in northern Oregon, the Klamath reservation no longer exists. In 1954 Congress passed the first of thirteen bills to terminate certain reservations (ultimately affecting 100 Indian groups in eight states) in a move to wean the Indians from federal supervision. By 1961, the remaining land and timber assets of the Klamath Tribe, slightly less than 1,350 square miles, had been sold and the proceeds distributed to its members.

The final perimeter of the Klamath Indian Reservation ran along an irregular path from approximately the northeast corner of Crater Lake National Park about fifty miles south nearly to Klamath Falls, then east about thirty miles, then north and west again. The Fort Klamath military post south of Crater Lake stood just outside the reservation's western border, while the Klamath Agency headquartered itself just inside the reservation a few miles farther south.

During its ninety-some years of existence, the Klamath Indian Reservation offered a fascinating study in the difficulties of federal Indian policy. For example, in 1906, in exchange for returning to the tribe certain land grants along a road that was never built through Klamath Marsh, the government alloted 87,000 acres near Yamsay Mountain to the California and Oregon Land Company without the Indians' consent. Congress authorized a meager $1.25 per acre, and forced the Indians to accept the payment in 1908. Twenty years and several legal struggles later, Congress reassessed the land's value at $2.98 million and resettled with the tribe.

Quitting the Old Ways

In the beginning, the reservation and acculturation program appeared successful. But several complicated factors working against it made that success less than complete. "Not all Indians wanted progress," writes Theodore Stern, even though the desire to own a farm or ranch, "to use the coffee, sugar, salt, beef, flour, and baking soda that had become the new necessessities ... now became available to any who would work hard and subject himself to an alien discipline." But the tribes and bands living together on the reservation did not readily accept the necessity of their all obeying the same laws and rules. A generation was too short a period in which to successfully abandon their many and varied customs and beliefs.

Transforming themselves into self-sufficient farmers, forsaking their religion and language, wearing "citizens' dress," and moving into "modern" homes, simply could not be accomplished as quickly as their white agents and teachers urged. Even such a simple matter as changing one's name presented obstacles.

Changing Names

"My name is *niskag* (young girl)," one Klamath woman recalls telling her teacher. How could that name be transated into English? "One-who-has-a-big-belly" is the literal translation for the name of a chief called *Momchnkasgitk*. Another individual later known as Allen David, was originally named "Black Anus."

It became one of the functions of the interpreter and clerk to rename Indians on the reservation. Usually they were delighted with their new names, such as Joe Wilson and George Brown. "This is your name," he would say, writing it on a card, "and if you forget what it is, ask someone who can read, and he will tell you."

Sometimes the new names became corrupted by the difficulty the Indians had pronouncing or remembering them. John Wesley became "Whistler"; Simeon became "Sammy Andy." The soldiers and settlers also administered some odd names: "Great Eastern," "Old Faithful," "Skinflint," and "Skedaddle."

Crops, Cattle, or Timber?

What did appeal to the Indians, though, was the prospect of abundant home-grown food. Corn, beans, turnips, carrots, peas, potatoes, artichokes, and onions offered the Indians much greater variety than the yampa roots common to their diet. And beets held special appeal because the color resembled meat.

Despite good crops the first year, this high, dry country took its toll in subsequent seasons. Early frost, prolonged cold, and summer drought led one agent to write his superiors of "the uselessness of trying to make this an agricutural reservation." With livestock, he wrote, "they would soon become self-sustaining."

In pre-reservation days, horses had constituted an important form of wealth. On the reservation, cattle became increasingly important.

In 1879, Agent Nickerson reported that the Indians owned two thousand animals, almost two head of cattle for each member of the tribe. "Some of the Indians are already raising beef cattle for the market," he wrote. "With the income they are able to supply their families with flour, coffee, sugar, etc."

He claimed that the reservation rangeland could carry ten times that number of cattle, making the Klamath tribe self-supporting within five years. But he reckoned without the weather. Within a year seventy-five percent of the cattle and forty percent of the horses died in an extremely harsh winter.

Though livestock-raising slowly recovered and, with winter-feeding, better shelter for the animals in severe weather, and improved ranching methods, remained an important source of income for the Indians, it became apparent that timber would be the principal economic resource of the reservation.

A small sawmill set up in 1870 to convert the reservation forest into boards for agency buildings soon produced enough lumber for a few good frame houses for some of the Indian leaders. They rode around the community urging others to follow their example. "You've got to quit the old ways, change your houses, live like white people," they said. Many of the older people resisted, preferring instead to live in their brush wikiups, despite their shabby appearance, simply because they found them more comfortable and familiar.

But the Klamaths continued to cut and mill lumber for their own uses and to sell to outsiders. The money derived from the sales went to the chief, who put it into tribal funds for the purchase of livestock. This operation proved so profitable that when the salary of the white man who ran the sawmill was cut off by a misguided government economy measure, the Indians decided to pay him themselves.

Typical of bureaucratic rulings then and now, a technicality threatened to cut off Indian income from the timber resource. But the Klamaths ingeniously found a way to get around the ruling that would have done credit to their more experienced white brothers.

An 1873 Supreme Court ruling specified that the trees, like the land they grew on, were in a trust status. Trees cut specifically as timber belonged to the government. But trees felled incidental to clearing the land remained tribal property.

Innocently asking for and receiving permission to cut and sell dead and fallen timber, the Indians, who already had the right to fell trees for the building of their own houses, soon discovered an amazing amount of "dead and fallen" timber on the reservation, and the amount of their needs for building their own houses grew dramatically.

"With the rise of towns around the reservation, the demand grew until in 1896 the sale of lumber to whites was estimated to exceed a quarter million board feet, three-fourths of it cut from green timber," historian Stern writes. "For the Klamath, their operations in the timber market were more than an exercise in resourcefulness and industry; they provided experience and allies in evading what must have seemed a senseless legal prohibition."

242

The Road to Termination

In the early 1890s, a federal law was passed allowing tribes to take individual pieces of land for each member, with the remainder held to benefit the tribe as a whole. More than 800 of the 933 Klamath tribal members voted to take claims.

An 1891 amendment to the act allowed each member to receive an allotment of 80 acres for farming, or double that for grazing. A govenment official named Emery declared that Klamath reservation grazing land was twenty-five times more abundant than farm land, so he recommended that double allotments be issued. That timbered portions of the reservation were deemed "worthless" meant only that they were not acceptable for grazing or farming. They would be held in common by the tribe as a whole, and eventually would prove to be of great value.

Because of conflicting claims by the California and Oregon Land Company, the state of Oregon, and other entities, final distribution of individual claims by Klamath members waited until 1906. Meanwhile, the fate of the "surplus" land was debated.

Alloting agent Charles E. Worden suggested setting aside 100,000 timbered acres along streams until demand increased sufficienctly to float the commodity to market. This proved to be good advice. A few years after the timber reserve had been set aside, the Southern Pacific Railroad reached Klamath Falls in 1909, and when it moved north across the reservation, tribal stands of prime timber were opened up. Cutting began in 1911 and sales commenced two years later. The Klamath Agency employed thirty-seven members in its forestry and grazing division until 1947, and timber cutting and sales became a vital part of the Klamath economy. Reservation timber was big business.

By 1926, per capita income from timber sales was $500. Thus, a family of four received $2,000 a year from timber receipts, an income sufficient to provide for all their needs and give them a measure of economic independence.

In 1900 ninety percent of the Klamath tribe lived on the reservation. By 1955 only sixty percent of the tribal members remained, and the downslide picked up momentum, the rest having scattered to adjacent communities in southern Oregon, northern California, or cities such as Portland.

Furthermore, a majority of them had lost their Indian heritage.

"By 1955, only twenty-eight percent of the absentee members could claim to be biologically of over one-half Indian ancestry, and even for those dwelling on the reservation the corresponding figure was no more than fifty-four percent."

In 1950, with timber payments at $800 per capita, a Klamath family of four exceeded the median national income. This, combined with yearlong hunting and fishing rights (which indirectly increased their income) left little incentive for families to work.

Discussion of liquidation of the assets owned by the tribe began in 1945. After proposals were considered and discussed for a number of years, it was finally decided in 1954 that a vote be taken so that enrolled members of the tribe could elect either to withdraw, receiving their pro rata share of tribal property, or remain in a surviving ecomomic entity.

"When the vote was held, over seventy percent of the tribal membership elected to withdraw," Stern writes, "the government purchasing their land and creating the Winema National Forest.... The outcome of the vote was in part an expression of confidence among the Klamath in their ability to handle their own affairs."

Each member of the tribe would receive a cash payment of $43,500. Though a small percent chose to have their money managed under a trust arrangement, most chose to take the funds in a lump sum.

In a letter to the Klamath people, Seldon E. Kirk, past chairman of the general council, summed up their feelings in these words:

> We have no power over what has been but we have it in our power to shape our future and the future of our children. Out of the discouragement, the bitterness of the past, and out of Termination, perhaps something good can be created. It is important that you and I work harder than ever so that we can continue to lift up our heads with pride, and if they were living today, our ancestors too, could be proud of us.

OR 66, I-5 (OR 140)
Klamath Falls—Medford
64 miles (75 miles)

In Klamath Falls, there are two historical museums well worth seeing. One is the Klamath County Museum, which occupies the former National Guard armory and is run by a regional historic preservation committee. The other is the Favell Museum of Western Art and Indian Artifacts, which is privately owned and a true labor of love created and maintained by the grandson of a pioneer rancher in the high, lonesome, starkly beautiful rangeland of southern Oregon.

Klamath County Museum

The Klamath County Museum was completed in conjunction with the County Library Building in 1854. In 1970 the museum was relocated to the National Guard Armory building, where it resides today. Designed by a local architect, it is fireproof throughout and made of local face brick with cast-stone trimming. Two statues dressed like World War I soldiers guard the entrance. Its extensive exhibits include anthropology, history, geology, and wildlife of the Klamath Basin.

Also under the management of the Klamath County Museum is the Baldwin Building, which at the time of its construction in 1904 was the largest building in the city. With its foundation on a solid rock hillside layered on a stair step pattern, this four-story structure was operated by George T. Baldwin as a hardware store until 1911, then was converted into a 65-room hotel. After it closed in 1977, it was taken over by the Klamath County Historical Museum as an annex. With full restoration and original furnishings, the Baldwin Hotel was dedicated as a state and national Historical Landmark in 1978.

The Favell Museum

Gene Favell found his first arrowhead when he was eight years old. After widening his search area from the shores of local lakes to the entire West, after a successful career as a businessman, and after he and his wife Winifred produced six childen, they established the museum in 1972. This outstanding family museum houses sixty thousand choice arrowheads and a collection of other artifacts as well as art.

"We've got it about the way we want it now," Gene said in a recent interview. The permanent collection on display is pretty well established and their original works of art from over 300 contemporary Western artists is about all they can handle. Of course, like collectors everywhere, the Favells can no more resist acquiring new pieces than they can refrain from parting with ones that have served their intended purpose. To private collectors, buying and selling are as important as exhibiting.

A few years ago the Favell Museum acquired a Charles Russell painting titled *The Scouts*, for which it paid the appraised price of $55,000 to its Montana owners. From the original work, the Favells made one thousand limited edition prints priced at $100 each. "Where this painting for eighty-seven years graced but one wall," Gene says, "it now will hang on one thousand. We are proud to display the original in our museum."

According to its previous owners, Charles Russell was paid $15 for the 14" X 21" oil—and was reluctant to take it.

Also on display at the Favell Museum are several paintings by John Clymer, who was second only to Norman Rockwell in the number of covers he did for the *Saturday Evening Post*—over eighty—and whose historically accurate paintings sell for more than $100,000.

The museum occupies 17,000 feet of floor space on three levels, and Gene and Winifred identify its theme as follows:

> This museum is dedicated to the Indians who roamed this land before the coming of the white man and to those artists who truly portray the inherited beauty which surrounds us. Their artifacts and art are an important part of the heritage of the West.

Southern Oregon Sentinel— Mount McLoughlin

The least known and most southern major peak in the Oregon Cascades is Mount McLoughlin, originally known as Mount Pitt. Rising to 9,495 feet only some seventy miles north of Mount Shasta, its name honors Dr. John McLoughlin, the final Hudson's Bay Company factor in charge of Fort Vancouver who so generously helped American emigrants.

The lakes and streams surrounding the mountain's base provide excellent fishing for the relatively few sportsmen who visit them, and are easily accessible from Oregon 140, between Medford and Klamath Falls. Hikers or climbers willing to stray from improved trails may find this peak relatively accessible. Says geologist Stephen Harris in his book *Fire and Ice*:

> The poetically christened Lake O'Woods is probably the most visited spot near Mt. McLoughlin, although Four Mile Lake is the best point of departure for a summit climb. Those willing to exert the energy necessary to stand atop McLoughlin's narrow crest are rewarded by a sweeping panorama of the southern Cascades.

Although not technically difficult, the six-mile trail to Mt. McLoughlin's summit should be attempted only by persons in good physical condition and then only in late July and August after winter's snows have melted. Be sure to carry water as there is none along the trail.

South of Mount McLoughin, the crest of the Cascades angles southwest and merges with the Siskiyous. By any name, these are rugged mountains covered with such a magnificent stand of trees that from time to time conservationists have proposed setting a portion aside as a national park. As might be expected in a region long dependent on the logging industry for its livelihood, this idea is not warmly embraced by loggers and sawmill workers.

But, while the trees are still there, Oregon 66 between Klamath Falls and Ashland is an excellent highway from which to see the big Douglas fir, sugar pine, and other varieties of trees in the old growth forest. This is the route laid out by the Scott-Applegate party called the Southern Oregon Emigrant Road. There are historic markers along the way showing fords, ferry points, and passes traversed by the emigrants. Even today's traveler must be impressed with the steepness of the mountains and the crookedness of the road.

Chautauqua's Legacy to Ashland

The state highway joins I-5 about fourteen miles northwest of the interstate's 4,310-foot Siskiyou Summit. From either route, the highway drops into Ashland in one of the loveliest mountain valleys in southern Oregon. People unfamiliar with Ashland might reasonably expect that this is a prime vacation and resort area; but few can leave here without learning that its chief attraction, for which it is renowned worldwide, is its quality production of Shakespearean plays.

Begun in the summer of 1852 by the English born Robert Hargadine and his friend Mr. Pease, the settlement started to grow five days later with the arrival of Abel Helman and Eber Emery, who hailed from Ashland County, Ohio. Like so many footloose men at that time, they had sought their fortune in the gold fields of northern California and failed to strike it rich, so they wandered north to check out the new bonanza near Jacksonville. Upon learning of the Donation Land Act of 1850, they filed adjacent claims in this pleasant 2,000-foot valley in the upper reaches of the Rogue River. To fill their need for lumber the early pioneers first built a sawmill, then a flour mill, and, when they got a post office in 1855, they officially accepted the name Ashland Mills.

Bound by mountains on all sides and accessible by wagons and stagecoaches only after traveling toll roads, Ashland Mills became a way station on the rugged 710-mile trip between Sacramento and Portland. When the railroad finally reached it in 1887, its contact wih the outside world improved somewhat, but at no time did it threaten to become a thriving metropolis. More than most communities, its entertainment and culture had to be homegrown.

Around the turn of the century, the Methodist Society started a small library, the forerunner of Ashland's public library. Eager for a school of higher learning, the same society started an academy, which teetered on total failure until the state took it over in 1925. After that it became Southern Oregon State College and began a slow growth.

Always interested in education and culture, the Methodist Society used its influence to secure Ashland a place from 1892 through the late 1920s on the chautauqua circuit. In Lake Chautauqua, New York, in 1874, a Methodist minister and a businessman organized this adult education movement, which brought lectures, concerts, and plays to small, isolated communities. In the 1930s, when the delapidated and condemned wooden shell in Lithia Park came down, a small, quiet-mannered professor of drama at Southern Oregon State College named Angus Bowmer remarked that the shell resembled drawings he had seen of the old Globe Theatre in England, where William Shakespeare's plays had been staged several centuries earlier.

Shakespeare Comes to Oregon

In 1935 the small town of Ashland, like the rest of the nation, was in the depths of the Depression. But local merchants and interested citizens cooperated to build an Elizabethan stage. Angus Bowmer's idea of celebrating the Fourth of July with two Shakespeare plays was only slightly watered down by the insistence of local merchants to schedule afternoon boxing matches to pay the cost of putting on the plays, which they were sure would lose money.

To their great surprise, receipts from the plays covered the deficit from the boxing matches. From then on, the local businessmen took Shakespeare seriously.

In the years that followed, attendance at the Shakespeare productions continued to increase; the season constantly lengthened as the reputation of the the quality of the plays spread far and wide. At first, four plays on a rotating basis were performed on a rather primitive outdoor stage each summer. In 1937 the Oregon Shakespearean Festival established itself as a non-profit organization. Scholarships for promising actors began in 1941. In 1970, a larger Elizabethan theatre for modern plays to be run in conjunction with the outdoor theater went up at a cost of $1.8 million. During the 1976 season, 277 performances in the combined theaters brought 221,296 people in attendance.

Attracting actors, directors, critics, and audiences from all parts of the United States and many foreign countries, Ashland now has the large outdoor theater, which hosts three Shakespeare plays six nights a week on a rotating basis from early June until late September, and two indoor theaters, which stage productions six nights a week from late February through October.

The Angus Bowmer Theatre seats 600, while the Black Swan has a capacity of 140. The outdoor theater continues the Shakespeare tradition. The two indoor theaters stage a wide range of plays, from classics such as Henrik Ibsen's *Peer Gynt* to modern sociological plays like Steven Dietz's *God's Country*, which is based on the controversial life and fiery death of the white supremacist Robert Jay Mathews.

The Fruitful Valley

Though it was the discovery of gold in the mountains bordering the Rogue River Valley that first attracted settlers in the early 1850s, those who remained after the bonanza peaked discovered more lasting treasures. The mild climate and balance between temperature, rainfall, and sunshine earned this area the nickname "Italy of Oregon."

Hops used for brewing beer and ale grew extremely well. And apples raised around here tasted excellent and brought premium prices in San Francisco. Pears grown in the Medford area were particularly prized. Freight costs posed a big problem for a while, for the roads in all directions wound through rugged mountains, but the arrival of the railoads in the late 1880s made shipping more reasonable.

In recent years, the Medford fruit growers have become highly successful by relying more on quality than quantity. One ingenious business has established a Fruit-of-the-Month Club, shipping small gift packages of premium fruit anywhere in the United States for shoppers who value quality over price. This same firm is also known as "the world's largest rose grower," filling mail order requests for roses from all over the country.

Retirement homes in a mild climate, boasting many leisure-time activities and good medical facilities in relatively uncrowded communities, further demonstrate that a more lasting treasure than that taken out of the ground still exists in the foothills and valleys of the Rogue River country. But for those few years when the gold boom lasted, the times were exciting.

Few tangible reminders of the bonanza days remain today, but for those interested in "where and when" it all happened, the tour suggested in the following pages is the best way to see the gold country.

Gold Country Roads

For the traveler hurrying through the 97 miles between Medford and Roseburg, Interstate 5 traverses the beautiful Rogue River Valley and the rugged Siskiyou Mountains quickly and painlessly, with few scenic distractions to block the endless stream of traffic moving along at sixty-five miles an hour. But for those with more time and an interest in regional history, a number of intriguing back roads and fascinating places offer a more scenic and edifying trip.

A good starting point from the southern end is Jacksonville, five miles west of Medford. Following the gold strike in California at Sutter's Mill in 1849, which first drew prospectors to the Sacramento River area, men who failed to make fortunes there moved north and east into the Sierras, Sikiyous, and Cascades in search of treasure. Having learned from the Spanish—experts in the field for centuries—that gold could most likely be found in regions where volcanoes had erupted, tearing the earth's crust asunder and spewing precious metals in the molten crucible formed far below, the eager prospectors sought remote mountain streams in which the primal rocks had been rent apart most violently, for it was there, they felt sure, that the greatest treasure would be found.

More often than not, they were right.

Jacksonville

Two of these roaming prospectors, James Cluggage and J.R. Poole, discovered gold in Jackson Creek in January 1852. Proclaimed by local newspapers as a great bonanza that would make thousands of men rich, the strike inspired what soon became the biggest city in southern Oregon—Jacksonville. Though its days of prosperity and glory soon passed, the thrill lasted long enough for an impressive hostelry called the United State Hotel to be built. On one memorable occasion, President Rutherford B. Hayes and General William T. Sherman spent a night at the hotel, which gave it considerable prestige. Unfortunately, the distinguished guests left without paying their bill. But the prestige remained.

The WPA guide to Oregon mentions a local legend that claims "the Methodist Church was built in 1854 with one night's take at the gaming tables," with gamblers, owners, and bankers all contributing nuggets into a collection plate.

As the gold boom faded, the valley's fertile soil and mild climate replaced the precious metal with equally precious fruit. The people and, in 1927, the seat of government moved from Jacksonville to Medford. But the boom town's historical significance is well maintained, making it an intriguing place to visit from spring to fall. Some of the worthwhile sites and activities include the Children's Museum and the Jacksonville Courthouse Museum, the early-day camera and photograph collection of Peter Britt, the Peter Britt Music Festival, trolley rides through the old town, and the Jacksonville Cemetery tour.

From Jacksonville, the Gold Country Road follows Oregon 238 southwest for a few miles before turning west along Applegate River, a tributary of Rogue River, which bisects the heart of the region in which gold was found. After thirty-five miles, Oregon 238 goes into Oregon 199, which heads southwest from Grant's Pass toward the California line. Though not nearly as crooked or steep now as it was as a cattle trail, then a prospector trail, and finally a stage road from southern Oregon to the California coast at Crescent City, it still gives the traveler an impressive view of awe-inspiring rugged mountains and big redwood trees.

This part of southern Oregon, which includes the Siskiyou's Chetko Ranger District, contains almost all of the the redwoods now growing in the state. A substantial portion of them is endangered. Chetko District Ranger Mike Frazier said of Oregon's roughly 1,350 acres of the old redwoods, only 720 acres are protected, leaving the remainder open to logging. Because some of the old growth redwoods are on private lands where sales cannot be restricted, these trees were threatened during the summer of 1990. But as of this writing, protests by the Portland Audubon Society and other conservation groups have saved them for the time being.

Illinois River

Along the mountain-girt banks of the Illinois River, which flows northward into the Rogue, many gold strikes in the early 1850s gave rise to boom towns that flared then fizzled, but only a few signs that they ever existed remain. Some of the towns bear intriguing names. How did the hamlet of Wonder, for instance, get its name?

According to the WPA guide: "The village was named by settlers who 'wondered' how a merchant who established a store at this point might hope to make a living."

During the boom days, three towns thrived along the Illinois River: Waldo, Kerbyville, and Browntown. First called "Sailor's Diggings," Waldo still exists, as does Kerbyville, though its name has been shortened to Kerby. But Browntown, originally the biggest of the three places, has vanished without a trace.

"In the earliest days Browntown had more renown and was the wildest of the three towns," writes local historian Ruth Pfefferle in her book *Golden Days and Pioneer Ways.* "It served a wide area along Althouse Creek, Bolan Creek, and Sucker Creek. Browntown was located on a large flat of several acres at the mouth of Walker Gulch, a tributary of Althouse Creek."

Two brothers, Frank and Phil Althouse, made the first discovery, giving the stream and the district their name. At the peak of the rush between 1852 and 1860, 6,000 miners worked the streams, gulches, and hills of the district. Reportedly, the largest nugget found weighed 204 ounces. In those days, when gold appraised at $16 an ounce, it was worth $3,264; today, at $400 an ounce, it would bring $81,600.

As in so many other gold-bearing districts throughout the West, where the miner was king and could do no wrong, mining in the Illinois River Valley escalated in method and destructiveness. First prospectors dug the banks and gravel bars with shovels and pans; then they dug deeper and diverted water for sluicing; next came mule-powered arastras, which pulverized gold-bearing quartz so that it would yield its treasure by heating and treating the dust with quicksilver; and finally, in the most environmentally destructive method of all, they blasted the hillsides with water hoses—hydraulic mining—chewing up, digesting, and depositing ugly rubble that countless generations would see and deplore.

Ruth Pfefferle points out that dredging turned a profit on soils valued at only four cents per cubic yard. In the East Fork of the Illinois River, near Takilama, a large steam-powered dredge operated early in twentieth century. Mounted on a large wooden hull, the machine ran an endless series of steel buckets, displacing the entire stream bed as it scavenged gold from its interior sluice boxes. Floating on a self-made lake, the dredge inched along, digging a new pool for its massive hulk as it discarded gravel and boulders behind it.

Chinese in Oregon

As time has consumed the towns that once thrived in this area, so too has it reclaimed evidence of the people who worked and lived there—the Chinese. Beginning with the California Gold Rush of 1849, many Chinese workers were drawn from their dire poverty in South China to what they called *Gum Shan*, "The Golden Hills" of California. Though not an accurate label, they acquired the name "coolies," a corruption of the Chinese term *ku-li*, or "muscle strength."

Manual labor was the chief asset of these strong young men drawn to America by the same get-rich-quick lure that brought many Europeans. A lack of understanding and misinformation brought on by a formidable language barrier and inaccessible records has hampered getting at the true history of the Chinese in the western United States. Almost all the West Coast records of the Chinese workers in the United States were kept in the secret headquarters of the Six Companies in the labyrinth of San Francisco's Chinatown and were completely destroyed by the fire following the Great Earthquake of 1906. Any corresponding records still in China never have been and may never be accessible to American scholars.

But we do know a few important facts about the Chinese immigrants who came to the western United States between 1850 and 1880. Most of them were young, single men willing to work hard for low wages and endure abuse without complaint. During that period, these Chinese workers made a great contribution to this country doing the work nobody else wanted to do. Though they paid taxes, they were denied citizenship and the right to vote.

During the 1880s, political rabble-rousers spouted and wrote a lot of nonsense to the effect that cheap Chinese labor took the bread out of the mouths of honest American workers; that opium dens run by the Chinese were debauching innocent Americans; that young white girls were being kidnapped and forced into prostitution by the criminal heads of Chinese Tongs; and that any white person foolish enough to venture into the Chinese district of a big West Coast city was apt to get his skull split open by a lather's hatchet, which was supposed to be the favorite Tong weapon.

At the same time, most miners' camps in the West employed Chinese washermen to do their laundry because they did it cheaply and well. Whites also employed Chinese to hew and haul firewood, to cook in the best family kitchens, to grow fresh vegetables, to take care of children, and to do anything else that required dependability and loyalty. Ninety-nine percent of the Chinese in the West were sponsored not by the gangster-type Tongs, but by one of the benevolent Six Companies, which compared more with the Odd Fellows, the Masons, or the Elks. Their main functions were to help poor Chinese workers get to America, find them jobs, send most of their earnings home to their families, and, in the event that they should die in this distant land, return their bones for burial in the country of their birth.

Politicians across the West, including Oregon, responded to what they perceived as a popular issue by proclaiming to groups they relied on for support *"The Chinese Must Go!"* A bill introduced in the legislative session of 1854 excluded the Chinese from Oregon Territory. It did not pass. But special taxes, such as the Mining Tax Law of 1857, were imposed on the Chinese, requiring them to pay for "the privilege of mining," as Ruth Pfefferle put it. "Twenty percent of the revenue thus derived was paid to the territorial treasury." Since the remaining eighty percent went to the local collector, we can be sure this law was strictly enforced.

In 1858, "The Chinaman Tax" of the preceding year was extended to include not only mining but also trading, selling, or whatever else the Chinese did to make a living. By 1859, the law in Josephine County read: "All Chinamen engaged in any kind of trade or barter among themselves are required to pay $50 a month for such privileges."

By the 1880s anti-Chinese sentiment reached such a fevered pitch that riots broke out from Wyoming to Washington, often resulting in injury or death for the Chinese. Oregon was not without incident, but no large scale riots occurred. Much of the credit for this is due Harvey Whitefield Scott, editor of the *Oregonian* and one of the first to graduate from Tualatin Academy in 1863. Though he did not endorse bringing more Chinese into Oregon, his editorials sympathized with those already here. While some blamed hard times on the Chinese labor glut, Scott contended that there was work for any man that really wanted it. But white men did not want jobs the Chinese were willing to do, such as work on the railroad and clear fields for farms, because the wages were too low.

The Oregon Caves

Twelve miles north of the California line, Oregon 46 goes east from US 199 to a truly remarkable natural wonder, the Oregon Caves National Monument. Known as "The Marble Halls of Oregon," they are a series of spectacular caverns in Elijah Mountain, a towering limestone and marble formation in the Siskiyou Range. The 7,000 foot peak was named for Elijah J. Davidson, a pioneer who discovered the caves in 1874 while pursuing a bear that had disappeared into the mountainside.

"The mountain is a labyrinth of chambers, corridors, and passageways of incredible beauty, carved by the relentless flow and drip of water in subterranean darkness," says the WPA guide.

About 150 million years ago, underground pressures squeezed, heated, and recrystallized an ancient sea floor of limestone into marble. Heat and cold ruptured it and water from melting glaciers found its way through the fissures, eventually carving grottos. Today, a stream probably much smaller than the original glacial river, gushes from the grotto and tumbles down a canyon betweeen forested hills.

> Carved through unreckoned ages are weirdly beautiful caverns in which clusters of intricately sculptured marble hang from frescoed ceilings like frozen lotus flowers. Stalagmite and stalactite join together, forming columns like vast organ pipes; they emit sweet, thin music when struck by metal. Out-thrust from the walls are shells adorned with bric-a-brac fashioned by nature, some of it

grotesque, but all of it arresting in its cold brilliance. Fluted columns and pillars rise along the passages, shimmering like pearl when the searchlights play upon them. Colored lights, at intervals through arched vaults, give the marble walls a blue and crimson translucence. A spoken word echoes and reverberates in the stillness.

President Taft named the caves and 480 acres surrounding them a national monument in 1909. The heavily explored and well-mapped caverns contain numerous points of interest, such as "Niagara Falls," a waterfall frozen eternally into marble and "Joaquin Miller's chapel," a vast, cathedral-like room named for the famed Oregon poet who visited there in 1907. Also a system of forest trails leads around Elijah Mountain, a distance of about four miles.

Grants Pass & Rogue River

To see the rest of the Oregon Cascades, head northeast on US 199 to Grants Pass, where I-5 leads north through the mountains and the Rogue River country to Roseburg. Contrary to some local historians, Ulysses S. Grant never passed through this part of Oregon, though, as noted earlier, he was stationed at Fort Vancouver in 1852, when he tried to supplement his meager captain's pay by raising potatoes. According to the WPA guide, "The town, which came into existence as a stopping place on the California Stage route, was named by enthusiastic builders of the road over the pass when a messenger told them of General Grant's capture of Vicksburg." At first named simply Grant, the citizens lengthened the town's name to Grants Pass after postal authorities informed them that there already was a settlement named Grant in Oregon.

For many years, a social and service club organization called the Oregon Cavemen has existed here, holding annual festivities and carnivals in which members impersonate their tribal forebears. "The Cavemen claim the marble halls of the Oregon Caves as their ancestral home. Symbolically their food and drink consists of the meat of the dinosaur and the blood of the saber-tooth tiger. The officers of the organization are Chief Big Horn, Rising Buck, Keeper of the Wampum, Clubfist, Wingfeather, and Flamecatcher."

Flowing from the mountains on the southwest slope of Crater Lake, the Rogue River tumbles westward toward the sea through two hundred miles of the wildest, most scenic, and pristinely unspoiled country in southern Oregon. From the 1920s, when Zane Grey (supported by fellow writer Jack London) regarded a long stretch of canyon along the lower river so much his own personal property that he was prepared to repel invaders with hot lead as though in a scene right out of one of his Western novels, through the 1930s when President Herbert Hoover, actors Gary

Cooper and Clark Gable, and many other famous people declared the Rogue to be the best steelhead, salmon, and trout fishing river in the world, to the present day when "running the rapids of the Rogue" still is a treasured experience for the thousands of ordinary people privileged to do it, the Rogue has been untouchable to those who would defile it.

Legend has it that when a critic suggested to President Hoover that a week he had spent fishing on the Rogue was a "waste of time," he made the statement that has forever endeared him to *compleat anglers*: "The hours a man spends fishing," he said, "do not count against his total life-span."

Even Harvey Scott, the editor of the *Oregonian*, rose up in righteous verbal wrath when a thoughtless reader wrote his paper asserting that the river should have been named *Rouge* ("red," in French) but was not because "them French couldn't spell." The reader claimed that early spring flood waters of the river ran red, thus, that should have been its name.

"This is fanciful, purely so, though the *Rouge* story is old!" Scott thundered. "There would have been reason for calling the Klamath River Rouge River, or Red River; for its waters are much discolored by the marshes of the lake basin which it drains. But Rogue River is one of the clearest of streams, and even in flood its waters are not red." He then went on to point out that Bishop Blanchet's account of the Catholic Church in Oregon stated that the French first called the Rogue by that name because the Indians living there were a peculiarly troublesome lot. "Hence," wrote Blanchet, "the name *'Les Coquins'* (the Rogues) and *'La Riviere aux Coquins'* (the Rogue River) was given to the country by the men of the brigade."

The actual truth, Scott concluded, was that the French themselves called it Rogue River—and spelled it correctly.

By any name, if, in time to come, proposals are made to dam, divert, pollute, or otherwise alter the character of the Rogue River, present-day defenders will prove to be a far more "peculiarly troublesome lot" to the would-be defilers than the pugnacious tribe of Indians that once lived along its banks.

Roseburg and Yoncalla

Between Grants Pass and Roseburg, a distance of 68 miles, the mountains remain rugged and heavily timbered, but in the descent from 948 feet at Grants Pass to 470 feet at Roseburg, one begins to feel the relatively benign climate of the upper Willamette Valley; the foothills are less steep, there are more open prairies, and less snowfall in the winter.

Roseburg's annual Rose Festival encourages its citizens to grow an abundance and variety of blossoms each year. But despite the quality of its flowers, the town was named for a man, not a bloom.

Settling in this remote valley in 1851, pioneer Aaron Rose soon opened a public tavern and became one of the community's leading citizens. In those days, of course, a tavern provided a variety of services—food, lodging, and a meeting place to discuss local problems—as well as thirst-slaking liquids. Aaron Rose proved so public spirited, in fact, that when his town got into a squabble with the residents of nearby Looking Glass Valley about which should become the seat of Douglas County, he offered up $1,000 and three acres of land for the courthouse.

The first territorial governor of Oregon, Joseph Lane, made his home in Roseburg. In 1860, he became a U.S. vice-presidential candidate. Even though there is some question as to whether he might be better remembered if he had won the election, the fact is he lost.

Like all pioneer communities, Roseburg passed some eyebrow raising local ordinances meant to deal with special problems. In 1882, for instance, the city fathers' concern over laundry led them to decree that "any woman who has been lawfully married and has a legitimate child or children to support may operate a hand laundry upon recommendation of the committee on health, and police." At that time of heightened anti-Chinese sentiment, it's natural to wonder if this was perhaps an attempt to put Chinese laundries out of business; if so, it failed.

"On January 14, 1889," according to the WPA guide, "an ordinance was passed to prevent the use of bells on cows and other domestic animals between the hours of 8 p.m. and 6 a.m. Previous to the ordinance one citizen frequently detached the bells from cows and threw them in the gutter when on his way home in the evening, thus hoping to get a good night's sleep."

Sage of Yoncalla

Twenty-four miles north of Roseburg, a turnoff west from I-5 leads to the small town of Yoncalla, which marks the southern limits of the Willamette Valley. It was here that Jesse Applegate and his brothers settled after coming west with the Great Emigration of 1843. All of the Applegate's played important roles in Oregon history. As patriarch of the clan, Jesse was fondly referred to by all who knew him during his later years as "The Sage of Yoncalla."

Roselle Applegate Putnam, Jesse Applegate's daughter, said of Yoncalla: "It is not a town, not a place of man's creation, nor of a white man's naming, but it is a hill, round and high and beautiful, ten miles in circumference and one and a half in height.... The hill is called after a chief who with a numerous tribe once inhabited these valleys."

According to Lewis McArthur, compiler of *Oregon Geographic Names*, Yoncalla meant "eagle" in the local Indian tongue, though he was never able to find any Indian or white experts to verify this.

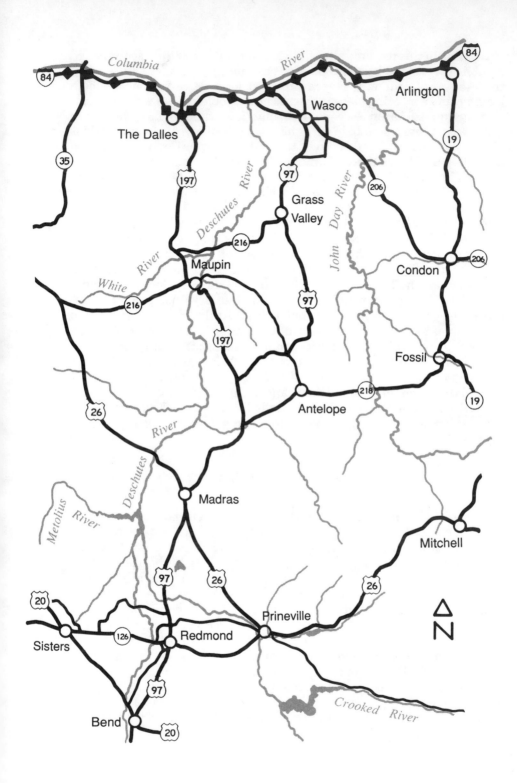

PART V

High Desert Country

Celilo Converter Station

A good place to launch an exploration of the wide open spaces of the high desert country, which looks much the same now as it did when humans first saw it, is a high-tech center situated on top of a bluff overlooking the Columbia River. Below lies the city of The Dalles and the bridge to Washington State; directly to the west is an unsurpassed view of Mount Hood.

This is the Celilo Converter Station. It processes all the electric power generated by the thirty major dams on the Columbia River system, plus that produced by coal, oil, nuclear, and other facilities in the Pacific Northwest.

Nothing else like it exists in North America.

As noted in Part One of this book, the primary argument in favor of building the Bonneville Dam in back in 1933 was that it would put men to work during the depths of the Depression. Grand Coulee, started a few years later, was also praised mostly for its employment value. The electricity generated by these two projects was incidental, almost a by-product.

"Who is going to use all that electricity?" eastern newspaper editorials sneered. "The jackrabbits? Grand Coulee should be called the 'Dam of Doubt.'"

The Army Corps of Engineers built Bonneville Dam; the Bureau of Reclamation built Grand Coulee. When the two agencies argued about which one should be in charge of distributing the power generated by the dams, President Franklin Roosevelt settled the dispute by creating a new agency, the Bonneville Power Administration. Quickly dubbed BPA, its purpose was to spread cheap electric power among farmer co-ops, owner-run public utility districts, and other agencies with a mini-

259

Celilo Converter Station with the Columbia River and bridge to Washington in the background. —Bonneville Power Administration

mum amount of fuss and bother so that the federal executive branch and Congress could devote their attention to more important matters.

Then came World War II, eventually requiring massive amounts of cheap electricity in the Pacific Northwest to help create the atomic bomb. This was followed by the post-war boom's demand for aluminum and other light metals, also requiring large quantities of electric power to produce. Though arguments between public and private power grew ever more vocal and heated, as did those between public agencies, the question of who should build the dams and their generating facilities remained. The fact that BPA existed and seemed to be doing a fairly even-handed job of distributing the power permitted that agency to grow in relative peace.

Today, the Bonneville Power Administration still has as its primary job the distribution of electrical power. But it does so on a scale undreamed of when the agency was created.

The Intertie

To visit the Celilo Converter Station, which offers a fascinating self-guided tour, turn south off I-84 at Exit 87 one mile east of The Dalles, follow US 197 south one mile, then go left up the hill to the top of the bluff. Through the station next to the parking lot flow incredible amounts of electricity generated by at least 150 units as far north as British Columbia, as far east as Montana, as far west as the lower Columbia, and as far south as Los Angeles.

Electricity cannot be stored. It must be used the instant it is generated. The Celilo Converter Station's single million-volt direct current (DC) line is enough to satisfy the needs of the city of Los Angeles. In addition to this high-capacity transmission line, which runs uninterrupted across 846 miles of high desert and mountain country to the Sylmar Station near Los Angeles, there are two 500,000-volt alternating current (AC) lines that run parallel to it for a ways before heading west toward the Oregon and California population centers. Another 500,000-volt AC line will soon go into service.

Collectively, these transmission lines are called the "Intertie." Its purpose since the 1960s is to carry electricity from a region that produces it in abundance to regions that use it in abundance.

Eighty percent of the electricity generated in the Pacific Northwest is hydro power, while that generated in the south is mostly thermal power. They each rely on spinning turbines, but one source uses the weight of falling water while the other uses the force of steam created by burning gas, oil, or nuclear fuel. Since falling water is free and a renewable resource, hydro generation is cheaper, costing only a cent or two per

Celilo Converter Station with Mount Hood in the background.
—Bonneville Power Administration

Celilo Converter Station. —Bonneville Power Administration

kilowatt hour. Thermal generation, which uses non-renewable resources, is more expensive, costing five to six cents per kilowatt hour. An exchange rate at three or so cents per kilowatt hour from an area with an energy surplus to one with an energy deficit benefits everyone.

Of the thirty major dams on the Columbia River system, only a few have any significant storage capacity. This means that during periods of high runoff, the water behind the dams must be "spilled," or allowed to leave the reservoir without making electricity. Usually this happens during the late spring and summer months, when southern California's needs for air-conditioning electricity are great. By sending the cheaper hydro power south, they can avoid generating expensive thermal energy. On the other side of the coin, during the winter, when river water in the Pacific Northwest is locked up as snow and ice but electric needs for heating and light intensify, the south can send thermal power north over the two-way Intertie.

In practice, the exchange is not quite that simple, of course; in fact, the energy exchange may turn around hourly, depending on sophisticated computer calculations monitoring who owes who for what and whether the debt will be paid with energy or cash. But the exchange is beneficial to all who participate in it.

DC and AC

Electrical power can be transmitted either by direct current or by alternating current. DC flows steadily in one direction. AC changes directions 60 times a second. Most appliances and consumer gadgets use AC, which is easily stepped up to higher voltages for transmission and stepped down for distribution. But DC is cheaper to send long distance because it requires only two cables while AC needs three.

AC can be converted to DC, but converter stations are expensive. "When the DC Intertie was built, the break-even distance beyond which DC transmission became cheaper was about 400 miles," says a BPA brochure on the Intertie. "So the DC Intertie to Southern California made good economic sense. BPA also has an AC Intertie to Northern California. It connects with other power lines along its route, so it is more efficient as an alternating-current line."

Balancing Act

When first conceived, the Bonneville Power Administration was given the simple task of distributing the electricity generated by federal dams equitably among the various public utilities in the region. Whether the companies were small, like the Lost River Co op and the Douglas County P.U.D., or large, like Seattle City Light or Tacoma City Light, the mandate called for distributing electricty at the lowest rate consistent with repaying the federal government for its expense in creating the system.

This simple task soon grew complex. Grand Coulee Dam included a million-acre irrigation project; costs for pumping, building canals, and clearing the land would be recouped through the sale of power. Some dam projects included slack-water navigation and locks to help move tug and barge traffic, so these costs also would be defrayed by power revenue. Then fish-ladders were needed to save the salmon and steelhead runs, and power sales also would pay for these facilities.

At first, privately owned companies in the region, such as Pacific Power and Light, Portland General Electric, and Idaho Power Company, ignored the growing field of cheap public power, producing their own electricity by building their own dams or thermal plants. For a time, a bitter battle raged between public and private rivals competing for the right to build the next dam at a choice location on the Columbia or Snake.

Finally, after a long and fierce struggle, they agreed that their common goal was to serve the people who lived in the region. A complicated set of ground rules was laid down. Public power would have first chance at half the electricity generated by the dams, and private power companies could buy the rest, with the retail cost to the public

Intertie lines head south from the Celilo terminal.—Bonneville Power Administration

averaged between the two. Private companies could buy or sell their deficits or surpluses through BPA.

But other players insisted on being dealt into the game. The fact that both the commercial and sport fishing industries are big income producers in the Pacific Northwest makes them watchdogs of the salmon and steelhead runs. If the rivers flow too high or too low during migration seasons, the fish could die. Commercial shippers play a hand, too. Tug and barge traffic requires adequate channel depths as far inland as Lewiston, Idaho, 470 miles from the sea. And migratory water fowl nesting along the shore below dams cannot withstand rapid fluctuations in the water level. Last but not least (financially, anyway) are the owners of resorts, marinas, and summer homes who depend on mostly full reservoirs for their livelihoods. Few of these varied players sympathize with power demands sometimes hundreds of miles downstream.

Dealing with all these complicated factors and trying to keep everyone happy often frustrates the BPA managers charged with making decisions that affect so many. One executive said: "When everybody gives us hell, we know we must be doing things about right."

Recently, a new concept has been factored into the "balancing act" equation—energy conservation. In the Pacific Northwest, as in other parts of the world, the idea of "unlimited resources" simply no longer applies. Until relatively few years ago energy was so cheap and abun-

264

dant that few people thought about using it sparingly. Now we recognize that our resources are finite.

Public and private power companies now encourage us to save electricity just as fervently as they once urged to use it. To this end BPA is a leader. By insulating homes, by using more energy-efficient appliances, and by conserving energy wherever we can, we can indefinitely postpone building another dam or another thermal plant. For the sake of our finite resources, we must try.

OR 206 and 19
Celilo Park—Fossil
71 miles

OR 218
Fossil—Antelope
39 miles

Zane Grey Country

Even though the mountainous, well-watered region where he lived and loved to fish in the 1920s was the Rogue River country of southwestern Oregon, most of Zane Grey's Western novels were set in the stark, lonely, thirsty American Southwest, where it was a long ride between water holes and a hundred acres of range barely fed one cow. Some modern historians believe the Old West is dead—its cowboys gone, along with the kind of country Zane Grey wrote about. Following the route suggested in this chapter will dispel that myth. Here, if anywhere, Zane Grey Country still lives.

Fourteen miles east of The Dalles, opposite the Celilo Park Exit on I-84, Oregon 206 goes south and east across miles and miles of country so remote and undisturbed by traffic that it takes little imagination to picture a party of Indians, trappers, explorers, emigrants, cowboys, sheepherders, or dryland homesteaders making their weary way across it toward a distant horizon.

John Day managed to get lost here in 1811, Peter Skene Ogden and his party of Hudson's Bay Company trappers passed through the region a couple of times during the late 1820s, and Captain John C. Fremont crossed and mapped the area during the 1840s; but none of them left a mark on the land that the incessant wind did not soon erase. Even

Hotel Shaniko, 1902. —Deschutes County Historical Society

though the railroad builders, Harriman and Hill, staged their fabled race up opposite sides of the Deschutes River canyon in the early 1900s, nothing remains of their rivalry but two parallel bands of steel, which, for most of the route, lay unseen in the depths of the canyon.

Names of local settlements such as Spanish Hollow, Wasco, Grass Valley, and Shaniko sound like the titles of Zane Grey or Louis L'Amour novels. Indeed, it was here that Grey's *Desert of Wheat* is said to have been set, near the small town of Kent. A description of the region published in the WPA guide in 1940 is as accurate today as it was then:

> Characteristic of this region are the alternate stretches of growing wheat and fallow land which in early summer resembles a vast checkerboard of tawny grain and dark, harrowed earth. To conserve the scanty moisture wheat is planted in alternate years, and where the soil is not being cropped it is harrowed repeatedly until the surface is a fine mulch that rises in slow-moving pillars of dust enveloping tractor-drawn harrows as they crawl across the long undulations of land.

Annual rainfall ranges between five and fifteen inches a year. One resident in a Condon cafe said over breakfast one morning: "We don't have enough moisture to argue about it." That may be true about rain, but not after the precious liquid runs into the John Day River, which is the chief water source for irrigation and fishing in the area. Any threat by a newcomer to take more than his share can start a deadly conflict.

Here, the wind blows much of the time. To escape it, ranchers build their houses in depressions or hollows, making the country look even emptier than it is—until harvest time in the late summer. Then the whole countryside comes alive with grain-threshing combines and labor crews on amber fields so large that cutting a single swath may take half a day. Tractors with air-conditioned cabs and music-playing tape decks ease the chore of harvesting for some, but it still is a lonely, time-consuming task.

Before the railroad came in 1897, jerk-line outfits bearing heavy loads of wheat to boat landings followed the tortuous course of the canyon into the Columbia gorge from the plateau above. The term "jerk-line" comes from the single rein stretched between the lead horse and the driver, who usually rode the nigh-wheel (left) horse and signaled a turn to the right or left by a single or double jerk on the rein. The last trip made this way was in 1926, when three wagons of wool went to The Dalles from Shaniko in parade-like fashion to commemorate the by-gone technology.

As the terminus of the Biggs-Shaniko branch of the Union Pacific Railroad, Shaniko was an important shipping point for wheat, wool, and stock. The town was named for August Scherneckau, whose ranch house served as a station on the old stage route from The Dalles to central Oregon. The difficulty folks had in pronouncing his name resulted in its more simplified version.

Some of the last battles between sheepmen and cattlemen were fought on the open range near Shaniko. "For about twenty-five years after the middle eighties," says the WPA guide, "the cattle barons stubbornly

Deserted Shaniko School.
—Deschutes County Historical Society

resisted the invasion of the sheepmen. Having ruled the public domain for a generation, the cattlemen had come to believe they had an inalienable right to its exclusive use and sheep were slaughtered by the thousands before the cattlemen gave up the vain struggle."

In 1909, as Harriman and Hill raced to build a railroad up the Deschutes River, Shaniko experienced a boom when it became construction headquarters. It was then that the two-story brick hotel, which is now a historic landmark and the most substantial structure in town, was built.

Where Oregon 19 and 206 intersect at Condon marks the 2,844-foot summit plateau of several mountain ranges: the Blue Mountains to the east, the Cascades to the west, and the Ochoco Mountains to the south. Though on the northern edge of the John Day Fossil Beds discovered in the 1860s by the world-famed geologist, Dr. Thomas Condon, the town was named not for him but for his nephew, Harvey C. Condon, an attorney from the Columbia River settlement of Arlington who developed the townsite a few years later.

Farther south, near Fossil, have been found many interesting bones of animals that no longer exist, such as the saber-toothed tiger, reminding us that the climate many centuries ago was far different than today. West of here on Oregon 218, the John Day River and Clarno State Park mark the halfway point between Fossil and the small town of Antelope.

Named for the herds of fleet, graceful, horned animals that once roamed the dry hills surrounding it, Antelope is famous for two historic events, neither of which has yet been commemorated by a statue or a plaque. The first is that H.L. Davis edited the town's weekly newspaper in 1928, eight years before his fine novel about the early days in Oregon, *Honey in the Horn*, won both the Harper and Pulitzer prize awards. The second is that between 1981 and 1985 Antelope stood at the center of a firestorm of controversy in the strangest chapter in recent Oregon history—the Rajneesh invasion.

The Rolls Royce Guru

Despite the reams of newspaper and magazine copy that have been written about it, the extensive regional and national TV coverage, and the stacks of court records detailing suits, trials, and appeals to governing bodies, historical interpretations of what happened during the reign of the Rolls Royce Guru will shift along with the ever-changing perspectives that the passage of time and the study of cause and effect offer. For now, relating the key events as reported by a number of writers will have to do.

In 1981, a group of people who always dressed in red paid $6 million for one of the biggest ranches in central Oregon, a hundred square miles of dry hills and hollows on the John Day River. In his 1984 book, *Rajneeshpuram: The Unwelcome Society*, historian Kirk Braun called them "a well-organized, dedicated, capitalistic-oriented movement of 350,000 world-wide followers who have planted $100 million American dollars into a 64,000 acre run-down, abandoned Central Oregon cattle ranch in an effort to convert it from an arid, semi-desert hell to a heaven on earth for their master and themselves."

The statement that the extensive piece of land was "a run-down, abandoned semi-desert hell" may well be questioned, for such properties do not normally sell for $93 an acre in that part of the country. But whatever its value, it did not remain empty very long. Soon six hundred members of the cult moved onto the land, coming from such diverse places as Poona, India, Montclair, New Jersey, and points in between. Though some of them were well educated, intelligent, affluent American citizens, many were not. A number of the non-citizens, who came to the United States with temporary permits of one kind or another, tried to become citizens by marrying Americans in ceremonies of questionable validity.

Bhagwan Shree Rajneesh. —Oregon Historical Society

Rajneeshpuram city limits marker, 1990.

Their leader was a bearded, impish-looking, fifty-year-old native of India calling himself Bhagwan Shree Rajneesh. Though disavowing his label as a spiritual leader or founder of a cult, he claimed that the colony was altruistic enough to be exempt from paying taxes. Though he had studied the teachings and philosophy of Mahatma Gandhi, he held no belief in the virtue in being either humble or poor. In fact, he was so strongly opposed to poverty that he readily accepted the gifts his faithful followers showered upon him—including Rolls Royces.

By 1983, they had given him twenty-one of the luxury cars. Two years later, the total rose to ninety.

As his spokesperson, he had chosen a handsome, dark-haired woman, also a native of India, named Ma Anand Sheela. She claimed to be president of the Rajneesh Foundation International, acted as personal secretary to the Bhagwan, called herself "mother" of the colony, became the Bhagwan's voice when he went into periods of silence (as he sometimes did), and did not object to the title Queen of Rajneeshpuram.

At first, the 136 inhabitants of the small town of Antelope, twenty miles away, and the 2,235 residents of Madras, seventy miles from the colony, viewed the "red people" with amused tolerance. These self-reliant Oregonians lived in a big country; they were used to roving prospectors, eccentric hermits, and rootless wanderers with values different from theirs. In this country, people killed their own snakes and lived as they wanted to. As long as no one's peculiar ways infringed on the neighbors, each person enjoyed a right to be left alone, crazy or not.

When a few curious local residents visited the colony, they told their friends that the newcomers "do a lot of hugging, dancing, and singing," and seemed to feel that, instead of cleanliness being next to Godliness, "it was sex, not soap, that was the speediest and surest path to a spiritual high." The institution of marriage did not seem to be considered sacred in the colony; children belonged to nobody or everybody; some of the newcomers smoked pot and perhaps took drugs.

The natives viewed this sort of behavior disapprovingly; however, there is no evidence that they threatened vigilante action. But when the Bhagwan and his red-clad followers started flaunting their Rolls Royces and promising to take over the governments of Antelope and Madras, along with those of the counties of Jackson and Wasco, the local people got very disturbed.

Parade to Madras

As a study of the Bhagwan's life in India indicates, he liked to stir people up by making outlandish statements and doing outrageous things. In India, he had been fired from several prestigious teaching positions in universities because of this behavior. Now, he exercised it in an offensive way by leading a caravan of his followers seventy miles each day from the settlement of Rajneeshpuram to the outskirts of Madras, for the sole purpose of indulging himself in an ice cream soda.

Accompanied by armed disciples in an escort Jeep, he would drive one of his Rolls Royces to Madras, where he would park near the weigh

The Bhagwan goes for a drive, July 1983. —Oregon Historical Society

station or supermarket. There, he would sit and smile enigmatically, while his companion, Ma Sheela, went in and bought him a soda. Often he was followed by one or more busloads of red-clad disciples, who, while he sat and enjoyed the soda, would surround the Rolls Royce, sing, dance, laugh, bow, jump up and down, and cry with apparently mystic meaning: *"Hoo! Hoo! Hoo!"*

The soda and the ceremony finished, the guru and his entourage would turn around and drive the seventy miles back to Rajneeshpuram.

As the practice continued day after day through January 1983, the Reverend Mardo Jimenez, pastor of the Madras Conservative Baptist Church, grew increasingly irritated. Born in Honduras, Jimenez had come to Oregon to minister to Hispanic migrant workers. He loved the United States passionately, and, just a year earlier had gained citizenship—a status the Bhagwan aspired to but had not yet achieved. Jimenez was a sincerely religious man.

In her book *Cities in a Hill*, sociologist Frances Fitzgerald summed up Jimenez's three main concerns over the Rajneesh presence: one, the cultists were an immoral people intent on destroying the institution of marriage; two, they had surrendered themselves to the man they called God; and, three, their political and territorial ambitions included two counties—Jefferson and Wasco—and possibly the state.

District attorney for Jefferson County was Mike Sullivan, a graduate of Washington University in St. Louis, whom Fitzgerald characterized as "a man of unusual intellectual detachment." In a legal sense, the Rajneesh were committing no crime, he knew. But he also knew that they were behaving with reckless arrogance and were pushing the local people toward the limits of their endurance.

Despite Sullivan's appeals that they act diplomatically, the newcomers treated the Antelope residents with contempt, insulting them, calling them "rednecks" and "ignorant old people," and harrassing them in all kinds of ways. In a country where pickup trucks dominate, many of which held rifles in the rear-window rack, this was a dangerous—if not stupid—way to talk.

Day by day, the crowd of participants and onlookers at the weigh station grew. The main highway, US 97, leading south to California across the wide-open spaces of central Oregon, went past the weigh station. Until now, it had been a dull stretch of road with very little to see except sagebrush for seventy miles in either direction. But now truck drivers and other travelers spread the word that on the outskirts of Madras an entertaining show was being staged every afternoon.

The conflict reached a climax one day when over-the-road truckers, pickup-driving local cowboys, the Bhagwan, Reverend Mardo Jimenez, four busloads of Rajneesh young people, and a contingent of highway

Bhagwan followers place hay around newly planted fruit trees, March 1982.
—Max Gutierrez (UPI), Oregon Historical Society

patrolmen and local police got into a confused melee of shouting, singing, flag-waving, and preaching that came very close to violent explosion.

Keeping a cool head when all those around him seemed about to overheat, district attorney Mike Sullivan managed to negotiate a settlement between Jimenez's group and the Bhagwan. But the truce at the weigh station did not end the conflict, it simply moved to a different arena.

Takeover in Antelope

With six hundred people in residence at Rajneeshpuram, and more arriving every week, the settlement was growing fast. They drew up elaborate plans to build a dam, a lake, an airstrip, a huge greenhouse, and develop fields to grow vegetables, grain, and fruit. Ignoring prior water rights of long-time residents, the Rajneesh asked for more water out of the John Day River than they were entitled to. Furthermore, the large population center they planned to establish in this dryland country threatened to destroy the area's fragile balance.

When the Rajneesh applied for building permits at the county level, they were turned down and told their land was for ranching and farming only. The nearest incorporated municipality was Antelope, so they applied for permits there. With only forty-two registered voters and no desire to have the outsiders build anything in their town, the Antelope City Council also refused to issue the permits.

In addition to having unlimited financial resources, the Rajneesh possessed a wealth of sharp legal talent. So their lawyers scrutinized local, county, and state laws. Soon they discovered that to vote in an incorporated town in Oregon, a person need only own a piece of property, spend twenty-four hours in town, and declare an intention to become a resident. The Rajneesh bought an old building, in which a number of its members slept for a night, then demanded an election for which they would supply four candidates for the seven-member council.

In desperation, the Antelope City Council called an election to disincorporate the town. If the measure passed, it would be the first time in Oregon history that a town in that state had voted itself out of existence.

Kirk Braun reports that over 100 media representatives attended, including eleven television crews, and Secretary of State Norma Paulus came to monitor the proceedings. By then, quite a few of the Rajneesh had moved into Antelope and registered to vote. When the final tally came in, 42 voted to disincorporate and 67 against it. Calling a second vote to elect a city council, the Rajneesh faction won a 4-3 majority, one of whom became the mayor.

In a demonstration of its power, the new council passed an ordinance decreeing that a portion of the municipal park—a small expanse of bare dirt containing a swing and a slide—be set aside for nude sunbathing.

The Red Tide

Now that they had taken over Antelope and learned how local and state laws could work in their favor, the red-clad people incorporated their own city on their ranch, calling it Rajneespuram. In an effort to curb the growing number of legal decisions favoring the Rajneesh, a group calling itself the "1000 Friends" organized a letter-writing crusade, addressing newspapers, Oregon legislators, and anyone who might help them stem the "red tide." Puzzled and amused, metropolitan newspaper columnists made wry comments. In the *Oregonian*, Larry Colton wrote in January 1983:

> He has 270,000 disciples worldwide, 27 Rolls Royces in his driveway and a farm in the central Oregon desert that's bigger than the city of San Francisco. Depending on who's speaking, he's described as a spiritual savior, a glorified pimp, a corporate genius or a big fat hoax.

Meanwhile, at the Madras Builders Supply, a box of baseball caps had just arrived, honoring the Bhwagman after a fashion. "On the front of each cap," writes Kirk Braun, "there was an emblem bearing a picture of a Rolls Royce framed in the cross hairs of a gunsight." Also in the carton were a number of white T-shirts showing the Bhagwan's head mounted as a trophy with hunting rifles underneath. The caption read: "I ain't got nuthin' agin gurus—Everybody should BAG WAN!"

Speaking for the Rajneesh while being interviewed on a TV show, Swami Prem Devalaya, who was fairly well up in the ranch hierarchy, jokingly declared: "We are going to paint Oregon red!"

More fuel was added to the growing conflagration when the Bhagwan predicted that a nuclear war would take place within ten years, which was one of the reasons the red people had located where they did, and that plans were being made to build huge underground vaults to store libraries of materials that would help people make a new beginning.

"Bhagwan Shree Rajneesh, whose message is love and life, predicts that World War III will begin in 1993," stated the *Oregon Journal*, "last six years and will destroy modern civilization. Or almost all of it; some Rajneesh communities could survive to give a start to a new world."

It is not clear whether open-mindedness, curiosity, or a maintainence of a long-standing tradition impelled the politicians to invite Ma Anand Sheela to give the invocation that opened the State Legislature session in 1983. But invite her they did. Unlike the fire-and-brimstone Baptist preacher, Joab Powell one hundred and thirty-four years earlier, who had bowed his head and said simply: "Father, forgive them, for they know not what they do, Amen," Ma Sheela rambled at length.

Afterwards, no one was sure what she said, let alone what she meant. She claimed to be reading from the Bhagwan's writings, which she probably was, but no one knew what he meant either. In part, the invocation proclaimed:

> Those who know, know God as the fragrance of life, the perfume of existence, the very ground of being. For them, God is not a concept, not a theory, not a hypothesis. For them, God is an existential experience. For them, God is not separate from man, for them God is man's innermost core. God is not an ideal as we have been thinking down the ages. God is man fulfilled, man is God on the way. God is not to be worshiped but realized.

Instead of a simple amen to signify the prayer was over, Ma Sheela then sang the Rajneesh invocation, raising her arms as she sang each part: "I go to the feet of the Awakened One, I go to the feet of the commune of the Awakened One, I go to the feet of the Absolute Truth of the Awakened One."

Veteran House Representative Max Simpson, whose district adjoined Rajneeshpuram, was not available to explain the meaning of either the prayer or the song. He had walked out of the session in a huff when Ma Sheela had been introduced.

15,000 Sannyasins

As owners of a million-dollar Mitsubishi aircraft and a 3,200-foot desert runway to land it on, the Rajneesh invited Governor Victor Atiyeh, state legislators, university professors, sociologists, agricultural experts, and public opinion makers in related fields to pay them a visit as guests. Though the governor and most of the legislators declined, others who were curious about the colony and wanted to see it for themselves came to call, acting, as sociologist Fitzgerald aptly put it "like foreign visitors to a Chinese commune."

Verdicts of the visitors were mixed. One agricultural expert concluded that there was no way the Rajneesh could ever raise enough food to be self-sufficient; another predicted that their growing processes would be the wonder of the Western world. After spending a million dollars on an immense greenhouse to produce food year round, the Rajneesh were more than a little chagrined when an expert pointed out that the structure's massive amount of glass had been installed in such a way that it could not possibly make use of the sun.

Sannyasins demonstrating at a U.S. Courthouse. —Oregon Historical Society

Liberal social historians gave high marks to the colony for its efforts to better the plight of mankind, while conservatives called it a refuge for intellectually bankrupt nuts. Both liberal and conservative sociologists compared the Rajneesh movement to earlier efforts at group living by the Mormon, the Shaker, and Amana colonies, predicting that it would *succeed* or *fail* for the same basic reasons that theirs did. Oddly enough, no one (at least, to my knowledge) compared the Rajneesh effort with the Aurora Colony, which existed in Oregon between 1855 and 1885 west of the Cascades.

In late July 1983, an act of violence broke out against the Rajneesh when a bomb struck a hotel they owned in Portland for the faithful to use when in the city. Though only the bomber, an obviously deranged man, was hurt and little damage was done, it caused the Rajneesh to tighten security at both the hotel and the ranch to the extent that strangers were frisked for arms and gun-carrying guards watched visitors with suspicious eyes.

Still another bit of bad news hit the Bhagwan when the Portland office of the Immigration and Naturalization Service denied his petition to remain in the United States as a religious worker. Furthermore, the INS turned down his application to adjust his status from that of a tourist to a permanent resident. The reasons given by the agency for this double refusal were as curious and contradictory as those the Bhwagan offered in his application.

Upon entering the United States, he had claimed that as a religious worker he had come to minister to his flock; he also said his poor health required medical attention available to him only in this country. In turning down his petition, the INS stated that his poor health rendered him unable to perform his designated role as a religious worker, and since he was at the moment in one of his "periods of silence," during which he communed only with God while Ma Sheela became his voice, he could not communicate with his followers and be a religious worker anyway. Ma Sheela became indignant over the ruling.

"The INS does not know what true religion is," she raged. "They are blind and have been looking for reasons to reject the Bhagwan's application rather than looking for the truth and what the Bhagwan has to offer America. They say on the one hand that he is too sick to be able to perform his role as a religious teacher adequately, and on the other they say he was not as sick as all his doctors said he was when he came to America for medical care. They can't have it both ways."

The INS ruling came late in December 1982. Whether it, warmer weather, or a vision caused the Bhagwan to decide to break his silence, is not clear. But he got his voice back in time to speak out at the biggest celebration Rajneeshpuram ever had staged. According to Russell Chandler, who wrote about it in the *Los Angeles Times* the following July:

The seven-day festival is an extravaganza of meditation, wild dancing and "transcendental therapy," recreation and nude sun-bathing
at one of two lakes created at the 100 square mile spread.

Festival in the Sun

According to writer Kirk Braun, who was there, it was "the most
photographed and written-about news event in the history of the Pacific
Northwest." Maybe. Writers and photographers from 61 publications
and twelve TV crews attended, he says. "Rows of tents covering the
valley floor—4,000 of them in all—clustered around the giant 2.2 acre
Buddha Hall, where 15,000 sannyasins gathered daily during the first
week of July under one sun-baked roof to celebrate the presence of their
master."

Now that he had broken his silence, the Bhagwan began to talk about
his plans for the future of Rajneeshpuram. Although his immediate goal
was a city of 4,000 by the turn of the century, eventually he had visions
on a much more grandiose scale. Surely the desert of Central Oregon
could accommodate such a dream, he said.

"The big city is going to be ours, a big experiment of 100,000 sannyasins
who have never lived together anywhere in the world at any time in

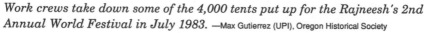

*Work crews take down some of the 4,000 tents put up for the Rajneesh's 2nd
Annual World Festival in July 1983.* —Max Gutierrez (UPI), Oregon Historical Society

history. This will be the first sannyasin city. This is going to be something of a unique experiment."

Though the July 1983 festival marked a high point in the growth of the Rajneesh movement, small clouds of doubt about its future were beginning to appear in the sunny central Oregon sky. Considering the relatively large number of Ph.D.s in the community, educational standards were unusually low, with a number of the teachers claiming that the children should learn math and languages but not history, because, as Henry Ford had said years before, "history is meaningless bunk."

Sociologist Frances Fitzgerald was surprised to learn that there were only fifty children in the community, even though the 800-1,000 adults living there were relatively young and in any other society would have been parents of many more children. Insofar as intelligent planning was concerned, all decisions seemed to made by the Bhagwan, who relayed them to Ma Sheela, who then put them into effect under her authority as Queen of Rajneesh. Though she met with people regularly and appeared to listen to what they had to say, she did only what she wanted to do and answered to no one.

By September 1983, Rajneeshpuram security guards checked everyone entering or leaving the ranch; visitors were body-searched, police dogs sniffed cars, and residents as well as visitors had to wear identification bracelets. Ma Sheela became increasingly arrogant, calling local people "ignorant and stupid, rednecks and bigots." In an open letter to the governor, which was reprinted in the Madras paper, Sheela wrote:

> Oregon can hardly prosper if it is filled with stagnant, dilapidated little towns like Antelope—places where indolent old people go to mark time until they die.

Schooling local children became a heated issue. In a raw display of voting power, the Rajneesh, who had set up their own school after refusing to send their children to the local tax-supported school, took over $50,000 in state funds, then told the local people to send their children to the colony school: "It will be good for them. They have no idea what a really good school is like."

That they were using public funds to support a private religious school apparently did not matter to them. But even as the battle over that issue began to develop, the Rajneesh were facing legal challenges on two other matters: first, the INS case against the guru; second, a land-use lawsuit which claimed that a city could not be incorporated and run by a religious insititution.

In October 1983, the state attorney general ruled that the municipal status of Rajneeshpuram violated the religious-establishment clause in the state and federal constitutions. That the city was actually owned and controlled by a church—that is, the Commune and the Rajneesh Foundation—was patently clear, he said. Backing up the ruling, Wasco County Circuit Court Judge William Hulse enjoined any further construction at Rajneeshpuram until the settlement of the incorporation case.

Relations with local people suffered further deterioration when Ma Sheela declared in a Portland TV interview that the children of the ranchers "looked retarded." After she called a local woman a "racist" and a "bigot," the woman sued her for libel—and won. But that did not slow her down.

"All publicity is good publicity," she declared after some statements she made on Ted Koppel's *Nightline* raised hackles nationwide, "and I can get it for free. Not even the governor can do that!" She paused, and then added in a harsh tone, "Donkeys can only understand a kick. The Antelopians are your average day-to-day bigots. Their brains are in the fifteenth century."

Decline and Fall

By the winter of 1983-84 many Rajneesh watchers in Oregon believed that some form of denouement was now inevitable, Frances Fitzgerald wrote:

> The Rajneesh lawyers were still quite masterfully holding back all the legal challenges to the commune's existence, but there were a great many forces arrayed against them, and the Rajneesh leaders seemed bent on a course of conflict.

Though there were rumors that the Bhagwan wished to sacrifice his life and become a martyr, the rate that he continued to accumulate Rolls Royces, diamond watches, jewelry, and other earthly treasures did not make him seem a very likely candidate for that role. More ominously, the Rajneesh were preparing for war.

The *Oregonian* reported that by the fall of 1984 two helicopter reconnaissance teams and 150 sannyasin security guards patrolled the Rajneesh ranch. They bought hundreds of human silhouette targets and $25,000 worth of ammunition, more than half of what the city of Portland spent that year. Their arsenal "included at least twenty-eight semiautomatic weapons.... They had tried to buy automatic weapons on a number of occasions, but the U.S. Bureau of Alcohol, Tobacco and Firearms had prevented the sales from going through."

According to Rajneesh financial statements, gifts to the commune and foundation for 1981-83 totaled $20 million, excluding income from the ranch and its related businesses. But gifts declined in the wake of rumors that the Bhagwan might "give up his body." Other well-known ministers in the United States made similar overtures to this tune about the same time, if contributions to their causes did not increase.

Ma Sheela frightened a number of reporters who visited her by brandishing a new acquisition, a Smith & Wesson revolver. When noticeably fewer people attended the 1984 Summer Festival, ranch personnel wrote or phoned every American who had ever stayed at the ranch to offer a six weeks to three months stay at reduced rates—practically free. But very few people came. So the Rajneesh came up with an offer too good to refuse.

Give Us Your Homeless

At the end of August the Rajneesh invited homeless people from big cities all over the United States to come and live on the ranch, paying bus fares to and, in the event the visitors did not want to stay, from the colony. Meanwhile, they enjoyed free room and board and work if they wanted it. Newcomers arrived in droves. By October, 2,000 "homeless" found a home, including derelicts, curiosity seekers, hitchikers, drunks, bums, petty criminals, and street hustlers. Noting that all the new arrivals were over eighteen, Frances Fitzgerald observed, "Rajneesh charity apparently did not extend to homeless families."

Knowing that the Rajneesh had accumulated an arsenal of weapons and observing that many of the "homeless" were tough-looking young men, local residents wondered what would be done with the newcomers. Would they be given terrorist training? Drugged into zombies? Turned loose on the streets of Madras with knives?

In view of Antelope losing even its name—changed to Rajneesh—many Oregonians feared that this most recent influx spelled trouble for Wasco County in the upcoming November elections, when two of three seats for county commissioner would appear on the ballot. They had, after all, recently voted to repeal Rajneeshpuram's comprehensive plan, delayed the festival permit, and denied tax-exempt status to Rajneesh Mandir—the greenhouse-turned-religious-meeting hall.

When the three county commissioners had visited the city in early September, two became ill. A week later there was a large and mysterious outbreak of salmonella poisoning in The Dalles, which was traced to the salad bars of eight separate restaurants, though it could not be connected to any common food source. About 750 people were affected. Many believed that the Rajneesh were responsible.

With only 12,000 registered voters in Wasco County, the importation of thousands of outsiders voting in a bloc threatened the election. After putting up two Rajneesh write-in candidates for the two commissioner positions, Ma Sheela bragged that there were now 7,000 people in Rajneeshpuram—1,500 residents, 1,500 paying guests, and 4,000 in the Share-a-Home program. This so frightened the residents of Wasco County that it inspired 2,000 new voters to register, bringing the voter rolls up to 14,000, and a fundamentalist group from Albany, Oregon, in the Willamette Valley, stood by to bring in 1,000 more to support the county's long-standing residents.

But this time Secretary of State Norma Paulus planned ahead. On October 10 she brought voter registration in Wasco County to a halt and set up a special hearing process for all prospective voters. Fifty lawyers stood ready to interview new voter registrants at a mass hearing in The Dalles and subjectively judge each applicant's intent to reside in Wasco County. The Rajneesh protested the order but lost. A week later, the Rajneesh declared the Share-a-Home program full and stopped recruitment of street people.

Thwarted in their attempt to dominate the democratic process, the Rajneesh announced on October 26 that they were urging all their people to boycott the election. On November 3, the date of the scheduled hearings for voter qualification, the fifty volunteer lawyers sat idle in The Dalles armory all day long. The street people never showed up.

Back at the ranch ten days later, a spokesman said that about half of the street people had left Rajneeshpuram and only 2,000 remained. Most of these soon left, too, not by means of paid bus tickets to cities of their choice but by being transported off the ranch to the nearest small town, where they were unceremoniously dumped and left for the churches or the Salvation Army to care for. The Salvation Army alone spent over $100,000 feeding them and buying them bus tickets home.

By their own admission, the Rajneesh had spent at least $1 million on the aborted effort to win the election.

Legal and Criminal Problems

By now, both civil authorities and individuals were bringing lawsuits against the Rajneesh. The land-use case and the church-state case were still in litigation. A lawyer representing seven street people claimed fraud, coercion, physical abuse, and theft. A woman who was deceived into giving the group $310,000 in Poona, India, won her case and was awarded $1.7 million in damages. Instead of sticking together to defend itself against the lawsuits, the Rajneesh leadership fell apart.

On Monday, September 15, 1985, the big bombshell exploded when the Bhwagan himself called a press conference to announce that Sheela and a dozen other leaders had fled to Europe after the "gang of facists" tried to poison his doctor, his dentist, his female companion, the Jefferson County district attorney, and The Dalles' water system. He accused Sheela of stealing money and mismanaging the commune's finances, leaving it $55 million in debt. The next day he leveled more accusations on her, including a plan to crash an explosive-laden plane into The Dalles courthouse and poison him, the Bhagwan.

Hearing this, one frustrated law enforcement officer reportedly said that officials had been looking for "a stool pigeon" for a long time. Now, he said, "We've got the biggest one of all. The Bhagwan himself. That's going to break it."

He was right.

The guru's strategy was to clear himself by blaming everything on Sheela. From her place of refuge in a resort in Germany's Black Forest, Sheela was doing the same thing by blaming everything on the Bhagwan, selling interviews to the German press in which she claimed it had been his insatiable greed for diamonds, money, and Rolls Royces that had brought the colony to the brink of ruin.

After obtaining evidence through search warrants and subpoenas, the investigators presented their case to a federal grand jury, which issued a thirty-five count indictment against the guru, Ma Sheela, and six other

Sheela and U.S. marshall. —Oregon Historical Society

disciples. The federal authorities claimed that the Bhagwan had lied on his visa application and had arranged sham marriages so that foreign disciples could remain in the United States.

While his attorneys dickered with officers about his coming to Portland to surrender, two chartered Lear jets secretly carried the guru and six of his disciples to Charlotte, North Carolina, where another chartered jet prepared to fly the group to Bermuda. But federal customs agents interrupted the escape party. After brief stays in jails in North Carolina and Oklahoma, the guru was returned to Portland, where he pleaded guilty to two felonies: making false statements to the authorities in 1980, and concealing his intent to reside in the United States.

The Bhagwan received a ten-year prison sentence, suspended upon his agreement to pay $400,000 in fines and prosecution fees and to leave the country within five days, forbidden to return for at least five years without explicit permission from the U.S. Attorney General. Boarding a plane for New Delhi, India, he declared that he never wanted to see the United States again.

Meanwhile, in Germany, Ma Sheela thought she was safe because immigration fraud is not an extractible offense under our treaty with Germany. But attempted murder is, and when the charge was brought against her and two others, they were arrested in their Black Forest resort hotel by German authorities and returned to the United States. By the time they arrived, additional charges of poisoning, burglary and arson of the Wasco County planning office, racketeering, immigration fraud, wiretapping, and causing the salmonella outbreak in The Dalles had been made against them.

A district court judge ruled Rajneeshpuram unconstitutional by summary judgment. Though for several years highway map-makers had been forced to show it and Antelope/Rajneesh on the map, the larger settlement was quickly wiped off the map, while the smaller quietly resumed its original name and started the long process of trying to forget everything that had happened during the five years previous.

Sheela and Puja, the woman in charge of Rajneesh medical services, against whom the most serious charges had been made, both pleaded guilty, were fined half a million dollars, and sentenced to twenty years in a federal prison in California. Among the portable assets owned by the ranch, the farming equipment and the ninety-three Rolls Royces were sold at auction. A used car dealer from Texas bought the luxury cars.

The $55 Million Mystery

To date, none of the commune's assets have been found. Authorities believed that the Bhagwan's throne, which he took on his attempted escape, was stuffed with millions of dollars worth of precious gems. But they x-rayed it, then broke it into little pieces without finding a thing of value in it. When the Bhagwan took its remains with him into exile, he listed it simply as "chair pieces."

Ma Sheela and Puja retained high-priced attorneys both in Germany and the United States to defend them without a single complaint of not being paid for their services. At least $200,000 of Sheela's half-million dollar fine was paid by a gift from an "anonymous donor." But when the state of Oregon tried to collect $270,000, she took a pauper's oath and underwent a rigorous debtor's exam—which disclosed no assets whatsoever. Her Portland attorney would only say of her $23,926 long-distance telephone tab ran up between May 1986 and April 1988 that she "does not have funds herself."

The *Oregonian* reported that in a letter to her parents—one of many she wrote from prison—Sheela claimed: "... the people of Oregon missed me immensely. It was clear to me that they had recognized their error of persecution. They finally had the glimpse that I and the Bhagwan had offered them meaning in their lives and in their dull existence." But after Sheela and the guru left the state, she wrote, "Oregon became a backward, low mentality, coward country again."

The Bhagwan stayed for a while in India, where he tried to establish a new commune, then he moved to Nepal, and then to Crete, as the guest of a Greek producer of X-rated films. He changed his name to "Osho." Though his health improved remarkably, he may have been preparing himself for reincarnation, for after he returned to India and began founding yet another colony, he died suddenly of a heart attack on January 19, 1990, at the age of 58.

Many questions remain unanswered. None of the $55 million in jewelry and cash contributions listed on the Rajneesh books has been found. When creditors closed in, the Rajneesh tried to sell what they claimed was a $100 million property for the best price they could get. First they asked $42 million, then dropped their price to $28 million. No buyers appeared. Though they had paid $6 million for the ranch, nearly two-thirds of it remained under a mortgage, and Wasco County had a tax lien against it for $1 million.

Finally, at a Christmas Eve auction in 1989, Connecticut General Life Insurance Company, the mortgage holder, bid $4.535 million for the property and received title to it after back taxes were deducted. But in this lonely land of wide distances, little rain, and eternal wind, it seems likely that nature itself will regain title eventually, for the marks man makes on the high desert country do not remain there very long.

Soon after the Bhagwan died in India, he was cremated and his ashes given to the sacred river. If federal investigators worry that he might reincarnate himself and return to the United States with a new identity, the guru's epitaph in Pune, India, may offer little comfort. A press release from Osho Commune International says the it reads: "Osho: Never born, never died, visited the planet Earth between Dec. 11, 1931, and Jan. 19, 1990."

OR 19 and 207
Fossil—Mitchell
47 miles

US 26
Mitchell—Prineville
49 miles

National Forest Islands

Resuming the route across the high desert country before our detour to Antelope, Oregon 19 continues south of Fossil. Green islands of high meadows and beautiful forests crossed by clear mountain streams offer relief from the monotony of sagebrush, sand, and scattered basalt rocks flanking such main highways as US 97. Invariably, these areas are shown in green on highway maps and are designated as national forests. Most range from 3,500 to 7,500 feet in elevation and are the western spurs of the main range to the east, the Blue Mountains.

While it is interesting and useful to have an altimeter in your car to check the altitude of mountain passes, most native eastern Oregonians who have hunted, fished, hiked, rock-hounded, or engaged in other outdoor pastimes that require observing one's surroundings can estimate elevation with remarkable accuracy—give or take a few hundred feet—simply by noting two factors: the type of vegetation and the amount of moisture available for its growth.

Wildflowers, grasses, trees, shrubs, and plants in this edge-of-the-desert country all have lower and upper limits of moisture and temperature tolerance. Though the kind and quality of soil also affects plant growth, it is overall less important than moisture and temperature. In

Painted Hills near Mitchell. —Deschutes County Historical Society

this part of the country, moisture and temperature are determined almost entirely by elevation.

Twenty-two miles south of Fossil, Oregon 19 turns east at Service Creek, which originally was named for a pioneer settler named Sarvis, then was changed by the postal authorities without consulting the local citizens, who still pronounce it *their* way.

Here Oregon 207 goes on south to Mitchell. Located on the main stage road between The Dalles and John Day, this small town sprouted from a big gold strike in the 1860s and was named for John H. Mitchell, who served for a time as a United States senator from Oregon. Though a quiet place now, Mitchell has survived some trying times. The WPA guide says:

> Burned out, washed out, beset at times by desperadoes, Mitchell has had an unusually dramatic existence. In 1884 a nine-foot wave rushed over the bluff above the town, filled the streets with boulders weighing as much as a ton, carried away houses, wagons and implements, and deposited mud and gravel on the floor of Chamberlain and Todd's saloon a foot deep. The town was attacked by fire March 25, 1896, and nine buildings destroyed. Again, in August, 1899, ten buildings were burned.

On July 11, 1904, a cloudburst precipitated a wall of water thirty feet high onto the town. Everything was destroyed except for a few buildings on higher ground. Because the terrific din of the onrushing flood warned the people, most escaped into the nearby hills and only two died. Two months later, a smaller flood struck the town, but there was little left to destroy.

At Mitchell, US 26, heads west toward Prineville through the heart of the Ochoco National Forest. Covering an area of 1,200 square miles, this is a surprisingly green, well-watered region after the long desert miles of the lower country, with campgrounds, lakes, wildlife refuges, and stands of stately pine trees that make it one of the loveliest drives in eastern Oregon. The highest point on US 26 is Ochoco Summit at 4,720 feet.

For a time during the late 1860s, this was a bloody battleground for determined white settlers and desperate Indians, who made a last-ditch fight to save their homeland in a bitter, undeclared war. No mercy was shown by either side. The grim details of how this brutal war eventually came to its inevitable conclusion are forthcoming. But first let's move on to Prineville, which, during its early years, suffered through a somewhat different kind of violence.

Where the West Was Really Wild

If a movie producer wanted to create a setting for a low-budget Western, Barney Prine would be a good man to hire for the job, for he spent money very frugally. The WPA guide reports that:

> Prineville, the seat of Crook County, was named for its founder. During the summer of 1868 Barney Prine started Prineville by building a dwelling house, store, blacksmith shop, hotel and saloon. He was all of one day building them. They were constructed of willow logs, 10 by 14 feet in size, one story high and all under one roof.... His first invoice of goods cost $80; his liquor consisted of a case of Hostetter's Bitters, and the iron for the blacksmith shop was obtained from the fragments of an old emigrant wagon left up on Crooked River.

As the biggest town in the area during the range wars of the 1880s, where sheepmen sometimes referred to cattlemen as "The Crook County Sheep-Shooters' Association," Prineville would seem the logical setting for a script dealing with that conflict. But a good story consultant might recommend a less hackneyed tale—one that has never been filmed, despite its alleged truth.

Russell Blankenship, in his apocryphal regional history of the Pacific Northwest, *And There Were Men*, noted that local communities took considerable pride in their badmen. Luminaries in the Southwest included Wyatt Earp, Doc Holliday, and Billy the Kid. Less notorious but no less rascally were Prineville's Charlie Long and, two hundred miles east of here in what became the "Round-Up City," Pendleton's Hank Vaughn.

Before reading this story in Blankenship's own words, you should know something about his brand of history. Though the term had not yet been invented when he published his book in 1942, Blankenship was a folklore preservationist—a scholar who specializes in collecting stories told by old-timers to younger people. These stories usually had been told so many times by so many people that they simply must be true, even though their veracity cannot be vouched for by any scholarly authority.

This is the story as Blankenship told it:

In the heydey of his lurid career Hank Vaughn heard that a fellow named Charlie Long had firmly established himself as the champion bad man of the lower John Day and Deschutes regions of Central Oregon. Such news always held a poignant interest for Hank. Carefully making inquiry, he ascertained that Long was sojourning at Prineville. Prineville was about two hundred miles from the Vaughn home, but despite the distance, Hank determined to make a personal investigation of the report. The investigation was not conducted in a mood of hot-headed impetuosity, nor was it animated by personal dislike. Hank had never met Long. Even if the Umatilla champion had left home in a fit of petulance, a solitary horseback ride of two hundred miles would certainly have given him enough time to consider his actions. He went in exactly the same spirit which impels a star golfer to take a long trip just to pit his skill against that of another player.

Hank arrived in Prineville and straightaway inquired where Charlie Long could be found. He was directed to Charlie's favorite night-and-day spot. With his usual urbanity he introduced himself and followed his introduction with an invitation to have a drink. Long had most assuredly heard of Hank, and he did not have to be psychic in order to divine why Vaughn was visiting in Prineville. The two stood at the bar and sized each other up with appraising eyes, both excessively polite but also excessively cautious. After the drink Hank politely suggested a game of cards. The two considerately went outside and sat down on the porch. By way of starting the game of seven-up with the proper tone, Long drew his bowie knife and pinned Hank's leather chaps to the board floor. Vaughn, unwilling to lag behind in an exhibition of savoir faire, did the same with Long's chaps. After a hand or two Long leaned over and said:

"Hank, you'd make a good cannoneer in hell."

Hank retorted in kind, and the reverberation of pistol shots shook the air of the little village. When the smoke cleared away, the two gunmen lay unconscious. The somewhat bored citizens of Prineville picked them up, put them to bed in the same room but in different beds, summoned a doctor, and went about their affairs, cheerfully hoping for the best. They were a bit discouraged the next day to discover that both duelists were recovering.

A few days later when Hank had regained consciousness, he weakly raised himself on an unsteady elbow and looked into the other bed. There was Long also feebly aware of his surroundings.

"Charlie," said Hank, "they oughtn't to waste two beds on a couple of damn fools. Lay over."

So saying, he tottered across the room and went to bed with his late opponent. This was widely regarded as a fine sporting gesture, indicating that Vaughn's trip was launched by no personal animosity.

Hank's friendly action completely won Long's heart. Several years after the Prineville affair, Vaughn was in bed from an injury which had not been received in the discharge of professional duties. Long was desolated by news of the unfortunate occurrence. Forthwith he saddled his horse and started to Pendleton to offer in person what condolence he might. At his destination he found himself momentarily nonplussed. Just how could he most delicately convey his sincere wishes for Hank's recovery? To bolster his judgment he sought the advice and services of a bartender.

A few drinks flooded his memory with mellow recollections of the chivalrous Vaughn, and in a sentimental mood he decreed that flowers could most adequately express his good wishes. But then came a real difficulty. The only flowers in Pendleton in those days were the bouquets blossoming on the noses of chronic drunkards. Three more drinks in quick succession suffused Charlie with the glow of plenary inspiration. Weaving unsteadily, he went to the only millinery store in town, bought its entire stock of artificial flowers, and sent them to assuage Hank's wounded body and spirit. Then brimming full of liquor and self-esteem he rode back to his bailiwick in Central Oregon.

Later Vaughn refused another chance to meet the man from Prineville. One morning he was sitting in a saloon, his straight chair tipped back against the wall. The bartender standing at the door recognized a passing horseman.

"Hank," he called, "there goes one of your friends. Charlie Long's in town."

Hank never stirred.

"Don't you want to see him?" persisted the bartender.

"No," said Hank, his voice a little weary. "I seen him once."

Prineville Builds a Railroad

Like many western towns at the close of the nineteenth century, Prineville dreamed of the day when a railroad through town would make it a city of importance. In this land of great distances, transporting grain, cattle, sheep, and timber products to market was a major problem, as was importing the finished goods needed to improve the quality of life.

By its very location, Prineville knew that there was no way a north-south or east-west railroad could miss it. Any civic booster could clearly demonstrate with paper and pencil how the town must become the crossroads of Oregon. The stage road from The Dalles to the John Day country passed through it, as did the road from The Dalles to California. Not only that, but a west-east route from the coast through the Willamette Valley, across the Cascades, then connecting with the Union Pacific in Utah or Idaho could very well cross the north-south route at Prineville, making it the most important transportation junction in Oregon.

Gasoline motor car, Prineville Railroad, 1919. —Crook County Historical Society

But as time passed, so did opportunities to get a railroad. The Oregon Pacific crossed the Willamette Valley, came as far up the Santiam River as the crest of the Cascades, then fizzled. The Columbia Southern Railway, which planned to tap the wheat, cattle, and gold country of eastern Oregon by stretching from Biggs south through Antelope, Prineville, and John Day, petered out at Shaniko.

When James J. Hill of the Great Northern and Edward Harriman of the Union Pacific locked horns in their big fight to gain control of railroading in the Pacific Northwest, Prineville was sure its day had come. Both men were building railroads south up the canyon of the Deschutes River, their lines headed for California. Regardless of the outcome, Prineville could not lose. No railroad would dare miss the metropolis of central Oregon.

"Unfortunately, Prineville preened itself too much," writes Randall V. Mills in his book *Railroads Down the Valleys.* "It overlooked two factors. First was geographic. Routes into Prineville from the north were possible, but to the east and west any road would have to squirm its way along the deep cut canyon of the Crooked River.... And second was strategic. Neither Hill nor Harriman was in fact after the business of Central Oregon; it was hardly worth it, for all of that whole region would scarcely support the shoddiest jerkwater."

When Hill and Harriman finally ended their feud and built a single line south through Bend and Klamath Falls, it missed Prineville by eighteen miles. Clearly, if Prineville wanted a railroad, the town would have to build its own. Which it did.

The Prineville & Eastern Railway incorporated in 1911, about the same time that new-fangled contraption called the automobile began appearing in the country. Occasionally a land promoter, trying to sell sites for farms or ranches, came to town with a carload of potential customers. On hearing about the railroad project, one of them offered to build it if the local boosters would supply him with the right-of-way, terminal grounds, and $75,000 in cash. But cash was hard to come by and eventually the promoter quietly faded away, along with prospects for the railroad.

In desperation, the Prineville City Council proposed a bond issue to get the project back on track. It was an ambitious undertaking for the population of only 1,200; in a magnificent demonstration of civic spirit, the measure passed 358 to 1. The lone dissenter was not identified.

By September 1916, with blueprints drawn, right-of-way obtained, and grading contracts let for the eighteen miles to Prineville Junction, where the railroad would join the Southern Pacific a few miles north of Redmond, events on another continent threatened this local project. Europe had gone to war. The price of raw materials quickly rose beyond the budget of the original bond issue. So voters had to approve increased funding, which they did, 202 to 14.

The steel shortage brought on by the war resulted in rail lines all over the country being torn up and shipped to Europe. Though the wartime dictator of railroads, William G. McAdoo, failed to see how this line from Prineville to the junction with the Southern Pacific would contribute to the downfall of the Kaiser, Oregon's Senator Charles McNary, who had considerable political clout in Washington, D.C., managed to convince him that the contribution would be vital.

Prineville received the track it needed and the first rails were laid in June 1918. The first locomotive on the new line rolled in gingerly in August while the track was still being aligned. But by the following January, its freight included "a full carload of automobiles," says Randall Mills, "an act something like that of a prisoner building his own gallows."

First train across Crooked River Bridge, 1911. —Crook County Historical Society

*City of Prineville
Railway Station
today.*

Speed on the uneven track was not breath-taking. On good days, it took an hour for the eighteen-mile trip. On O'Neill Grade twelve miles west of town, the route climbed sharply out of the canyon with a sharp reverse curve at the top. If there were too many freight cars for the locomotive's ability on one trip, "doubling" might be required, taking even more time. But it beat walking or freighting by wagon.

Eventually trucks took over a larger share of freight traffic while automobiles cut into passenger travel, diminishing the original enthusiasm for the railroad. But the bond indebtedness, which had grown to half a million dollars, remained to be paid whether or not the railroad operated, so the line kept running. Editorials in the local paper urged businesses to ship by rail, but it was not enough to pay the debt. The City Council, advised by months of committee and citizen meetings, took desperate measures.

It passed Ordinance No. 300, which required all businesses to have licenses and to report the means of all freight shipments in or out of town. Any loads not carried by either the City of Prineville Railway or the business' own trucks had to pay the city a tax of ten cents per pound.

The trucking firms wailed to high heaven that their rights were violated and that the whole Constitution had been toppled from its base. But the city stood firm, asserting the legality of such a tax that merely encouraged the use of a municipal utility; it added no costs, for if the merchant did not ship by the municipal railway, he still had to pay property taxes to cover the road's deficit.

Thanks to this "railroad ordinance" and improved business conditions, the amount of freight hauled by the railroad increased and the deficit grew smaller. In August 1940 the railway proudly declared itself out of the red. Though the railway was held together with baling wire and fence posts during the war years, the lumber business boomed. After the war it went through a general upgrade of equipment and maintenance. As of this writing, the Prineville City Railroad is still running and Ordinance 300 is still on the books.

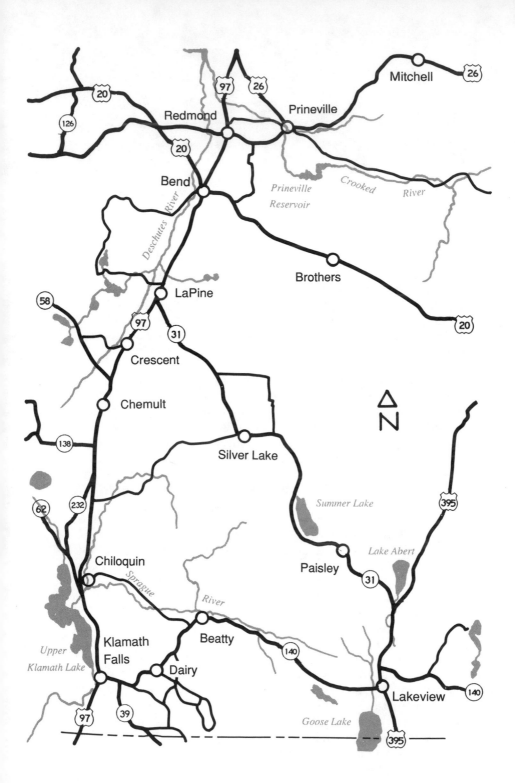

294

OR 126, US 97
Prineville—Bend
35 miles

US 97
Bend—La Pine
30 miles

OR 31
La Pine—Lakeview
175miles

The Desert Ten Looks Across

Though slogans promoting the state of Oregon always have called it the "evergreen land," a place where rain falls much of the time, in fact 24,000 square miles of Oregon—one-quarter of the state—qualifies as desert land where less than ten inches of rain falls annually. Almost all of the desert is located in four large counties: Deschutes, Lake, Harney, and Malheur, the area covered in the next few chapters.

By far the best book ever written about the region is *The Oregon Desert*, by E.R. Jackman and R.A. Long. The interesting thing about the book is that neither man pretended to be a writer. Reub Long was a cowboy and E.R. Jackman worked for the Extension Service of Oregon State University. "Long is a cowboy who thinks like a scientist," the bookjacket plug states, "while Jackman is a scientist who thinks like a cowboy."

Reading their thoughts and feelings about the high desert country is like sitting beside a campfire listening to good cow-country talk.

"You don't measure desert distances by miles," Reub Long says, "but by looks. It [the Oregon desert] is ten good looks across."

Several interesting facts about this region may not be apparent to visitors. One is that roughly two-thirds of the area is still owned by the federal government as national forests, Bureau of Land Management holdings, or wildlife refuges, which means that the government, rather than the people who live here, has final say about how the land is used. Another is that although most maps show a number of large lakes scattered over the region, the water in them disappears from time to time, and, even when an unusually wet season leaves these "sometime lakes" full, they have no outlets, so not a drop drains to the sea—it evaporates.

This puzzled emigrants at Goose Lake in southern Oregon during Oregon Trail days. Says the WPA guide to Oregon:

"Modern" haying methods in eastern Oregon, 1927. —ZX Ranch

> For years settlers had seen the weathered wagon ruts of early emigrant trains leading up to the lake shore, and continuing from the water's edge on the opposite shore, though the lake was too deep to ford.... The mystery of the tracks remained; but years later the lake dried up, and there were the wagon ruts leading across its bed and connecting with those on the two shores.

South of Bend, historically curious travelers can take a number of side trips. The first two sites worth mentioning are the High Desert Museum, which is covered in Part Four on the Cascade Mountains, and the Ice Caves. In these caves, water seeping down through crevices and lava tubes freezes and remains ice, even on the hottest days of summer.

Thirty miles south of Bend, just beyond LaPine, Oregon 31 heads southeast toward Silver Lake and Lakeview. Slightly more than halfway to Silver Lake from LaPine and a few miles east of the highway stands Fort Rock, where stark relics of the desert country remain little changed from the way they looked when the first settlers came.

The huge, cresent-shaped basalt column rising 325 feet a mile north of the fort gave this place its name. The Indians used it for defense. It once served settlers in the same way, according to the *WPA Guide*, when a party of wagons discovered a band of hostiles following them. "Reaching Fort Rock ahead of the enemy, they blocked the approach with wagons and successfully stood off their assailants."

Later settlers who tried to form a dryland farming community in 1908 were not as successful. Only a few decades later, the WPA guide described the remains of their effort:

Now a weather-beaten huddle of crude frame buildings, the town once supported three stores, two saloons, a newspaper with a circulation of five hundred, creamery and cheese factory, church and grade school. The town had its being through the attempt to farm the almost waterless valley, but after a decade of struggle the attempt was abandoned.

From Fort Rock, an unnumbered but paved highway goes east six miles, then south eighteen miles to rejoin Oregon 31 fifteen miles north of Summer Lake. The explorer John C. Fremont first saw this lake on December 16, 1843, from a vista far above it called Winter Ridge. He stood in snow three feet deep looking down at this ice-free lake and its surrounding valley and dubbed each for its respective contrast. Though he and his men had difficulty descending to the lake, its draw was irresistible. Covering roughly sixty square miles, Summer Lake has no outlet; consequently, its waters are extremely alkaline, as are all those in the high desert country.

Paisley, farther south, received its named in 1873 from Charles Ennis, after his native city in Scotland.

"Cowboys ride through the streets and the watering trough and hitching post still stand," the WPA guide stated in 1950. "Paisley is headquarters for the Chewaucan Land & Cattle Company, the largest of Oregon's stock-raising enterprises, which has 32 subsidiary ranches."

Today, little has changed. Now called the ZX Ranch, this is the second largest ranch in the United States, covering 1.6 million acres, which figures out to be 2,500 square miles.

When Congress passed the Homestead Act in 1862, its intent was to grant a piece of land to any family head who would live on it for five years

Cook wagons used in the desert were pulled by mules in the 1920s. Cowboys on the ZX Ranch still use cook wagons, but the mules have been replaced with pickups. —ZX Ranch

and bring it into productive use. Because of the high desert's aridity and remoteness, few settlers filed claims on it between 1870 and 1910. Hostile Indians posed a problem at first, though transportation remained poor throughout the period, and the fertile, well-watered land west of the Cascades made the desert country unattractive to all but stock raisers. Most of them simply filed claims where there was water, then let their sheep or cattle range over public land.

But the transcontinental railroads, which controlled alternate sections along their right-of-way, wanted the land settled; for people meant freight and revenue. So they concocted all sorts of schemes to entice eastern and foreign immigrants. One was the slogan "Rainfall follows the plow," which theorized that when dryland country was plowed and cultivated, the annual rainfall of the region would increase to the amount needed for a successful crop. Conceived by some nameless promotional genius, this notion lacked any factual statistic for support. But thousands of land-hungry people who *wanted* to believe it bet years of their lives on it—and lost.

With most of the good land gone by the turn of the century, a new kind of speculator—encouraged by the 1909 "Enlarged Homestead Act," which permitted 320-acre claims to those who would irrigate the desert— began to operate in eastern Oregon. Reub Long, who saw these types first hand, describes one:

> A man who decided he was an unhappy medium—too light for heavy work and too heavy for light work—could set up an office in Prineville, Bend, or Lakeview, and advertise that he would locate all the land-hungry people right out in a neglected part of paradise. These ads filled Eastern papers and proved irresistible to school teachers, bank clerks, and others who believed in fairies. The butcher, the baker, and the candlestick maker all wanted land.

Because the maiden school teacher from Bangor, Maine, did not know where the section corners were before she picked out a choice piece of land near Lakeview, Oregon, she would pay a fee to a "locater," who charged in direct proportion to the size of the nest-egg she had to invest. If it were $2,000, say, $1,000 for his services seemed about right. The fact that the land claim made in her name by the locater was one she herself could have made without charge had nothing to do with the transaction, of course. She wanted a piece of land. He got it for her.

Once the maiden school teacher, the butcher, the baker, or the candlestick maker came to Oregon and saw the particular piece of paradise they had bought, there was nothing most of them could do but build some kind of living quarters on it and try to eke out an existence. Most failed after a few years. Others succeeded—usually by marrying a rancher or his widow, and merging their claims. Still others sold out cheap and left, cursing the country; others simply left.

Curiously enough, the hunger for land still is so strong that a January 1990 article in the *Oregonian* told how hundreds of people from cities such as Seattle, intrigued by advertisements for land in an unspoiled desert paradise on the shore of a beautiful lake, with a golf course, park, clubhouse, and other amenities soon to come, invested in one-acre parcels for $499 down and $19.99 a month for five years.

Later, when those who bought the land came to inspect their property, they learned that at least some of the promises made in the ads were true: The country was unspoiled by people because no one had tried to live in it for fifty years. There was a lake and there was a shore, though there had been no water in this particular lake since the wet spring of 1983 and the shore was encrusted with alkali dust that obscured the horizon whenever the wind blew.

Where *was* that beautiful blue, mountain-surrounded lake pictured in the four-colored ad? Why, that was Ice Lake, high up in the Wallowa Mountains, two hundred miles to the north. And what of the agency that had promoted the development? Its only address was a post office box with overdue rent.

One Seattle lady who had planned to build her dream house and retire in this "unspoiled paradise" was so disappointed she didn't even bother to get out of the car. "I just had a good cry, turned around, and drove back to Seattle."

When there is enough water to irrigate desert land, it can be extremely productive, as has often been proved in the West. But few streams of any size flow through the high desert country of eastern Oregon. Not only that, but its average altitude is so high that frosts come early and stay late, limiting the growing season. Lakeview, for example, has an elevation of 4,800 feet. Admittedly, the high country air is bracing, clean, and pure. Wild game, sheep, cattle, and horses do well in it, but these are animals that require a lot of space—as do the people who make their living in occupations related to hunting and stock-raising.

Because space was so abundant in southeast Oregon, southwest Idaho, northwest Nevada, and northeast California during the 1860s, there would seem to be room for both the Indians and the white men to live in it together without conflict. But since the members of both races wanted the same things—water, grass, and meat, all in short supply—it was inevitable that the two races would clash.

On this vast, unmarked battlefield, a bloody, bitter war took place over a period of fifteen years. Despite its scope and the appalling number of its casualties, it is the least-known of all the conflicts in the West.

General George Crook, Indian Fighter

Gold strikes in eastern Oregon, Nevada, and Idaho Territory had caused an influx of population into towns such as John Day, Boise City, and Virginia City in the early 1860s. Soon, stage lines crossed what had been empty desert country. Between Sacramento, The Dalles, and Boise City, stage stations to feed, care for, and keep horses were built at intervals of ten miles across a lonely, desolate land. To supply beef for the mining towns and horses for the stage lines, equally lonely, isolated ranch houses were built across this same territory.

For the always-hungry Indians of the region, both the stage stations and the ranch houses offered tempting targets to raid and pilfer. These were not horse Indians like the Nez Perce, Shoshone, Crow, and Sioux, who lived on the well-watered ranges farther north and east. These were desert Indians who usually traveled on foot, had no buffalo in their country, and lived on roots, nuts, fish, and small game. Predominantly, they were Paiutes living in small bands, existing as best they could in a harsh land short on both food and water. It was not their nature to attack

General George Crook in field dress.
—National Archives

wagon trains of any size, towns, or fortified places. But a stage station or a ranch house, inhabited and defended by only a few people, posed a tempting prize to them, particularly if cattle or horses were available.

In all that vast expanse of country, only Fort Boise, built near the city of that name in 1863, could be called a military post. As Indian fighters, the troops stationed there during and after the Civil War tended to be poorly trained recruits with minimal military skills. That of their officers was not much better, according to contemporary newspaper accounts.

For example, when a stage station or a ranch fell victim to an Indian raid in Oregon fifty miles away, it would take a day for the news to reach the post, three days to decide upon, equip, and dispatch a punitive expedition, and a week riding around the country looking for hostiles Typically none were found, so the troops would spend another week riding back to the fort, exhausted.

"The way the Army goes after Indians," a Boise editor exclaimed in exasperation, "is like hunting ducks with a brass band."

After several ineffective commanders at Fort Boise, the San Francisco-based Department of the Pacific finally put the right man in the right place at the right time. His name was George Crook.

"From what I have observed of this country," he told a reporter shortly after his arrival in Boise City, "it is in a state of siege. My job is to settle the Indian problem once and for all. That is what I intend to do—by extermination, if necessary."

As an Army officer, Colonel George S. Crook, who was usually called by his Civil War brevet rank of general, was not a spit-and-polish man. He did not drink whisky, coffee, or tea; he did not use tobacco in any form; and, instead of a braid-embellished dress uniform, he much preferred a black slouch hat, a canvas hunting jacket, heavy brown wool trousers, and thick-soled, moderately low-heeled boots suited for walking or riding. When mounted, his taste ran to a steady, sensible mule rather than a high-spirited horse. And, where duty was concerned, he had a one-track mind.

Winter came early in December 1866, promising a cold and bitter season. Exactly a week after his arrival in Boise City, General Crook received word that a band of Indians had stolen some stock and shot at some settlers in the lower valley twenty miles west of town, following which they apparently had fled into the Oregon desert in the Malheur River country. Taking along a toothbrush, a single change of underwear, and Captain Perry's company of the First Cavalry, General Crook left Fort Boise within an hour of receiving the report, determined to have a firsthand look.

"Sir, the men are wondering how long we will be gone," Captain Perry said as they rode west under the leaden, threatening sky. "With Christmas coming next week..."

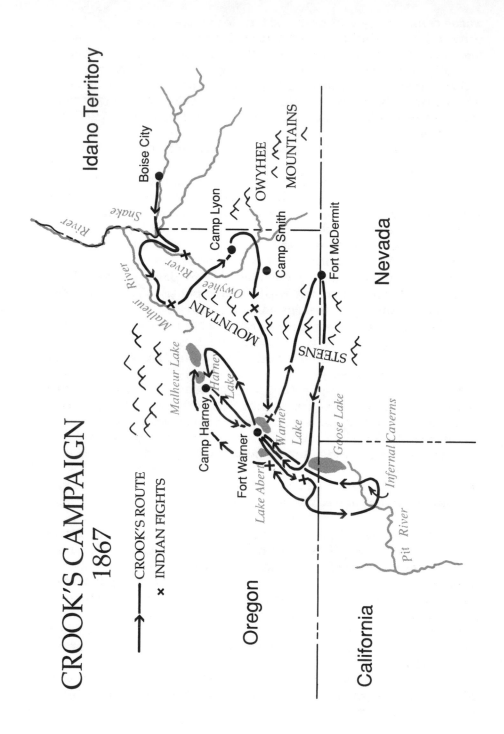

CROOK'S CAMPAIGN 1867

CROOK'S ROUTE
× INDIAN FIGHTS

Idaho Territory

Boise City

Snake River

Camp Lyon

OWYHEE MOUNTAINS

Camp Smith

Fort McDermit

Nevada

Malheur River

MOUNTAIN

Owyhee River

Malheur Lake

Harney Lake

STEENS

Camp Harney

Fort Warner

Warner Lake

Goose Lake

Lake Abert

Infernal Caverns

Oregon

California

Pit River

302

"Oh, we'll be back by Christmas, I imagine."

"May I tell them that, sir? Just to raise their spirits."

Crook shook his head. "Let's wait, Captain. Just in case we get interested after the Indians..."

Though contingents of troops under him were rotated back to Fort Boise from time to time, Crook himself became "interested after the Indians" and stayed in the field for the next two years. One of the secrets of General Crook's success as an Indian-fighter was that he went after the hostiles when they were most vulnerable—in the winter time. Another was that once he began a campaign he never quit until the hostiles were eliminated or surrendered.

Crook had a way of finding scouts who knew the country, supplied him with reliable information, and offered him their complete loyalty. One was Archie McIntosh, who came to him from the Warm Springs Reservation in central Oregon, looking for employment as a scout. Though known as an excellent scout, he liked to drink.

If it struck the officers and enlisted men as strange that a teetotaler like General Crook and a moody, habitual drunk like Archie McIntosh could establish a mutual respect and trust that lasted a lifetime, it was because they did not understand their commander. Being a completely practical man, Crook required only one thing from a scout: accurate information. If he got that, sobriety could go hang.

Whatever demons controlled the half-Scotch, half-Indian soul of Archie McIntosh and forced him to drink himself into complete oblivion whenever he could, he had a memory that retained every image imprinted upon it, a shrewd intelligence that weighed impressions precisely and realistically, and an inborn instinct for direction, time, and space that was as infallible as that of a wild animal. If sober enough to talk, his information could be relied upon. If sober enough to ride, he could lead Crook where he wanted to go.

"A blizzard was howling when we set out that day," Crook wrote in one of his reports, "and I could tell from Archie's attitude that he thought us foolish to travel. But he made no objection, for he never gave me advice unless I asked for it. We traveled all day and for several hours after dark, with Archie leading us. His route never deviated one foot to either side of the trail we wanted to follow, though the snow was falling so thick we could see no landmarks of any kind. Late at night we arrived safely at our previous camp. What was truly remarkable was that Archie had been in that place but once previously—and on that occasion had been so drunk he could barely ride."

Through the bitter winter of deep snow and punishing cold, Crook stayed "interested after the Indians," remaining in the field, leading his chilled, weary command back and forth across the high desert country of eastern Oregon, northern Nevada, and southwestern Idaho, flushing bands of hostiles out of their camps in sheltered canyons, fighting them when they chose to stand their ground, pursuing them when they scattered and ran, accepting their surrender when they became too weary to resist any longer.

Now and then Crook risked his own life in charges against Indian villages. In one case, his charge was inadvertent, caused by the absence of his favorite mount. Approaching a sleeping village of hostiles, he arranged his troops so they would make simultaneous charges from all sides, when given the signal. As commander, he intended to remain in the rear to make sure the attack was properly carried out. But because the mule he customarily rode had turned up lame that morning, he mounted himself on a spirited, nervous horse. When the order to charge was given, the horse lost its head.

"Taking the bit between his teeth, he led the charge," Crook wryly admitted in a report. "Instead of obeying my injunctions, the troops behind me began firing at once. The balls whistled by me, and I was in more danger from the rear than I was from the front. My horse ran through the village, and I could not stop him until he reached some distance beyond...."

After that, if General Crook's mule was not in shape for battle, he commanded his troops on foot.

The weather played freakish tricks in this country. Following a week of sub-zero cold on the high plateaus of eastern Oregon, Crook led his frozen command down into a sheltered canyon in late January and found the sun so warm and the temperature so mild that they saw grasshoppers bouncing about. A month later, while the command was making a scout through the Dunder and Blitzen country to the southwest, a raging blizzard left powder-dry snowdrifts fifteen feet deep in which the horses sank almost out of sight. Temporarily camped on the shores of Warner Lake because deep snow and bitter cold had made travel impossible, the command was awakened in the middle of a March night by the eerie sighing of a Chinook wind which, in minutes, raised the air temperature sixty degrees and melted the snow so rapidly that by morning the party hastily moved their camp to higher ground for fear of being flooded out.

Sportman's Paradise

To a passionate sportsman like Crook, the lake and marsh country of south-central Oregon was veritable paradise. Swans, geese, ducks, cormorants, and coots nested by the thousands among the tules and bullrushes. Getting a skilled Indian craftsman to fashion him a canoe from a pine log, Crook spent many hours exploring the shallow lakes. He discovered that when the weather grew colder, a well-concealed hunter could get in several shots before the wildfowl took alarm and flew, mistaking the gunshots at first for the common sharp sounds of ice cracking.

One day he collected sixty-seven dozen cormorant and coot eggs and brought them back to the camp cooks to supplement the troops' meager diet. "The coot eggs were good eating," he reported, "being about the size and color of a guinea fowl egg. But the white of the cormorant egg was bitter and strong when cooked, and the eggs were not healthy."

With the coming of April and milder weather, Crook went after the hostile Indians with renewed vigor. Under his direct command he now had some two hundred men. Camp Smith, Camp Lyon, Camp McDermit, and the other Army posts strategically located in the heart of the Indian country sent out more and more troops. The campaign he planned for the coming months was a simple one: go to the hostiles, fight them, chase them, and wear them down until they got so sick of war they would sue for a permanent peace.

With a number of his horses worn out, strayed, or stolen, he ordered his quartermaster to advertise in northern California newspapers for 450 well-broken saddle horses, 80 pack mules, and 40 draft mules. This summer's campaign, he promised, would be a big one. It took two months before the horses and mules arrived. By then, more soldiers, three separate companies of Indian allies, and a newspaper correspondent had joined the command. Thanks to the correspondent, Joe Wasson, who previously published the *Owyhee Avalanche* and possessed a wry sense of humor, the campaign received excellent newspaper coverage.

Wasson wrote:

> I came on this trip in search of new life, and I certainly found it. Last night, while sleeping in the tent assigned to me, I had no more than rolled into my blankets when I felt new life creeping upon me from all directions. These Oregon graybacks have no abiding loyalties; they like white meat fully as much as red....

Before the command left Camp McDermit, the horses and mules arrived from California. But somewhere along the line there had been a slight error. The animals had not been broken to the saddle, aparejo, or harness and were as wild as deer. The command had recently been strengthened by two companies of infantry, made up chiefly of of German, Dutch, and Irish immigrants, who had never ridden, packed, or harnessed a four-footed animal in their lives. Determined to mount his entire command, Crook gave the foot soldiers and the unbroken animals just forty-eight hours to get acquainted.

"Put a Dutchman who's never ridden a horse on a horse that's never carried anything on its back but hair," Wasson wrote, "and they're both bound to learn something new right away. For a while around here, it literally 'rained' soldiers."

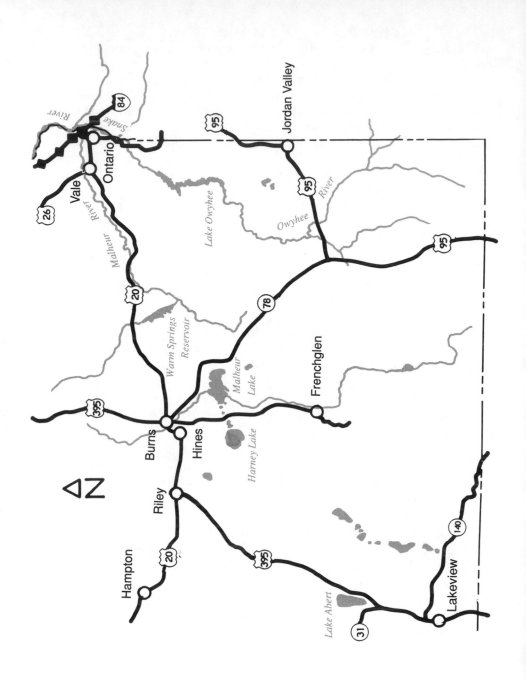

US 395
Lakeview—Burns
139 miles

OR 205
Burns—Frenchglen
60 miles

War of Attrition

Though correspondent Joe Wasson yearned for a major battle and a great victory to report, General Crook was not fighting that kind of war. By the end of July, despite continuous effort, the campaign had killed or captured just thirty-five Indians, and only half were warriors.

On the grimmer side was the recently compiled Army statistic that in the Pacific Northwest since settlement had begun, over one thousand whites had died at Indian hands, excluding soldiers killed in battle.

The mid-summer heat and a ride over a bare, black, lava-strewn mesa prompted Wasson to write:

> It was so hot at noon yesterday I was reminded of a story told me by an officer who had recently served at Fort Yuma, Arizona. A soldier died of sunstroke, he said, went to Hell, and slept badly his first night in that place. When Old Scratch caught him trying to sneak out the gate, next morning, and asked him where he was going, the soldier answered: "Back to Fort Yuma to get my blankets."

General Crook admitted to Wasson that he put little faith in a summer campaign. The most he could hope for in this one was to keep the hostiles moving, to wear them down, and to pick up a few stragglers. But in the eight months since he left Fort Boise with a toothbrush, a change of underwear, and a single company of cavalry, he had gained a knowledge of the country, learned what must be done, and made considerable progress toward putting together the forces required to conquer the Indians. Wasson asked him how much time he would need to get the job done.

"A year. If the authorities will just leave me alone for one more year, the Indian problem will be settled—I promise you that."

The most strategic spot for a permanent post, Crook now was sure, was Warner Lake (a few miles northeast of present-day Lakeview). Being relatively low in elevation, this valley had a fairly mild winter climate; water, grass, and game were plentiful; in the nearby mountains was timber; and supply lines to the towns of northern California and

Wounded soldier on horse stretcher, 1868. —National Archives

western Oregon were not excessively long. Contracts for the construction of log buildings to house officers, men, and animals were let to civilians; arrangements were made for the cutting of hay and grain; and Crook now let it be known that he had decided to extend the campaign an additional thirty days, which meant that the troops would not be returning to this place until late October.

Meanwhile, one of the Army surgeons, Dr. Tompkins, gave Joe Wasson a questionnaire he had received from the Smithsonian Institution requesting information about the Indians of the region, and suggested that he answer it. One dull Sunday afternoon, Wasson attempted to do so, reporting his labors to his newspaper.

> Q: Ordinary duration of life?
> A: Extraordinary—say the settlers.
> Q: Can photographs be taken of individual Indians?
> A: Yes—if the camera is mounted on a Henry rifle.
> Q: Do they practice agriculture?
> A: Mostly they raise settlers—hair and all.
> Q: Do they practice scalping?
> A: Don't need to. They've got it down perfect.
> Q: What are they called?
> A: Usually they come without calling.

A section of the instructive pamphlet that particularly intrigued Joe Wasson was the one in which the Smithsonian professor had written: "... a great obstacle in the way of making alcoholic collections while on the march is the escape of the spirits and the friction of the specimens."

308

Indeed, Wasson commented, this was a knotty problem.

"... a fourth proof whisky will be found best suited for collections made at permanent stations," continued the pamphlet, "but the specimen must not be crowded."

On the contrary, Wasson begged to differ, around many permanent stations in this part of the country he had seen a number of "specimens" fuller than ticks with fourth proof whisky, who hadn't minded being crowded a bit.

"Skins of reptiles may be stuffed with either sand or sawdust," advised the pamphlet, "or they may be simply flattened out."

It had been his own experience, Wasson observed, that the reptiles he came across kept better flattened out.

To the Smithsonian professor's statement that "among the first of the *desiderati* is a full series of skulls," Wasson replied that such a series would require more "skullduggery" than he felt like expending, then gave up the project as a bad job.

Though the newspapers of southwestern Idaho and eastern Oregon solidly supported Crook, Wasson knew that the Portland and San Francisco editors would overlook no opportunity to play up Indian unrest in the interior country and the Army's ineffectiveness against it. To maintain their monopoly on freight and passenger traffic to the interior, they unscrupulously distorted truth.

"Why risk lives and goods on the long, dangerous, Indian-infested desert route from California to Idaho?" they asked in their editorials, "when such a safe, sure, comfortable sea and river route to Idaho exists?"

A further source of irritation to Crook, Wasson knew, was the ill-conceived reservation system, which placed bands of Indians that had never really been conquered or tamed on refuges run by incompetent civilian appointees. Indians could leave at will with firearms sometimes more modern than those issued to the soldiers. Ostensibly, the Indians

Camp Warner, Oregon, 1873. —National Archives

left to hunt wild game, but their broad definition of "game" often included the horses and cattle of white ranchers.

Though some of the best fighters in Crook's command were the fifty Warm Springs Indians led by Archie McIntosh, they were poorly armed. Wasson wrote: "If Archie's scouts could exchange their weapons for some others not bearing the brand of 'Harper's Ferry, 1845,' and get revolvers swung to them also, their confidence would be enhanced and better accounts rendered in these skirmishes."

Apparently Crook's persistent appeals for better arms were at last heard, for Wasson added a P.S. to his dispatch that very day:

> Several of the Boise wagons arrived here last night, and among other things brought Spencer carbines for Lt. Parnell's Co., and today Archie's men got the best of the Sharp's guns. He has done most of the rough work so far with the poorest tools, and it is time that his outfit be improved.

General George Crook in later years. —National Archives

Left alone by the authorities over the next year, General Crook brought the long, brutal war to a close in late July 1868. He estimated that the Army had killed, starved, or frozen out at least half of the hostiles in the high desert country. He had laid down peace terms that made sense.

"The hostiles that wished to do so could go live on the established reservations," regional newspapers reported him as saying. "Those that did not could remain free as long as they kept the peace. White settlers who had lost livestock were not to attempt to retrieve it themselves but were to leave that chore to the Army."

No treaties had been signed with the hostiles and no promises had been made them. They were to keep the peace. If they did not, the Army would resume its war of extermination against them.

Hart Mountain Antelope Range

The largest expanse of wildlife refuges in the United States is in this area of Oregon. Besides the 215,000-acre Hart Mountain National Antelope Refuge northeast of Lakeview, Malheur National Wildlife Refuge encompasses over 180,000 acres more south of Burns along Oregon 205. Antelope, deer, and elk roam freely throughout these protected areas, as do a variety of smaller animals and predators.

Hart Mountain National Antelope Refuge is home to roughly 12,000 antelope, the fleetest, most graceful animal in the West, capable of sprinting up to sixty miles an hour. Split by an enormous scarp or fault reaching 8,000 feet, the plateau and Warner Peak overlook the Warner Valley to the west and the Catlow Valley to the east, both of which lie about 3,000 feet lower. In the high desert, a rise of 1,000 feet can result in a precipitation increase of perhaps five inches a year.

This refuge has four climatic zones by altitude, according to E.R. Jackman in *The Oregon Desert*; they are Sonoran, Transition, Canadian, and Hudsonian, each accommodating certain plants and animals.

All the lakes in this upper Great Basin region are shallow, ranging from about four to six feet deep. Since their beds are wide and flat, the difference of an inch or two annual rainfall or a variation of a few degrees in the temperature, which affects the evaporation rate, can make their shorelines approach or recede by as much as a mile. In dry years a lake may vanish completely; in wet years the same lake may cover the valley floor like an endless sea. While farmers in other parts of the West complain that bad conservation practices erode priceless topsoil and wash it out to sea, Jackman and Long explain that not a grain of soil in his country ever washes out to sea since no streams from this region connect with it.

Rocks piled into wire baskets serve as corner posts in the desert country where wood is scarce.

Wagontire, forty miles southwest of Burns on US 395, marks the western boundary of Harney County, the largest in the United States. Wooden wheels commonly shrank in this dry desert air, sometimes enough to loosen or even lose their iron rims, or "tires." Usually when this happened, the driver had to get the wheel repaired at a blacksmith shop. For two-bits the smithy would heat the rim in his forge, cut a piece out of it, then refit it snugly to the wooden wheel.

The wagon tire that lay beside the road and gave this settlement its name may have fallen off its wheel; some say the iron rim was all that remained after Indians attacked and burned a wagon train. Whatever happened, the rim lay in plain sight for years near the road and a spring of good water used by travelers and their animals. Homesteaders and cattlemen fought one of their many feuds over this spring. In 1942, the WPA guide told the town's story, listing its elevation at 4,725 feet and its population at seven. Forty-five years later, Ralph Friedman's *Oregon for the Curious* said "one family" lived there, so the town does not seem to have grown much in this century. Though Wagontire is small, Harney County covers 10,132 square miles. Named after Brigadier General William S. Harney, commander of the Pacific District in 1858, this county is bigger than half a dozen eastern states.

Harney county seat is Burns. South of there, Oregon 205 passes through the Malheur Wildlife Refuge, with Harney Lake to the west and Malheur Lake to the east. In French, *malheur* means "bad luck" or "misfortune." The river, the lake, and the region probably were given that name by French-Canadian Astorians in 1811, when several of their party were killed by Indians in the area. To the local Indians, who for thousands of years had found the game and wildfowl that frequented the marshes and shores a marvelous food supply, it had always been a good luck region. To them, bad fortune came only with the invasion of the white man.

Malheur Wildlife Refuge

In 1850, Congress passed a law granting Arkansas all of the swamp or overflow lands within its borders. In 1860, it extended the act to Oregon and Minnesota. Having just become a state in 1859, Oregon made no claim under the act for ten years, then, in 1870, its legislators decided to take advantage and lay claim to just about every piece of land in the state where water ever had overflowed. Under the law, this land then could be sold to private citizens for as little as one dollar an acre. By 1872, 323 individuals had applied for 5,828,715 acres. The state whittled this figure to half a million, of which it eventually sold 215,000 acres.

To the Indians of the region, Malheur Lake had long been known for its teeming birdlife, writes E.R. Jackman in the beautifully illustrated, historically accurate book *Steens Mountain.*

> The Indians gathered there to hunt waterfowl and watch the wild geese as they came in from the north in November with their lonesome echoing cry. Sighting where thousands would alight,

Bird-watching tower on Malheur Wildlife Refuge, near the old "P" Ranch House site.

turning a brown field into a white sea of geese, the Indian hunter would walk slowly toward them, shielded from their sight by his pony. When within range, he stepped out and sent his arrow whistling into the white cloud. He could often get as many as three arrows on the way.

Today on the Malheur National Wildlife Refuge, the same white sea of geese may be seen in season, along with hundreds of other varieties of waterfowl. Between 1880 and the early 1900s, this paradise for wildlife nearly became a graveyard for extinct species. Jackman continues:

> The prize was a few plumes from the beautiful snow-white egrets. They lived in colonies during nesting season and Malheur Lake was one of their principal homes. The plume hunters came in after the young were hatched when the old birds had to come back to feed the young. Every bird was killed, leaving the young to sure death by starvation.

Thanks to a few early-day conservationists, who included the owners of several area cattle ranches and President Theodore Roosevelt, the marshlands were withdrawn from settlement and the plume collectors were stopped in 1908. Fortunately, the birds are still there. In a *Steens Mountain* chapter called "The Marshes of Malheur," wildlife author Dallas Lore Sharp is quoted as he poetically expressed his feelings in his book *Where Rolls the Oregon*, published in 1914:

> The sedges were full of birds, the tules were full of birds, the skies were full of birds ... I was beside myself at the sight—at the sound— at the thought that such wildlife could still be anywhere upon the face of the earth, to say nothing of finding it within the borders of my own land. Here was a page of the early history of our country; no, an actual area of that wild, unspoiled, unslaughtered country as the Indian knew it, as Lewis and Clark saw it....

"Clouds of birds!" he repeats in awe. "Acres of them, square miles of them—one hundred and forty-three square miles of them!"

In a rare example of the preservation of wetlands in a land of little rain, the Malheur National Wildlife Refuge now contains twice the area Sharp saw in 1914. As quoted in *Steens Mountain*, John Scharff, who had been superintendent of the refuge for thirty-two years, explained the growth of the preserve:

> In 1935 the Blitzen Valley portion of the Refuge was added by the purchase of 64,000 acres from the Eastern Oregon Livestock Company. In 1940, the famous old Double-O Hanley ranch was purchased and added to the Refuge west of Harney Lake. Other small tracts were purchased to round out the present boundary. The Malheur Wildlife Refuge now contains 180,850 acres, or 282.5 square miles.

Its goals include a safe nesting, feeding, and breeding area for wild birds; a haven for migratory waterfowl; a sanctuary for rare species; and a study/observation area for the management and habitat of migratory waterfowl, wild birds, and mammals.

Though it attracts thousands of bird-watchers, wild animal lovers, camera enthusiasts, and a limited number of hunters whose harvests of game are rigidly controlled, the nature of the land, vegetation, and water is little changed from what it has always been, except for a few lightly traveled access roads. Vistors can obtain information from the visitor center and refuge headquarters on the south shore of Malheur Lake.

Sixty miles south of Burns on Oregon 205, just beyond the Malheur Wildlife Refuge, is the historically important Frenchglen Hotel, now operated by the Oregon State Parks Division. With a decor from the turn of the century, when cowboys roamed the region's vast rangelands, the eight-room hotel is open from March until mid-November, serves breakfast, lunch, and a by-reservation family-style dinner daily.

A few miles to the east looms a significant geological feature, Steens Mountain. Called one of the world's largest fault blocks, Steens Mountain is thirty miles long and has an elevation of 9,670 feet. Its history is as dramatic as its appearance.

Steens Mountain

In the high desert country, as we have noted, a 1,000-foot increase in elevation can mean an additional five inches in annual precipitation. So if the level of the lower country is 4,500 feet and its rainfall seven inches a year, a mountain of 9,500 feet might receive twenty-five inches more, making its total annual rainfall thirty-two inches.

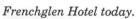

Frenchglen Hotel today.

Pueblo Mountains south of Fields.

Along the thirty-mile crest of Steens Mountain, most of this moisture falls during the winter months in the form of snow. Melting slowly during the late spring and summer months, it naturally irrigates the lower country surrounding its base, with none of it ever going into a stream that reaches the sea. This makes the area a veritable paradise for waterfowl, wildlife, horses, and cattle.

In 1860, Major Enoch Steen came through the Harney Lake area with instructions to lay out a wagon road west that would serve as a shortcut across the Cascades to the Willamette Valley. According to a biographical sketch in *Encyclopedia of Frontier Biography* by Dan L. Thrapp: "On August 8 Steen struck a band of hostiles and had a fight and pursuit over a lofty butte which today bears the name of Steens Mountain, a landmark in southeastern Oregon." Called off the job because of more pressing matters, one of which was acting as commandant of Fort Walla Walla, Major Steen never finished laying out the proposed road. But the name Steens Mountain stuck. Good grass, abundant water, and thousands of square miles of empty land soon attracted ranchers from California.

Beginning in 1872, men like Peter French, John Devine, and Henry Miller began buying up swampland claims for $1.25 an acre, filing homestead claims, timber claims, and desert claims of their own and in

Steens Mountain, a landmark in southeastern Oregon.

Steens Mountain viewed from the east.

the names of their hired hands, always making sure they got control of the best sources of water, until each of their ranches covered tens of thousand of acres. Within twenty years, four big owners controlled most of the range land in southeastern Oregon, which they ruled in classic cattle-king style.

At first, they had little competition from the homesteaders, for most of this country was ill suited to farming. When a "sodbuster" filed a claim on what he thought was a good year-round spring and attempted to eke out a living as a farmer, the big rancher had the resources to let nature take its course, which usually meant waiting until the spring dried up, frost or hungry deer destroyed the crops, or the lack of markets and roads brought the homesteader and his family to the brink of starvation. When that happened, the big rancher often put the sodbuster to work for wages. If the farmer grew so desperate for meat that he killed and butchered one of the rancher's steers, the cattle king took no drastic action; he was more likely to have his cowboys haze the prime steers away from the hungry homesteader's claim and run older, thinner cows his direction to make meat for the homesteader's table without cutting so much into the cattleman's profit. The big rancher knew that eventually the home- steader would give up, sell out, and leave the country—which was never meant for farming anyway.

Henry Miller— ## Butcher Boy to Cattle King

Born in Germany in 1827, B. Heinrich Kreiser learned the butcher's trade as a youth, came to New York at the age of twenty, changed his name to Henry Miller, and followed the Gold Rush to Califoria in 1850. In San Francisco, he operated a meat market until 1857, when he formed a partnership with an Alsatian named Charles Lux, and went into the cattle business. Though he lived to the age of ninety and became a very

317

wealthy man, he never learned to speak English very well. But he did learn how to make money the traditional American way—which in those days meant by fair means or foul.

In 1863, the firm of Miller & Lux bought its first ranch in the San Joaquin Valley with funds supplied by wealthy San Francisco friends. Before long, fifteen other ranches came under the firm's control, making it the largest ranching enterprise on the Pacific slope. Expanding north into Nevada and southeast Oregon, the company eventually controlled over 800,000 acres of land, grazing 80,000 cattle and 100,000 sheep. In his broken English, Henry Miller could and did boast that he could get in a buggy and drive from San Francisco to Burns—a distance of 520 miles—staying every night in a ranch house sitting on land he owned.

Lux died in 1887. After engaging in a twenty-year court battle with the heirs, which he won, Henry Miller formed the Pacific Livestock Company. It was said that at one time a million head of cattle grazed on lands Miller either owned or had an interest in. His critics said he paid the courts to steal for him what he couldn't steal himself.

The Steens Mountain country is rich with stories about his passion for detail, his thick German accent, and his rare moments of generosity, only two of which we have space for here. While visiting one of his ranches, dressed in rough clothes and riding alone, he came across a homesteader who had killed and started cutting into a company-owned beef. Without revealing his identity, Miller got down off his horse and expertly helped the homesteader butcher the carcass. He asked the homesteader what the steer's owners would say if they caught him.

"Aw, hell!" the homesteader replied, "they stole so many themselves, they'll never miss this one."

"Vell, I'm Henry Miller," the butcher replied, "und if you von't tell on me, I von't tell on you."

Though he was not an educated man, Henry Miller read a bit on scientific matters now and then. Somewhere he came across an article on atoms and molecules that fascinated him, and he looked for a way to put the new knowledge to practical use. "Every year he had to spend many dollars on new pitchforks," writes E.R. Jackman in *Steens Mountain*. "He studied the pitchforks, tested new ones and old ones, and found it was easier to break the old ones. Therefore, the molecules must have drained down into the wrong position or drained out the ends of the tines or something. So whenever he visited a ranch, he went through all the barns and stood every fork with the tines up."

Teaching the cowboys and ranch hands about scientific matters proved a losing battle, but Henry Miller kept trying. "I tell all dese poys to upshtand dem mit de handles down. Dey forget. But I keep telling dem yust de same."

When Henry Miller—America's largest cattle operator—died in 1916, he owned a million acres of land in California, Nevada, and Oregon, did not owe a dime, and had $10 million in the bank.

Killing of Peter French

Though relations between the cattle kings and the homesteaders usually were fairly good, now and then an act of violence broke out. The most fabled of these was the shooting of cattle baron Peter French by homesteader Ed Oliver. A small-statured man, French was a dynamo of energy and quick-tempered. Ed Oliver, also small, was outwardly phlegmatic, but stubborn and often angry.

After the custom of the times, Oliver had filed a homestead claim on a piece of land which, over the years, had become completely surrounded by property French owned. Growing tired of the way Oliver kept riding and driving animals and vehicles across his land, French tried to limit the homesteader's access by taking him to county court. Much to the cattle baron's disgust, Oliver won the suit, being granted a "reasonable" easement across French's land.

Apparently a difference of opinion festered and grew as to what constituted "reasonable," with Ed Oliver belligerently crossing any place he pleased without regard to fences and gates, contrary to the common rules of the range. The conflict came to a head late in December 1897. Historian Peter K. Simpson tells in *The Community of Cattlemen* what happened:

Pete French's "White House," built in 1880s on the "P" Ranch at Frenchglen, burned to the ground in 1940.

So when Oliver wandered across the field during a winter roundup the day after Christmas, French rode over to him and, within sight of several witnesses, dismounted and accosted Oliver. Accounts vary, but French made his points in an angry way, and as he walked away, Oliver drew a pistol and shot him in the head.

All the witnesses present worked for Peter French, who died instantly. French was unarmed, except for a limber willow stick with a strip of leather attached, which he used to prod cattle. There had been no physical contact between the two men, the witnesses said, and French was walking away from Oliver when the homesteader shot him from behind.

Ed Oliver's trial in Burns was a classic rich-man-poor-man contest. Though the cattle kings had the money and the power, the homesteaders had the numbers and the sympathy of the community at large. The prosecution witnesses were all French employees. Pleading self defense, Ed Oliver's four attorneys, all of whom lived in Burns, brought forth a number of people who, though they had not seen the killing, testified to French's violent temper, Oliver's good character, and the terrible effect his conviction would have on his loyal wife and loving children. The community raised enough money to hire Oliver's lawyers and sustain his family during the trial.

Since the jury was made up of homesteaders, the "not guilty" verdict came as no surprise. But when Ed Oliver, who had been portrayed as such a solid citizen and good family man, left his wife, his children, and the community shortly thereafter, taking the money his friends raised— as he did—a number of people *were* surprised.

OR 205
Frenchglen—Fields
52 miles

County Road 201
Fields—Jct OR 78—Crane
107 miles

County Road 312
Crane—Jct US 20—Ontario
110 miles

Names on the Land

When names were given mountains, streams, ranches, and brands in the high desert country, the residents often distorted their spelling and pronunciation. For instance, a stream born high up on the western side of Steens Mountain, which then runs north through the heart of Malheur Wildlife Refuge, is designated on the map as the Donner und Blitzen River. This strange mixture of English and German evolved because that's the way locals pronounced it. This happened with many foriegn words, regardless of whether the new version made sense.

Colonel George B. Currey named the stream appropriately when he crossed it in 1864 during an expedition against the local Snake Indians, and it should have stuck without alteration. In *Cattle Country of Peter French*, author Giles French tells how it came about:

> It was storming that day, and the little river was high and boiling at Rock Ford—the only spot with bottom solid enough for a ford. With lightning flashing and thunder rolling, the well-read colonel remembered his German lessons and named the the river the *Dunder und Blitzen*. But when less well-read people moved in, it became the "Donner und Blitzen"—and has been called that ever since.

Because Peter French's livestock brand was the letter P, most people assume that it stood for the first letter of the cattle baron's first name. Not so, says Giles French, a distant relative. In 1872, when Peter French first came into this region with 1,200 cattle driven up from California, a man known only as Porter wandered into French's camp one evening. The cattleman fed Porter and listened to his sad story about getting ready to leave the Blitzen Valley after long, weary months of prospecting for gold. Sure, this was good cattle country, he admitted; he ran a string

Alvord Desert east of Steens Mountain.

of a dozen or so cows and had even registered a brand. Porter's branding iron formed a P. French bought Porter's cattle and brand.

Peter French remained a bachelor until the age of thirty-three. Then he married the twenty-two-year-old Ella Glenn, whose father, Dr. Hugh Glenn, had supplied most of the money for the cattle business. Truth was, Dr. Glenn was more interested in wheat than he was in cattle. At one time, the central California farms he owned raised so much grain that he was called the "Wheat King." Like Henry Miller, Glenn was a multi-millionaire—which was a good thing because his wife, daughter, and grandson, all in turn, spent money almost as fast as Dr. Glenn and Peter French could make it.

But tragedy struck when a disgruntled, alcoholic bookkeeper shot and killed Hugh Glenn only ten days after Peter and Ella got married. When French built his big ranch house, he named it Frenchglen, but neither his wife nor their son, who turned out to be a weakling, ever visited the place. After eight years of marriage during which they seldom lived together, Ella divorced Peter and left him in charge of the operation with a twenty percent share of the profits, though he surely was entitled to much more.

Like the other big ranchers in the area, Peter French brought in Shorthorn and Durham bulls to improve the weight and quality of his animals, gradually eliminating the tough but skinny Texas longhorns and Mexican strains. Though the Steens Mountain region had seemed immune to harsh weather, the bitter winter of 1888-89 killed off three-fourths of the cattle in the area. With so much more invested now, the ranchers could not continue to rely on the declining quality of the open range. They turned more and more to fencing and cross-fencing their fields, putting up hay, and keeping a close eye on their cattle—in a word, becoming stock-raisers rather than ranchers.

The High Desert Country Today

On Oregon 205, just south of the Malheur Wildlife Refuge, is the small town called Frenchglen. The Frenchglen Hotel originally built in 1916 as a stop for teamsters and stagecoaches traveling between Burns and Winnemucca is now owned and operated by the Oregon State Parks. Open from March to November, the hotel has eight rooms, serves good family style meals, and is a popular place to stay for wildlife and bird-watchers. During the popular summer season reservations are a good idea.

The original house built by Peter French in the 1880s occupied a beautiful site on the Donner und Blitzen River two miles east of the Frenchglen Hotel. In its day, it was something of a showplace. He built the "P" House for his bride, but she never came there to live. The place burned to the ground in 1940, leaving only the brick chimney standing; today tall poplar trees over a hundred years old mark the spot. Nearby, a steel observation tower for bird-watchers overlooks the Donner und Blitzen River and the teeming life of the Malheur refuge.

Fifteen miles south of Frenchglen, one of the largest cattle operations in the area, Roaring Springs Ranch, once was part of the French-Glenn empire. Though most highway maps show the pavement ending here, it continues all the way south to Denio, Nevada.

To get a close-up look at the Steens Mountain, turn northeast on the good gravel road at Fields, which runs straight and level for sixty-five miles between the base of the forty-mile long mountain and the Alvord Desert until it intersects Oregon 78 southeast of Burns. In the "rain shadow" of the 9,500-foot Steens Mountain, these extensive flats, with no drainage to the sea, are as white as snow.

Once you reach the highway, the small town of Crane lies forty-two miles northwest toward Burns. Because this region is so sparsely populated, Crane has the largest consolidated school district in the

The school in Crane serves the nation's largest consolidated school district.

United States. Being bused to school is a fact of life here. Some students ride up to 175 miles each way—a long trip in good weather but impossible in bad, so when the students get to school they stay dormitory-style for extended periods of time. Boys on the first floor, girls on the second, and never the twain shall meet on the stairs. From all reports, most of the students like the Crane school and take great pride in its activities and sports.

Two Myths Dispelled

Before leaving the high desert country, let's dispel two widely accepted myths about it. The first has to do with the notion that the pre-white-man West was a paradise for game, some of which the newcomers soon killed off to near extinction, such as the buffalo. While it's true that the American bison suffered tremendously in its natural habitat, Oregon's high desert country was never buffalo range. The principal game animal here was the mule deer; and it was not nearly as plentiful then as it is today. E.R. Jackman and his friend Reub Long testified to that in *The Oregon Desert*, after hunting deer in the same place for thirty-four years.

> This is in an area where the pioneers, both emigrants and trappers, reported a great scarcity of deer. Early-day cattlemen tell of riding for days without seeing a deer, and at night, if someone reported he had seen one, they all gathered around him, asking questions.

For years later the annual take of deer by hunters had been larger in Oregon than in any other state, Long says. In one recent year, the Oregon Department of Fish and Game sold over 265,000 hunting licenses and allowed at least 164,000 deer harvested, about a quarter of which came from the desert counties. The state game commission gets a lot of flack about the yearly kill rate, but the deer population has managed to withstand and even depend on this rate of loss; otherwise, many would surely die from starvation.

Reub Long points out that Peter Skene Ogden found few deer in 1826; as did John Fremont in 1843. He states flatly: "Deer are at least ten times as numerous in Oregon now as they were seventy years ago" (in the first decade of the twentieth century).

Killing off predators such as the cougar has probably helped increase the deer population, though, despite a concerted and sustained effort to eradicate or thin out the greatest deer-killer of all, the coyote, its numbers have not diminished and probably never will. Like most desert people, Reub Long admits having ambivalent feelings about the coyote, in that he hates some of the things it does to calves and lambs but admires its ingenuity for staying alive in a land where every man's hand is turned against it.

The second myth that should be laid to rest is the cattleman-sheepman controversy. When properly cared for, sheep are no more inclined to destroy grass than are cattle. Improperly herded, either can destroy the range beyond repair. It is a matter of record that in the days of the great livestock barons, all of them raised both cattle and sheep, often on the same expanse of rangeland, with no ill effects.

The Taylor Grazing Act of 1934 established grazing districts administered by the U.S. Grazing Service, until 1946, when the newly formed Bureau of Land Management took over. Prior to this, as Reub Long states:

> ... feed on the public lands of the desert belonged to the fellow who got there first. The sheep are under the command of herders and go in flocks of a thousand or more. A thousand sheep are the equivalent of two hundred cattle. On the desert, two hundred cattle will be scattered over maybe ten thousand acres, but a [sheep]herder must be able to see his flock all the time. If they scatter, the lambs will soon be adorning the quick-lunch counters of coyotes and bobcats.

Whether the sheepherders were Irish, Basque, Scotch, or Portugese—all of whom came to the high desert country—they were men skilled in the art of tending their flock. To make best use of the available pasture, the herder moved the sheep daily in a circle around his wagon, while one or more well-trained dogs guarded the flock by night. Good herders lost few sheep and allowed the range to recover fully before returning their sheep to graze it again.

In the case of the cattlemen in Oregon, most of their hired hands were Spanish-Indian vaqueros from California, with a deep, abiding loyalty to the ranch owner's foreman as well as an understanding of cattle and horses. Usually the sheepman or cattleman used the same range from year to year, either through ownership or a long-term lease, so he took good care of it and certainly did nothing to destroy its quality.

The trouble between these two groups stemmed from the abusive habits of "itinerant" flocks of sheep. These flocks stayed on the move, driven by herders working for big companies that bought or leased water rights barely adequate to quench the sheeps' thirst while passing through a region where they might cross ten miles of open, unfenced rangeland to the next water hole. As they moved, the sheep devoured every blade of grass in sight.

> Nothing riled a cattleman any more than to try to save grass for later use, only to find from one to twenty bands of sheep on it, the range eaten bare and clean. If the year turned dry, the grass treated that way might die. I want to repeat that with sheep it didn't need to be eaten so closely, because the herder has absolute control, but when the grass belonged to no one, the herder knew that if he didn't get the last spear, someone else would, so there was no point in grazing lightly, as he did on privately owned land.

The Faithful Sheep Dog

A final story about the mystic of the high desert country came to me from a long-time friend and is my favorite dog story. Wesley Slaughter joined the U.S. Forest Service as a firefighter in the John Day country at the age of sixteen before working several years as a full-time ranger, then earned a degree in forestry from Washington State University so he could describe in technical terms what he had been doing most of his adult life. After several years of leading firefighting crews from southern California to the Canadian border, he rounded out his career building trails in primitive areas—where the use of power tools is prohibited—with crews of husky young college students he had to train from scratch. He is the only man I know that can give the Latin name of a tree, a shrub, and a plant tied together in a three-way symbiosis, explain why one of them is never found without the other two, then fall a hundred-foot tree with a pair of wedges and a chain saw and drop it within six inches of where he wants it to go. This is his story:

When a sheep herder takes his flock into remote country, his home is a wagon—usually rubber tired—equipped with a stove, a bed, a lamp, and enough food staples to last him for several weeks. In addition to the thousand or so sheep he is tending, he has a horse or two to ride or pull the wagon, and three or more dogs to help him look after the sheep. At intervals of every three weeks or so, someone resupplies the herder with food, reading material, mail, and whatever else he needs for creature comforts.

In a routine the dogs know as well as he does, the flock of sheep is moved daily in a circular pattern so that the range will not be overgrazed. If there are three dogs, one will be the boss and the other two helpers. The two helper dogs stay with the sheep constantly, while the boss dog goes back and forth with the herder from the flock to the wagon.

"When we went out to supply this particular herder's camp," Wesley Slaughter said, "we found no evidence of him at the wagon, though its back door was standing ajar. As we sat on our horses wondering where he was, his boss sheep dog came trotting across the meadow where the wagon was parked, and, without paying us the slightest attention, climbed the steps at the back of the wagon and disappeared inside.

"When we got off our horses to see what it was doing, we saw it stand on its hind legs and take a biscuit off a pan setting on the sheepherder's stove. Apparently cooked a few days before, there had been twelve biscuits in the pan. Counting the one the boss dog had in its mouth, five were now missing.

"Still paying no attention to us, the dog climbed down out of the wagon, trotted back across the meadow, and into the fringe of scattered pine that bordered it higher up the slope. We got back on our horses and followed. A mile or so away, we found the herder. He was dead."

Wesley Slaughter and his friend determined that the herder had died from natural causes five days ago. Supervised by the boss dog, the two helper dogs had moved the sheep each day, even though their master was not there to supervise. Whether the boss dog thought his master was just taking a long nap from which he would wake up hungry, no one could say. But as the two riders watched, the boss dog carefully deposited the biscuit he had taken out of the pan near his dead master's hand.

There were four other biscuits beside it...

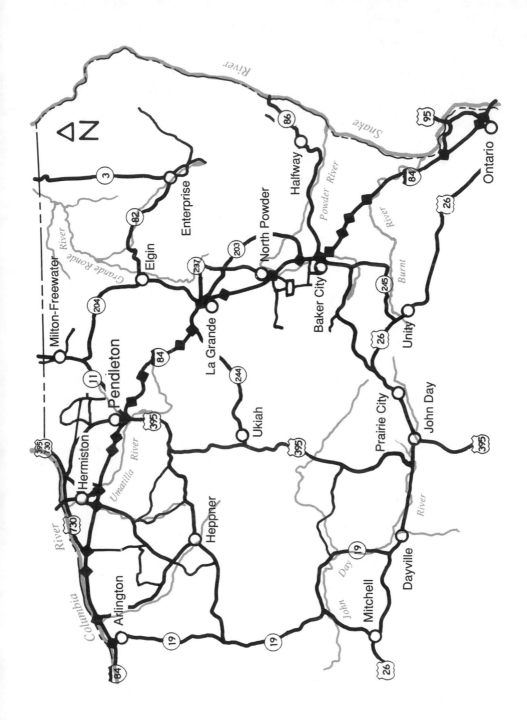

PART VI

The Blue Mountains

I-84
Ontario—Pendleton
168 miles

Death in the Mountains

Crossing the Blue Mountains between Ontario and Pendleton on I-84 is not a problem for modern travelers—the divided highway has a few long but relatively gentle grades, its curves are open and gradual, and the speed limit is sixty-five miles per hour (except for in the immediate vicinity of La Grande). Motorists on this super highway can take for granted this crossing that has proven a hazardous, sometimes deadly barrier for others, from the first party of Astorians, followed by British and American fur trappers, explorers, and emigrants, then by stagecoachs, railroads, and finally earlier car and truck traffic.

The area around Ontario, where I-84 crosses the Snake River boundary between Idaho and Oregon, is like a fertile oasis today; irrigation, excellent soil, abundant sunshine, and a benign climate make it a garden spot for fruits and vegetables, and give us no hint of how bleak it appeared to the early explorers and emigrants. As the highway rises a few miles northwest of Ontario, we get a glimpse of how the land looked when white men first saw it. The sagebrush-covered, desolate foothills seem to go on forever. After some twenty-five miles I-84 descends for a final contact with the Snake River at Farewell Bend. This historic spot is commemorated by a state park (and a truck stop); here your eyes and imagination can help you visualize what faced the first white people to reach this spot.

329

Major Lee Moorehouse, agent on the Umatilla Reservation near Pendleton around 1900, developed a hobby into professional-quality photography. —Umatilla County Historical Society

Washington Irving provides some additional detail from his book *Astoria*:

> Here, on the night of December 22, 1811, the starving Astorians under the command of Captain Hunt crossed the ice-filled Snake River. Mr. Hunt caused a horse to be killed and a canoe to be made out of its skin. The canoe proving too small another horse was killed and the skin of it joined to the first. Night came on before the little bark had made two voyages. Being badly made it was taken apart and put together again by the light of the fire. The night was cold; the men were wearied and disheartened with such varied and incessant toil and hardship.

Early the next morning, they crossed with much difficulty, breaking the new ice that formed during the night for some distance from either shore. "At length they all got over in safety to the west side; and their spirits rose on having achieved this perilous passage."

But then the Hunt party faced another formidable task—finding a route across the immense mountain range in the dead of winter. The local Indians were of no help. Also in a starving condition, they skulked on the party's fringes, ready to steal any strayed or injured horses and rob or kill any white man that lagged behind.

330

This 1898 photo of the Cayuse twins, A-lom-pum and Tox-e-lox, became famous all across the country. —Lee Moorehouse, Smithsonian Institution National Anthropological Archives

Feeling the twins' mother was being neglected, another Pendleton photographer took her picture in 1899. —W.S. Bowman

Traveling with the party of thirty-two men was a half-blood hunter-interpreter, Pierre Dorion, Jr., whose father had gone up the Missouri River with Lewis and Clark as far as the Mandan country, where he had persuaded several chiefs to go downriver with the explorers on their return east in 1806 to St. Louis and Washington, D.C. With a well earned reputation as a hard drinker and just plain ornery, Pierre, Sr., had been a problem to the white explorers. But his son, Pierre, Jr., was even worse; in fact, he was so violent and quick-tempered that on one occasion he got into a quarrel with his father and came close to scalping him during a drunken brawl. The only person who could handle him when he flew into a rage was his Indian wife, Marie Dorion.

This remarkable woman, who played a much more significant role in the history of the Pacific Northwest than she has received credit for, was born around 1784, so was about the same age as Sacajawea. But from all accounts that have survived, she was a much stronger person and played a much larger part in the development of Oregon than Sacajawea did, for, unlike the famed Lewis and Clark guide, Marie Dorion spent most of her life in the country.

When Wilson Price Hunt hired Pierre Dorion, Jr., in St. Louis and learned that he planned to take along his Indian wife and two children, Hunt told the interpreter that such a thing was out of the question. In that case, Dorion replied, he would tender his services to some other leader who would not object. Reluctantly, Hunt gave in and advanced Dorion $200, which was about two-thirds of his first year's salary.

According to historian Jerome Peltier, whose *Madame Dorion* comprises the most accurate account of the Indian woman's life, Pierre had a few drinks to celebrate the deal, then came home and told his wife of the great scheme he had devised for making even more money.

> After the excitement had subsided, he would find another job, keeping the two hundred dollar advance. The Dorion woman would not hear of this proposed act of treachery and told Pierre that they would join Hunt as agreed. During the quarrel that followed the besotted Pierre struck Marie, who then proceeded to pick up a club and knock him out with a well-aimed blow to the head. She then walked out into the darkness with her bundle of belongings and her two sons.

Also, no doubt, with the two hundred dollars.

When Pierre regained consciousness, he recalled his promise to Hunt that he and his family would join the party at St. Charles, a few miles upriver, so he hurried there. Marie hid out in the bushes with her two sons, Baptiste, four, and Paul, two, for a couple of days to make sure her husband was going to fulfill his contract, then she appeared and resumed her duties as a faithful helpmate. There is no record that Pierre Dorion ever attempted to beat his wife again.

Sweat Lodge. —Jane Gay

By the time the Hunt party reached the Snake River desert area in mid-November and decided to break up into four sub-groups, Pierre had managed to trade a buffalo hide for a horse so that his wife, then eight months pregnant, could ride and carry the two children. After crossing the ice-choked Snake and heading northwestward into the snow-filled mountains, Marie Dorion's time had come. Washington Irving described the action in *Astoria*:

> Early the following morning [December 30, 1811, in the Grande Ronde Valley] the squaw of Pierre Dorion, who had hitherto kept on without murmuring or flinching, was suddenly taken in labor and enriched her husband with another child. As the fortitude and good conduct of the poor woman had gained for her the good will of the party, her situation caused concern and perplexity. Pierre, however, treated the matter as an occurrence that could be arranged and need cause no delay. He remained by his wife in the camp, with his other children and his horse, and promised soon to rejoin the main body, who proceeded on their march.

The physical condition of some members of the party was poor. Hunt allowed one man (named Labonte) to ride a horse after he collapsed, assigning himself to carry the horse's pack; three other men decided to abandon the party and stay with the Indians, even though the natives were as destitute as the Astorians. But none of this affected Marie Dorion. Again, Irving paints the scene:

> In the course of the following morning the Dorion family made its reappearance. Pierre came trudging in advance, followed by his

333

valued, though skeleton steed, on which was mounted his squaw with her new-born infant in her arms, and her boy of two years wrapped in a blanket and slung at her side. The mother looked as unconcerned as if nothing had happened to her.

Though the mother came through the ordeal in good shape, the baby, whose gender remains unknown, was not so fortunate. On January 7, 1812, Hunt briefly noted: "In the course of this day's march the recently-born child of Pierre Dorion died."

The best so far determined is that the unmarked grave of this first part-white child born on what later became the Oregon Trail was near Duncan Station, a now-vanished whistle-stop on the Union Pacific Railroad near La Grande.

The Ordeal of Marie Dorion

After reaching Astoria and spending a year or so there, Pierre and Marie Dorion, with their two children, returned to the area where they had made the winter crossing of the Snake with John Reed and nine other men to begin trapping in the area. The local Bannock Indians, often referred to as Snakes, were decidedly unfriendly. Because Marie was Indian, a sympathetic Bannock warned her that his people were planning an attack on the white men's winter quarters. But she could not get word to her husband and the other trappers in time. When it was over, her husband, Pierre, John Reed, and eight other Astorians lay dead. The sole survivor, Giles LeClerc, was so severely wounded that he fell off the horse Marie Dorion struggled to keep him on, reopening his wounds and dying shortly thereafter.

Snow blanketed the entire region, even in the lower area where the post stood. Alone with her two sons, now four and six years old, Marie Dorion decided to make her way back to more friendly country. She found two horses healthy enough to travel and scrounged a few pieces of dried salmon and several deer hides from the stores not stolen or burned. After crossing the Snake River somewhere near Farewell Bend, she faced 150 miles of mountainous terrain before getting to the land of the Umatillas and Walla Wallas on the western slope of the Blue Mountains around present-day Pendleton.

Jerome Peltier tells what happened:

> She had to cross the Snake River, which she likely swam despite the intense cold. She pushed along in a northwesterly direction for nine days until one of the horses could no longer continue. Faced with this serious dilemma, she proceeded to kill both animals for additional winter food. She lit a fire and smoked the meat so there would be no waste.

Worth noting is that this woman, then in her late twenties, was not native to the mountains. She was native to the Plains tribe of Iowas and grew up in the lowlands of Arkansas and Missouri. But she could swing a club, among other things, when she needed to.

She decided to build a shelter and stay put through the worst of the winter. She chose a site at the foot of a rocky precipice near a small stream in the vicinity of La Grande and built a hut of cedar branches, grass, and moss. Her only tool was a knife. She waited fifty-three days for winter to break. Peltier believes that Marie Dorion and her two sons lived in the winter camp from January 30 to March 23, 1814.

Thinking the weather mild enough to travel, she then resumed her journey. But the valley and the mountains were so brilliant white with snow that she became snowblind on the second day and spent three days recovering. When she regained her sight and set out again, it took fifteen days to reach the western slope of the Blues. Through breaks in the trees, she could see the plains of the lower country in the distance far ahead. Out of food for six days and her strength nearly gone, she saw smoke rising from what she hoped was a friendly Indian camp. As a safety precaution, she concealed the children as best she could, then went on through the drifts of melting snow alone.

> She crawled, being too exhausted to walk. Occasionally, she slept. At noon she reached a camp of Walla Wallas, who proved to be friendly. She told them where her children could be found. Her hosts immediately sent a search party to find the children. They found it easy to follow the trail made by her body as she had dragged herself along.

After resting with the Walla Wallas for a few days, she got them to take her on west to the Columbia River, where she hoped to encounter a party of Astorians sent to check on the John Reed party. When such a party did come a month later, she told its leader, Alexander Ross, what had happened. He offered to take her and her children back to Fort George at the mouth of the Columbia or send them east to St. Louis with a returning fur brigade. But she declined. This was her country now, for here was where her husband and her baby had died. She did not intend to leave it.

And she never did.

Apparently living with the Walla Walla tribe for a while, she married a French Canadian named Louis Joseph Venier in 1818, the same year Fort Nez Perce (precursor to Fort Walla Walla) was built. After he left the area or died (the record is not clear), she married John Baptiste Toupin, an interpreter of French and Indian blood, in 1824. Though this probably was a ceremony read by a company clerk or factor, she legitimized it on July 19, 1841, with Father Francis Norbert Blanchet (later the archbishop of Portland) officiating.

The Dorion name is well represented in the history of Oregon. Baptiste Dorion, Marie's older son, married an Indian woman who bore seven children. Marie and her second husband, Louis Venier, had a daughter named Marguerite, who married a French Canadian and bore six children.

As the years went by and tales of her courage were told and retold, Marie earned a title of respect seldom granted an Indian woman; all who knew her called her Madame Dorion. Dr. Elijah White, appointed Indian agent for Oregon in 1846, reported that he:

> ... saw this woman living comfortably in the Willamette Valley with a Canadian Frenchman, to whom she had long been married. She presented him with several pairs of moccasins, very neatly executed, after the most approved fashion of her tribe. He was very much impressed with her noble, commanding bearing.

On September 5, 1850, she died at the age of sixty-four in the small Willamette Valley town of St. Louis, Oregon, and was buried under the steeple of the parish church. On April 7, 1935, the Oregon chapter of the *Daughters of 1812*, placed a marker at the site. Appropriately enough, Champoeg, the birthplace of Oregon, is only a few miles away.

Search for a Trail

Early explorers searching for routes across North America generally followed this simple rule: Find a river flowing the direction you want to go and follow it to either its source or its mouth. It seemed to work pretty well.

In 1805, Lewis and Clark ascended the Missouri River deep into the heart of the Rocky Mountains to a place now known as Three Forks. There they had to decide which of the three streams—the Gallatin, the Madison, or the Jefferson—would take them closest to where they wanted to go. After a few hours of indecision, a bit of shrewd geographic reasoning, and a few days of exploring the three possibilities, they chose the right stream, the Jefferson. Ascending the Jefferson, then the Beaverhead, they reached the continental divide, where water flowed to the Atlantic Ocean on one side and to the Pacific on the other. One member of the party exulted that he had stood "with a foot on either side of this little rivulet and thanked God that [he] had lived to bestride the mighty & hitherto deemed endless Missouri."

West of the divide and with the help of local Indian guides, the Lewis and Clark party had no trouble following first the Lemhi, Salmon, Clearwater, and Snake rivers westward down the Pacific slope to the Columbia and eventually to the sea. Later travelers who failed to follow that route and tried to find a new way west without the help of Indian guides ran into all kinds of trouble, mostly because of the turbulent nature of the middle reaches of the Snake River.

Geologists say the Snake may be a "captured river," which means that some fairly recent geological activity may have caused it to change course, or perhaps even reverse its direction of flow. A prime piece of evidence for this theory is Hells Canyon.

Beginning a few miles north of Farewell Bend State Park, the Snake enters the deepest gorge in North America, a fearsome canyon 6,500 feet deep, with rugged mountain ranges nine to ten thousand feet above sea level on either side. For a hundred miles through the gorge the walls are too steep for anything less sure-footed than a mountain goat. In the river's channel, white rapids make the Snake impossible to navigate by any craft less powerful than a specialized jet boat.

Hells Canyon forced early explorers, fur trappers, emigrants, railroad builders, and highway engineers to choose between the difficult and the impossible. Invariably they opted for the difficult, which meant leaving the river and turning northwest to climb up and over the Blue Mountains along a route closely followed by the highway today.

Captain John C. Fremont wrote in 1843:

> Leaving Snake River, which is said henceforth to pursue its course through canyons, amidst rocky and impracticable mountains where there is no possibility of traveling with animals, we ascended a long and somewhat steep hill; and crossing the dividing ridge, came out into the valley of the Brule or Burnt River, which here looks like a hole among the hills.

Though Fremont ascribed the blackened color of the bluffs along Burnt River to the Indian practice of setting fire to the grass each autumn in order to make it grow more lush next spring, later travelers discovered veins of coal in the rock strata, which they tried to put to use as fuel for the boilers of steamboats on the Snake. When it proved to be of such poor quality that it took "a cord of wood to keep a ton of coal burning," they gave up the effort. The low-grade coal is there still.

After crossing the first crest of the Blue Mountains, the highway drops down to a broad, wide, beautiful valley twenty or so miles across. Here, during the gold rush days of the 1860s, miners built the thriving metropolis of Baker City. After the gold petered out, the metropolis continued and thrived as a center for cattle, grain, and timber products.

For a time the ten-story Baker Hotel was one of the tallest buildings in the state. Prominent even from the freeway, it is now a historic landmark. As a sign of its coming of age, Baker's leaders dropped "City" from the town's name but lately have rekindled a liking for the sound of Baker City.

The town honors its heritage today with the Oregon Trail Regional Museum. Once scheduled for demolition, much of the 32,500-square-foot brick Natatorium Building has now been converted into a marvelous exhibit of historical artifacts and semi-precious stones, with a rock collection valued at over a quarter million dollars. Its black-light display of mineralized rocks is outstanding. Presently it is open only from May through September, but well worth the visit.

Oregon Trail Interpretive Centers

Incidentally, Oregon Trail sesquicentennial celebrations have spawned at least four new interpretive centers of historical interest. All commemorate the opening of the trail in 1843, when over one thousand people made the epic trek to the Oregon country and helped assure that it would become American rather than British territory. The first interpretive center, a $10 million facility, opened in May 1992 a couple of miles west of Baker City on Flagstaff Hill. The second was scheduled to open in 1993 on the Umatilla Reservation near Pendleton; the third at The Dalles; and the fourth at Oregon City. Each is expected to draw 200,000 visitors annually, and the Oregon State Tourism Bureau has issued a free map identifying forty historic sites along the Oregon Trail.

Of Baker's gold-boom days, the WPA guide says:

> Travelers passing through saw more exciting life in Baker City than in any town between Portland and Salt Lake. Notwithstanding the two-fisted character of the town, the city commissioners in 1881 passed an ordinance prohibiting small boys from shooting marbles or riding velocipedes on the sidewalk.

Sumpter Valley Railroad. —Baker County Library District

Typical of hillsides covered with evergreen trees, the atmosphere in this part of the country often has a bluish tinge to it. Fremont wrote: "It is probable that they have received their name of the Blue Mountains from the dark-blue appearance given to them by the pines."

Standing near the ford of the Powder River on the western edge of the valley, with no other trees nearby, once soared a pine so distinctive that travelers from the 1820s on called it "Lone Tree Crossing." But after traffic began rolling on the Oregon Trail in 1836, its doom was sealed.

"Cooked dinner at *L'Arbor Seul,* a lonely pine in an extensive plain," Thomas J. Farnham's journal reads at his entry for September 19, 1839. Four years later Fremont wrote: "From the heights we looked in vain for a well-known landmark on Powder River, which had been described to me by Mr. Payette as *l'arbre seul* [the lone tree]; and, on arriving at the river, we found a fine tall pine stretched on the ground, which had been felled by some inconsiderate emigrant axe. It had been a beacon on the road for many years past."

After the tree fell, the WPA guide says the place became known as "Lone Pine Stump."

Northwest of Baker City the land rises again, becoming steep, rocky, and heavily timbered, then drops down into the Grande Ronde Valley. Fremont in 1843 was among the first of many who later described it:

> About two in the afternoon we reached a high point of the dividing ridge, from which we obtained a good view of the *Grand Rond*—a beautiful level basin, or mountain valley, covered with good grass on a rich soil, abundantly watered, and surrounded by high and well-timbered mountains; and its name descriptive of its form, the great circle. It is a place—one of the few we have seen on our journey so far—where a farmer would delight to establish himself, if he were content to live in the seclusion it imposes.

Indian Trading Place

The Nez Perce, Umatilla, Cayuse, and Walla Walla Indians had long treasured the Grande Ronde Valley as a garden spot. Horses raised by these tribes on the naturally good range became recognized throughout the West as among the best anywhere. Soon whites referred to any tough, wiry, small horse of the kind ideal for working cattle as a "cayuse."

When Meriwether Lewis observed the quality of the horses raised in the Nez Perce country, he remarked that they equaled any horses he had seen in his native Virginia. He was particularly impressed with the fact that the Nez Perces practiced selective breeding, being as skilled with the use of the knife when it came to gelding as any Virginia horse-breeder, as well as with the use of green rawhide ligatures in the gelding process, much as veterinarians use rubber bands today, to eliminate the problem of infection.

Captain Bonneville, who came through the valley in 1833, commented on its good winter pasture for elk. The Indians often hunted here and dug for camas roots, which Bonneville said were so abundant that their blue blossoms made the whole valley look "like the ocean when overcast by a cloud."

During the years of heavy travel over the Oregon Trail between 1843 and 1859, the Grande Ronde Valley was a welcome oasis in a bleak and thirsty land. Behind emigrants on this leg of their journey lay the hot, dry Snake River desert, where the Bannocks and other hostile tribes constantly shadowed the wagon trains, wounding and stealing stock, picking off stragglers, and boldly attacking and killing parties too small to put up a stiff defense.

Here the bone-weary emigrants and their exhausted oxen found plenty of water, wood, and grass; the cooler air and tall shade trees made for a comfortable camp. The Indians around here followed the Nez Perce example of friendship toward the whites, first tested on the Lewis and Clark expedition. The only potentially negative trait these Indians had was their shrewdness in trading.

Once a yoke of oxen became worn out by too much heat and not enough food and rest, its chances of recovering strength on the trail were nil. Though the Indians had no use for oxen or draft animals of any kind, they soon learned that worn-out animals from one year's wagon train could be traded back at a profit the next year after growing fat and strong on the valley's rich grass.

To paraphrase (and slightly twist) an expression later widely applied to European immigrants, the Indians said, in essence: "Give us your hungry, poor and skinny animals in a two-for-one trade this year, and we'll trade them back to next year's wagon train, also two-for-one." Such crafty bartering led one exasperated emigrant from Missouri to comment: "The Nez Perces can beat a Yankee peddler in a trade!"

Another feature about the pause in the Grande Ronde Valley the emigrants welcomed was its relative closeness to the only civilized American settlement between Fort Laramie and the Willamette Valley—the Whitman Mission. A slight detour north of only a few days could offer a brief respite on the long journey to the Willamette Valley.

A few miles west of the present-day town of La Grande, after topping the final crest of the Blue Mountains, emigrant trains in good condition began the long, winding descent to the Umatilla River and the Columbia. If winter threatened safe passage through to the Willamette Valley, or if the people in the train were sick or simply too physically and spiritually exhausted to travel any further, the emigrants could make their way along the Walla Walla River to the Whitman Mission.

Though the mission stood in Oregon country during its eleven-year existence between 1836 and 1847, it is within the modern political boundary of Washington State. Anyone interested in the history of Oregon should make a point of visiting the Whitman Mission National Historic Site, six miles west of Walla Walla on US 12. The visitor center is open year round and effectively explains the role Marcus and Narcissa Whitman played early in this region's development.

To get there, you can go northeast from Pendleton on Oregon 11 across rolling farmland, or, for a more scenic route, take Oregon 82 north from La Grande to Elgin, then Oregon 204 northwest over the last spur of the Blue Mountains to Weston, where you join Oregon 11 and head north to Milton-Freewater and the Washington state line. The trees along the western slope of the Blues thin out below 3,500 feet, then wide vistas of rich, fertile land come into view. Even on steep-graded slopes, wheat and peas grow in abundance here.

Due to variations in rainfall, altitude, and temperature, farmers can begin harvest in early June on the lowest-lying fields and continue working at ever-increasing elevations through the summer until finally reaching the highest fields in early September. Normally, wheat around here and in southeast Washington yields more than one hundred bushels an acre, and one third of all frozen and canned peas in the United States comes from this area. Fruit orchards, strawberries, and a special species of onion called the "Walla Walla Sweet" also grow here.

More About Hank Vaughn

Between Milton-Freewater and Pendleton along Oregon 11 lie the small communities of Adams and Athena. Hank Vaughn, a man of dubious character first mentioned in the Prineville section of Part Five, lived and gained notoriety around here. No plaques, fountains, or statues have been erected in his honor, but this is where old-timers in the 1930s proudly pointed out to writer Russell Blankenship the bullet holes in bars made years earlier by Hank when he was in a playful mood. They also showed him scars gouged in the floor of the local saloons by the shoes of Hank's horse, when he chose to ride into the bars for his drinks.

Blankenship credits Hank Vaughn's fondness for guns and horses with first getting him in trouble. At the age of eighteen, he and a man named Dan Burns stole a large band of horses off the range near Pendleton and headed them across the Blue Mountains to market in Boise. Umatilla County Sheriff Frank Maddock and his deputy, O.J. Hart, tracked them to the Baker City area, where they found the two horse-thieves sound asleep in their their blankets. Sheriff Maddock told his deputy to cover young Vaughn while he took care of the older Burns. As the officers jerked the blankets off the two sleeping thieves and ordered them to surrender, both men came up shooting. The lawmen replied in kind. When the powder smoke cleared, Deputy Hart and Burns lay dead, while Sheriff Maddock and Hank Vaughn were badly wounded.

Though he got away briefly, Vaughn was captured and hauled into court. Recovering from his wound, Sheriff Maddock could not swear whose bullet had killed his deputy, so, considering his youth and the circumstances, the judge sentenced Vaughn to prison rather than hanging.

During his eight years in prison Vaughn learned blacksmithing, but never worked at it after his release because he found a career that beat working all hollow. He married a widow with enough Indian blood in her veins to be allotted a good wheat farm on the Umatilla Reservation near Athena. Fortunately, her children were old enough to do the farm work so Hank could attend to other matters. Mostly, he drank whisky and fooled around with horses.

"Hank was a fancier of horse-flesh and an expert driver and rider," wrote Blankenship in *And There Were Men*. "As the old-timers around Pendleton say, he could drive a six-horse team where most men would be afraid to drag a halter-rope." Even so, a team of runaway horses nearly killed Hank one day, along with his bosom buddy, Doc Whitley.

Other than the fact that he came to Umatilla County from Arizona shortly after the Earp-Clanton feud at Tombstone's infamous O.K. Corral, nothing was known about Doc Whitley's past. No one was impolite enough to ask. Opening a saloon in the small hamlet of Adams, Doc Whitley took a liking to Hank Vaughn. Blankenship reported the saloon's regular patrons attested it was an orderly place most of the time; when it was not, usually Hank or Doc were to blame.

One day Vaughn, pretty well illuminated, drove up in front of Doc Whitley's saloon with a half-broken team of lively young horses hitched to a light buggy. Doc came out to admire the animals, then twitted Hank: "It seems to me that you're scared of your team, Hank. Why don't you hire a man to break them for you?"

Hank answered by inviting Whitley to take a ride, so Doc jumped into the buggy, seized the whip, and lashed the horses. Instead of trying to control the team, Hank threw the lines to the ground and gave an Indian yell. Blankenship writes:

> The runaway was one of the most successful that Adams ever saw. Down the street the team dashed pell-mell, Doc whipping the horses and Hank yelling. The team was going much too fast to make a turn, and the frantic horses, the smashed buggy, and the men all ended up in a heap beside the road. Doc and Hank were so severely injured that for a few days hope was entertained for their demise, but the reckless devils were too wiry. Hank survived to plague the community for years.

Four Indian cowboys in their angora wool chaps about 1910. Clockwise from left: Gilbert Minthorne, Green Fly, Johnson Chapman, and Jim White (sitting).
—Walter Bowman

During the 1880s and '90s Athena was a lively town, old-timers say, with one row of store buildings housing a saloon in every structure. One of Hank's favorite diversions was spurring his horse into one saloon after another until he paid his respects to every bartender and took a drink at every bar. Then he would race his horse along the street, yelling and firing his pistol at random. After each spree, Vaughn would come back to town sober and pay in cash whatever damages he caused.

There were never any train robberies in Umatilla County, but Hank Vaughn once prevented one on a return visit from Idaho with his wife. They were in a day coach seat when three bandits, armed with revolvers, rushed into the car and ordered the men to stand and raise their hands. Literally caught napping, Hank had no choice but to obey.

Dressed in a long Prince Albert coat, white shirt, and tie, Hank also wore a gunbelt and two holstered pistols around his waist. As he stood up, he whispered to his wife to reach up under his coat and unbuckle his belt. She did, and "as he felt the weapons slide beneath the bottom of the Prince Albert, he swiftly stooped and came up with two guns blazing. One of the bandits fell dead; the others ran, but they were soon taken by officers. For his bravery Hank received a life pass from the grateful railroad company."

Uncharitably, some local detractors said that Hank was not being brave; he was just expressing his anger that the bandits were encroaching on what he regarded as his territory. For whatever motive, he now had a lifetime pass on the railroad to ride free to the scenes of his depredations.

343

Sad to say, it was an extremely rude encounter with what passed for the amenities of civilization that did Hank in. Reasonably sober on a bright June day in 1893, Hank spurred his horse onto the only piece of concrete sidewalk in eastern Oregon, which happened to be in Pendleton. The horse slipped and pitched Hank's head into a telephone pole. Wooden barrooom floors, the horse could handle. But not concrete sidewalk.

His skull fractured beyond repair, Hank lingered unconscious for a week while three doctors, including a surgeon brought up from Portland, tried to save him. But their efforts failed. When he died, the editor of the *East Oregonian* wrote a fitting tribute:

> Ah, Hank, that was a fateful ride, the last time you mounted your trusty sorrel in the streets of Pendleton and sped with him like a tempest until his sure feet could not keep pace with your impetuosity, and you were plunged headlong upon the rocks.

Pendleton—The Round-Up City

Over much of the West, Pendleton, Oregon, is famous for two things: Pendleton wool and the Pendleton Round-Up. In the heart of sheep country, the Pendleton Woolen Mills started fabricating quality western-style shirts and pants many years ago. Though the company has since expanded and now has plants in other the parts of the Pacific Northwest, the expression "It's a Pendleton" means quality outdoor clothes.

When anyone mentions the Pendleton Round-Up, rodeo fans and cowboys all over the country recognize the reference to the top rodeo in the country since 1910. When it first began in 1909, this event celebrated

Old Stage Coach Race, Pendleton Round-Up, 1916. —Pendleton Public Library

Round-Up Hall-of-Famer Jackson Sundown, c. 1920.

the Fourth of July with a few local white and Indian cowboys competing with one another for modest purses in bronc and bull riding, bulldogging, wild horse racing, and other contests. But because summer is harvest time, the promoters decided to put off the Round-Up till mid-September, after harvest. Excepting an interruption by the Second World War in 1942 and 1943, the Pendleton Round-Up has been held every year in September.

Famous riders and horses have made rodeo history at the Round-Up for many years. Though the bucking horse named Midnight inspired a legend and a song about "the bronc that never was rode," Midnight *was rode* three times at the Round-Up, and the cowboy who rode the outlaw horse *was throwed*—five times.

Rodeo fans should visit the Round-Up Hall of Fame in Pendleton. Old-time Western movie stars and stunt men such as Hoot Gibson and Yakima Canutt often competed in the Round-Up. My favorite hall-of-fame member is a Nez Perce Indian named Jackson Sundown.

In 1855 a treaty made in the Walla Walla Valley established an 800-square-mile reservation in the foothills of the Blue Mountains just east of Pendleton for three related Indian tribes—the Umatillas, the Walla Wallas, and the Cayuses. The much larger Nez Perce tribe received a

10,000-square-mile reservation overlapping the current states of Oregon, Washington, and Idaho. Since that time, these native Americans have exchanged friendly visits, intermarried, and moved back and forth from one reservation to the other.

Like their cowboy counterparts, these horse-loving Indians undertook any kind of activity that kept them riding. As riders, they excelled. So when the Pendleton Round-Up started, the Indian contestants more than held their own. Now enshrined in the Round-Up Hall of Fame, Jackson Sundown won the title World Champion Bronc Rider in 1916. Any professional cowboy can tell you that riding broncs is best left to young men, but when Jackson Sundown won the coveted prize, he was fifty years old.

One of the most tragic chapters in the history of Indian-white relations was the Nez Perce War of 1877, when Chief Joseph led his people across 1,300 miles of mountain wilderness with the U.S. Army in

Blanket of the Sun, who Americanized his name to Jackson Sundown, won the title of World Champion Bronc Rider at the Pendleton Round-Up in 1916 at the age of 50. —De Lancey Gill, Smithsonian Institution National Antropological Archives

hot pursuit. From their Wallowa home in northeast Oregon, across the Bitterroots that divide Idaho and Montana, down through Yellowstone Park, and then north towards Canada, the chase ended only a day's ride from freedom. With Chief Joseph on that epic flight was an eleven-year-old Nez Perce youth who, when he reached manhood, adopted the name Blanket of the Sun. Years later, when he returned to the Nez Perce Reservation and took up a career riding the rough ones, he Americanized his name to Jackson Sundown.

Accounts of exactly what happened the day Sundown won the Bronc Riding title vary. But I found an eyewitness who wrote me a letter explaining what he had seen. Some said the judges of the contest were reluctant to give the top award to an Indian and required Jackson Sundown to re-ride. Finally, public sentiment in the crowd forced the judges to award the prize to him. At first I doubted that story, for when it comes to bronc riding only one thing counts among cowboys—making the ride without pulling leather.

Pioneer photographer Waible Patton, who was there with his father, confirmed the story: "They made Sundown do several re-rides ... [be-cause] he was wearing the old-fashioned angora wool chaps, which had wool about six inches long." Just before his last ride another cowboy loaned him a pair of smooth chaps. "It was getting late in the day, and the sun was going down in the west. It seemed like everybody in the crowd was yelling 'Sundown! Sundown! Sundown!'"

In addition to the title of World Champion Bronc Rider, Jackson Sundown received a golden belt buckle from the Police Gazette for being the outstanding rodeo performer of the year. He was in good company. Hoot Gibson, the Western movie star, won this award in 1912, and Yakima Canutt, the famous Hollywood stuntman and action-movie director, won it in 1917 and again in 1919.

US 395 and US 26
Pendleton—John Day
127 miles

US 395 and OR 74
Pendleton—Heppner
59 miles

OR 207-19 and US 26
Heppner—John Day
118 miles

Two Roads South

Two historically interesting routes run between Pendleton and John Day. One traverses the Blue Mountains while the other skirts their lower western slopes. The over-mountain highway, US 395, is fifty miles shorter because it crosses three summits over 4,000 feet, winding through broad mountain valleys in between. The longer route takes about the same amount of time behind the wheel, but over straighter roads through open, semi-desert country. Either route offers a number of attractive stops for the history buff.

Heppner, southwest of Pendleton, once was completely wiped out by a flash flood whose scope was exceeded only by the famous Johnstown Flood in Pennslyvania. Unlike Johnstown, where a dam above the city gave way following torrential rains, Heppner had no dam to fail at the time of its epic disaster. But the clouds let loose a tremendous burst on June 14, 1903, and Willow Creek swelled too quickly for a third of the town's people to find safety. At least 247 died. In recent decades the creek has overflowed its banks again, but never with so much devastation.

In the early 1980s, compelled by the federal government either to relocate the Morrow County seat or agree to a Corps of Engineers plan to build a 165-foot flood-control dam across Willow Creek south of town, Heppner's 1,375 residents narrowly approved the federal project. Built in 1983, it is the world's first dam constructed entirely of roller-compacted concrete, a technique calling for sand, rock, cement, and water to be spread onto one-foot-thick layers and compressed rather than poured into forms. The process economizes both building time and materials, say the engineers.

County Courthouse, Heppner, Oregon.

Soon after the dam was completed and its reservoir filled, a problem developed. The dam sprung a leak. Its consequences remain a matter of controversy and debate among experts and townspeople. But the cause of the problem, experts agree, is animal waste and fertilizers used upstream that collect in the nutrient-rich reservoir and slowly dissolve the dam's concrete.

Remedial action taken by the Corps of Engineers has reduced the seepage by 95 percent. Supposedly, the dam's structural integrity will last another twenty to thirty years. Yet, so much vegetation grows on the lower face of the dam that one local resident claims has considered pasturing a flock of sheep on it. Septugenarian Neva Matteson, who lives just a quarter-mile downstream and fishes for trout and bass in the Willow Creek Reservoir every day, says she's not going to worry about it or move.

In times before the dam, the volunteer fire department sounded sirens when flash floods threatened the town. Someday when the dam's condition eventually deteriorates and poses a renewed and heightened danger to Heppner's residents, let's hope they remember what the siren means and head for the tops of the "scaredy-cat hills" surrounding the town. Meantime, the owner of the Wagonwheel Cafe and Lounge says he's got a plan to save himself and his customers. "If we're in the restaurant and it breaks, we're going into the bar."

John Day Fossil Beds

Eighty miles south of Heppner, a Congregational minister interested in geology, Dr. Thomas Condon, took credit for discovering the John Day Fossil Beds some years after coming to Oregon with a wagon train in 1852. The WPA guide to Oregon tells us:

> A cavalry officer member of a punitive expedition against the natives of central Oregon in the 1860s brought the first specimens from this area to The Dalles and to Mr. Condon's attention. Soon Mr. Condon had visited the beds himself in the company of other Indian fighters. In 1870 he sent a small collection of teeth from the beds to Yale University, bringing the natural museum to the attention of scientists. In 1889 a Princeton University expedition removed two tons of specimens from the beds and many other groups have also worked here.

In 1974 the John Day Fossil Beds National Monument was established in three different sites: Clarno, Painted Hills, and Sheep Rock. Clarno is twenty miles west of the town of Fossil on Oregon 218; Painted Hills is a few miles west of Mitchell and north of US 26; Sheep Rock, two miles north of US 26 on Oregon 19, is the main exhibit and visitor center for all three units. The visitor center is the converted ranch house of an early sheep grower. All three units of the fossil beds have extensive self-guided tour trails.

Legend of the Lost Blue Bucket

Before reports of California gold spread in 1849, few emigrants on Oregon-bound trains wasted time panning creeks for signs of color. In 1845, for example, a train led by an inept guide hoping to establish a new route west much farther south than the usual path (roughly along I-84) took his group up the Malheur River, where US 20 runs today. After getting completely lost, they stumbled into the John Day area, and eventually down that stream toward The Dalles. If the starving, desperate emigrants could have laid hands on their leader, they would have hanged him, survivors said, but he prudently made himself scarce and left the folks who hired him as a guide find their own way west.

Somewhere between Fort Hall and the John Day country—a stretch of 250 miles—children playing in a stream at the end of a day's travel found some pretty yellow rocks, tossed them into a blue bucket, and forgot them. Years later, after their family settled in the Willamette Valley, a man from California saw these trinkets, recognized them as gold, and asked the children where they had found them. In a stream, they said, one afternoon along the way. Which stream? Which afternoon? Where along the way?

They did not remember.

Thus, the legend of the Lost Blue Bucket Mine began. That it never was a mine, that it even existed, that it later was found, or not, or that it may yet be found—all adds to the fabled richness that is not a part of the region's folklore. What is of interest historically is that this legend and others of its kind inspired a search for gold in eastern Oregon and, as a result, the precious metal eventually turned up in many places, including a narrow canyon a couple of miles soulth of John Day in a town called Canyon City.

The trail of gold and history leads along the streams and gulches of Oregon's ruggedly beautiful northeast corner, where the heedless pursuit of treasure helped despoil some of the most beautiful landscape in the state. But first I must tell the poignant, unusual story of two highly respected Chinese residents named Lung On and Ing Hay and the renouwned Kam Wah Chung Company.

China Doctor of John Day

One of the least known facets of history in the inland portion of the Pacific Northwest is the role played by the Chinese in the development of the region. Between 1850 and 1882—when Congress closed the immigration door on Chinese laborers with passage of the Chinese Exclusion Act—tens of thousands of Asians willing to toil long hours for low pay came to Gum Shan (the Golden Hills) from the port of Canton in southern China. These (predominantly young) men were sojourners seeking their fortune in a distant land. They sent most of their earnings home to support their parents or the families they had started shortly before leaving heir native village, to which they fully intended to return some day.

The letters they wrote or dictated home have not been made available to American historians by the Chinese government, and may of the records once kept in the United State wer destroyed by fire after the 1906 earthquake in San Francisco (as explained earlier in Part Four), so our knowledge of their thoughts and feelings about his country remain sketchy. But we know that after their labor was no longer so desperately needed for mining and railroad-building, many returned to China. Inland, once-thriving colonies of Chinese gardeners, laundrymen, and restaurant owners in such towns as Boise, Spokane, Walla Walla, Baker, and Pendleton gradually dwindled away.

Only in the Kam Wah Chung Building in John Day has a complete record of Chinese life in the United States during the past half century been preserved. In their excellent book, *China Doctor of John Day*, historians Jeffrey Barlow and Christine Richardson state: "The building and its contents are the greatest singl surving group of original

Dr. Ing Hay, shortly after he came to John Day. —Oregon Historical Society

materials dating from the nineteenth-century influx of Chinese immigrants into the American West."

Ing Hay

Ing Hay, who later became known in John Day as Doc Hay, was born in the village of Hsia Pin Li in southern China in 1862. Like many others in that place and time, his family was desperately poor. In a country wracked by war and famine, the remedy for poverty was migration. Five of his father's brothers had gone to the United States; when word came back in the early 1880s that they were doing well, Ing's father took his twenty-year-old son and decided to join them.

Whether they entered the United States legally is not clear, but their first stop was Walla Walla, where the five brothers lived. When they arrived in 1885 work opportunities in both mining and railroads had dwindled significantly, but for a couple of years they managed to find enough unskilled labor to keep themselves going.

Failing to learn English or adapt to American ways, as his five brothers had done, Ing's father decided in 1887 to return to China. In a letter that has been preserved and translated, Ing told him: "Let the old go back home and rest. Let the young seek their fortune abroad."

Though his five uncles remained in Walla Walla, young Ing Hay, speaking very broken English, decided to find his fortune two hundred miles to the south, in John Day, Oregon. When he arrived, the population of Canyon City stood at 1,500; two miles away, 500-600 Chinese lived in "Lower Town." Attracted first by gold mining in the area, then by the empty promise of work on a railroad, the Chinese community in what later became John Day centered around a unique stone building erected in the early 1860s.

Constructed of locally quarried stone, the building stretched thirty feet on a side with three-foot thick walls pierced only by small windows covered with steel shutters outside and wooden ones inside. Probably built originally as a trading post and fort, by 1885 the Chinese community owned the stronghold and used it as a store. It was here that Ing Hay and Lung On came together in 1887 and began their lifelong association.

Lung On

Lung On, who was about the same age as Ing Hay and from the same part of China, landed in San Francisco in 1882. Well educated, cultured, fluent in English, and a shrewd (if sometimes reckless) businessman, Lung On was as adventurous and outgoing as Ing Hay was quiet and retiring. Learning that Ing had training in classical Chinese medicine and intended to establish a practice as a traditional Chinese herbal doctor, Lung proposed that they become partners in an enterprise called the Kam Wah Chung Company, which would purchase and be headquartered in the stone building. Ing Hay agreed; thus, they joined forces in a business that endured for over fifty years and made them men of substance.

Chinese medicine had been a subject for scholarly study for 2,000 years; in many ways, its practitioneers were far ahead of their American counterparts. "To name one example," write historians Jeffrey Barlow and Christine Richardson, "the herbal physician had far better cures for blood poisoning and infection than did western science at that time." In time, Doctor Hay reaffirmed this in dramatic fashion, saving lives in the white community; but, at first his patients were limited to those of his own race.

Lung On was an exceptionally personable man, with a great deal of confidence and courage. Several white people who knew him said that he was the smartest man they knew. The authors of *China Doctor of John Day* write:

Lung On in Baker Oregon when he first came to John Day.
—Oregon Historical Society

Lung On's intellectual capabilities were bicultural. He was an accomplished person by both Chinese and American standards. He was raised as a young scholar and was familiar with the Chinese Confucian classics, a very esoteric and demanding body of documents. He could speak fluent English and communicate with Americans on their own terms rather than in the demeaning pidgin, which Americans found so comical.

Learning more than English in a remarkably short period of time, Lung On also liked the American traditions of horse racing, gambling, and chasing women. Though many Chinese liked to gamble, he was unique because he won more often than he lost and his stakes often were in real estate. He dealt in profitable business ventures, succeeded, and became a wealthy man.

Kam Wah Chung

A source of strength in the Chinese community was the way they helped one another by forming credit associations. Each member contributed a small sum, the aggregate being loaned by a committee of elders to some venture that promised to yield a profit. As needs to pay legal fees or bribes in assisting relatives enter the country or return home, the money was available.

One term of the Exclusion Act passed in 1882 was that only scholars, merchants, or persons related to those who were already residents of the United States would be allowed to enter the country. There is evidence that Lung On "sponsored" an extraordinary number of nephews and cousins that came to America as students or merchants. He had a special friendship with an immigration officer in Portland, with whom he corresponded, visited, and went to the races.

Almost all Chinese in America belonged to one of the "Six Companies"—fraternal organizations that looked after the welfare of their members. Both Ing Hay and Lung On were members of the Sze Yup Association, which predominated in the John Day area. Lung On led the society. Though Americans often confused these benevolent societies with "Tongs," which really were gangs committed to crime and violence, the Sze Yup Association wielded a great influence for maintaining order in the Chinese community.

The fortified building that headquartered the thriving Kam Wah Chung Company served as a post office, hiring hall, religious center, and residence for both Ing Hay and Lung On. Card playing, fortune-telling, gossiping, and opium smoking which was legal until 1906—flourished there.

Although gold mining in the John Day area boomed briefly during the 1890s and a contingent of Chinese laborers worked on a narrow gauge railroad built from Sumpter to Prairie City, the wave of immigrants Lung On and Ing Hay expected from China never arrived, even though

Kam Wah Chung building, 1909. —Oregon Historical Society

*Kam Wah Chung &
Co., John Day.*

they had added a partial second story to the Kam Wah Chung building
to help house them. By 1900, the thousand or so Chinese living in Grant
County had dwindled to one hundred. Of these, only eight were women.

With the passage of the federal Pure Food and Drug Act of 1906, which
outlawed opium, white residents of the community raised a brief hue and
cry against Chinese drug users. Though some whites used opium in its
pure form, many more unwittingly suffered its addiction through a
variety of opium-based patent medicines.

"Several Chinese, including Lung On—who, ironically, did not use the
drug—were hauled off to jail," write Barlow and Richardson. "The
excited mob initially ordered the entire Chinese community to get out of
town." But Lung On hired a local law firm that raised a blizzard of
objections and even tried to generate pressure from the Chinese Em-
bassy in Washington. The lawyers succeeded in getting the case dismissed.
To compensate for any hard feelings, "the Chinese offered the community a face-saving contribution to the local education fund and the matter
was forgotten."

Chinese Country Doctor

Ing Hay's medical reputation soon spread to the white community.
Herbal cures were different than the folk medicine commonly practiced
in the West at that time. Empirically "based on observations, experi-
ments, and clinical trials," as Barlow and Richardson note, Chinese

medical knowledge was rooted in the 2,000-year-old eighteen-volume *Nei Ching*.

In addition to his training as an herbal doctor, Ing Hay had perfected the rare craft of pulse diagnosis, or "pulsology," the central theory of Chinese medicine. "The doctor skilled in pulse diagnosis can, without ever speaking to the patient and simply by touching the radial artery of the wrist, arrive at a correct diagnosis in minutes."

Like a surgeon or safecracker today, Doc Hay took special care of his hands. He protected his sense of touch fervently, avoiding even coarse paper, which might rub the sensitive skin from his fingertips. According to Wing Wah, his nephew: "He would wear a glove on his hand, just like a movie star or a woman; he never handled anything rough."

Making up his prescriptions from herbs imported from China, Doc Hay sometimes used as many as eighty ingredients in them, cooking, mixing, and brewing each one to the patient's special needs in the tiny Kam Wah Chung kitchen. As his fame grew, his practice spread over an area bounded by the cities of Portland, Walla Walla, Boise, and Winnemucca.

"Rather than ride for several days to the doctor, which in many cases would have killed them, Doc Hay's patients could write to him and describe their illness, then have him diagnose their disease and mail them medicine."

At a time when infection following a serious accident killed as many people as the accidents themselves, Doc Hay became renowned for his success at curing blood poisoning. In one case, a ranch hand's ankle became badly infected from a barbwire wound. His leg too swollen and

Interior of the Kam Wah Chung building after the restoration in 1972. —Oregon Historical Society

painful to bend, he rode to John Day in a wagon with his leg hanging over the side. Doc Hay prescribed an herbal tea at three doses per day until the man recovered.

Doc Hay's big break into the white community came when he cured a prominent local rancher's son who got blood poisoning from a wound in his upper arm, write Barlow and Richardson. Another rancher's wife, so the story goes, had advised the desperate father to try the China doctor after the boy's condition worsened under the care of a Western doctor. Hay required implicit trust from the boy's father and stayed at the ranch six days, his charge was $1,000. But this success established Doc Hay's reputation as a specialist in treating blood poisoning.

As might be expected, some of the local white doctors became jealous of Doc Hay's success and tried to put him out of business. In 1905, they pressed charges that he was practicing medicine illegally, but they could not make the indictment stick; no jury in Grant County would convict him.

None of Hay's patients died during the terrible flu epidemics that ravaged the area in 1915 and 1919. Later he had remarkable success treating the often fatal disease, meningitis. "The white doctors got ahold of them and they'd die," one person said, "but this Chinaman would save them."

Golden Flower of Prosperity

In Chinese, *Kam Wah Chung* means "The Golden Flower of Prosperity." Now that Ing Hay had become a respected doctor in the white community, his and Lung On's fear of being forced to leave the United States and go back to China faded. Financially, both men prospered in a partnership that functioned in almost perfect harmony.

Before leaving China many years ago, both men had married and fathered children—Ing Hay a son, Lung On a daughter—but unlike most of their countrymen, these two maintained little contact with their families, sent little money home, and had no desire to return to the land of their birth.

So religious that he created a small shrine in his living room to make daily offerings to his traditional gods, as well as an altar in the kitchen to the Kitchen God, Ing Hay eventually was accepted into the society of Masons. Dedicated to his profession of healing, he lived very frugally despite his growing affluence. He never learned to speak English very well, would not ride a horse or drive a buggy, and, when the age of the automobile came, never attempted to drive a car.

In contrast, Lung On spoke and wrote English very well, loved to make and spend money, owned a race horse and liked to gamble, and was so intrigued with mechanical gadgets such as check-stampers, mice-catchers, or string-dispensers that he always bought the newest versions. He

Kam Wah Chung building, 1972.
—Oregon Historical Society

installed one of the first telephones in the area in the Kam Wah Chung and Co. Building. He also made substantial investments in real estate, and even opened a Pontiac dealership with a white friend, which was the first such enterprise east of the Cascades. Lung On quickly learned to drive cars, and chauffeured the Nervous Nelly Ing Hay on house calls.

Early in 1940, Lung On's usual good health gave in to illness. After a brief period of increasingly serious symptoms, he died in April at the age of sixty-eight, despite his friend and partner's best efforts to save him. Leaving an estate of nearly $90,000 to Ing Hay, he stipulated that half of it should go to his daughter in China upon the doctor's death.

By this time, Ing Hay was going blind, so he had to be led to the grave site on a hill overlooking the town of John Day and the Kam Wah Chung and Co. Building. He was hard hit by his friend's death. Write Barlow and Richardson:

> They had been together for fifty-three years. He was not only Ing Hay's skilled translator and chauffeur but his last link with the Old China, and with the frontier of the gold camps and the boom towns to which they had each been drawn as youths.

Alone now, Doc Hay feared life without Lung On. But two brothers who also practiced herbal medicine, one in Portland and one in Idaho,

359

came to his aid. The one from Idaho, Bob Wah, moved to John Day to look after and work with Hay.

> Bob Wah, his wife Rose, and their four children all loved the old man and took him into their family. For the first time since he had seen his father off for China in 1887, Ing Hay had a family relationship. He continued to live in the old Kam Wah Chung and Co. Building but took most of his meals with the Wah family.

With Bob Wah's assistance, Ing Hay got along fine until he fell and broke his hip in 1948. This was the first time in a life that spanned eighty-five years that he had been stricken with an ailment he could not treat himself. Taken to a hospital in Portland, where the broken hip was pinned, he was put in a nursing home, where he lived, bedridden, for four years. There, he died in 1952 at the age of eighty-nine.

His years of generosity to his patients left behind an estate of only a few thousand dollars. "In his old bed in the Kam Wah Chung and Co. Building, the heirs and friends who cleaned up after his death found more than twenty-three thousand dollars in uncashed checks from patients. Bob Wah had known that Hay had not been cashing the checks and had asked him why. He had answered: 'Good people. I don't need the money. I no cashee. They need it.'"

In 1955, Bob Wah deeded the Kam Wah Chung and Co. Building to the city of John Day, as Ing Hay had instructed, with the provision that the building be made into a museum, a monument to the contribution of the Chinese community of John Day to the development of eastern Oregon. For many years it sat idle. Then, in 1967, while surveying the land around it to develop a city park, the city of John Day found that it owned the Kam Wah Chung Building and its contents.

> Professional assistance from the National Trust for Historic Preservation, the Oregon State Parks Bureau, the Oregon Historical Society, and students and faculty from the University of Oregon and Lewis and Clark College all combined with community volunteers and financial donors to rebuild the building, clean and inventory its contents, and replace them as they had been in 1940, just before the death of Lung On.

There to be seen today is the entire history of the Chinese community of John Day—and the life stories of Lung On and the China Doctor.

Chinese Tunnels in Pendleton

Though the Chinese population in the Pacific Northwest between 1887 and 1914 has been estimated at over 150,000, it's only a wild guess. Undoubtedly Portland, John Day, Pendleton, and Baker had sizable Chinese communities, but the inhabitants did their best to make themselves invisible.

According to local legend recently enhanced through research, the Orientals living in Pendleton stayed hidden by an extensive network of underground tunnels. In his recently published book *The Pendleton Story*, local historian Rufus Crabtree writes:

> We know that the city started with a few tunnels beneath the sidewalks. The Chinese then connected those together to create quite a catacomb of pathways for travel to and fro, across and under the streets.... Those Chinese who had been lucky enough to own businesses in Pendleton, would house up to 20 families at a time in the little basements under their restaurants or laundries.

They dug the tunnels to protect their valuables and their lives. "It was an unwritten law that the Chinese could not occupy the streets of Pendleton after the sun went down," lest they become targets for bored cowboys.

When the nation outlawed liquor in 1919, the network of tunnels became supply routes from the airport on the hill to clandestine bars in downtown hotels. "Down the trap door and into the tunnel Kim and Soo would take the goods. They would load as much as they could carry into wheelbarrows or onto hand trucks, and off they would go, traveling the subterranean floor to a basement somewhere in downtown Pendleton."

According to a few of the old-time "elbow benders" Crabtree interviewed, the Chinese workmen were much more dependable than white laborers, who tended to sample the goods along the way.

When chuckholes recently mysteriously appeared in the streets, the system of tunnels was rediscovered. Some of them have been cleaned out so that an organization called Pendleton Underground Tours could conduct tours under the Old Town area, featuring such attractions as the Shamrock Tavern and the Cozy Rooms Bordello.

US 395
John Day—Pendleton
127 miles

US 26, OR 7
John Day—Baker
80 miles

Gold Country

Basing their searches for gold on the theory that the richest deposits lie in regions where the crust of the earth had been fractured most violently, early prospectors explored the roughest, most mountainous country they could find. In northeast Oregon, their quest brought them first to Canyon City in the John Day area, then east and north to Sumpter, Baker City, and then down into deepest gorge in North America, the 6,500-foot chasm of Snake River now called Hells Canyon. If you do not mind crooked though perfectly safe roads, this route awaits your visit nearer the end of this book.

Prospectors looking for the site of the Lost Blue Bucket vein discovered gold near Canyon City in 1862. Over the following thirty years, placer and hydraulic miners took gold worth more than $26 million from the area. At the same time, homesteaders filed land and timber claims in the 4,528 square miles that became Grant County. Long after the gold played out, ranching and logging held the economy intact.

Canyon City's population dwindled to less than 700 once the gold was gone, though it remained the county seat, while two miles to the north John Day's grew to over 2,000 souls. Today, the Grant County Historical Museum in Canyon City contains many relics from the early days, several extensive rock collections, Indian artifacts, and Chinese items. The historic Joaquin Miller cabin and the Greenhorn Jail are located next to the museum building.

Thirteen miles east of John Day, Prairie City marks the westward limit of the 1890s-era narrow-gauge railroad from Sumpter. The historic Sumpter Valley Railroad Depot, relocated in Prairie City's Depot Park, is home to the Dewitt Museum. This museum exhibits memorabilia from the gold rush and from early ranching and business ventures, as well as a collection of Chinese items. The Sumpter Valley Railroad hauled logs, gold ore, cattle, passengers, and supplies between Prairie City and Baker from 1891 to 1947.

Before moving on to Sumpter, where seven miles of the narrow-gauge railroad has been restored and is open for business, I want to pass on a

Narrow-gauge railroad, Sumpter.

few personal reminiscences of a pioneer in the John Day country, which will give an idea of what life was like in this rugged region before the turn of the century.

Wesley Slaughter Story

James Fremont Slaughter, who had enlisted in the Union Army in 1863 at the age of fifteen, survived the Civil War, got a good education from a college in Iowa, then came to Oregon in 1881. Living first in Pendleton, he homesteaded near Ritter Hot Springs on the Middle Fork of the John Day River at a time when no roads and very few trails crossed the mountains.

His son, Wesley Slaughter, who was born in 1885, later set down his recollections of a long, active life spent in the John Day country, which, in manuscript form, have been made available to us by the grandson, Wesley Slaughter, who, like his father, spent much of his life working for the U.S. Forest Service in the still-rugged area.

In those early days, survival came before all other needs. For example, when the senior Wes Slaughter told his son of girdling the big, fine, old yellow pine trees growing on the land, then later cutting them down and burning them to free the space for farming, the son asked his father why he would do such a thing.

"You could not eat pine trees," his father answered grimly. "You *could* eat potatoes."

In those days, boys became men at a very early age. Wes Slaughter senior wrote about a cattle drive he went on in 1899. Three boys—himself, at age fourteen, Jim Tozier, age eighteen, and the boss-boy Joe Wilmoth, age sixteen—drove 500 head to market in Pendleton. At daylight the first morning the three cowboys had their herd strung out on the trail heading north.

> We landed on the North Fork early in the afternoon and it was very warm. We wanted the cattle to go up Trail Canyon but they wanted to stay on the river. So we decided to let them bed down and then drive them up the Canyon in the evening when it would be cooler.

Meanwhile, with the afternoon only half gone and the sun blazing, the three young, thirsty cowboys decided to go to Billie Anderson's "tent saloon" a couple of miles up the river and slake their thirst with a few beers.

> The saloon was in a tent at the foot of the hill and a cellar dug into the bank to keep the liquor cool. The bar consisted of a few boards under the tent. Many a thirsty traveler came along the road and stopped for a beer or a drink of whiskey.... We rode to the tent saloon and met a sight to behold. I will not ever forget it. Wild Bill Hale was lying on the floor in a pool of blood with a bullet hole in his head. We could see that he was dead.

The proprietor, Billie Anderson, had gone to town to tell the sheriff what had happened. Two regular customers, Tom Tuttle and Tim Townsend, who appeared to have been involved in the fracas, now were tending bar. Obligingly, they informed the three young cowboys that "the man on the floor would not hurt anyone; they had fixed that."

While the account is somewhat vague (perhaps deliberately so), Tuttle, Townsend, and Hale apparently had fought over their horse-stealing proceeds, exchanging bullets and knife slashings before resolving the dispute. Upset that a killing had taken place in his saloon, Billie Anderson nervously paced the floorboards afterwards until Tim Townsend finally offered to let him use his horse to get the sheriff. Meanwhile, the dead man's cohorts tended the bar.

Whether the three cowboys got their beer, Wes does not say. But before sundown they rode back to the herd and, in the cool of the evening, drove their cattle up the steep slope called "Old Stairsteps," then bedded them down on Bridge Creek Flat for the night. Wes later wrote: "I took the first turn [on watch] and made it fine, but as I rode around the cattle I could ever so often see Wild Bill lying there in his own blood and his face where the bullet went through and took out part of his mustache."

At 10:30. p.m., Wes rode in and woke up Joe Wilmoth to take the next watch until 1 a.m.; then Jim Tozier took the shift lasting until dawn. Suddenly, Jim came riding into camp at a gallop, yelling: "The cattle have all gone on a stampede!"

Alerted by the rumble of hooves, Joe and Wes were already on their way. But it was too late.

By using the whole day we finally got them back, except for nine head short. I stayed with the sign and found the missing steers high up on Bridge Creek and got them back to the herd just before dark. We were compelled to camp with them in the same place another night. We never knew what startled them.

After that, the drive went better. Seven days later the three young cowboys reached Pendleton, where they weighed in their herd and turned it over to the Union Meat Company. At $1.50 a day, Wes's total wages came to $10.50, "the most money I had seen in my whole life."

When I got back home from the first beef drive that I ever was on, I had seen and learned about everything that a cowboy had to learn—or thought I had. I did not smoke cigarettes. But I sure could chew tobacco. I learned to be so expert at the art of spitting tobacco juice, I could sit straight up on my horse, spit over his head, and never get a drop on his ears.

Range Management—
Blue Mountain Style

Between 1863, when the Homestead Act went into effect, and 1905, when the federal government made its first attempt at regulating the use of public lands by establishing the U.S. Forest Service, there were virtually no laws designed to protect the rights of settlers who had filed legal claims. Contrary to the myth of the greedy land-holding rancher abusing the small sodbuster, the usual villains of that place and time often were owners of itinerant herds of sheep, who drove and pastured their flocks wherever the grass grew, regardless of who owned the land. In the John Day country, many of the local settlers undertook to defend their rights by what Wes Slaughter, who saw what happened but prudently did not comment on it in writing until many years later, calls a special kind of range management of their own.

The land on the high ridges was not considered by the public as of very much value. The settlers were along the creeks. A few lanes were fenced from the ridges down to the creeks so stock could come down and get water, but otherwise the only fences in the country were around a few of the settlers' fields.... Sheep kept coming from other counties and taking the range, the settler or homesteader being left without feed for his stock.

When settlers complained to roaming sheepherders, their pleas fell on deaf ears. Sheep owners followed the grass, wherever it grew. Fences made little difference; grazers of the public range generally regarded them as annoyances and did not respect the intended division between "yours" and "mine."

In the John Day country at that time, a number of the big sheepmen were Irish, Wes writes, men who had immigrated to America, worked for a few years as policemen in New York City, then decided there was a lot of money to be made "Out West" grazing sheep on free public lands. Other views regarding the sanctity of owning and using the land came from the many homesteading Civil War veterans who, by service to their country, had earned land alotted to them as military scrip. It was inevitable that the two groups should clash.

Among the range management rules Wes Slaughter learned while still young, he notes:

> Never put anything in print or writing. Never kill a man. Take all firearms before anything is done. Don't kill many stock; take just enough to show them we need "Range Management." Spend at least three days scouting, and do it with different riders. When you talk to a Sheriff or Judge the motto is: Know nothing, say nothing, and stick with it.

Even in his "Reminiscences" written many years later, Wes Slaughter abides by these rules, naming no names, reminding the reader time and again that he was only ten years old at the time the troubles began, and that every incident he records is simply something he "heard," without specifying when and where he heard it.

For example, he writes:

> There was a sheep camp under a rimrock near the Smith River Ranch above Susanville. Some "Lawless Marauders" threw a keg of black powder over the rimrock with a fuse burning at a band of sheep. The burning fuse scared the sheep so they scattered and ran, but nevertheless there was eight head killed. I don't remember who the sheep belonged to, but I talked to at least three men who said they were Heppner sheep. The herders moved the sheep out of the country as soon as it got daylight, they said, and they were there and saw the sheep moving out.

The most serious clash occurred on Brush Creek around 1895, he says, where a large flock of "Outside Sheep" had been held for several weeks on range commonly used by by cattle-raisers who had homesteads and fenced fields in the area. When the owner of the sheep had bluntly told them, "I will herd these sheep wherever there is grass," the settlers decided to take drastic action.

After carefully scouting the Brush Creek camp for several days, at least thirty men armed with Winchester rifles surrounded it. "At the camp below, near the creek, the sheep were bedded down," Wes writes. "Five men were in the camp; one man had started to make bread and had his hands in the flour sack; one man was washing his face. Their guns mostly were stacked against a tree."

Describing the action that followed "as I remembered it talked about," Wes writes that the leader of the cattlemen shouted:

"Don't pick up a gun or you are dead!"

One of the herders took a step toward the tree where the guns were stacked, then. when the order was repeated from another direction, changed his mind, stopped, and stood very still.

> Then one man walked into the camp and tied five men to trees. As I have heard it talked over, there was at least fifteen men on each side of the canyon with Winchesters pointed into the camp. There was a continual clicking of gun levers and hammers, to show there was a lot of business going on in those rimrocks.... After the business of tying up herders and guards, the sheep were taken out of the canyon onto the rocky flat south of Kilkenny Crossing, and I always heard that there was 600 of them shot.

Then the cattlemen burned the sheep camp.

"This was the most sheep that was ever shot that I know of," Wes writes. "I know only what I heard, of course, and I could tell more than I heard. But this will give you an idea of what I mean."

OR 7
Austin Jct—Sumpter
54 miles

Birth of Sumpter

North of US 26 along Oregon 7 (almost midway between John Day and Unity) is the heart of an area that yielded a great deal of treasure between 1862 and 1954. The five men who made the first discovery of gold here sympathized with the Confederacy, so in honor of the Civil War's first conflict at Charleston, South Carolina, in 1861, they named the new settlement Fort Sumter.

When the town grew large enough for a post office in 1883, the Postal Department insisted on dropping "Fort" and inserting a "p" in the name. A year later the transcontinental railroad reached Baker; and Sumpter began to boom as mining operations changed from placer to hard-rock and hydraulic methods. By 1896, when the narrow-gauge railroad arrived, Sumpter was "a rip-roaring place," say local historians, boasting five hotels in 1901, an opera house, a school, and a population of 3,000.

Near Sumpter in northeast Oregon, this dredge recovered $4.5 million in gold operating from 1935 to 1954.

Following the boom years of 1899-1903, gold production dwindled and the population declined over the next ten years. Then, in 1913, dredging operations in the valley breathed new life into the town. Prosperity reigned through the valley for four years, until a disastrous fire consumed virtually the entire business district and many homes in a twelve block area on Sunday, August 13, 1917.

Dredging residue, Sumpter.

Narrow-gauge railroad, Sumpter.

Though the town was never again the same, the Sumpter Valley Dredging Co. in 1935 built a monstrous dredge to clean the overburden of its valuable deposits. Except for the war years from 1942 to 1945, this dredge operated continuously until 1954, when the company shut it down and left it at the eastern edge of town, where it still sits. Local historians say this single dredge recovered more than $4.5 million in gold, and the entire valley yielded over $10 million.

A legacy of those years is the environmental destruction still visible from placer, hydraulic, and dredge mining. Along the once beautiful streams of the gold country lie ugly piles of rock rubble ruthlessly washed down from the hills or excavated from below, mile after desolate mile. Throughout the West, the still-valid Mining Act of 1872 gives miners a free hand to follow any vein of precious metal wherever it leads—under a town street, a city building, or a private home—with no responsibility for supporting above-ground structures or restoring the area to its original condition.

Even in this modern age of environmental awareness little has changed. In fact, a new gold rush into eastern Oregon is under way, using deadly cyanide poison to leach out "micron gold" from the soil in enormous open pit mines. *Oregonian* correspondent Dick Cockle wrote on September 17, 1989:

> The technique involves sprinkling a weak cyanide solution on enormous piles of ore to leach out disseminated specks of gold. Farm sprinklers are commonly used to wet down the ore, and the gold-laden cyanide is caught at the bottom of the pile by a plastic or clay liner, reclaimed, and used again.

Though mining proponents claim the process is safe and will not harm the environment, others worry that the wide-open spaces of southeastern Oregon may never again be the same. From Ontario, where the activity is centered, environmentalist Gary Brown says wildlife and birds have been known to drink from cyanide recovery ponds near mines in Nevada, where an estimated 80 million pounds of cyanide are used annually in the leaching process.

Glenn Miller, a professor of biochemistry at the University of Nevada, Reno, said in a recent three-year period 6,000 birds died of cyanide poisoning. Historians of the future will tell us if modern mining methods reap another toll on our environment.

Railroad Revived

For now we can only speculate about the ills of cyanide-solution mining; but the results of past processes are clear. To see them, take a ride on the seven miles of track that has been rebuilt on the Sumpter Valley Railroad. For a small fee, travelers can ride in old-time passenger cars pulled by wood-burning locomotives to the end of track through the very heart of the dredge-destroyed terrain.

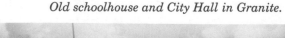

Old schoolhouse and City Hall in Granite.

Old cemetery, Granite.

Fondly called the "Stump Dodger" by the Baker County railroad buffs who restored it, the Sumpter Valley Railway Co. received its charter as a common carrier on August 15, 1890. At first it mostly carried logs to sawmills from the vast forests south and west of Baker City, and did not reach Sumpter until October 1896. Then the "Polygamy Central," as it was called, started carrying passengers and gold ore as well. By 1910 service extended to Prairie City, hauling cattle, seed, and farming supplies to the John Day valley.

Increased automobile traffic and the Great Depression hurt business. By 1935 some stretches of tracks were pulled up, and passenger service ended two years later. Then in 1947 the little railroad that had played such a significant role in the development of this region ceased operation. All the tracks had been removed by 1952, except for a short section in the Oregon Lumber Co. yard. For almost twenty years, what little rolling stock was left silently rusted away.

But a small group of railroad lovers in Baker County refused to let the "Stump Dodger" die. In December 1970 they formed a non-profit organization dedicated to acquiring, restoring, preserving, maintaining, and operating a portion of the abandoned Sumpter Valley Railroad as an historical and educational museum.

They acquired rolling stock from such diverse sources as the Boise-Cascade Corp. in Idaho, the Denver and Rio Grande narrow gauge operation in Durango, Colorado, and the White Pass and Yukon Railroad in Skagway, Alaska. Then the volunteers relaid seven miles of track and persuaded Baker County to build Dredge Station and a day park nearby. Retired railroaders run the little train through a wildlife habitat area, where passengers can see beaver, muskrat, geese, herons, and other game species reclaiming the old dredging ponds. Unable to turn around, at the end of the track the train backs up for seven miles to its starting point.

When funds become available, the Sumpter Valley Railroad Restoration, Inc. plans to extend the rails into Sumpter, two miles away.

Ghost Towns

Scattered through the rugged, high, timbered country in all directions from Sumpter are old mining towns: Austin, Granite, Bourne, Greenhorn, Galena, and others that have long since disappeared from maps. Here and there a few weathered buildings remain, with nearby cemeteries filled with long-forgotten prospectors and pioneers. In this high country the snow comes early and stays late, but in good weather the paved roads are easy enough to drive, if one is not in a hurry.

One scenic loop topping 7,000 feet adds about seventy or so miles to the I-84 distance between North Powder and Baker. (If coming from North Powder, reverse this route.) From Baker, go south then west on Oregon 7 to Sumpter, then northwest to Granite, then north and east across the top of the Blues to Anthony Lakes, a locally popular ski area, and on to the town of North Powder and I-84.

Anthony Lake south of La Grande.

OR 86
Baker—Oxbow Dam
70 miles

Road to Hells Canyon

Why any pioneer should wish to homestead in the remote depths of Hells Canyon during the 1880s puzzles many visitors today. The determining factor—according to Earl Hibbs, whose father, Martin, did such a thing—was finding a place where a person would not be bothered by too many neighbors. Earl said his father believed: "You just can't raise cattle where you can hear a train whistle or a church bell."

Martin's brother-in-law, Ralph Barton, is credited with naming the infernal gorge. As Martin told the story to his son: Ralph and some other fellows were riding after cattle one day when a dog they had with them jumped a brown bear and took out after him. But the bear disappeared before anybody could get a shot at him, so those fellows asked Ralph where the dog and the bear went. Ralph said, "They went down that hell of a canyon."

By any name, mining operations deep in Hells Canyon in the 1890s faced formidable obstacles. Little evidence of them remains today, but interested explorers can drive to the occasional ruin by staying on Oregon 86, which descends the broad valley of the Powder River from Baker, then drops down Pine Creek to Oxbow Dam.

To reach that portion of the Snake that slithers naturally through Hells Canyon, cross the river into Idaho on the bridge just below Oxbow Dam, then go north twenty-two miles alongside the turgid green backwaters of the pool backed up by Hells Canyon Dam. By crossing this dam back into Oregon and continuing another mile, you'll arrive at the launching site for white-water rafting and kayak trips down the Snake. From this spot to a few miles above Lewiston the Snake flows free for ninety of its 1,036 miles.

Rightly called the "deepest canyon on earth," the Snake in this sector is 5,500 feet below the rimrocks immediately above it on either side, 6,500 feet below the ridges a mile or two back from the canyon walls, and more than a vertical mile and a half if measured from the peaks of the Seven Devils Mountains in Idaho and the crest of the Wallowa Mountains in Oregon.

Hells Canyon at China Gardens Dam site. —Army Corps of Engineers

When the River Ran Free

Though buried now by the backwaters of three Idaho Power Company dams—Brownlee, Oxbow, and Hells Canyon—there was a time when the Snake River between Farewell Bend and Lewiston was the wildest river in the West. Because boats ran on its lower reaches, the federal government classified it as a "navigable river," but in Hells Canyon only the superhuman efforts of a very few men made it so.

In all its long history, only one man ever succeeded in bringing a craft upstream through the countless rapids that tumbled down the canyon. Only two men ever succeeded in taking boats built above Farewell Bend downstream through the hazards of the river.

In the first case, it was the red-haired giant, Donald MacKenzie, who bossed a crew of six French-Canadian *voyageurs* as they paddled, poled, pushed, and pulled a barge from the mouth of the Clearwater to Farewell Bend. This was in the spring of 1819, when he was working for the North West Company. After he had accomplished the feat, he wrote with qualified elation:

> *Point Successful, Head of the Narrows, April 15th, 1819.* The passage by water is now proved to be safe and practicable for loaded boats, without one single carrying place or portage; therefore, the doubtful question is set at rest forever. Yet from the force of the current and the frequency of the rapids it may still be advisable, and perhaps preferable, to continue the land transport.... We had often recourse

to the line. There are two places with bold cut rocks on either side of the river, where the great body of water is compressed within a narrow compass, which may render those parts doubtful during the floods, owing to rocks and whirlpools, but there are only two, and neither of them are long.

Requiring two months of dangerous and concerted effort, the trip was not repeated. In fact, forty-five years passed before a boat of any size ventured into the treacherous rapids of Hells Canyon again.

In 1864, the stern-wheeler *Colonel Wright*, with Captain Thomas J. Stump in command and eighteen-year-old William Polk Gray, already a veteran riverman, as assistant pilot, undertook to explore the limits of navigation on the middle reaches of Snake River. William Gray later wrote a vivid account of the venture:

> We went up the river to about twenty-five miles above Salmon River. In attempting to make a dangerous eddy at this point, the boat was caught in a bad eddy, thrown into the current and upon a sharp rock reef jutting out from the Idaho shore. It carried away eight feet of her bow, keel, and sides to her deck. Things looked desperate for a moment. Captain Stump gave an order from the pilot house to get out a line on shore. You never saw such a universal willingness to get on shore with that line. Every deckhand, the mate, the chief engineer, the fireman and our two passengers, who were standing forward watching the boat, seized the line by both ends, the middle and wherever they could get a hold of it and jumped ashore.
>
> The only people left on the boat were Captain Stump and myself in the pilot house, the second engineer, who was below, and old Titus, the cook. Before they could make the line fast, the boat was caught by the current and went down the river half a mile. Here Captain Stump succeeded in beaching her. We here were joined by the ambitious line-carriers, who walked down the shore.

South of Hells Canyon in the Farewell Bend area, two boats assembled and launched there tried to operate in that stretch of river. The boilers, engines and metal parts of the first steamer, the *Shoshone*, had to be transported up the Columbia to Umatilla Landing, then freighted across the Blues over nearly impassable roads. Indian snipers occasionally made workmen scramble for shelter. But on April 20, 1866, the *Shoshone* was launched with enthusiastic ceremony.

For a time, the boat plied the 100-mile stretch between Olds Ferry and the mouth of the Bruneau River. But trees for fuel were in short supply and the available low-grade coal was so poor that it would not run the boat. When travel to the mines dwindled, the *Shoshone* ceased operation. Eventually the directors of the Oregon Steam Navigation Company (OSN) decided to risk bringing the steamer downriver through Hells Canyon.

"A more perilous and uncertain adventure has never been undertaken in these waters," wrote an editor of the period, "and we shall watch its progress with interest. The canyon between Powder River and the mouth of the Salmon is said to be seventy miles long and ... a continuous succession of rapids the whole way.... River men have always considered it an impossibility to navigate the canyon even with a small boat."

Captain Cy Smith and his crew floated the inland-built steamer to Hells Canyon by late June 1869, then tied her up near a stream still known as Steamboat Creek to await higher water the following spring. Then another OSN crew under Captain Sebastian Miller, supplied with plenty of fuel and heavy rope, maneuvered her through the hazardous rocks and rapids of the canyon and delivered her badly battered hulk to Lewiston in late April 1870.

Eventually, the *Shoshone* shot the tamer rapids of the lower Snake, descended the Columbia's Celilo Falls, and ran the upper and lower cascades under the skill of a handful of daring pilots when the river was in flood. Later, the steamboat returned to service on the upper Willamette above the falls at Oregon City until she wrecked near Salem in 1874. Next spring, when high water cast her hulk ashore, a farmer detached her pilot house and converted it into a chicken coop—the final ignominy for a well-traveled lady that never was really at home in any river.

A second boat, the *Norma*, was built on the banks of the Snake near Huntington. Oregon, in 1891. Soon after her launching, she made a successful run to Seven Devils Landing and back. But when the Union Pacific refused to remove an inconsiderately built bridge a few miles upriver, which limited the boat's operations and profits, the owners decided to bring her downriver.

The captain chosen for the job was William Polk Gray, who by 1895 had become the dean of river boat pilots. Since Gray's letters are as colorful as his long career, his first-person account of the *Norma*'s trip down the Snake ought be read in its entirety for full appreciation. (See "She Will Strike About There . . . Steamboating in Hell's Canyon" by Merle Wells, *Idaho Yesterday*, summer 1957.) A few of its high points:

Like many river pilots who knew how quickly and often channels could change in a river, Captain Gray did not have a very high opinion of the U.S. Army Corps of Engineers, whose duty it was to study and chart the nation's navigable rivers. He also had good reason to believe that they were very careless with where they left their tools. On May 17 1895, he writes:

"At Bay Horse Rapids three miles down, while drifting in a channel improved by government engineers (a copy of their report was in the pilot house) we touched on what afterward proved to be a piece of two-inch steel which had been broken off and left when the engineers were working there some years before. The drill ripped several holes through

the bottom and the boat swung around and damaged the sternwheel badly."

After pulling into a landing and patching the boat, Captain Gray cautiously moved on down the river, steering the boat while his brother, the mate, studied the government chart. While passing through what the chart showed to be a clear channel, the *Norma* struck an unmarked underwater reef with such force that it ripped a hole in the starboard side forty feet long and four feet wide. That was enough for Captain Gray.

"I grabbed the chart and flung it out of the window, and we touched no reefs or rocks thereafter."

The most dangerous part of the canyon was Copper Creek Falls, where the river dropped vertically some eighteen feet, while immediately downstream a sharp turn and a sheer bluff made it inevitable that any boat going over the falls would collide violently with unyielding rock. But Captain Gray was prepared to deal with that, for he had loaded forty cords of wood below decks and had the carpenter build in six strong bulkheads the length of the keel. Before going over the falls, he conferred with the chief engineer, saying:

"Charlie, this boat is worthless up here. What do you think about going back."

"We came up to get her," the engineer replied. "I say go on or put her where they can't find her."

377

Stern-wheeler Norma *at Lewiston, Idaho.* —Oregon Historical Society

When Captain Gray conferred with the carpenter, who had been construction foreman for the OSN for years and had asked to go on this trip for the "excitement," the man listened to him dubiously as Gray put his foot on the deck about ten feet behind the bow, and said:

"She will strike about here. I want you to run a bulkhead six feet back of that to the midship keelson, then have the mate back it up with cordwood in case the water should rush in hard enough to tear away your bulkhead."

"You ain't intending to go over that place, are you?" the carpenter asked as he stared apprehensively at the falls. "You will drown us all."

"Tom, you never had much notoriety, did you?"

"No, why?"

"They have all our names that are on this boat, and if you should be drowned your name would be in every paper in the United States and Europe."

"Oh, go to hell!"

"Put in the bulkhead, Tom, and we'll chance the other place."

Going below decks, the carpenter went to work, though for a brief time when the sound of hammering stopped, Captain Gray heard him muttering aloud.

"Damned old fool—going to be drowned because a damned fool wants notoriety."

But the bulkhead went in good, Gray says.

Captain Gray knew that going over the falls would require precise timing, as well as an accurate estimate of what the tremedous force of the water would do to his boat. He wrote:

> When we dropped over the falls we seemed to be facing certain destruction on the cliff below, but I knew my engineer was "all there" and would answer promptly. We backed slowly and within ten feet of the rocks to starboard her bow passed the mouth of Copper Creek, where an eddy emptying gave her a slight swing out and I backed strong with the helm hard to starboard—the bow must take its chances now, the stern must not.
>
> Almost before one could speak the bow touched the point of the cliff just hard enough to break those guard timbers without touching the hull, and we bounded into the still water below. The carpenter, who had stationed himself on the hurricane deck just outside the pilot house with two life preservers around him, stepped out in front of the pilot house and shouted: "Hurrah, Cap! You start her for hell and I'll go with you!"

Law Lady of Copperfield

Though no vestige of it remains today, one of the wildest boom towns in the West briefly existed in the depths of Hells Canyon just below Oxbow Dam on the Oregon side of Snake River. Named Copperfield because some of that metal had been mined in the area, the town from its very beginning was dedicated to hell-raising.

Soon after four land speculators from Baker set up a town site in 1908, they turned a quick profit by selling lots to entrepreneurs who planned to live off the large labor crews working on the power plant and a railroad tunnel. According to the WPA guide: "The boom town soon had every conceivable type of business, both legal and illegal, with the latter in the ascendancy."

The inhabitants boastfully aped the wickedness of the mining towns of the 1860s, says the guide. The railroad gangs often clashed in "free-for-alls." One conflict said to last more than an hour was accompanied by the tinny tunes from the mechanical piano in Barney Goldberg's saloon. Rocks, beer bottles, and fists flew, but when exhaustion led to truce the enemies drank from the same bottle, bound up each other's wounds, and set a date for the next encounter.

"The leading citizens of Copperfield, including the mayor and members of the council, either ran saloons or were financially interested in them. A few peaceful citizens finally tired of the disorder and appealed to the governor for help. He ordered the Baker County authorities to clean up Copperfield by Christmas; but they refused to act."

So the governor declared martial law; but not in the conventional sense. He would not call out the National Guard or anything like that.

Instead, Governor Oswald West sent his secretary, Miss Fern Hobbs, to Copperfield with the authority to put the order into effect.

"Judging from her past work," he told the press, "I have not the slightest doubt she will succeed. If these men who are sworn to enforce the law and have the great arm of the law back of them cannot close the saloons, we shall see what a woman can do."

This response by the Oregon governor was similar to what happened down in Texas during the heydey of the Texas Rangers when the citizens of a wild and woolly town appealed to state's governor for help in preventing a riot. When the "help" appeared, it consisted of a single Texas Ranger, who, when questioned as to why he had come alone, drawled laconically:

"You all got more than one riot?"

Governor Oswald West, you may recall from Part Two of this book, was the man whose far-sighted vision convinced the people and the legislature that the entire Oregon Coast should be preserved for public use. He was a shrewd politician and a keen judge of human nature. Aware of the fact that both Prohibition and Women's Suffrage were just around the corner, he decided to defuse a potentially violent confrontation by using the two popular issues to good effect.

His secretary, Miss Fern Hobbs, though a young lady of grit and determination, did not look at all like a Texas Ranger. Weighing only 104 pounds, standing just five foot three inches tall with her boots on, she had been admitted to the Oregon State Bar as an attorney a year earlier at the age of twenty-four. But pitting her against the lawless, muscular rowdies of Copperfield was such a ridiculous mismatch that it was laughable.

And the town did laugh. Notified that she was aboard a train due to arrive January 2, 1914, Copperfield literally roared with laughter as it prepared to greet her.

Says the WPA guide:

> Flags and bunting hung in the streets, and all bars were embellished with pink and white ribbons and such flowers as were available. The entire town was lined up to greet the train. Accompanied by her army of war correspondents, photographers, and almost the entire populace, the secretary marched at once to the town hall, mounted a platform, gave the governor's orders for the resignation of all officials connected with the saloon business; said that if they refused she would hand over the governor's declaration of martial law, disarm everyone in town, close all saloons, burn all gambling equipment, and ship all liquors and bar fixtures out of town.

When the rowdies of Copperfield learned that a colonel of the National Guard, who also happened to be warden of the state penitentiary, two penitentiary guards and five National Guardsmen had accompanied her incognito on the train and were with her now, they stopped laughing. Still, the town's officials refused to comply with her orders.

> The secretary immediately commenced to carry out her threats. The audience was silent throughout the proceedings, and there was little protest when the expeditionary force collected all six-shooters present and piled them on the platform. Just 80 minutes after her arrival the secretary boarded the train for her return journey. The men remained to mop up. A few months after the departure of the guardsmen, fire, of suspected incendiary origin, left the town in ruins, and it was never rebuilt.

Many years later during a bitter dispute over who should build the dam in the Oxbow area, long-retired Governor Oswald West expressed his feelings regarding his former secretary when he wrote a letter to the *Oregonian* on July 11, 1953:

> The only mistake I made while governor, was when I sent my secretary, Miss Fern Hobbs, to settle the Whiskey dispute at Copperfield, on the Snake—where the Idaho Power Company was then undertaking construction of the Oxbow project—that I did not give her further instructions to settle the Hells Canyon-Idaho Power matter while on the ground. Thus she could have saved the U.S. Government, the several states and the politicians much worry and expense. All my fault!
>
> —Oswald West

Chinese Massacre in Hells Canyon

In the gold country of northeast Oregon one hundred years ago, the Chinese took the white men's leavings. The Chinese often reworked and occasionally purchased "unprofitable" claims white men had abandoned. It was just such a group of men working a sandbar on the Oregon side of the Snake in Hells Canyon who became victims of the most notorious massacre of Chinese in the history of the Pacific Northwest.

A few years ago Marilyn Sparks, Penrose Library research specialist at Whitman College in Walla Walla, made an inquiry to the State Department about the Chinese massacre. An archivist there asked her "which tribe of Indians was involved."

Even today, it seems, the word "massacre" evokes Indians as the likely culprits.

But the savages who committed this "massacre" belonged to the most brutal race in the West—the whites. Though many fanciful stories have been written about it, my extensive research leads me to believe this is what actually happened.

Contrary to the assumption held by many Americans at the time, these were not nameless, impoverished coolies smuggled into the country and forced to work as slaves for the enrichment of their Chinese masters. Each man had a name, and each name was meticulously recorded by the individual's sponsoring company along with his credits and debits. As discussed earlier, the very word "coolie" is a corruption of *ku-li*, which means "muscle strength" in the Cantonese dialect. Then, as now, muscle strength was the greatest resource China possessed.

The ten Chinese miners were clansmen from the district of Punyu near Canton. Their names were Chea-Po, Chea-Sun, Chea-Yow, Chea-Shun, Chea-Cheong, Chea-Ling, Chea-Chow, Chea-Lin-Chung, Kong-Mun-Kow, and Kong-Ngan. All were members of the Sam Yup Company. In their homeland village they undoubtedly had parents, wives, and children whose only hope for a better material existence was the gold these sojourners abroad would send or bring home after years of privation and hard work.

With a boat load of provisions, the party arrived at Douglas Bar, in the heart of Hells Canyon, at the beginning of the ninth month of the Chinese twelfth year of *Kwong Su*—by our calendar, this was October 1886. The Snake River ran low at that season, exposing a maximum expanse of the gold-bearing sand and gravel; until next summer's high water reclaimed their bar, the industrious placer miners could anticipate profitable diggings.

Deep Creek, China Gulch on the Snake River. —Army Corps of Engineers

Scenically and historically, the Chinese worked in a dramatic place. For twenty-five years, placer and hardrock miners had been stripping the upriver valleys, hills, and mountainsides of fine and coarse gold worth hundreds of millions of dollars. But each summer's flood carried their gold-laden tailings down the Snake, forming new deposits where the current slackened or eddies formed.

Douglas Bar, known by the local Indians as "Nez Perce Crossing," one of the few safe places to cross the Snake during flood stage, created an eddy where the Chinamen dug for gold. From the beautiful meadows, lakes, forests, and streams of the Wallowa Valley, homeland of Chief Joseph's band, a relatively easy trail followed Little Sheep and Big Sheep creeks down to the Imnaha, then on to the Snake. On the east side of the river, the trail wound through a series of narrow, rocky canyons, eventually leading to Lapwai, headquarters of the much-reduced Nez Perce Indian Reservation to which the Army insisted Chief Joseph's band move in 1877—only to precipitate a senseless war.

Joseph and his people crossed the flood-swollen Snake in June, miraculously losing no human lives and only a few animals. But after the Indians had swum 6,000 head of cattle and horses across the cold, treacherous river, the Army had not given them time enough to round up all their livestock. So, for years afterwards, white men caught and claimed these stray cattle and horses. With little law enforcement in this remote, lightly settled part of Oregon and Idaho Territory, a breed of men euphemistically called "cowboys" began to infest the area, making a profitable business of rounding up Nez Perce animals left behind in Oregon and selling them in Idaho—with no questions asked or answered.

In late spring 1887, several such "cowboys" swam the river at Nez Perce Crossing, saw the ten Chinamen working the bar, and decided that there was an easier way to acquire gold than by stealing livestock. So they brutally murdered the Chinamen, tossed their bodies into the river, and stole all their gold dust. Several months passed before the killings became known, but eventually the Chinese consul, Chang Yen Hoon, investigated and wrote to the American secretary of state, T.F. Bayard:

> A person named Jackson told a Chinese named Hung Ah Yee that he had witnessed some cowboys, eight in number, forcibly driving Kong Shu and his party out of the bar in their boat and throwing their provisions overboard. Kong Shu and his party fled, being afraid to offer any resistance; since then, he learned of the murder of Chea-Po and nine others, and came to the conclusion that the cowboys had committed the crime.

Certainly there was evidence that a crime of major proportions had been committed, for during the next few weeks bodies were found in the shoals on both sides of the river, some as far away as Log Cabin Bar, 150 miles downriver, and Penawawa, ten miles farther. Because it is so cold, the Snake River is slow giving up its dead. This scattering of bodies on shores under the jurisdiction of the state of Oregon, Idaho Territory, and Washington Territory caused an almost insoluble snarl of red tape.

Hearing about the murders, the Sam Yup Company sent its own investigator, Lee Loi, to Lewiston. After gathering what facts he could from Chinamen in the area, he enlisted the aid of U.S. Commissioner J.K. Vincent, who also held the title Justice of Peace for Nez Perce County, Idaho Territory. In a curious relationship, Vincent was employed by the Sam Yup Company as a "private eye" to find out what had happened, identify the guilty men, and bring them to justice. He apparently did a good job, as evidenced by his correspondence to the Chinese consul in San Francisco:

> I am still in the employ of the Chinese company, ferreting out the crime. From what I have so far found, things seem to show that white men were the murderers, as some of the provisions taken from the Chinese miners I have traced directly to them. I have been following up for six days a white man who was at their camp. He has told me some very curious stories.... But there is in that vicinity some twenty or thirty bad men and I was watched very closely for nine days. I plan to start again up Snake River and will get into their camp by some means and know what is done.

Acting on evidence supplied by Vincent, a Wallowa County grand jury met, deliberated, and indicted six men on charges of murder. On April 28, 1888, the Walla Walla *Union* reported:

> A party of men, consisting of Bruce Evans, J.T. Canfield, Homer LaRue, Robert McMillan, Carl Hughes, H. Maynard and Frank Vaughn, entered into an agreement to murder these Chinese miners for the gold dust which they thought they possessed, and agreed that if any of the party should divulge it, the rest should kill him.... As near as we can learn, all the men except Hughes went down to the Chinese camp and opened fire upon them, killing them all. They then secured all the money and gold dust they could find, amounting to between $4,000 and $5,000.

Evans, Canfield, and LaRue were never found, though the indictment against them remained on the circuit court docket for several terms. Frank Vaughn apparently got off the hook by cooperating fully. The other three, McMillan, Hughes, and Maynard, stood trial in Enterprise, Oregon, on August 30, 31, and September 1, 1888. The jury acquitted them.

Grand jury proceedings cannot be revealed, even after all these years, so that record, if it exists, is still sealed. The trial record is not privileged, but it's missing. Often such old records cannot be found, which exasperates historians who prefer to review the testimony and draw their own conclusion. A record that is available raises more questions than it answers; it is the deathbed confession from sixteen-year-old Robert McMillan, one of those acquitted, as told to his father.

The September 30, 1891, Walla Walla *Statesman* carried this story:

> On the 3rd of August last Hugh McMillan, who lives in Walla Walla and works at his trade of blacksmithing, appeared before the Hon. W.M. Clark, notary public of the legal firm of Brents & Clark, and made the following statement:
>
> "I make this statement from the statement made me by my son, Robert, aged sixteen, just prior to his death, and by me then reduced to writing. In the latter part of April, 1887, my son and Bruce Evans, J.T. Canfield, Mat LaRue, Frank Vaughn, Hiram Maynard and Carl Hughes were stopping in a cattle camp four miles from Snake River. My son and Evans, Canfield, LaRue and Vaughn went to the Chinese camp on Snake River. Canfield and LaRue went above the camp and Evans and Vaughn remained below. There were thirteen Chinese in the camp and they were fired on. Twelve Chinese were instantly killed and one other caught afterwards, and his brains beaten out. The party got that evening five thousand five hundred dollars in gold dust. Next day eight more Chinese came to the camp in a boat. They were all killed and their bodies with the others thrown into the river. The party then took a boat and went to another Chinese camp four miles distant where thirteen Chinese were working on a river bar. These were all killed and their bodies thrown into the river. The camp was robbed and fifty thousand dollars in gold secured. My son was present only the first day, but was acquainted with the facts as they were talked over by the participants in his presence. The circumstances here detailed occurred on the Oregon side of the Snake River in Wallowa County near the northeast corner of the state."
>
> Dated Walla Walla, Aug. 3, 1891. W.M. Clark, Witness.

Commenting on the confession, the editor of the *Statesman* said: "We take no stock in the statement that fifty-five thousand dollars was realized by the murderers for the reason that such rich diggings never did exist in that vicinity. Still, the Chinamen must have had considerable gold dust, as they had been working for six months."

The deathbed confession of young Robert McMillan, which for some reason his father wished published, raises many unanswerable questions. If Robert McMillan were sixteen at the time of his death in 1891, he would have been only twelve years old at the time he took part in the murders. Why was a mere boy riding with such a violent gang? What happened to the $55,000 in gold stolen from the Chinese? His account lists thirty-four dead Chinamen; so why would the Sam Yup Company list only ten?

No one knows.

But we do know that buried gold later was found at the site of the massacre. A Lewiston newspaper reported in 1902:

> A few weeks ago the tragedy was revived at Joseph, Oregon, when two young men appeared there with gold dust to the amount of $700. They had been prospecting in the vicinity of the old Chinese camp and encountered the cache where the murderers had hidden the wealth, and had failed to take away the flask worth $700.

The massacre of Chinese along the Snake River is one of many brutal acts whites carried out against Orientals during the 1880s. In California alone, the Chinese consul wrote the State Department, an estimated 100,000 of his countrymen were deprived of their property and driven from their homes. In a token gesture, the American Government agreed on October 19, 1888, "to pay, out of humane consideration, and without reference to the question of liability therefore, the sum of $276,619.75 to the Chinese Government as full indemnity for all losses and injuries sustained by Chinese subjects within the United States at the hands of residents thereof."

In view of the fact that since 1850 China had been America's best Asian friend—and would remain a friend for many years—the "humane consideration" seems minuscle indeed.

Eureka—
The Hells Canyon Bubble That Burst

Nothing remains of the fabled mine, smelter, and town called Eureka—a Greek word meaning "I've found it!"—except a long tunnel through the base of a mountain spur between the mouth of the Imnaha River and a back eddy of the Snake. But during its boom years, hundreds of men worked there, thousands of investors bought stock, and close to $3 million went into Eureka's hole in the ground, from which very little precious metal ever came.

In relating how his father, Martin Hibbs, made the original discovery, Earl Hibbs says:

> Him and a man he kind of partnered with were looking all the time for mine outcroppings. They were down at the mouth of the Imnaha and they run across these two ledges full of copper ore. They broke off some samples, put them on their pack horses, and went back up the Imnaha and met Bas Hibbs, who was a cousin of my dad's and a mining engineer. After looking at the samples, he told 'em: "You boys have got it made."... They staked out some claims. In less than a month, they sold them to what later became the Eureka Mining Company for $15,000. So far as I know, that was the only money ever made on those claims.

Gopher Hole Mine in Hells Canyon, 1900.
—Wallowa County Museum

Developing a mine in this area offered many problems. No wagon roads came within twenty-five miles of the site, and the pack trails were steep and dangerous. At river level, no trees grew—a serious handicap in the days when it was axiomatic that "it takes a forest to support a mine." They needed lumber for buildings and for shoring tunnels and firewood to stoke the steam boilers in the stamp mills and the smelter.

For forty years, Lewiston, Idaho, fifty-five miles down the Snake River, had been the supply center for north-central Idaho mines. Waterways normally seemed the natural and logical avenues for transportation, but the Snake ran downhill in such a hurry that no regular boat traffic had ever been established on its turbulent, surging course. In this stretch of river, no less than thirty-two rapids were distinctive enough to have names—and several of them were killers.

But the lure of precious metal in Hells Canyon prompted the founders of the Eureka Mining and Smelting Co. to build a boat suitable for transporting men, animals, and supplies between Lewiston and the site on a regular schedule. It would be named the *Imnaha*. While its keel was laid and its hull began to take shape in Lewiston, work went on at a feverish pace upriver.

"At their Imnaha camp, a force of 30 men are now driving extensive tunnels into the bowels of the mountains," wrote a reporter for the Lewiston *Tribune* on February 27, 1903. Forty others worked on a wagon road leading to the timber supply, where a sawmill would operate. "W.E. Adams, the engineer, is now engaged in surveying a townsite at the mouth of Deer Creek, about a mile and a half from the smelter. Eureka has been selected as the name of the new town, which ought to become a place of considerable importance in the near future."

Far from being a homemade boat, the *Imnaha*'s boilers came from Portland, her engines from Wisconsin, and some other machine parts from Pennsylvania. Several special features enabled her to cope with the wildest river in the Pacific Northwest. Sturdily built and heavily cross-braced in the bow, she stretched 125 feet with a 26-foot beam. Able to carry 100 passengers and a large cargo of freight, she drew only twelve inches of water when fully loaded. It was estimated that on trips upriver she could handle 50 tons of freight; coming downriver, 125 tons. To breast the heavy currents of the Snake, her steam boiler operated at pressures up to 250 pounds per square inch.

If the power of her engines proved unequal to the task of driving the boat through the rapids, she carried 1,500 feet of steel cable wound around a power capstan in her bow with which she could pull herself through the white water.

After making a trial run downriver to Riparia, Captain Harry C. Baughman pronounced the *Imnaha* ready to tackle the job for which she had been built. Carrying only its crew, a few passengers, and a reporter for the Lewiston *Tribune*, the new stern-wheeler left its dock Tuesday afternoon, June 30, 1903, cheered on by several hundred spectators.

For the first twenty miles, the rapids were mild, giving the boat little trouble. Reaching what was known as the Earl Place a mile below Buffalo Rock, the *Imnaha* tied up for the night.

Next day, she resumed her journey, passing through rapids every mile or so as the riverside bluffs rose higher and higher above either shore. Pulling in to the mouth of the Grande Ronde, the boat paused long enough to take on a supply of fuel and water, then made ready for the three-mile run to the foot of Wild Goose Rapids, long regarded as a major obstacle to navigation upriver. The *Tribune* reporter gives a graphic description of its nature:

> The rocks in fact unnaturally force an immense volume of water against the natural flow of the river and a wall of seething, swirling water results. At the right of this channel the bluff extends almost perpendicular to the water line and a boat is forced to the left and into the face of the steep, rough climb. The *Imnaha* crept along the right bank of the island slowly and then plunged into the rapid.
>
> The steam gauge showed 210 pounds and the boat steadily crowded forward, while water dashed in roils to the rim of the lower deck. In two minutes the crest of the rapid had been reached. Cheers were heard above the rush of the waters and the din of the heavy engines. Then the steam gauge began to fall, and slowly, inch by inch, the boat was carried back. Bad coal had defeated the noble craft, and when she drifted into the lee of the island the gauge registered but 160 pounds.
>
> The bells in an instant rang ahead, the boat was pointed to the left channel, and in just three minutes Wild Goose had been conquered

The Imnaha *approaching the Eureka mine site landing in the summer of 1903. The stern-wheeler wrecked near here a few months later.*
—Idaho Historical Society

and the boat nestled calmly under a bluff in the peaceful waters above.

When questioned about the loss of power, Captain Baughman told the reporter: "The coal is inferior and the boiler fouled. With a few more pounds of steam, we could run the main channel. In fact with good fuel, the *Imnaha* could climb a tree."

Poor or scarce fuel long had been the curse of steamboat operations on Snake River, both below and above Hells Canyon. Pitch-filled wood burned better than low-grade coal, but no pine forests grew at river level. Cord wood cut at higher elevations, as it would have to be at Eureka, and then hauled by wagon eight or more miles down to the river over narrow, twisting roads, was both expensive and scarce.

Leaving her moorings above Wild Goose, the *Imnaha* spent more than three hours fighting her way twelve miles upstream to the mouth of the Salmon River. Two strong rapids—Cougar and Coon Hollow—were negotiated with no more than 182 pounds of steam pressure. Above the Salmon the craft entered waters traveled but once by an upriver-bound steamboat.

At Mountain Sheep Rapid, two miles below the Eureka mine, the *Imnaha* encountered her first serious trouble. The river bends sharply at the foot of the long rapids. The *Tribune* reporter explained the problem:

> On the right hand bank for a distance of several hundred feet, huge boulders have rolled into the channel, forming innumerable cross-currents and swirls. Then the roils from the upper rapids are met, which leads to "The Narrows." The latter, as the name suggests, comprises a chute of water that pours down with a steep fall between

a long ledge of rocks and an immense rock that has fallen from the mountains above into the stream.

Directly back of the rock lies an eddy which forms a back current of perhaps five miles an hour. The water presented an innocent appearance to the passengers. But Captain Baughman saw trouble ahead. A driving rainstorm with a strong wind was prevailing when the boat shot into the race of the narrows. The *Imnaha* made a game fight for a minute and poked her nose beyond the point of the rock to the left. But a swirl from the current veered her to the right and she was crowded back. Captain Baughman rang to go ahead, but like a flash the sternwheel was caught in the back current and the boat shot to the opposite shore, turning completely around. She then faced downstream and a landing was made beneath the right bank.

It was decided to put out a line and the cable was strung for a distance of a quarter of a mile along the right hand shore. The boat again shot out into the stream and tackled the strong current, but she had approached to a point within only ten feet of the rock when the heavy current of the eddy again caught her.

Straight toward the bluffs on the right bank she darted, and as the bow turned with the current the cable "deadman" gave way. Captain Baughman signaled for a back wheel, but the bow grazed the bluff. The bow then swung back across the stream and the hull slid on a sloping rock, where the craft was temporarily lodged. She was soon, however, backed off the rock and the run to the opposite bank was made, where the craft was tied up for the night.

The captain sent to the Eureka mine, two miles upriver, for explosives and a crew to blast away the obstructing rock. Mining engineer W.C. Adams arrived at ten o'clock Wednesday night; he examined the rock the next morning and estimated the task might take several days to accomplish. After a full day of drilling, setting charges, and blasting out the ledge on the right (west) side of the channel, he decided that the big rock on the left side must be destroyed, too.

Captain Baughman went to the head of Mountain Sheep Rapid to have a look Friday morning. It was July 3. He returned to the boat and announced that he intended to take it through "The Narrows" immediately. "The *Imnaha* will run it," he said, "and we will not wait on the rock."

A line was again run out and a cable was coiled on a rock at the right of the channel. Attached to the cable was a line and a deckhand was stationed there.

At exactly 10 o'clock the *Imnaha* left the bank and tackled the current for the fourth time. She "walked" up to the crest between the two rocks where she was held for fully three minutes. The man on the rock made an unsuccessful throw with the light line; there followed two unsuccessful casts by deckhands on the boat, and then Mate Bluhn shot out a line that reached the goal.

In a minute the cable was pulled aboard, the line tightened, and the wiry craft crept inch by inch over the top of the torrent to smooth waters. From the time the *Imnaha* left the rapid till the period the cable was slacked and taken aboard a period of only fifteen minutes had elapsed. The run to Eureka was then made in forty-five minutes and the boat tied up at exactly 11 o'clock. She had made the run to Mountain Sheep Rapid in ten hours. A wild demonstration occurred at Eureka when the boat was seen in the canyon below. On the highest peaks, the miners could be seen waving their hats with enthusiasm, and loud blasts resounded through the valley.

The *Imnaha* returned downriver to Lewiston in three and a half hours. The minor damage caused by the rocks was repaired, and a schedule of regular runs was established.

But first, the U.S. Army Corps of Engineers, whose responsibilities included eliminating navigation hazards, employed the *Imnaha* for two months as they blasted boulders from the channels and installed iron rings into the rock walls above both Wild Goose and Mountain Sheep rapids. At each place, a 1,500-foot steel cable secured upriver by the heavy iron ring stretched through the white water to a water-tight barrel floating free in the quiet pool below, enabling the *Imnaha* to winch herself through the current.

Resuming her regular upriver run in early October, the *Imnaha* suffered her first serious accident when the current threw her against a rock that punched a hole in her hull. Repaired downriver at Riparia, a week later she returned to Eureka and brought several horses and forty tons of granite downriver from a newly opened quarry. Below the mouth of the Salmon, the Snake River's flow was so low that additional trips were postponed until autumn rains raised the water level.

By November 8, 1903, the rains had come, the Snake began to rise, and the *Imnaha* embarked on her fourteenth and final trip to Eureka.

Wreck of the Imnaha

Leaving the Lewiston dock Sunday morning, the first part of the stern-wheeler's trip went smoothly. Only a few minutes before pulling into the landing at Eureka, disaster struck without warning. Captain Baughman tells what happened:

> We had successfully ascended the rapid and cast off the line when in some manner the wheel picked up a bight of the line, which caught in the eccentric rods. As a result, the rods were bent, the rock shaft broken, and the engines rendered useless. At the time this occurred, the boat was about four hundred yards above Mountain Sheep Rapids, and the helpless steamer drifted stern on onto the sharp rock that has been a menace to navigation since the boat was first placed in commission.

Hells Canyon, where the stern-wheeler Imnaha *sank, looking upstream from the mouth of the Salmon.* —U.S. Army Corps of Engineers

The wheel struck the rock squarely and was doubled back over the boat. The bow then swung to the Oregon shore where it remained but a moment when the stern slipped from the rock and swung to the Oregon side while the bow turned against the big rock, completely filling the channel.

The Snake River at this point is only 62 feet wide, so the 125-foot boat now turned broadside felt the tremendous force of the current. Fortunately, it hung there long enough for the fifteen crew members and twenty-five passengers to scramble ashore. Quick thinking by Chief Engineer L.H. Campbell prevented what could have been a murderous explosion.

> Knowing that great danger existed from the escaping steam in case the boat was badly injured by striking the rock, my first move was to start the pumps and open the siphons. By the time the boat commenced to go to pieces the steam was so reduced that no danger of an explosion existed. As the boat struck the rock, I swung out of the engine room at the side door, but as the jar was not sufficient to break the pipes the dangerous period had passed and I returned to the engine room to find that the entire stern had been stove in and that the abandonment of the boat was sure to follow.

Only seconds after the last of the crew and passengers got safely ashore, the bow of the disabled boat dipped. The *Imnaha* slipped off the rock upon which she had lodged and drifted into deep water downstream. In the eddy there, she spun around several times. Taking water rapidly now, the hull tilted, the boiler tore loose from its supports and rolled into the water carrying a large portion of the pilot house with it.

The *Imnaha* was finished.

Though no human lives were lost, several horses tied to stanchions on the freight deck were forgotten by the crewmen scurrying ashore. Their whinnies of fright as the boat sank were pathetic to hear, said the survivors, but nothing could be done to save them.

As with all such disasters, rumors, guesses, and attempts to place blame lasted for months, with no conclusive results. Had an inexperienced deckhand thrown the barrel attached to the slack cable into the river on the wrong side of the boat? Had the helmsman turned the boat the wrong way, making the stern-wheel hook into rather than avoid the looped winching line? Had an order been carelessly given, not heard, or recklessly disobeyed? No one could say.

Built at a cost of $35,000, the *Imnaha* had not been insured by its owners, so had to be written off as a total loss.

End of the Eureka Mining Company

Dependable river transportation was vital to the businessmen of Lewiston as well as to the mining operations in Hells Canyon. They quickly raised $22,000 to begin building a new boat. Launched by late September 1904, the *Mountain Gem* was skippered by the veteran pilot, Captain William Polk Gray.

But the Hells Canyon mining bubble had burst. Angry investors filed lawsuits against the corporation directors because their money went into the ground much faster than any profits came out. The digging stopped.

The Mountain Gem *at Lewiston, Idaho, shortly after being launched in 1904.* —Idaho Historical Society

With no ore to bring downriver, the *Mountain Gem* ceased runs to Eureka and began hauling freight and passengers on the Snake River below Lewiston. Eventually, smaller boats were built to carry mail, groceries, farm and ranch supplies, and sightseers to remote cabins and camps above Lewiston.

Prospectors continued to pan for gold on the sandbars of the Snake, occasionally exposing a vein that merited drilling, blasting, and excavating in "gopher hole" mines. But the bonanza promised at Eureka never was realized. The tunnel between the mouth of the Imnaha and the Snake is still there, though access to it is limited since the creation of the Hells Canyon National Recreation Area in 1975 because of the danger of falling rocks.

From time to time, mineral experts have reassessed various mines in the area, reporting far less potential treasures than did the stock peddlers working for the Eureka Mining and Smelting Company. In 1942, a group searching for copper and tungsten to help the war effort concluded that the width of the veins in the area should have been measured "in inches rather than feet." Assays by the U.S. Bureau of Mines in 1968 failed to find more than a trace of copper.

Like so many boom-and-bust mines, Eureka's real value may well have been more in its paper stock certificates than in its copper and gold. Firm money figures are even more difficult to come up with today than they were in 1904, but one court suit instituted by stockholders then stated that the Fargo, which was contiguous to the Eureka, had been capitalized with three million shares of stock valued at one dollar a share. Since one million of these were treasury shares, it must be assumed that the other two million were sold to the general public, whose descendants—the American taxpayers—now own the site.

Challenge of Hells Canyon

From the time of its first discovery to the present day, the Snake River in Hells Canyon has offered an irresistible challenge to explorers and adventurers. For example, the ubiquitous Captain Bonneville tried to force a passage through the canyon the hard way during the winter of 1833-34. After supposedly settling into a winter camp on the Portneuf River toward the eastern edge of the Snake River desert, Bonneville grew restless. What he should do, he decided, was go down the Snake and Columbia and look into the possibility of establishing a post in direct competition with the British.

No sooner decided than done. On Christmas Day, 1833, with three companions, he rode away from the Portneuf camp, blithely telling the detachment left behind that he would return in early March.

"They were obliged to travel slowly to spare the horses," Washington Irving wrote in his extremely popular book, *Adventures of Captain Bonneville*, published in 1837, "for the snow had increased in depth to eighteen inches; and though somewhat packed and frozen, was not sufficiently so to yield firm footing."

Thus began one of the most incredible journeys ever taken across the Snake River country. Because Irving never saw the region, he misplaced streams and landmarks, but through his specific dates we can trace Bonneville's route with reasonable accuracy. Moving along the south and west bank of the Snake, he reached the vicinity of Farewell Bend January 12, 1834. There, instead of crossing the Blues by the route taken by the overland Astor party and many Hudson's Bay Company brigades, Bonneville hired an Indian guide, who gave him a bad piece of advice: "Stick to the river; there will be less snow."

This was true. But the guide neglected to add that the river route led into Hells Canyon—impassable in any season. After a few days, the guide deserted, and Captain Bonneville found himself and his three companions in serious trouble.

> The river forced its way into the heart of the mountains, winding between tremendous walls of basaltic rock.... The snow was from two to three feet deep, but soft and yielding, so that the horses had no foothold.... Sometimes the crags and promotories forced them onto the narrow ribbon of ice that bordered the shore ... to scramble over vast masses of rock that had tumbled from the impending precipices,... to cross streams on bridges of ice and snow,.... to pass along narrow cornices.... Two of their horses fell into the river, one saved, the other lost.

In desperation, the four men considered killing and skinning their horses, making bullboats out of the hides, and committing themselves to the uncertainties of the river. If they had done so, Bonneville's death would have cast a dreary note on his heroics and Washington Irving would not have written his book. Instead, the freezing, exhausted, starving men deserted the water's edge and climbed out of the canyon, probably in the vicinity of Oxbow Dam. It is likely that they ascended North Pine Creek, crossed a 6,000-foot high spur of the Wallowa Mountains to the headwaters of the Imnaha, descended that river to its lower valley, then climbed over the towering ridge dividing the watersheds of the Imnaha and Grande Ronde rivers, and at last descended into gentler country near the present-day border between Oregon and Washington.

They were fifty-three days from camp on the Portneuf; twenty from Farewell Bend.

Today, a few experienced outdoorsman with mountain-climbing skills have attempted to duplicate the feat over the same route in the dead of

*Looking down into
Hells Canyon from
the Oregon side.*
—Dave Jensen

winter—without success. In the summer time, some have made the
climb out of the canyon, but even this is serious, disagreeable work.

When Captain Bonneville reached the mouth of the Grande Ronde, he
found himself in the winter home of Chief Tu-eka-kas' band of Nez
Perces. As always, these Indians treated the whites hospitably, providing food, shelter, guides, and an escort west to Fort Walla Walla.

Four years later the missionary Henry Harmon Spalding, found Tu-
eka-kas receptive to Christianity, baptized him, and named him Joseph.
Making a summer home for himself and his band in the beautiful
Wallowa Valley in the high country to the southwest, Joseph led his
people along the path of peace all his life, then counseled his son, called
Young Joseph until his father's death, to do the same. Through no fault
of his own, Young Joseph failed in an epic tragedy detailed in the final
section of this book.

War of the Dams

In settling the West, more men were killed in disputes over water than in quarrels about gold, women, livestock, and land combined. During modern times, uses and control of water still inspire more vocal violence, legal controversy, editorial polemics, and political rhetoric than any other subject.

Until the last quarter-century or so, two basic assumptions about the waters of the Snake and Columbia rivers were treated as sacred: the first, that dams meant progress; the second, that irrigation rights exceeded all others. That a case might be made for migrating fish, recreational uses, or even the wilderness notion that a few rivers should be left in their natural state was not taken seriously by policy-makers.

Following the building of Bonneville and Grand Coulee dams in the 1930s, the concept of "multi-purpose" became popular. Since a dam could produce cheap electricity, prevent floods, aid navigation, preserve irrigation water, and provide recreation for water skiers, the question was not whether a dam should be built; it was simply a matter of *where* it should be built and which agency should build it.

The Army Corps of Engineers, the Bureau of Reclamation, small and large public utility districts, and private power companies all laid claims on dam sites and applied to the Federal Power Commission for licenses to build dams on the Columbia and its tributaries. By 1970, the watershed as a whole contained 161 large and small dams divided about equally between public and private entities. By then, the only place left to build major dams was in the one hundred miles of free-flowing Snake River between the foot of Hells Canyon Dam and Lewiston, Idaho.

Public and private power companies fought over these few sites. Inevitably, their prolonged and expensive disputes went through the legal process until they reached the United States Supreme Court. The two questions before the Court seemed simple enough:

(1) Should the federal power commission license an association of private power companies called Pacific Northwest Power to build High Mountain Sheep Dam in the heart of Hells Canyon, forever flooding the white water sector?

(2) Did the association of public utilities, backed by the Corps of Engineers and the Bureau of Reclamation, have a preference claim on the site?

But even as the High Court pondered this, a third party entered the contest—the environmentalist. Environmentalists appeared in many forms: the Indian protesting the loss of his traditional fishing grounds; the bird watcher concerned over the loss of nesting areas for migratory waterfowl; the sports fisherman worried about the future of steelhead and salmon runs; the Sierra Club member in love with wilderness; the white-water boatman bent on preserving a few challenging rapids; the naturalist, the antiquarian, the maiden lady in tennis shoes, and other assorted "little" people who, for obscure reasons, insisted on throwing their fragile bodies down before the juggernaut of progress.

The question, they quietly insisted, was not *who* should build the next dam but whether *any* dam should be built. For a long while, private power advocates, public power boosters, the federal power commission, and the courts, which were being called upon to referee the frequent quarrels, paid them little heed.

But the mouse had roared.

On June 5, 1967, in a 6-2 decision, with Justice William O. Douglas writing the majority opinion, the Supreme Court issued a surprising decree: "The test is whether the project will be in the public interest. And that determination can be made only after an examination of all issues relevant...." One highly relevant issue, the opinion stated, was "the public interest in preserving reaches of rivers and wilderness areas, the preservation of anadromous fish for commercial and recreational uses, and the protection of wildlife."

As so often happens when the highest court in the land makes a ruling, it was not clear who had gained or lost yardage. But to all the players involved in the contest, one thing was evident: the game had changed.

Hells Canyon National Recreation Area

With the playing field now changed from the court system back to area itself, hearings were held in Baker, Lewiston, Portland, and other towns nearby, with enough testimony being taken from interested parties to fill the High Mountain Sheep Dam site with paper, if not with concrete. I testified for preservation at a Senate hearing held in Lewiston in December 1973, while covering the story for the *Walla Walla Union Bulletin* and the *Seattle Times*. Comments from other witnesses varied.

"My dream is to float the Snake in a rubber raft," one middle-aged woman said. "I want a minimum flow guaranteed below Hells Canyon Dam so I won't bump my bottom on a rock."

"Environmentalists are a selfish lot," a southern Idaho farmer dependent on water for irrigation declared. "We refuse to give up any of our water for them."

Senator Frank Church said: "We all know we need electrical energy. But you know you're going to have to turn to thermal sources sooner or later. Why don't you turn now—and leave Hells Canyon alone?"

Testifying for the National Federation of Wildlife, Ernest Day pointed out that the use of electricity had doubled every ten years. Projecting those figures against the generating capacity of dams in the Hells

Canyon area, he said: "These dams would satisfy the growth in electrical demand for half a year. But we would lose Hells Canyon forever."

In southern and eastern Idaho, upriver from Hells Canyon, there are at least three million acres of arable desert land being brought into production at the rate of 50,000 acres a year. Since the Snake is the region's major water source, farming interests flatly refused to permit any minimum-flow guarantee written into legislation, in case they might need this water in the future.

"You have two choices," Idaho Senator James McClure told fish and boating advocates. "A bill with no minimum-flow guarantee—or no bill at all. Which will it be?"

But they wanted the bill, even without a minimum-flow guarantee. Actually, there is a de facto minimum-flow, Senator Church pointed out; the terms of its license require the Idaho Power Company to release 5,000 cubic feet per second at all times from its dam at the upper end of Hells Canyon.

"I don't think the Snake is going to dry up," Senator Church said. "There always will be water flowing through Hells Canyon."

After minor amendments, the Hells Canyon National Recreation Area Act was passed by Congress and signed into law by President Ford December 31, 1975. It authorized $10 million for the acquisition of land and $10 million more for the development of recreational facilities. Administered by the U.S. Forest Service, the project soon got under way, and continues today.

Like all compromises affecting unique ecological treasures, the final act does not please everybody, but it is a reasonable solution given the circumstances. Some people felt designation as a national park, wilderness area, or wild and scenic river might be too restrictive, or might attract too many special-interest groups.

Currently, 67.5 miles of the Snake between Hells Canyon Dam and four miles south of the Oregon-Washington border has been federally designated as wild and scenic. Banned are such non-traditional watercraft as jet skis, wind surfboards, and water skis. Jet boats may come upriver to Granite Creek, a few miles downstream from Hells Canyon Dam, beyond which such rapids as Wild Sheep make navigation too dangerous.

When water conditions permit, the Forest Service allows float trips in rubber rafts or kayaks from just below Hells Canyon Dam to Lewiston, but because of limited camping facilities on the sandbars through the canyon, permits are required between late May and mid-September. The Forest Service distributes these equally among qualified, well-equipped amateur river-runners and professional tour guides. Headquarters for the Hells Canyon National Recreation Area is at the U.S. Forest Service in Enterprise, Oregon.

While those who knew Hells Canyon and the Snake River when it ran wild and free regret the changes forced upon the area by a growing population wanting to enjoy it, we should all be grateful that at least some of its timeless beauty has been preserved for future generations.

OR 86, Forest Road 39
Oxbow Dam—Enterprise
101 miles

Following Bonneville and Joseph

If you are interested in retracing the trail taken by both Captain Bonneville and Chief Joseph, a very crooked paved road climbs out of Hells Canyon, crosses a 6,000-foot shoulder of the Wallowa Mountains, then descends 1,500 feet to the high valley where you'll find the towns of Joseph and Enterprise. Though this scenically beautiful area has been called the "Switzerland of Northeast Oregon," its wonders need no European comparisons—its 10,000-foot peaks, alpine lakes, crystal clear streams, and pure air are unique enough to stand on their own.

From Oxbow Dam follow Oregon 86 southwest eleven miles, then turn north on Forest Road 39 toward Indian Crossing, Imnaha, and Joseph. Not recommended for motor homes or cars pulling big trailers, the road is perfectly safe for automobiles, so long as the driver does not mind

Arrival of the Nez Perces, Walla Walla council, 1855. —Washington State Historical Society

*Tu-eka-kas, Old Joseph,
the father of Chief
Joseph.* —Gustaf Sohon sketch,
Washington State Historical Society

Joseph *Taawo-tak-hes.*
Cchief of the Nez perré Indians

crooked, narrow roads. After ascending the winding valley of North Pine Creek, the road climbs up and over a high spur of the Wallowa Mountains, then descends to the upper Imnaha River. Here, the road forks, with the right-hand branch going down the Imnaha to the small town of that name, while the left hand branch winds up and over another mountain spur to Joseph. From the town of Imnaha, intrepid travelers with four-wheel-drive vehicles can go up to Hat Point for a spectacular view of Hells Canyon, or on down the river to Dug Bar, but these roads can get ticklish in bad weather; even in good weather, it is wise to ask locally about the current conditions.

On the road to Joseph and Enterprise, the view of the broad, fertile valley and the Wallowa Mountains which hem it in is stunning from a ridge six miles east of town. From time immemorial this was the home of the Wallowa band of Nez Perces, a tribe friendly to white men in general and Americans in particular since their first meeting with the *Suyapos*—"crowned ones"—in late September 1805. During the many conflicts between Indians and whites in the Pacific Northwest, the Nez Perces steadfastly maintained the friendship they had pledged to William Clark, even though time and again white men betrayed their trust.

In the first part of this book, I told how two elderly, respected Nez Perce chiefs, Twisted Hair and Tetoharsky, accompanied Lewis and Clark down the Snake and Columbia as far as Celilo Falls, guaranteeing by their presence as representatives of the most powerful Indian tribe in the Pacific Northwest that the white men would not be harmed. Later, in 1831, a delegation of Nez Perces journeyed to St. Louis, where their friend William Clark was then in charge of Indian Affairs for the Far West. They told him they wanted to learn the white man's religion.

Tu-eka-kas, Old Joseph, converted to Christianity in December 1838, when Reverend Henry Spalding took him into the Presbyterian Church. When his son was born in 1840, the religious Indian asked Spalding if he could pass on his Christian name to his son. Yes, he could, Spalding said, if he would promise to raise the child according to the tenets of the church. This he would do, Old Joseph answered.

"All his life he will follow the ways of God and the path of peace."

In an attempt to settle mounting Indian-white problems once and for all in the Pacific Northwest, Washington Territory Governor Isaac Ingalls Stevens and General Joel Palmer, superintendent of Indian affairs for Oregon, held a council in June 1855. Of the five inland tribes in attendance at the Walla Walla Council, the Nez Perces were the largest, numbering 3,500. Traditionally, the Nez Perces had roamed over some 27,000 square miles of mountains, plains, and river valleys in what became southeastern Washington, northeastern Oregon, north-central Idaho, and a portion of western Montana.

Assured by the U.S. Government that they still could hunt and fish in their "usual and accustomed places," the Nez Perces agreed to accept a reservation of 10,000 square miles. One portion of it was in the Wallowa country, the traditional home for about two hundred Nez Perces led by Old Joseph.

By then raising both horses and cattle, the Wallowa Nez Perces normally spent the late fall, winter, and early spring in the sheltered valleys near the mouths of the Imnaha and Grande Ronde. In late spring they moved their lodges and livestock up to the lush, green, well-watered plateau below Wallowa Lake and along nearby rivers and creeks, where they remained through summer and early fall.

Since the Wallowa country was well removed from the Oregon Trail and had no known gold, the prospect that this small, peaceful, religious band of Nez Perces would ever be bothered by Americans coveting their land seemed remote. But east of Snake River, in the heart of the main section of the Nez Perce Reservation, gold was discovered in 1860. Despite the treaty stipulation that white men would not be permitted to trespass on the reservation, gold-hungry prospectors swarmed in by the thousands. Though the Indians protested, they did not resort to violence; they knew that in a war with the whites they could not win.

Chiefs at Dinner, Walla Walla Council, 1855. —Gustaf Sohon sketch, Washington State Historical Society

The government followed its usual course when its citizens violated Indian treaty rights: the authorities convened a new treaty council to redraw reservation boundaries, further restricting the Indians. This council was held at Lapwai, east of the Snake, in May 1863.

Many Nez Perces attended, including Old Joseph and his handsome twenty-three-year-old son, Young Joseph, who eventually assumed the mantle of leadership over the Wallowa band. Years later, Joseph remembered his father's words: "When you go into council with the white man, always remember your country. Do not give it away. The white man will cheat you out of your home. I have taken no pay from the United States. I have never sold our land."

This was true. Many of the Indian leaders who signed treaties in 1855 had received goods, houses, schools, and clothing for their people, as well as annual cash payments of $500 over the next twenty years. But Tu-eka-kas, even though he had touched the writing stick after the "X, His Mark" beside his name on the paper, had not accepted so much as a blanket or a dollar. To him, signing the treaty was only a token of goodwill and a confirmation that he accepted the white man's promise that the traditional home of the Wallowa band would be theirs forever.

But to white authorities, "forever" meant only as long as nothing else came up—in this case eight years. That the Nez Perce Reservation as set

Chief Joseph in 1901.
—Major Lee Moorhouse, Smithsonian

up in 1855 stretched across three political entities—Washington Territory, Idaho Territory, and Oregon State—made its regulation by the federal government an administrative nightmare. Some bureaucrat back in Washington, D.C., reasoned that the reservation should be tightened and contained within just one entity to make things simpler. Why did the Indians need all that land, anyway? So the new treaty council was called.

After several days of talks, the majority of the Nez Perces agreed to the new boundaries, which reduced the size of their reservation from 10,000 to 1,250 square miles. Some, whose traditional haunts did not fall within the reduced reservation, refused to sign the new treaty. In fact, they opposed it so vigorously that they suggested dissolution of the Nez Perce Nation to a grand council of tribal leaders—a majority of whom planned on signing the treaty—seeking permission to go their own way, which, by long-standing tradition, any dissenting band could do.

Faced with five chiefs who refused to sign the treaty—Old Joseph among them—the white commissioners appointed new chiefs who *would* sign. Operating on the "majority rule" principle, the commissioners pretended to take a vote of the Indians present, which resulted in one-

404

third of the tribe signing away seven-eights of the original 1855 reservation. From that time on, the dissenting Indians called this the "steal" or "thief" treaty.

Young Chief Joseph aptly summed up the treaty's essence like this:

> Suppose a white man should come to me and say, "Joseph, I like your horses and I want to buy them." I say to him, "No, my horses suit me, and I will not sell them." Then he goes to my neighbor and says to him, "Joseph has some good horses. I want to buy them, but he refuses to sell." My neighbor answers, "Pay me the money, and I will sell you Joseph's horses." The white man returns to me, and says, "Joseph, I have bought your horses and you must let me have them." If we sold our lands to the Government, this is the way they were bought.

Prelude to War

Feeling in his heart that his small band of peace-loving Indians was in no way bound by the new treaty, Old Joseph and his son returned to the Wallowa country, where Old Joseph is said to have torn up his Bible and a copy of the 1855 treaty. As markers delineating the western boundary of his territory, he set poles ten inches thick and ten feet long in rock cairns along the summit of Minam Grade, telling a white man through an interpreter that they showed "where his line was to the Wallowa country."

Known as "Old Joseph's Deadline" to early settlers in the area, the markers were maintained by the Nez Perces and seen, if not respected, by the whites for a number of years. As his eyesight and strength failed, Old Joseph came to depend more and more on his son to take responsibility as the leader of his people. Young Joseph later told a writer that his father sent for him just before he died in 1871, took his hand, and admonished him:

> When I am gone, think of your country. You are the chief of these people. They look to you to guide them. Always remember that your father never sold his country. You must stop your ears whenever you are asked to sign a treaty selling your home. A few years more, and white men will be all around you. They have their eyes on this land. My son, never forget my dying words. This country holds your father's body. Never sell the bones of your father and mother.

In an effort to eliminate graft and corruption and improve the spiritual life of the Indians throughout the West, a number of reservations were turned over to various religious orders to run. In 1871, the Nez Perce Reservation was allotted to the Presbyterians under John Monteith, whose father, William Monteith, ministered a church in the Willamette Valley.

Young Joseph, though a quietly religious man in his own way, expressed doubts about organized religion in 1873 when asked if he would welcome Christian ministers in the Wallowa country. He said:

> They will teach us to quarrel about God, as the Catholics and Protestants do on the Nez Perce reservation. We do not want to learn that. We may quarrel with men sometimes about things on this earth, but we never quarrel about God.

At agency headquarters in Lapwai, John Monteith resented the fact that Chief Joseph and his small band of Wallowa Nez Perces accepted neither his spiritual nor civil authority over them. Rich with horses and cattle, excellent hunters in a country teeming with game, skilled fishermen in the rivers and lakes full of salmon and trout, and such shrewd bargainers that even the white newcomers admitted, "A Nez Perce can beat a Yankee peddler in a trade," the Wallowas were proudly independent and completely self-sufficient.

To teach or Christianize a young Indian boy, the white missionaries knew they first had to catch him and set him afoot, for the chances of getting that boy to attend school regularly when his family owned many fine horses ranged from slim to none. On the Lapwai Reservation, even owning a spirited horse that might be used for racing or riding across the mountains to hunt in the buffalo country was frowned upon by the agent, whose every effort was bent toward turning wild Indians into tame Indians content on eking out an existence on a small subsistence farm.

Another thing that Agent Monteith deplored was the fact that the Wallowa Nez Perces refused to stay in one place. Living along the lower Grande Ronde and Imnaha in winter and in summer moving to the

Troops set up a Gatling gun battery during the Nez Perce War, but they never used it. —Oregon Historical Society

higher Wallowa Valley, they persisted in visiting their relatives and friends on the reserve. Keeping those relatives and friends from returning their visits (i.e., keeping them on the reservation) was as impossible as damming a stream with a sieve.

As Old Joseph had predicted before his death, white settlers began coming into the Wallowa Valley as soon as word got out that it no longer was part of the Nez Perce Reservation. But the number of white settlers was relatively small and most of them got along well with the Nez Perces in this vast region with plenty of room for all. According to Grace Bartlett, a native of the region and among the best of local historians, when the first white settlers drove a herd of cattle into the country in 1871: "There was some question of how the Indians would receive them, but not much fear, due to the attitude and actions of those with whom they had mingled up until then." In fact, when Old Joseph died in October 1871, several white settlers attended the burial services on terms of perfect goodwill with the Indians.

Shortly thereafter, the Nez Perces headed for their traditional winter village along the lower Grande Ronde, escaping the bitter cold and heavy snows of the high valley to the relative warmth and abundant grass in the lower region. To the white ranchers, such a seasonal move was the height of irresponsibility. When whites settled on a piece of land, they moved there to stay. They built well-chinked cabins and solid outbuildings to keep people and livestock snug and warm. To supplement their cattle and horses during the winter, they cut wild hay and broke the sod to plant and harvest grain.

Even so, the white settlers respected Indian rights to the extent that most of them did not file homestead claims near Wallowa Lake or in the higher, more broken country of the valley's eastern half, preferring instead the open areas better suited to ranching and farming in the western half. Chief Joseph and a friendly white settler named A.C. Smith agreed to let a commission take a census of the valley and recommend an equitable division of lands between Indians and whites. The three commissioners found only sixty-seven white claims in the eastern half of the valley, so suggested those white settlers sell their holdings to the Indians for $67,800; this would allow the Nez Perces exclusive rights to the upper, eastern half of the valley, while the whites could occupy the lower—or western—half, and both parties would be happy.

President Grant signed an executive order making the division legal. But in a classic example of bureaucratic stupidity, some nameless clerk in Washington, D.C., looked at a map and decided that "upper" meant north and "lower" meant south, so drew the dividing line from east to west. Both Indians and whites ended up with only half of the land they agreed to. A bit of common sense and patience might have rectified the error, but then, as now, correcting a bureaucratic snafu proved nearly as impossible as stopping an avalanche with a broom. Pressured by white rabble-rousers and greedy Oregon politicians during the election year of 1874, President Grant rescinded his executive order and the dispute moved back to square one.

Still, Chief Joseph and his many white friends in the Wallowa Valley continued to live together in peace.

Even in June 1876, when a white settler named A.B. Findley killed a Nez Perce named Wil-lot-yah in a dispute over a missing horse, Joseph insisted that his people keep the peace while he patiently collected and sorted the evidence. When he concluded that the white man, Findley— who always had treated the Indians fairly—was less guilty than Wells McNall—another white man who long had abused the Indians and had started the trouble that caused the shooting—both his own people and the white settlers accepted Joseph's judgment as fair.

But events unfolding a thousand miles away quickly and drastically affected the government's policy toward all Indians. On June 25, 1876, George Custer's Seventh Cavalry met its fate at the Little Bighorn. This occurred just two days after Findley shot Wil-lot-yah, so it is not difficult to understand why the death of a single Indian in a remote part of Oregon drew little attention from military leaders stunned over the loss of so many of their comrades. From that time on, the Indians' right to live away from reservations as free men found few champions in the American government, the press, or the public.

Chief Joseph—a Man of Peace

One of the most cherished myths in the poignant, sad history of the Nez Perce War is the one created by white newspaper and magazine writers who followed the epic flight of the Indians from the army in 1877. Conditioned by the recent Civil War to treat all great battles and campaigns as personal contests between generals—U.S. Grant versus Robert E. Lee, for example—war correspondents and their editors insisted on creating bigger-than-life leaders they could glorify. In the Nez Perce War, reporters found two men so unique and colorful that they could only be compared with Hannibal and Napolean.

Major General Oliver Otis Howard, a Civil War hero who had lost his right arm during the battle of Fair Oaks, had become commander of the department of the Columbia, headquartered out of Portland. An extremely religious man, he respected Chief Joseph and sympathized with his people's desire to remain in the Wallowa country. After meeting with Joseph, he reported to the government:

> I think it is a great mistake to take from Joseph and his band of Nez Perce Indians that valley. The white people really do not want it.

408

They wish to be bought out. I think gradually this valley will be abandoned by the white people, and possibly Congress can be induced to let these really peaceable Indians have this valley for their own.

Still, he was a soldier and would obey any order given him. As the pressure increased to move the Wallowa band from their homeland to the Lapwai Reservation, Chief Joseph tried time and again to reason with with the government. In February 1877, he said:

I have been talking to the whites for many years about the land in question, and it is strange that they cannot understand me. The country they claim belonged to my father, and when he died it was given to me and my people, and I will not leave it until I am compelled to.

On May 15, 1877, the final order was issued. The Wallowa Nez Perces must move to the Lapwai Reservation by June 15 or be put there by force. Chief Joseph protested: "Our stock is scattered and the Snake River is very high. Let us wait till fall, when the river will be low. We want time to hunt up our stock and gather supplies for the winter."

Anna Kash Kash, Umatilla. —Oregon Historical Society

Reasonable though the request for a few months' delay was, General Howard refused to grant it, saying: "If you let the time run over one day, the soldiers will be there to drive you on the reservation, and cattle outside the reservation at that time will fall into the hands of the white man."

On the face of it, the task confronting the Wallowa Nez Perces—rounding up all their livestock and moving all their people and possessions a hundred miles in a month's time—was impossible. Incredibly, the Indians managed to find most of their stock and crossed the flood-swollen Snake River to within one day's travel of the Lapwai Reservation boundaries by June 12, two days before the deadline. There, near Tolo Lake, they camped with four other non-treaty bands from east of Snake River, also being forced to move onto the reservation.

The five bands totaled about six hundred people, of whom, by actual count, only 191 were warriors. During a final salute to a way of life they would live no more, the Indians staged a parade. Riding double on a single horse were two young men from White Bird's Salmon River band, Wahlitits and Sarpsis Ilppilp. Known as fine, upstanding young men of good family and character, they were first cousins—or, in Indian parlance, "brothers."

By accident, their horse stepped on some roots Heyoom Moxmox's (Yellow Grizzly Bear's) wife laid to dry in the sun. Seeing this, the older Indian chided the two riders in angry derision. He said if they wanted to act like braves, they should go kill the white man who slayed one of their fathers.

A few years earlier Wahlitits' father, Eagle Robe, had owned and farmed a piece of land near Slate Creek, a tributary of the Salmon River. He allowed a white man named Larry Ott to settle nearby. Though at first promising not to trespass on Eagle Robe's garden spot, Ott gradu-

Nez Perce Indian camp near Wallowa Lake, 1890.
—Wallowa County Museum

ally took more and more land, until finally one day he built a fence that excluded the Nez Perce from his own property. Eagle Robe protested, an argument ensued, and suddenly without provocation Larry Ott grabbed a gun and shot the Indian.

Not wanting to start a war, Eagle Robe, as he lay dying, told his son, who at that time was still a boy: "Do nothing to the white man for what he has done to me. Let him live his life."

Growing to manhood, Wahlitits had respected his father's command. But now, stung by the taunt and burning with resentment at being forced by the whites to give up his freedom and leave his homeland, he decided to prove that he was a man. With the support of Sarpsis Ilppilp and several other young men who begrudged the whites, he formed a war party that killed several white settlers over the next few days.

When word of the killings reached the military post of Fort Lapwai, the army sent two companies of cavalry under Captain David Perry to subdue the Indians; no need to parley with them first and see if they would surrender the guilty young men. As Perry's column rode away from Fort Lapwai in the summer twilight, Captain Perry saluted General Howard.

"Goodbye, General!"

"Goodbye, Captain. You must not get whipped."

"There's no danger of that, sir."

After the soldiers had disappeared into the growing darkness, General Howard retired to his quarters, where for the next several nights and days he paced the floor in deep concern for his officers and men. But he was confident enough to write in one of his official dispatches:

"Think they will make short work of it."

Custer had thought that, too...

First train for Wallowa, crossing the river at Rondowa, September 20, 1908.
—Wallowa County Museum

Other than its beginning and end, the epic story of the Nez Perce War is beyond the scope of this book. Covering 1,300 miles of mountain wilderness across Idaho, Yellowstone Park, and Montana over a period of four months, it made Chief Joseph a legend in the minds of the public. It was his genius as a military leader, newspapers said, that enabled this small band of Nez Perce warriors to defeat the best the army could throw against them time after time in battle after battle.

In truth, Chief Joseph was not the "red Napolean" news accounts made him out to be; he devised no clever battle strategies and probably never fired a shot until the final battle, if then. From long before the conflict began until his surrender speech at the Bear Paw Mountains battlefield, he was a peace leader, wise enough to know that his people could not win a war against the overhwelming military power of the United States. Because he was the Nez Perce leader whom General Howard knew best, and because all the other Nez Perce leaders were dead or fled to Canada, he became the spokesman and symbol for a gallant people whose tragic plight had captured the sympathy of the nation.

"Tell General Howard I know his heart," he began his surrender speech. "What he told me before I have in my heart. I am tired of fighting. Our chiefs are killed. Looking Glass is dead. Toohoolhoolzote is dead. The old men are all dead. It is the young men who say yes or no. He who led the young men is dead. It is cold and we have no blankets. The little children are freezing to death. My people, some of them, have run away into the hills, and have no blankets, no food; no one knows where they are, perhaps freezing to death. I want time to look for my children and see how many of them I can find. Maybe I shall find them among the dead. Hear me, my chiefs! I am tired. My heart is sick and sad. From where the sun now stands, I will fight no more forever."

End of the Trail

After eight years of exile in Indian Territory (Oklahoma), the Nez Perces who survived the war were returned to the Pacific Northwest. Those who professed to be Christians were put on the Lapwai Reservation in Idaho; those who did not were sent to the Colville Reservation in northeast Washington. Until his death in 1904, Chief Joseph continued to act as an eloquent spokesman for his people, being strongly supported by the man who was once his enemy, General Howard.

Time and again, Joseph asked the government to let him return to the Wallowa country—"Land of the Winding Waters"—the place he loved above all others. But other than brief, closely supervised visits, he was never permitted to go. Even in death, his remains were interred in alien soil on the Colville Reservation.

Old Joseph, however, later was honored after a fashion by having a small town at the foot of Wallowa Lake named for him. First buried in October 1871, near the junction of the Lostine and Wallowa rivers on a plain called "Indian Town," because it was a traditional camping place for the Wallowa Nez Perces, his body was accompanied to the spirit land by a favorite horse which had been killed and laid beside his grave, while a bell hung on a pole tinkled with every passing breeze.

The white settler who homesteaded the area respected the grave site by ploughing around it for many years. In 1923, with the war long over and most of the white and Indian survivors gone, the citizens of Wallowa County set aside a small knoll overlooking the lower end of Wallowa Lake as a small park, reinterred Old Joseph's remains there, and erected a stone marker and a bronze plaque commemorating the site.

For whatever it may be worth to his spirit, no lover of beauty and freedom could ask for a more spectacular view than the one overlooking this lake, its mirror-like surface reflecting the mighty Chief Joseph Mountain rising steeply from the evergreen-covered foothills just a few miles to the south.

It is fitting that here our long, immensely enjoyable journey around the magnificent state of Oregon should end.

Bibliography

Abbott, Carl. *The Great Extravaganza*. Portland: Oregon Historical Society Press, 1981.

Alt, David D. and Donald W. Hyndman. *Roadside Geology of Oregon*. Missoula, Montana: Mountain Press Publishing Co., 1978.

Ashworth, William. *Hells Canyon, the Deepest Gorge on Earth*. Binghampton, New York: Hawthorn Press, 1977.

Barlow, Jeffrey and Christine Richardson. *China Doctor of John Day*. Portland: Binford & Mort, 1979.

Bartlett, Grace. *The Wallowa Country 1867-77*. Enterprise, Oregon: Chieftan Press, 1976.

Beal, Merrill D. *Intermountain Railroads*. Caldwell, Idaho: Caxton Printers, Ltd., 1962.

Binns, Archie. *Lightship*. New York: Reynal and Hitchcock, 1934.

_____. *Peter Skene Ogden: Fur Trader*. Portland: Binford & Mort, 1967.

_____. *You Rolling River*. New York: Charles Scribner's Sons, 1947.

Blankenship, Russell. *And There Were Men*. New York: Alfred A. Knopf, 1942.

Boyle, John C. *Fifty Years on the Klamath*. Medford, Oregon: Klocker Printery, 1976.

Braun, Kirk. *Rajneeshpuram: The Unwelcome Society*. West Linn, Oregon: Scout Creek Press, 1984.

Case, Robert Ormond. *Last Mountains*. New York: Doubleday, 1946.

_____. *The Empire Builders*. New York: Doubleday, 1947.

Caverill, W.S. *Marie Dorion and the Trail of the Pioneers*. Milton-Freewater, Oregon: Valley Press, 1971.

Chittenden, Hiram Martin. *The American Fur Trade of the Far West*. 2 vols. 1904. Reprint. Stanford, California: Academic Reprints, 1954.

Conley, Cort and John Carrey and Ace Barton. *Snake River of Hells Canyon*. Council, Idaho: Backeddy Books, 1979.

Crabtree, Rufus. *The Pendleton Story*. Pendleton: East Oregonian Press, 1990.

Cranson, K.R. *Crater Lake, Gem of the Cascades*. Lansing, Michigan: KCR Press, 1982.

Culp, Edwin. *Stations West*. Caldwell, Idaho: Caxton Printers, Ltd., 1972.

DeVoto, Bernard, ed. *The Journals of Lewis and Clark*. Boston: Houghton Mifflin Co., 1953.

Downey, Fairfax. *Indian Fighting Army*. New York: Charles Scribner's Sons, 1941.

Evans, Elwood, ed. *History of the Pacific Northwest*. Vol. 1, Oregon and Washington. Portland: North Pacific History Company, 1889.

Federal Writers Project, Works Progress Administration. *Oregon, End of the Trail*. Portland: Binford & Mort, 1950.

Fitgerald, Frances. *Cities on a Hill*. New York: Simon & Schuster, 1986.

Fogdall, Alberta Brooks. *Royal Family of the Columbia*. Fairfield, Washington: Ye Galleon Press, 1978.

Franchere, Gabriel. *Narrative of a Voyage to the Northwest Coast of America*. 1820. Reprint. New York: Redfield, 1854.

French, Giles. *Cattle Country of Peter French*. Portland: Binford & Mort, 1954.

Friedman, Ralph. *Oregon for the Curious*. Caldwell, Idaho: Caxton Printers, Ltd., 1987.

From Tillamook Burn to Tillamook State Forest. Oregon State Department of Forestry, 1983.

Gibbs, James A. *Oregon's Salty Coast*. Superior, 1978.

_____. *Pacific Graveyard*. Portland: Binford & Mort, 1964.

_____. *Shipwrecks of the Pacific Coast*. Portland: Binford & Mort, 1957.

_____. *Tillamook Light*. Portland: Binford & Mort, 1976.

Gulick, Bill. *Chief Joseph Country: Land of the Nez Perce*. Caldwell, Idaho: Caxton Printers, Ltd., 1981.

_____. *Snake River Country*. Caldwell, Idaho: Caxton Printers, Ltd., 1971.

_____. *They Came to a Valley*. New York: Doubleday, 1966.

_____. *Treasure in Hell's Canyon*. New York: Doubleday, 1979.

Harris, Stephen L. *Fire and Ice: The Cascade Volcanoes*. Seattle: The Mountaineers Press, 1980.

Holbrook, Stewart H. *Burning An Empire*. New York: MacMillan Publishing Co., 1943.

_____. *Promised Land*. New York: McGraw Hill, 1945.

Hussey, J.A. *Champoeg: Place of Transition*. Portland: Oregon Historical Society Press, 1967.

Irving, Washington. *Astoria*. 2 vols. 1837. Reprint. Philadelphia and New York: J.B. Lippincott Co., 1961.

_____. *Adventures of Captain Bonneville, U.S.A., in the Rocky Mountains and the Far West*. 1838. Reprint. Norman: University of Oklahoma Press, 1961.

Jackman, E.R. and R.A. Long. *The Oregon Desert*. Caldwell, Idaho: Caxton Printers, Ltd., 1982.

Jackman, E.R. and John Scharff. *Steens Mountain*. Caldwell, Idaho: Caxton Printers, Ltd., 1968.

Kemp, Larry J. *Epitaph for the Giants*. Portland: Touchstone Press, 1967.

Klamath County History. Klamath Falls, Oregon: Klamath County Historical Society, 1984.

Lapham, Stanton C. *The Enchanted Lake*. Salem, Oregon: Statesman Publishing, 1931.

Lyman, William D. *The Columbia River*. New York & London: G.P. Putnam Sons, 1911.

Martin, Albro. *James J. Hill and the Opening of the Northwest*. New York: Oxford University Press, 1965.

McArthur, Lewis A. *Oregon Geographic Names*. Portland: Oregon Historical Society Press, 1982.

Mills, Randall V. *Railroads Down the Valley*. Palo Alto, California: Pacific Books, 1950.

_____. *Sternwheelers Up the Columbia*. Palo Alto, California: Pacific Books, 1947.

Morwood, William. *Traveler in a Vanished Landscape*. New York: Clarkson Potter Publishers, 1973.

Nevins, Allan. *Fremont, Pathmaker of the West*. New York: D. Appleton Century, 1939.

Newell, Gordon, ed. *The H.W. McCurdy Marine History of the Pacific Northwest.* Seattle: Superior, 1965.

Nielsen, Lawrence E. *In the Ruts of the Wagon Wheels.* Bend, Oregon: Maverick Publications, 1987.

Peltier, Jerome. *Madame Dorion.* Fairfield, Washington: Ye Galleon Press, 1980.

The People of Warm Springs. Warm Springs, Oregon: Confederated Tribes, 1984.

Peterson, Emil R. and Alfred Powers. *A Century of Coos and Curry.* Coquille, Oregon: Coos-Curry Pioneer and Historical Association, 1977.

Pfefferle, Ruth. *Golden Days and Pioneer Ways.* Grants Pass, Oregon: Josephine County Historical Society, 1977.

Philips, Susan Urmston. *The Invisible Culture: Warm Springs.* New York: Philips, Longman, 1983.

Price, Richard L. *Newport Oregon, 1866-1936: Portrait of a Coast Resort.* Newport, Oregon: Lincoln County Historical Society, 1975.

Reynolds, Helen Baker. *Gold, Rawhide and Iron: Biography of Dorsey Syng Baker.* Palo Alto, California: Pacific Books, 1955.

Ross, Alexander. *Fur Hunters of the Far West.* London, 1855. Reprint. Norman: University of Oklahoma Press, 1956.

Simpson, Charles D. and E. R. Jackman. *Blazing Forest Trails.* Caldwell, Idaho: Caxton Printers, Ltd., 1967.

Simson, Peter K. *The Community of Cattlemen.* Moscow: University of Idaho Press, 1987.

Stern, Theodore. *The Klamath Tribe.* Seattle: University of Washington Press, 1965.

Sutton, Jack. *110 Years With Josephine.* Grants Pass, Oregon: Josephine County Historical Society., 1966.

Supham, Robert J. *Oregon Indians II, Ethnological Report on the Wasco and Tenino Indians.* New York: Garland Publishing, 1974.

Terrell, John Upton. *Furs by Astor.* New York: William Morrow and Co., 1963.

Thrapp, Dan L. *Encyclopedia of Frontier Biography.* Spokane: The Arthur H. Clark Co., 1988.

Timmen, Fritz. *Blow For the Landing.* Caldwell, Idaho: Caxton Printers, Ltd., 1973.

Wright, Edgar Wilson, ed. Lewis and Dryden's *Marine History of the Pacific Northwest*. 1895. Reprint. New York: Antiquarian Press, 1961.

Periodicals

East Oregonian, Pendleton, Oregon.

Lane County Historian, Eugene, Oregon.

Oregon Historical Quarterly, Portland, Oregon.

Oregonian, Portland, Oregon.

Oregon Journal, Portland, Oregon.

Quarterdeck Review, Astoria, Oregon.

Union Statesman, Walla Walla, Washington.

Western World, Bandon, Oregon.

Index

429